W9-CHS-331

Nova Scotia &
Prince Edward Island

The Bay of Fundy low tide leaves the red mud visible on the Shubenacadie River, next to the Fundy Tidal Interpretive Centre in South Maitland.

A COMPLETE GUIDE

1ST EDITION

Nova Scotia & Prince Edward Island

Nancy
English

The Countryman Press
Woodstock, Vermont

To the people of Nova Scotia and Prince Edward Island who work to make their homelands so hospitable and beautiful.

We welcome your comments and suggestions. Please contact Great Destinations Guide Editor, The Countryman Press, P.O. Box 748, Woodstock, VT 05091, or e-mail countrymanpress@wwnorton.com.

ISBN   978-1-58157-096-0

Front cover photo © Mike Grandmaison Photography
Interior photos by the author unless otherwise specified
Book design by Bodenweber Design
Composition by Melinda Belter
Maps by Mapping Specialists © The Countryman Press

Published by The Countryman Press, P.O. Box 748, Woodstock, Vermont 05091

Distributed by W. W. Norton & Company, Inc., 500 Fifth Avenue, New York, NY 10110

Manufactured in the United States of America

10 9 8 7 6 5 4 3 2 1

GREAT DESTINATIONS TRAVEL GUIDEBOOK SERIES

Recommended by *National Geographic Traveler* and *Travel + Leisure* magazines

A crisp and critical approach, for travelers who want to live like locals.
—*USA Today*

Great Destinations™ guidebooks are known for their comprehensive, critical coverage of regions of extraordinary cultural interest and natural beauty. Each title in this series is continuously updated with each printing to ensure accurate and timely information. All the books contain more than one hundred photographs and maps.

Current titles available:

The Adirondack Book
The Alaska Panhandle
Atlanta
Austin, San Antonio
    & the Texas Hill Country
The Berkshire Book
Big Sur, Monterey Bay
    & Gold Coast Wine Country
Cape Canaveral, Cocoa Beach
    & Florida's Space Coast
The Charleston, Savannah
    & Coastal Islands Book
The Chesapeake Bay Book
The Coast of Maine Book
Colorado's Classic Mountain Towns
Costa Rica: Great Destinations
    Central America
Dominican Republic
The Finger Lakes Book
The Four Corners Region
Galveston, South Padre Island
    & the Texas Gulf Coast
Guatemala: Great Destinations
    Central America
The Hamptons Book
Hawaii's Big Island: Great Destinations
    Hawaii
Honolulu & Oahu: Great Destinations
    Hawaii
The Jersey Shore: Atlantic City to Cape May:
    Great Destinations
Kauai: Great Destinations Hawaii
Lake Tahoe & Reno
Las Vegas
Los Cabos & Baja California Sur:
    Great Destinations Mexico
Maui: Great Destinations Hawaii
Memphis and the Delta Blues Trail

Michigan's Upper Peninsula
Montreal & Quebec City:
    Great Destinations Canada
The Nantucket Book
The Napa & Sonoma Book
North Carolina's Outer Banks
    & the Crystal Coast
Nova Scotia & Prince Edward Island
Oaxaca: Great Destinations Mexico
Palm Beach, Fort Lauderdale, Miami
    & the Florida Keys
Palm Springs & Desert Resorts
Philadelphia, Brandywine Valley
    & Bucks County
Phoenix, Scottsdale, Sedona
    & Central Arizona
Playa del Carmen, Tulum & the Riviera Maya:
    Great Destinations Mexico
Salt Lake City, Park City, Provo
    & Utah's High Country Resorts
San Diego & Tijuana
San Juan, Vieques & Culebra:
    Great Destinations Puerto Rico
San Miguel de Allende & Guanajuato:
    Great Destinations Mexico
The Santa Fe & Taos Book
The Sarasota, Sanibel Island & Naples Book
The Seattle & Vancouver Book
The Shenandoah Valley Book
Touring East Coast Wine Country
Tucson
Virginia Beach, Richmond
    & Tidewater Virginia
Washington, D.C., and Northern Virginia
Yellowstone & Grand Teton National Parks
    & Jackson Hole
Yosemite & the Southern Sierra Nevada

The authors in this series are professional travel writers who have lived for many years in the regions they describe. Honest and painstakingly critical, full of information only a local can provide, Great Destinations guidebooks give you all the practical knowledge you need to enjoy the best of each region.

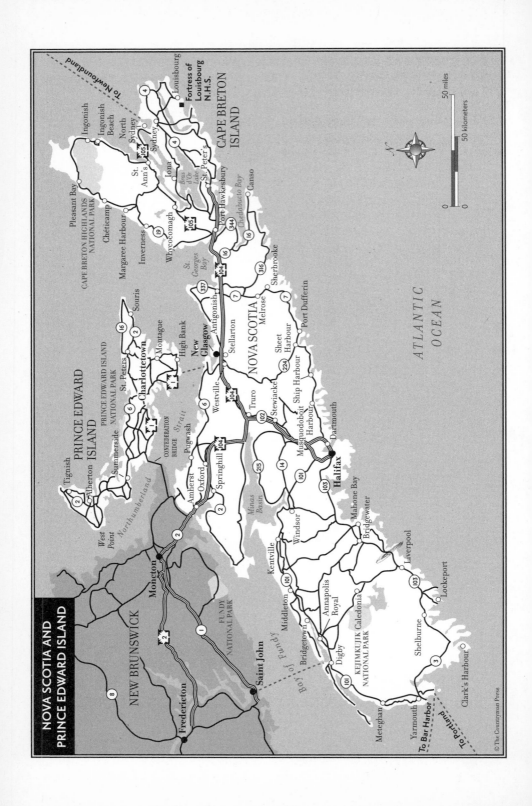

NOVA SCOTIA AND
PRINCE EDWARD ISLAND

© The Countryman Press

Contents

Acknowledgments

First thanks go to the many staff people at information centers across Nova Scotia and Prince Edward Island who respond with unfailing courtesy to questions. Although asked by the government not to share their full names, they are still at the top of the list—from Diane at the Yarmouth, NS, Information Centre to her fellow workers at Mahone Bay, Halifax, Canso, Guysborough, St. Peters in Prince Edward Island, Ingonish on Cape Breton Island, and many more. Anita, who works at the Fundy Tidal Interpretive Centre in South Maitland, helped me understand how the water moves in and out of the Bay of Fundy—and where to go mud sliding. And thanks to Duetta at the Digby Tourist Bureau, who knew the easiest route to the Maude Lewis House Replica.

The generosity and hospitality of the innkeepers whose businesses are in this book cannot be too highly praised. Janet Palmer at the 1775 Solomon House Bed & Breakfast in Lunenburg knows exactly where to go for the best of everything in her area. Elizabeth and John Measures, innkeepers at Whitman Wharf Bed & Breakfast, have the same expertise in Canso, and they make great coffee.

Penny Steele, innkeeper at English Country Garden B&B helped with the whole northern end of Cape Breton Island. On Prince Edward Island, Cairns Motel owners Aaron and Kendra Wedge knew where to dine and hear music.

George Driscoll, vice president at Bay Ferries, introduced me to his company's great ferry service. John Duggan, general manager at Cambridge Suites Hotel in Halifax, introduced me to the good wine made by Jöst and the fine accommodations of his hotel.

The owners of the Painted Saltbox, artists Tom Always and Peter Blais, make their own guide to their area's restaurants and studios; thanks to them for that promotion of the area around LaHave. Gail Martin, owner of the Trail Stop in Moser River, has the same area-wide knowledge.

Thanks to Peter Llewellyn, mayor of Georgetown, PEI, who gave me a red sandstone carving he made of the outline of Prince Edward Island, and told me all about his hometown.

Randy Brooks, media relations manager for Nova Scotia Tourism, helped with accommodations, and Kristen Pickett, media relations assistant, made all the arrangements with speedy competence. Thanks to them both, and to Nova Scotia Tourism for that help, and for its fine resources on the Web and in publications.

Douglas Vaisey made sure Patrick Power Library at Saint Mary's University, got the write-up it deserved. Jen and Rob Thomson, vacationing on PEI from Halifax, came from the Antigonish area and knew exactly where to find perfect fish and chips—at Murphy's of course—and many other bests.

Thanks to Lisa de Melogue who with her husband runs Dayboat Restaurant in Oyster Bed Bridge, PEI. Art lover Nora MaKay, who plans to visit the Halifax Public Gardens every day of her retirement, was a great help with Halifax. So was Dennis Johnston, owner and chef of Fid.

Thanks to Ken Pribanic, architect in charge of the "Big House" in Lunenburg, who showed me how to find my way round that pretty town. Aileen Raphael and her coworker,

encountered on Middle Head Trail in Ingonish Beach, helped with more recommendations, as did John Baldwin, headed to a golf weekend at Highlands Links, who shared his
favorites while waiting for the Englishtown ferry.

Thanks go to my publisher and editor, Kermit Hummel, who approved this new title,
and to Kim Grant who acquired it. Thanks go to Jennifer Thompson, managing editor, who
will be missed as she pursues other career opportunities. Thanks to Lisa Sacks, now managing editor at Countryman Press, for overseeing the production of this book. Finally,
thanks go to Philip Rich, who worked with me on my first guidebook in 2001, took on this
project with enthusiasm in 2008, and has always been a joy to work with.

Introduction

Rich, fertile red soil lies like a sleek blanket over Prince Edward Island, growing crops that feed festival goers through the summer and fall. On the southwestern coast of Nova Scotia, 50-foot tides tear into the coastline on the Bay of Fundy, carving rock into sculptures that visitors marvel at from their kayaks, or from parkland walks at low tide. Another discard, after the tide retreats, is the gooey red mud some like to roll in and slid down, perhaps at Anthony Provincial Park on the edge of the Bay of Fundy.

Tourism is a profoundly important part of the economy of both Nova Scotia and Prince Edward Island, and the provincial governments are deeply involved in its promotion. Visitor Information Centres are open daily all summer in most cities and towns, with friendly staff happy to help. The provinces both publish thick books stuffed with every last detail about accommodations and cottages. In this book, I list high-quality inns and B&Bs that a tourist could be sure to enjoy, and restaurants and cafes with good cooks and great meals.

A traveler intent on tasting the best of these provinces would start with Digby scallops at one end of Nova Scotia, and Aspy Bay oysters at the other. Malpeque oysters from Prince Edward Island are not to be missed, and neither is snow crab from the north Atlantic. You will be able to enjoy all this with some good wines grown and bottled on both provinces, like Gaspereau Vineyard wines near Wolfville. If you get a fishing license in Cape Breton, you may be able to taste North Atlantic wild salmon—the catch-and-release license does allow four keepers, as long as they don't exceed the size limitation.

A lobster boat tied up at the wharf in Morell, Prince Edward Island

But lobster is abundant and easy to order everywhere you go. Clams and haddock are ready to hand too, and deep fried with skill. Mussels are everywhere you look, and they taste wonderful in these provinces where they are never long out of water before arriving on your plate.

Lamb, beef, and pork are raised here, and served here. Cheese is made with rich milk, and ice cream is too. Fruit is abundant in the fertile Annapolis Valley of western Nova Scotia, with apples just one of the many kinds of fruit grown in huge quantity. Prince Edward Island's Preserve Company is a big success because of that province's fertile farm-land and fine crops.

I think any food item makes the best kind of souvenir. A jug of maple syrup, a bottle of blackberry mead or L'Acadie Blanc, a Nova Scotia white wine, a can of Chicken Haddie, which is codfish, a local woman told me, for fishcakes, or a jar of preserves bring the best of the Maritimes home with you.

THE WAY THIS BOOK WORKS

Though nowhere near as vast as Canada's western provinces, Nova Scotia, like all the Maritime Provinces, is still pretty big. Accordingly, we divide the province into geographical regions, placing everything you need for a drive of a day or two within one chapter. (Within each region, you'll find descriptions of available lodgings, restaurants, food purveyors, recreational possibilities, and shopping.)

After two introductory chapters on the history of the region and the various ways you can get there, Chapter Three is devoted to the provincial capital, Halifax, and the rugged Eastern Shore that runs northeast from Halifax to the town of Canso. Chapter Four takes us down the southeast coast to Cape Sable Island, then north along the Gulf of Maine to Yarmouth, and finally to the charming French Shore up to St. Bernard.

Chapter Five covers fertile Annapolis Valley and the Fundy Coast from Digby to Wolfville and Grand Pré. Chapter Six describes the north end of the Fundy coast, including Truro and Amherst as well as the charming villages in between.

Chapter Seven takes us along the north side of Nova Scotia, beside the relatively warm waters of Northumberland Strait. And Chapter Eight covers the most remote and possibly most fascinating part of the province, Cape Breton Island.

Chapters Nine and Ten are devoted to Prince Edward Island, which, like Nova Scotia, is divided geographically into three regions for travelers' easy access, using the county lines. Kings and Queens Counties are in Chapter Nine, with the exception of one village, Victoria-on-the-Sea, which is included with Prince County in Chapter Ten.

Chapter Eleven provides a miscellany of practical information to make your visit to Nova Scotia and PEI run more smoothly.

For most of the inns and restaurants and some cultural sites, brief introductory text blocks provide the hard-core details—address, time to visit, and so on. (Establishments of especially high quality and interest are indicated by a ✪ next to their names.) It is always desirable to phone ahead to confirm this information, since it is subject to frequent change, especially from year to year.

Prices

	Lodging	*Dining*
Inexpensive	Up to $110	Up to $16
Moderate	$190 to $130	$12 to $24
Expensive	$120 to $200	$21 to $38
Very Expensive	$149 and up	$60 or more

Prices are stated in Canadian dollars. For further information, see Chapter Eleven, *Information*.

This monument marks the site of Fort St. Louis, defended by Charles de la Tour, in present-day Port La Tour.

1

History

Native Peoples, Acadians, and the British Lion

On a map, Nova Scotia looks like a long lobster wearing a wind-blown cloth cape. The claws at the northeast form Cape Breton Island, where Cape Breton Highlands National Park draws summer visitors with a yen for dramatic landscape and seacoast. The "cape" is the part of Nova Scotia that ties it to the mainland, at the border with New Brunswick. On its north shore is Northumberland Strait, full of warm water from temperate ocean currents. The wide tail section of this massive creature has Yarmouth on its very southern end and Halifax on its eastern midpoint. All along its back is the Bay of Fundy, with its world's highest tides.

Prince Edward Island was called Abegweit by its native Canadians, the Mi'kmaq, which means Cradle on the Waves, and indeed, that is what the island looks like in a map's outline. With the Northumberland Strait on its southern shores, the Gulf of St. Lawrence on the north, and the Atlantic Ocean to the east, any point along its length is near a beach.

Natural history and social history, introduced here, are braided together like destiny in the provinces' stories. Nova Scotia came into existence because it made a good, safe harbor for the British navy. Today, one of the many reasons to visit is the natural beauty found at every point of the endless coastline. And many visitors come seeking to trace their ancestry or learn about cultures that arrived in waves, like the British and the Scots, or were dispersed in exile, like the Acadians, or pushed into smaller and smaller territory, like the Mi'kmaq.

NATURAL HISTORY

At the northernmost tip of Cape Breton Island in Nova Scotia the oldest rocks of the Atlantic Maritime provinces are found, and their age exceeds almost anything on earth. More than a billion years ago these rocks were created by the collision of continents that brought a supercontinent into existence, called Rodinia.

According to *The Last Billion Years—A Geological History of the Maritime Provinces of Canada, Atlantic Geoscience Society*, presented on the Parks Canada Web site, these rocks are probably part of the core of the North American continent.

Half a billion years ago, Rodinia succumbed to the pressures of continental drift and began to come apart. One new continent is today called Amazonia; igneous rocks that seeped up near it form the ground of the Bras d'Or Lakes, in the middle of the long claw-like northern end of Nova Scotia.

The glaciers cut valleys out of the highlands plateau during successive ice ages.

About 360 million years ago a continent called Euramerica and another called Gondwana were pushed toward each other. The forces pulling them together pushed the land up in folds and created the Appalachian Mountains of North America—the Cape Breton Highlands are the northernmost end of this range, once higher than the Himalayas but now far lower, after millions of years of erosion.

Between the mountainous highlands were deep basins. Most of the rest of the province was part of those basins, flooded and filled with sediment for eons. Lowlands above the water level were forested swamps that subsequently turned into the coal beds mined on Nova Scotia in the 1800s and 1900s.

A climate shift about 290 million years ago turned the forests to deserts; after millions of years of erosion these red-rock deserts created the red sands of the beaches along the Northumberland Strait, between northern Nova Scotia and southern Price Edward Island, and the fertile red soil on top of the bedrock that grows PEI's potatoes and other crops.

About 250 million years ago the Maritimes and Spain and Morocco were all fused, but another continental drift pulled the Maritimes west of the widening Atlantic. (Even today the land beneath us is drifting a few centimeters of inches each year.) Later the glaciers of repeated ice ages tore valleys out of the highlands of Cape Breton and created the deep basin that holds the Bras d'Or Lakes.

SOCIAL HISTORY

Nova Scotia's first residents left their mark in stone.

Their fossilized traces were eroded from the top of the highlands, but elsewhere, under sediment that is only recently being worn away, the fossils of the dinosaur age are still being discovered. The Bay of Fundy at Blue Beach, north of Wolfville, and Joggins, a World

Heritage site near Amherst, is renowned for its fossil prizes. Another discovery area is on the Northumberland Strait.

First People

The ancestors of the Mi'kmaq lived on Nova Scotia and Prince Edward Island more than 10,000 years ago, when Prince Edward Island was still connected to the mainland and the Gulf of the St. Lawrence had not yet formed.

These people hunted animals like the wooly mammoth (a skeleton of one was found in a gypsum mine in East Milford), following them into grasslands that appeared after the glaciers retreated. With caribou skins to keep out the cold and cover dwellings, they outwitted the winters—when, wearing snowshoes, they would hunt the caribou again, and deer. In spring they made weirs on the rivers to catch the incoming schools of herring, sturgeon, and salmon. Geese and ducks in enormous numbers were another easy prey.

The population of different nations interacted and traded across the territory, and traveling to summer hunting regions and winter refuges was part of their hunting and gathering existence. Eventually the skill needed to harpoon seals and swordfish added another food source.

Before Europeans arrived, and even for centuries afterward, the incredible abundant fisheries and oyster beds of seemingly unending bounty made some aspects of life easier than it would ever be again.

European Trade

Some believe a 1398 visit by Henry Sinclair was the real "discovery of America." An admiral who became Lord Chief Justice of Scotland, Sinclair supposedly sailed with a family of Venetians. In 1497 John Cabot arrived in North America, including the future Halifax harbor, a feat that made him a celebrity in Europe. Fishing in the Grand Banks, inspired by Cabot's description of catching cod with baskets, was soon pursued by all of Europe throughout the 1500s.

Samuel de Champlain mapped the region in 1603 and prophesied its future as Acadia. In 1604, a merchant named Pierre Dugua de Monts first sighted land at Cap de la Hève— present-day LaHave, south of Lunenburg. His group intended to found a colony. After a brutal winter on St. Croix Island, Port Royal won favor and its first French settlers, who were pleased with Annapolis Basin's qualifications as a natural harbor.

The French showed good manners and appreciation to their trading partners, the Mi'kmaq, and converted some to Christianity. But as British ships were moving into the same waters, wars in Europe turned into raids in the New World. Port Royal was burned and looted in 1613, and though Mi'kmaq cared for some of its inhabitants, the British would soon declare the whole of Acadia a New Scotland. Because the city would be traded back and forth for decades between the English and the French, it rarely enjoyed a long peace. Finally, in 1710, Port Royal was taken by the British for the last time—and its name permanently changed to Annapolis Royal.

Competition for the fur that was so desired in Europe created territorial disputes. And meanwhile disease eradicated far more of the Mi'kmaq than any of the weapons of the time. According to Harry Bruce, author of *An Illustrated History of Nova Scotia*, by 1700 the number of Mi'kmaq had decreased to a "few thousand."

While Acadians continued to dike the marshlands along the Bay of Fundy, turning them into fertile farmlands, their situation remained precarious and undecided.

This recreation of a salt marsh dyke at Annapolis Royal Historic Gardens shows what the early Acadians made with back-breaking labor here and on Minas Basin.

New Englanders from across the water traded rum and cloth for Acadian grain, despite treaties banning trade signed by European powers. The New England population grew with British immigrants eager to get away from religious persecution to 50,000 by 1670, vastly more than the population across the Bay of Fundy in Nova Scotia. By 1750 there were perhaps 10,000 Acadians in Nova Scotia. They pursued their lives without submitting to English rule.

Yet the British kept on arriving, and by 1718 they were pushing out the French. They established a town on Grassy Island, off present-day Canso, to salt and dry and pack the fish and ship it back to Europe. That town was attacked by Mi'kmaq in 1720 and then retaken by the New Englanders and British. But in 1744 the settlement was wiped out by the French.

The French had taken a last stand on Cape Breton Island, which had been given them along with Prince Edward Island as a settlement under the Treaty of Utrecht of 1713. The French king was willing to pour money into the Fortress of Louisbourg to protect this colony, and the work began based on the strategic design of Le Prestre de Vauban, with the lavish expenditure from King Louis XV. There were 2,000 people here by 1740. The expensive work of building went on and on—until finally Louis XV asked if its streets were being paved with gold.

Meanwhile, New Englanders taken prisoner in Canso were released from Louisbourg prison and took home a deeper understanding of that fortress's point of vulnerability—across land behind it, not beneath the wall facing the sea. In 1745 a group composed of 4,000 New England militia returned and seized the fortress after a seven-week siege. Bad luck and bad weather destroyed a huge French convoy that was then sent to take Louisbourg back.

But then, with the 1748 Treaty of Aix-la-Chapelle, France won back Louisbourg after all—to the rage of the New Englanders and British on Nova Scotia. England tossed it back into France's lap for an exchange of "an office in Madras" and other concessions, infuriating New England, but setting up her own lucrative colonization of India.

Halifax, capital of Nova Scotia, was settled in 1749 by English, Irish, Scots, and Welsh traveling in a flotilla of a dozen ships from England. Its founding marks the moment England decided to invest heavily in this region to protect its colonies in New England.

Le Grand Dérangement; The Great Upheaval

In the 1750s, yet another military conflict with France led Charles Lawrence, the British governor of Nova Scotia, to look into what kind of citizens he had in the Minas Bay and Chignecto Acadians—people who had earlier refused to swear to fight on the British side. It was fear of disloyalty that made the governor require a loyalty oath from the Acadians, threatening them with expulsion from their land.

They refused to agree, having been allowed to remain neutral before. But this time Governor Lawrence did not back down. In 1755 Acadians up and down Nova Scotia were put on ships to be scattered around the world, in what became known as the "Great Upheaval." (The story of this time became familiar to later Americans through Henry Wadsworth Longfellow's poem, *Evangeline.*) The Acadians' farms were destroyed to keep the settlers from returning, though some managed to find a way to return eventually.

A quote from *History of Annapolis Royal* by W. H. McVicar, quoted in Frank Call's *The Spell of Acadia*, gives a poignant description. "With hearts wrung with anguish, they saw merciless flames devour the very shrines of their devotion; saw their barns and granaries that were bursting with the offerings of a generous harvest, reduced to blackened ashes; heard the plaintive lowing of their cattle, the bleating of their flocks, the mournful lament of the faithful watchdog."

During the French and Indian War, the Louisbourg Fortress came under British assault in the summer of 1758 by 14,000 men in 157 war ships. After two months of bombardment, the city surrendered. The next year the British won the rest of the territories that France had settled; in 1760 Montreal was also in their hands.

Scots Farmers

With battles in the Scottish highlands leading to a defeat of the highland chiefs, who were now forced to pay steep taxes to the British king, Scots who could not pay expensive rents needed a place to start again. Nova Scotia was their destiny. The *Hector* is the famous first ship that brought 71 Scots to Pictou in 1773; today its replica is an attraction on the Pictou wharf. Many more Scots followed, turning Cape Breton and the Northumberland Strait coastline, including Prince Edward Island, its own colony as of 1769, into a New Scotland indeed.

The Loyalists

The next enemy Nova Scotia would encounter—although it was itself attacked only once, ineffectually—was the Americans. Because of the American Revolution, Nova Scotia once again became an important military outpost, supplying ships with everything needed to battle the American colonists.

When Britain was defeated, Nova Scotia became the land its loyalists would resettle in. The city of Shelburne became the largest of all destinations, with land grants doled out among the rich and powerful, creating an instant hierarchy. But the most rich and powerful often decided against too long a stay, once the winter took hold.

The poor and defenseless were less able to rearrange things to their liking. Yet, even without the land grants promised, some black loyalists who had fought for the king in exchange for freedom found a way to seek another land. Many took the opportunity devised for them to immigrate to Africa. Others would struggle to survive in Canada's harsh climate, without any of the help dispensed to the white British around them.

Some Acadians who were now willing to take the oath of allegiance returned—to find their land had been taken over. They found less fertile land elsewhere on the coast and stood their ground. The Acadians of Tor Bay, for example, settled there after sitting in prison in Halifax.

The War of 1812

The 1803 Town Clock was built on the side of Citadel Hill facing the harbor in Halifax. Some historians say that this gift from Prince Edward, Duke of Kent, commander of British North American forces at the time, was meant to solve the lack of punctuality among the soldiers. In any event, as the city grew more elegant throughout the 1800s, enjoying the support of the British Empire, Halifax remained a military stronghold.

It was the site of thundering cheers when the victorious British navy ship, HMS *Shannon,* returned to Halifax harbor after defeating USS *Chesapeake* in the War of 1812.

Privateering, the legal seizure of enemy ships and their cargo, had been the quickest way to get rich though the long years of war with Napoleonic France, and Halifax enjoyed its share of seized shipping and redistributed wealth. The Americans did the same in the War of 1812, with an eye to their long-held dream of seizing part or all of Canada as well; but by the end of the war in 1814, they had lost. That was the end of American ambitions to take over Canada for itself.

Shipbuilding, Fishing, and Canada

All along the coastline of Nova Scotia the little towns built and settled by the turn of the 19th century display their history in museums and architecture. Shipbuilding was largely responsible for the growth of Lunenburg and many other powerful towns. In addition, the ability of a working man to fish with a line—and later a line with multiple hooks—meant that most could make a living on a dory. Schools were built and roads cut into the dense woods throughout the 1800s, while slowly the residents began to think of themselves as something other than British. Attempts to exert greater self-rule and to throw off some of the demands of England won wider support. "Responsible government" was wrested from the empire—and provincial parliaments convened to rule themselves. By 1867, when provincial governors met in Charlottetown, Prince Edward Island, and formed a Confederation, the Canadian identity was born.

The American Civil War, and its threat to British trade, had forced once again a large British investment in Nova Scotian facilities and brought about the construction of a railroad that would transform the Canadian economy. The steam age, and the invention of the telegraph, brought more investments and wealth, with coal mines and a steel industry in Sydney.

Modern War

A catastrophe, the sinking of the *Titanic* in 1912, brought survivors and the dead to Halifax, where some of the dead remain buried.

Two years later the outbreak of World War I led to busy factories, busy ports, and ever greater dangers. The Halifax Explosion on December 6, 1917, came on a cold clear day. The French ship SS *Mont-Blanc,* stuffed with explosives, was traveling up the harbor when a

Norwegian ship, SS *Imo*, took a course that forced the pilot of the *Mont-Blanc* to veer away—into its path. The ships collided despite a last-minute attempt to throttle the engines "full speed astern," and some of the explosives in *Mont-Blanc* were set off and started a fire. The terrified crew took off in lifeboats, and the ship drifted to the Halifax side, where firemen attempted to put out the fire. At 9:05 in the morning, the ship exploded, killing more than 1,900 people within minutes. The north end of Halifax, 325 acres, was destroyed.

At the time of the explosion, CSS *Acadia*, which had been launched in 1913 to map the waters around Atlantic Canada and had ventured far north amid the icebergs of the Arctic Sea, was moored in Bedford Basin—in supposed safety. The Halifax explosion abruptly changed that; fortunately the ship survived the blast, and it has been an attraction on the Halifax dock since 1982.

Desperate Times

In the 1900s, Maritime industries were bought up by larger Canadian companies and often shut down or moved to central Canada—creating a long, slow-burning resentment against the rest of the country in the smallest Atlantic provinces. Many believed that Confederation had ruined their chance at economic success. High freight rates turned the railroad into a force that shut down businesses as Nova Scotia and Prince Edward Island companies could no longer support the expense of shipping their goods.

The 1920s and 1930s were brutal decades in the Maritimes, and in particular on Cape Breton Island. Miners who felt stripped of both rights and adequate wages organized strikes—and met with troops who forced them to agree to a bad contract. Steelworkers attempting the same were brutalized by police on Bloody Sunday, in 1923. A huge miners' strike followed within days, an expression of outraged sympathy. In 1925, during another strike, policemen fired on the striking miners, killing one miner named Billy Davis—and a riot ensued. But miners lost in the end, forced to work for even worse wages to keep from starvation.

During Prohibition, other resourceful Canadians took up rum running to make a living. That heritage is a frequent part of village museums and stories.

Still others took part in the Antigonish movement, which was the first development of credit unions and would spread around the world to help finance the lives of small town citizens.

World War II

World War II brought energy and wealth back to Halifax, which sent convoys that brought goods and soldiers to Britain through predatory submarines. But though the Nazis sank 119 ships, they never stopped the vital transport of goods.

Riots that broke out in Halifax on Victory Day ruined some of the pleasure of that triumph. Townspeople were appalled at a two-day spree of looting and drunkeness, and they were only appeased when a catastrophe was averted at an ammunition stockpile, by sailors who risked their lives to put out a dangerous fire.

Another downturn followed the war, and poverty and declining populations defined the economies of Maritime Canada. But the late 20th century saw a turnaround, as Halifax blossomed into a vital and busy city. The countryside remains modest—and certainly picturesque and unusually friendly. Canada offers its residents incentives to settle here, and recent census reports show a slight increase in population. Many innkeepers, I noticed, are from Europe and elsewhere in Canada, and a few are American. But most are natives whose kindness is as natural to them as breathing.

Motorcyclists wait to ride on to the PEI Wood Islands Ferry in Caribou, Nova Scotia.

2

Transportation

Getting Here, Getting Around

By Car

Travelers who drive to Nova Scotia (instead of taking the ferry partway—see the section on ferries, below) will almost always enter the province via the Trans Canada Highway. Prince Edward Island is accessible by car over its **Confederation Bridge** (confederationbridge .com), opened in 1997. Built at a cost of $1 billion, the bridge is 12.9 kilometers or 8 miles long and takes about 12 minutes to drive across. You will pay a toll for the trip, but only when you leave the island. When you come to the island, no toll is collected. In 2008 the toll for a passenger car was $41.50 and for a motorcycle $16.50. Pedestrians pay $4 and cyclists pay $8 to ride in a shuttle bus that leaves New Brunwick from the Cape Jouriman Nature Centre at Exit 51 on Highway 16 and departs from PEI at Gateway Village in Borden-Carleton. The bridge follows Highway 16 through New Brunswick, which becomes Highway 1 in Prince Edward Island. This route enters Prince Edward Island in Borden-Carleton, where a visitors' information center is located.

By Bus

Acadian Lines (800-567-5151; smtbus.com), 300 Main St., Unit B2-2, Moncton, New Brunswick E1C 1B9. The bus line loops through Cape Breton Island, Nova Scotia, heads south to Truro where it travels west to Amherst (and other inland provinces) and south to Halifax. From Halifax you can take a bus farther south to Digby. From Amherst you can travel via bus across the Confederation Bridge to Prince Edward Island, stopping first in Summerside and second in Charlottetown. Student discounts and discounts for children ages 5 to 12 are available; children four and under ride free if they're with "a person who has bought a return ticket."

A bus is an inexpensive way to tour a city, and Halifax offers a free one in the summer called **FRED** (902-423-6658; halifax.ca/metrotransit/fred.html), for "Free Rides Everywhere Downtown." This bright green shuttle bus is sponsored by the Downtown Halifax Business Commission, and in 2008 it ran from July 5 to October 24, daily, from 10:30 AM to 5 PM. This bus travels from the Pier 21 Museum entrance to Lower Water Street, the casino, Upper Water Street, Barrington Street, Spring Garden Road to Citadel Hill and back to Pier 21 Museum.

The public bus and ferry system in Halifax is called **Metro Transit** (902-490-4000; halifax.ca/metrotransit/), and schedules and ticket information are available online. In 2008, an adult ticket for the bus or the ferry was $2.

The Abegweit Sightseeing Tours double-decker bus takes in Charlottetown or Anne's Land on the north shore.

In Charlottetown, Prince Edward Island, visitors can take a tour with **Abegweit Sightseeing Tours** (902-894-9966), 157 Nassau St., Charlottetown PEI. Adults ride for $10, children $2. A double-decker bus takes you on an hour-long tour of Charlottetown, while a guide narrates the historical details. Another tour, the North Shore Tour, covers 100 miles and leaves daily at 10:30 AM for a full day at North Rustico and Anne of Green Gables sites.

By International and Inter-provincial Ferry

Bay Ferries: The CAT
Bay Ferries operates three ferries that make a visit to Nova Scotia and Prince Edward Island convenient and relaxing.

The **CAT**, short for Catamaran Car Passenger Ferry, can carry as many as 250 cars and 14 buses or RVs. Taking the CAT from Portland, Maine, instead of driving north to Amherst, Nova Scotia, to reach the province, will save a driver hours behind the wheel in exchange for five or six hours of relaxation on the commodious passenger deck. Slot machines start up once the ship reaches international waters, for anyone who likes to gamble. Otherwise, three different screens in separate areas play two movies for the length of the trip, one devoted to children's features. A quiet area in the fore, port side of the passenger deck is the perfect place for a nap. Two counter service food and drink stations sell coffee, tea, beer, wine, and food, and a duty-free shop sells liquor and souvenirs.

The schedule is subject to change, but in 2008 the CAT left Portland Friday, Saturday, and Sunday morning at 8 AM and left Yarmouth, Nova Scotia (an hour earlier than Eastern Standard Time) at 4 PM on Thursday, Friday, Saturday, and Sunday.

Also in 2008, the CAT left Bar Harbor, Maine, for Yarmouth, Nova Scotia, a three-hour trip, each Monday at 9 AM and Tuesday through Thursday at 8 AM. It left Yarmouth for Bar Harbor Monday at 5 PM, and Tuesday and Wednesday at 4 PM.

Contact information for **Bay Ferries:**

877-283-7240
catferry.com

Portland Maine Terminal
207-761-4228
14 Ocean Gateway Pier (off Commercial St.)
Portland, Maine

Bar Harbor Maine Terminal
207-288-3395
121 Eden St.
Bar Harbor, Maine

Yarmouth Nova Scotia Terminal
902-742-6800
58 Water St.
Yarmouth, Nova Scotia

Bay Ferries also operates another ferry, the *Princess of Acadia*, from St. John, New Brunswick to Digby, Nova Scotia. Canadian visitors or tourists leaving Nova Scotia for a tour of New Brunswick depend on this three-hour ride. In 2008 the ferry left St. John twice daily late June to early September, and at least once a day every day of the week for the rest of the year, except Christmas Day and January 1. Call 888-249-7245 for up-to-date information.

Bay Ferries' third important ferry service connects Caribou, Nova Scotia, to Wood Islands, Prince Edward Island, with two vessels, the *Confederation* and *Holiday Island*,

The LaHave Ferry cuts driving time if you want to stay on the coast of Nova Scotia.

running this route year-round. Multiple trips each day, and up to nine a day in the summer, make this trip the most casual of the three: Although reservations are recommended,
it is often possible without one to drive up to the ferry dock and find a spot for your car or
motorcycle. The trip takes about 75 minutes. Summer passage is made even more enjoyable with an impromptu *ceilidh* (KAY-lee), or house party, in one of the passenger decks,
featuring PEI musicians. Again, call 888-249-7245 for up-to-date information.

Other Ferry Companies

Another ferry company, **Marine Atlantic** (800-341-7981; marine-atlantic.ca), operates a
car ferry that travels to Newfoundland from North Sydney, Cape Breton Island. Four ships
take passengers and cars to Port au Basques, Newfoundland, a six-hour trip, or in the summer to Argentia, a 16-hour trip, arriving within a 90-minute's drive to St. John's,
Newfoundland.

From Souris, Prince Edward Island, a ferry operated by **CTMA Group** (418-986-3278,
888-986-3278; ctma.ca) travels to Îles-de-la-Madeleine, also known as the Magdalen
Islands, a chain of islands rimmed by white sandy beaches about as far away from it all as
you can get. The five-hour trip arrives in Cap-de-Meule, and almost all the trips during
2008 left Souris at 2 PM.

Local Ferries

The Dartmouth Ferry (902-490-4000; halifax.ca/metrotransit) Metro Transit, Halifax
Regional Municipality, 200 Ilsey Ave., Dartmouth, NS B3B 1V1, the oldest continuous salt-
water passenger ferry service in North America, has taken folks across Halifax Harbour
since 1752. Today it travels to two places on the Dartmouth side, Woodside and Dartmouth
Waterfront Park. It's still a pleasanter way to cross the water than in your car on either of
the two bridges that were built to do the same thing. Park and Ride lots, some with fee,
allow you to leave your car behind. The Dartmouth Ferry leaves every 15 minutes during
commuter hours and midday, every 30 minutes otherwise and in the evening until 11:30 on
weekdays, and every 30 minutes on weekends. The **Woodside Ferry** leaves every half hour
in the morning and late afternoon on weekdays, with no service on weekends. A one-way
adult ticket is $2, seniors 65 and older and children 5–15 $1.40, and it includes a transfer
to take a bus on the other side.

Nova Scotia's **Department of Transportation and Infrastructure Renewal** operates
seven ferries. The three ocean-crossing ferries give a traveler a way to get to islands with
no other way across the water, bridging the mainland at Chester to Tancook Island, and
from Digby Neck to Petit Passage and to Grand Passage.

Four cable ferries cross wide river mouths to shorten distances on a drive from one part
of the coast to another. The boats pull themselves across wide rivers with a cable laid
underwater, and they typically take only a few minutes. Most leave every five minutes, like
the *LaHave II* from LaHave to Bridgewater.

The *LaHave II* crosses the LaHave River 24 hours a day year-round, with a five-minute
passage. From 11 PM to 7 AM, the ferry stays on one side of the river, but it can be sum-
moned by the intercom on either side. Winter ice might cause a short delay, but hasn't shut
it down.

In Victoria County, Cape Breton Island, Little Narrows and Englishtown are both sites
of cable ferries, shortening the drive, for example, from Sydney to Ingonish.

The Englishtown ferry, *Angus MacAskill*, is new to the service and bigger and faster than the previous boat. It runs 24 hours a day with a five-minute passage. In February or March there may be ice, although that hasn't been an issue in the recent past. Local information centers will know if the ferry isn't running. If you arrive in the middle of the night, the boat will come to get you, and you can call it from either side.

The Little Narrows ferry, *Caolas Silas,* also runs 24 hours a day with a five-minute passage, and there is a box at either side with a button to push to summon the ferry.

From July 5 to September 1 the *Stormont* in Country Harbour, north of Sherbrooke, runs every 15 minutes from 7 AM to 6 PM.

The sign for the LaHave II *Ferry*

Later it crosses the river every half hour, and off-season, from September to June, it runs every half hour all day. Phones to call the ferry from either side are used from midnight to 6 AM, when the ferry operates only when a car arrives. The ferry stops operating for a week in early June for maintenance, depending on tides; signs of the closing are posted.

Off Digby Neck, the *Petit Princess* is the first ferry that takes you from the mainland, first to Long Island, leaving from East Ferry. That ferry takes you to Tiverton, and it leaves on the half hour. From the other side, it leaves on the hour. A 10-mile drive, which takes 15 to 17 minutes, brings you through Long Island into the village of Freeport on Highway 217. At the end of the road you'll find the *Joe Casey,* which leaves on the hour. The schedule has enough time built into it for people to catch both ferries, either coming or going. Brier Island, a distance of half a mile, is the final stop. When you leave Brier Island, the ferry departs at 25 minutes past of the hour, leaving enough time to get back to the Tiverton ferry.

The ferries tie up at midnight at Tiverton and Freeport and stay there until they're needed. They will start operating again at 6 AM. Between midnight and 6 AM you can call for a ferry to pick you up, using the little green call box at the other side. There is always someone in the wheelhouse who will bring the ferry, though only at the same point in the hour as it regularly arrives. The second ferry will be alerted that a vehicle is coming, if you are going that far.

These ferries both require a $5 ticket, but only once. "We collect only going to the island," said the captain of the *Joe Casey,* Troy Frost, who explained all these details. Visitors who are staying on the island and plan to explore the region can buy a book of 20 tickets for $25.

By Airplane

Three commercial airports and many private landing strips and smaller airports can take visitors to the Maritimes.

To Nova Scotia

Halifax Stanfield International Airport (halifaxairport.com) sees more than 3 million passengers annually. Airlines include:

Air Canada (888-247-2262; aircanada.com)
Air St. Pierre (902-873-3566; airsaintpierre.com), with flights to Cape Breton Island and
 Newfoundland
Air Transat (877-872-6728; transatholidays.com)
American Airlines (800-433-7300; aa.com) and **American Eagle** (800-433-7300)
CanJet (877-835-9285), with flights to Canada and the United Kingdom
Continental Express Airlines (800-784-444; continental.com)
Delta (800-221-1212; delta.com)
IcelandAir (800-223-5500; icelandair.com), with flights to Iceland, **Northwest Airlines**
 (800-225-2525; nwa.com)
Prince Edward Air Ltd. (902-873-3575)
United Airlines (800-241-6522; united.ca)
WestJet (888-937-8538; westjet.com), with flights across Canada, to New York City and
 cities in the southern United States.
Sydney Airport (Sydneyairport.ca) is served by flights from **Air St. Pierre** (902-873-
3566; airsaintpierre.com) and **Air Canada Jazz** (888-247-2262; flyjazz.ca).

To Prince Edward Island
Charlottetown Airport (flypei.com) lists airlines including **Air Canada Jazz** (888-247-
2262; flyjazz.ca); **WestJet** (888-937-8538; westjet.com), with flights across Canada, to New
York City and cities in the southern USA; **Northwest Airlines** (800-225-2525; nwa.com);
Delta (800-221-1212; delta.com); and **Prince Edward Air** (800-565-5359; peair.com), a
charter company.

By Train
VIA Rail Canada (888-842-7245; viarail.ca), Customer Relations, VIA Rail Canada Inc.,
P.O. Box 8116, Station "A," Montreal, Quebec H3C 3N3. The train that crosses all of Canada
ends its eastern route in Halifax, making two stops in Nova Scotia between Halifax and the
westernmost city of Amherst. The Web site allows you to book a trip and lists the stations
and schedules for the province. There is no train service to Prince Edward Island.

American travelers could take an Amtrak train to Montreal and travel VIA Rail Canada
to Nova Scotia—but the leg from Montreal to Halifax would take 21 hours. Or you could take
the train out of Halifax, from its station near the waterfront at 1161 Hollis St., Halifax, NS
B3H 2P6, next to the Westin Halifax hotel.

Between Halifax and Amherst the train stops in Truro Centre, 104 the Esplanade St.,
Truro, NS B2N 2K3, and in Springhill Junction, Station St., Springhill Junction, NS B0M
1X0 (but only if requested), which is close to Amherst.

By Foot
NovaTrails.com is a great resource for finding a trail wherever it is you already are. The
Web site is arranged by region and offers graded hikes from easy to extreme. Waterfalls
and lighthouses are also listed on the site. All of the provincial parks listed under "Parks"
in the individual chapters of this book have hiking trails.

By Bicycle

Bike shops, clubs, events, and tours are listed at the Web site bicycle.ns.ca.

More than 35,000 kilometers of roads in Nova Scotia and Prince Edward Island present an adventure to bicyclists. Some of the narrow, twisting roads require careful riding, but the rewards of natural beauty are not to be missed. A tour map of the Halifax Regional Municipality itself is available from the **HRM Call Centre** at 902-490-4000, or at area bicycle shops, HRM Customer Service Centres and Visitor Centres, and the Nova Scotia Tourism Visitor Information Center on Lower Water Street.

Halifax Metro Transit has some bike racks so you can skip biking in heavy downtown traffic. The city is slowly adding bike lanes when a road improvement project gets under-way. The area is definitely bike friendly.

In Prince Edward Island, bicycling is both easy and safe, especially on the Confederation Trail, an old Trans Canada Railroad bed transformed into a wide path that runs from the North Cape almost to the East Point. Bike rental shops are listed in Chapter Nine, on Queens and Kings Counties.

By Motorcycle

Huge numbers of motorcyclists arrive in Nova Scotia every year to drive up and down the switchbacks on the Cabot Trail, which many call the best riding they've ever experienced. Helmets are mandatory in Nova Scotia. For the best motorcycle tour guides available in Nova Scotia, contact 866-250-7777 or go to motorcycletourguidens.com. Ridenovascotia .com is another online resource. Motorcyclepei.com is a resource for that flatter province with longer vistas.

Coopering is one of the historic skills demonstrated at the Quaker Whaler House in Dartmouth. Lisa O'Neill

3

HALIFAX AND THE EASTERN SHORE

From Urban Sophistication to Rural Calm

A most lovely public garden, a waterfront casino, and festivals like the Royal Nova Scotia Tattoo—a military re-creation involving thousands—along with theater companies, fine hotels, and restaurants, mark this old city as the most modern stop in the book. Its airport is an increasing arrival point for tourists, with direct flights from Washington, Boston, New York, Frankfort, and London.

Today Halifax and several other cities have been merged into Halifax Regional Municipality, which includes Dartmouth, Bedford, Sackville, Cole Harbour, Timberlea, Hammonds Plains, and other communities. The total population of the municipality was 372,858, according to the 2006 census statistics.

The Halifax Citadel is a huge British fortification in the center of the city; a gun has marked noon every day for generations.

Citadel Hill will host special events when the Tall Ships visit Halifax in 2009, and when the Royal Canadian Navy celebrates its 100th anniversary in 2010 with a historic ship arriving from Quebec.

All dollar amounts are given in Canadian dollars, and that dollar varies in value compared to the American dollar. In the summer of 2008, after years of being valued much lower, the Canadian dollar rose to equal the American dollar. Check the exchange rate whenever you are thinking of taking a trip as its value changes daily.

LODGING

These listings include some of the big hotels in downtown Halifax that have particularly attractive features. Later in the listings are intimate places for travelers who prefer to stay in a small place, enjoying some of the comforts and ambiance of an attractive house. But Halifax offers many more places to stay, and if rooms are hard to find, one way to seek a last minute reservation is to call the **Nova Scotia Tourism** telephone number, 800-565-0000. The Web site, a cornucopia of information, is at www.novascotia.com. November through March bring lower rates. Note: Motels on the Bedford highway, with the exception of the Comfort Inn, are not recommended.

HALIFAX AND SURROUNDING AREA

Hotels

CAMBRIDGE SUITES HOTEL HALIFAX

John Duggan, General Manager
902-420-0555, 800-565-1263
cambridgesuiteshalifax.com
1583 Brunswick St., Halifax, NS B3J 3P5
Just east of the Citadel
Price: $99 in off-season to $269
Credit cards: Yes
Handicapped Access: Yes, except to fitness center

Special Features: Free Wi-Fi, parking garage with fee, fitness club with hot tub and sauna and outdoor patio, continental breakfast included, CAA/AAA discount

Cambridge Suites offers 200 one-bedroom and studio suites, each with a mini-kitchen—including a microwave, sink, small refrigerator, and dishes—standing in for your kitchen back home, and making the stay wherever you are that much more relaxing. In Halifax on the harbor side, the view adds allure to the expansive accommodations. I happened to stay in Room 527 on Canada Day, July 1, when a fireboat showed off its power with double plumes of seawater, and the late-night fireworks were extraordinary. Other guests could gather in the sixth-floor fitness center, a short walk upstairs from the elevator, which has an outdoor patio with a great view of downtown. The steep hillside that runs down from the Citadel, just outside the door, to the waterfront means that anyone who visits will get some exercise, but every block is a revelation, with handsome bronze sailors and pontificating politicians among the statues—and possibly the passersby.

THE HALLIBURTON

902-420-0658, 888-512-3344
thehalliburton.com
5184 Morris St., Halifax, NS B3J 1B3
Price: $85 to $350
Credit cards: Yes
Handicapped Access: None
Special Features: Free Wi-Fi in library (with fire in fireplace in cool season), $10 fee per day for Wi-Fi in rooms; garden courtyard with seating; Stories, a fine dining restaurant; deluxe continental breakfast included; free limited on-site parking plus one-block-distant parking lot; CAA/AAA discount

Part of this hotel is carved inside an 1809 townhouse that once belonged to the Chief Justice of the Nova Scotia Supreme Court, Sir Brenton Halliburton. The rooms vary in size and amenities. Some have wood-burning fireplaces (but fires are lit only when the weather is cold). Some rooms overlook the flowering central courtyard, with their own balconies, and other rooms are simply small—one has just one single twin bed—a deal for a single traveler in the off-season. A deluxe buffet continental breakfast offers guests baked beans, fruit, cereals, Black Forest ham, hard-boiled eggs, pastries baked at the hotel, and more.

LORD NELSON HOTEL

902-423-5130, 800 565-2020
lordnelsonhotel.com
1515 South Park St., Halifax, NS B3J 2L2
Next to Halifax Public Gardens
Price: $129 to $449
Credit cards: Yes
Handicapped Access: Yes, four fully accessible units
Special Features: Free Wi-Fi in conference areas and mezzanine, fee with standard rooms of $9.95 a night (no fee in high-end rooms), fitness room, pets welcome with no fee unless cleaning is necessary, underground parking with fee, CAA/AAA discount

With 261 rooms and suites, plus the most charming English-style pub in the city, the Lord Nelson Hotel is the kind of refuge any traveler wants to land in, from the paneled lobby to the superior beds. Renovations have transformed the older rooms, adding fresh white bedding and modern dark-wood furniture. Some bathrooms have tiled walls. Rooms with views of the Public Gardens are in demand, and they would give a gorgeous prospect in May. From rooms overlooking Spring Garden Road a guest can watch parades held during the Nova Scotia International Tattoo (see "Seasonal Events" in the Recreation section below).

THE PRINCE GEORGE HOTEL

902-425-1986, 800-565-1567
www.princegeorgehotel.com
1725 Market St., Halifax, NS B3J 3N9
Price: $149 to $249
Credit cards: Yes
Handicapped Access: Yes, one available
Special Features: Free Wi-Fi in rooms and business center, Gio Restaurant, heated indoor pool, covered walkways to waterfront, parking with a fee, pets welcome, $20 fee for entire stay, CAA/AAA discount

Two hundred rooms, undergoing a hotel-wide updating, are all outfitted with handsome furniture and big, soft beds at the Prince George Hotel, right in the center of Halifax. An enclosed pedestrian walkway or pedway is the favorite passage of Haligonians in the winter, offering a means of getting to the casino or the waterfront out of the cold, and it does just as well protecting you from the heat in summer. It's connected to the Marriott, the Casino Nova Scotia, the World Trade and Convention Centre, the Metro Centre, and more. Back in the hotel, there's a whirlpool and sauna ready after a workout in the cardio room. One of Halifax's best restaurants, Gio, is on the premises; see the review in the Restaurants section of this chapter.

THE WESTIN NOVA SCOTIAN
902-421-1000, 888-679-3784
westin.ns.ca
1181 Hollis St., Halifax, NS B3H 2P6
Price: $99 to $299, higher for suites
Credit cards: Yes
Handicapped Access: Yes, one available
Special Features: Free Wi-Fi in lobby, high-speed Internet access in rooms with a $9.95 fee; Café Pronto with Starbucks coffee in lobby; Eve, a cocktail lounge; Elements, the restaurant; indoor pool, hot tub, workout facility; CAA/AAA discount

Originally called The Nova Scotian, this 1930 property began its existence as an elegant hotel owned by Canadian National Railways. Alterations in the 1950s added 161 rooms, and the hotel hosted Great Britain's Queen Elizabeth II, who returned for a second stay in the 1970s. In the 1980s the hotel changed hands twice, and millions of dollars were invested through the 1990s to upgrade the rooms, ballrooms, and meeting areas. Westin has been in charge since 1996, offering 297 rooms that have all been groomed by upgrades and attention. Now if only the Commonwealth Ballroom, all 8,400 square feet of it, still hosted a supper club with dancing, as it did when the hotel got off to an auspicious start.

Small Inns and Bed & Breakfasts

✪ AT ROBIE'S END BED & BREAKFAST
Fran Bazos, innkeeper
902-405-2424
robiesend.com
836 Robie St., Halifax, NS B3H 3C1
Price: $100 to $140, includes taxes and parking
Credit cards: Yes
Handicapped Access: None
Special Features: Free Wi-Fi, breakfast and parking included

This tiny spot offers the intimacy and tranquility that some travelers prefer, with two attractive bedrooms, private washrooms with showers and private entrances, allowing a stay in Halifax to feel like a visit to friends. The garden suite has a deck and garden space to call your own, and the southwest suite comes with a king-size bed and a spacious sitting area; both have a fridge and coffee maker. The location beside St. Mary's University puts Point Pleasant Park, a jogger's paradise, within a few minutes' walk. In the other direction is the downtown area of Halifax, a 20-minute walk.

Hot dishes might include strata made with potatoes, ham, eggs, and cheese, and the classic, bacon and eggs. Fresh fruit is always served, as is premium-quality coffee.

THE PEBBLE BED & BREAKFAST
Elizabeth O'Carroll, innkeeper
902-423-3369, 888-303-5056
thepebble.ca
1839 Armview Terrace, Halifax, NS B3H 4H3
Price: $125 to $225
Credit cards: Yes
Handicapped Access: No
Special Features: Wi-Fi, small pets welcome

The Pebble Suite really does "boast," as they say, a flared soaker tub with air jets, separate shower, and an immaculate new-old sink in a wainscoted washroom. The pale walls of the bedroom are echoed in the white-covered duvet on the bed. The Armview Suite's name evokes the view from the armchairs of a garden, and a semiformal living room with a fireplace sustains the elegant décor of the rooms and the palate of cream, taupe, and brown. This B&B is located near the yacht club on the "Arm," the long arm-shaped inlet south of Halifax Harbor. A 10-minute drive to downtown Halifax.

DARTMOUTH AND OUTER AREAS

ARBOR VISTA BED & BREAKFAST

Lynn Hardy, innkeeper
902-434-9598, 888-484-9598
arborvistabb.com
28 Lake Charles Dr., Dartmouth, NS B2X 2T2
Price: $90 to $150 (no tax)
Credit cards: Yes
Handicapped Access: None
Special Features: Wi-Fi, on the water with a dock, garden, and gazebo

The dining room overlooks 4-mile Lake Charles and so does the common room, where guests can enjoy a cup of coffee or tea. Two bright rooms are offered, both with private bathrooms, a view of the lake, and a queen-size bed; one of the rooms offers an additional a single bed and a bathtub as well as a shower. Across the lake is Shubie Park, part of the Shubenacadie Canal System. Choices for breakfast might include bacon and eggs, waffles, and coddled eggs in a bone china dish. It's a traditional Canadian breakfast, and it often includes apple bran muffins.

"Lake lice," as jet skiers are called in Nova Scotia, are infrequent on this lake, where there is no public access for public boating. Loons call on the lake in the evening. Fifteen minutes to downtown Halifax.

HERITAGE HIDEAWAY BED & BREAKFAST

Martin and Diane Gillis, innkeepers
902-835-3605, 877-437-4433
heritagehideaway.com
36 Rutledge St., Bedford, NS B4A 1W9
Price: $115 to $139
Credit cards: Yes
Handicapped Access: No
Special Features: Wi-Fi, on the Heritage Walking Tour from Bedford's Scott Manor House

Two suites at the 1870 Heritage Hideaway hold more comforts than home—like goose-down duvets, terrycloth robes, and stationery, as well as a view of Bedford Basin. The four-poster canopy bed in the Heritage Suite is covered with gorgeous red and gold damask, and the Victorian chairs in the Carriage Suite are typical of the fine furniture used here. Innkeeper Diane Gillis has a reputation for her breakfasts, always with fresh fruit and yogurt, house granola, and freshly baked breads and tea biscuits, served on one of five sets of bone china in the soigné dining room with its ornate curtains (made by the innkeeper, who also irons everything here). A favorite of guests are apple crisp pancakes. Located 15 minutes from downtown.

OCEANSTONE INN & COTTAGES BY THE SEA

Ron and Carole MacInnis, innkeepers
902-823-2160, 866-823-2160
oceanstone.ns.ca
8650 Peggy's Cove Rd., Indian Harbour, NS B3Z 3P4
Price: $95 to $365
Credit cards: Yes
Handicapped Access: Yes, one suite
Special Features: Wi-Fi; massage; fully equipped cottages on the ocean; Rhubarb

Grill, a fine-dining restaurant on the property (see the Restaurants section below); 20 acres with trails

Throughout the assortment of accommodations spread around this landscaped oceanfront property, there is an atmosphere of bountiful peace and tranquility. Perhaps it comes from the family in charge, and their attitude of thankfulness detailed in the story of the business on their Web site—a saga of years of ambition and the realization of a dream. Six suites, five rooms, and eight cottages were all built within the last eight years and are furnished with taste and consideration. "All of our cottages are built with old Nova Scotia designs; we wanted the character in keeping with the coastline," said Carole MacInnis. An on-site eco-concierge takes guests on hikes and out on kayaks (fee).

RESTAURANTS

For a traveler who is contemplating dinner, the evening arrives in Halifax with an air of excited anticipation. There is such a good range, with dinners of seafood at every corner, and Greek, Lebanese, French, and Italian places vying with Maritime cuisine to tempt you inside one of the hopping restaurants, bistros, and cafes. A drink to start any evening could be enjoyed at **Economy Shoe Shop**, where you might also eat if you didn't have the energy to walk a few blocks. **Salty's** is a sturdy tourist magnet on the Waterfront, but not the place locals usually care to recommend, and it's not listed here. **Fid Cuisine**, with a plateful of something grown in the province that is expertly prepared, might be a destination. The **Wooden Monkey** keeps vegetarian and vegan items in mind, while serving a succulent, fabulous lamb burger and rosti. **Jane's On the Common** is so well loved by this town that everyone told me to go there—and voted it Halifax's Best

Restaurant. But there are Greek, Thai, Japanese, and more choices to consider. It certainly is clear that a few nights in this town will not be enough.

HALIFAX

Fine Dining

⊘ FID RESTAURANT
902-422-9162
fidcuisine.ca
1569 Dresden Row, Halifax
Open: Lunch Wed.–Fri. 11:30 AM–2 PM, dinner Tues.–Sun. 5–10 PM
Price: Dinner $24 to $29
Credit cards: Yes
Cuisine: Modern and inventive, French and Asian
Serving: L, D
Handicap Access: No
Special Features: A concentration of local foods

Maître d' Monica Bauché and chef Dennis Johnston are the team that has brought this business to the tip of the tongue of everyone lucky enough to dine here. They also have an impressive collection of awards given to both themselves and the staff. One menu item, lamb shoulder confit with charred tomato, corn, and heirloom beets, gives a clue to their inventiveness and sure touch with flavors and textures.

"We have a local farmer who supplies me with fresh veal," said Johnstone. "We're serving that with long flattish beans called the Marvels of Venice. We called them the marvels of Lakeville, because these beans are from Lakeville, Nova Scotia."

Butter-poached fennel and zucchini with flowers on the end were additional dishes that Johnston had devised to accompany the veal, served in a cut the size of beef tenderloin and sautéed in butter. Berkshire pork belly roasted in the style of Asian barbeque with an apple-jelly glaze was also on the menu, at this clean, spare, restaurant noted for its modern décor and fine dining.

A fid, by the way, is a pointy cone used by sailors to splice rope; Fid the restaurant splices flavors.

FIVE FISHERMEN

902-422-4421
fivefishermen.com
1740 Argyle St., Halifax
Open: Daily from 5 PM
Price: $28 to $54
Credit Cards: Yes
Cuisine: Seafood and steak
Serving: D
Handicapped Access: No, steep stairs to enter building
Special features: Free mussels with every entrée

Executive chef Renée Lavallée has put together a popular menu with touches of local inspiration and lots of pizzazz from the Mediterranean. Four Nova Scotia vineyards have wines on the list here, and some could easily pair with the complimentary mussels that come before any entrée. Lobster, of course, or blackened haddock with Creole shrimp and cheddar grits, are two meals out of the ocean. Tatamagouche lamb rack is accompanied by lamb and chèvre sausage, roasted eggplant and zucchini, grape tomatoes, and olives. The pork belly is from Nova Scotia and intelligently put together with creamed cabbage and Mostarda di frutta, a savory-sweet side. Neither is cheap, at $38 and $35 each—in fact, Five Fishermen is downright expensive.

The restaurant opened in 1975, in a building that once had been a school with many indigent students; at another time it had been a funeral home that sheltered the remains of John Jacob Astor, one of those who perished during the sinking of the *Titanic* in April 1912. Servers have seen ghosts on the staircase, or in the kitchen, or in the bar. But none of the spectral visitors have ever done any harm.

GIO

902-425-1987
giohalifax.com
Prince George Hotel, 1725 Market St., Halifax
Open: Lunch on weekdays, dinner daily
Price: $27 to $60 for Kobe beef
Credit cards: Yes
Cuisine: International, with a focus on local ingredients
Serving: L, D
Handicap Access: Yes, from the front doors of the hotel
Special Features: A large, chic lounge area is an inviting place for a drink

On one summer night we visited, elk with herbs and horseradish was served with oyster mushrooms, sweet potato gnocchi, and grilled watermelon. The lobster was poached in butter, and the swordfish was flavored with bacon. The expensive indulgence of Kobe beef, the Japanese specialty from cattle that get regular massage, came with cauliflower purée and short rib and stilton pierogies. The lunch menu is more fun, with a bento box of noodle salad, pork gyoza or dumplings, and katafi shrimp. Shrimp fatoush held seared shrimp, couscous, and a salad of romaine, peppers, cucumber and garlic, parsley and mint to enjoy with crisped flatbread. The crab club or the spinach and ricotta ravioli would be perfect another time.

HAMACHI HOUSE

902-425-7711
www.hamachihouse.com
5190 Morris St., Halifax
Open: Daily 11:30 AM–midnight
Price: Entrées $8 to $20, nigiri sushi $4 to $6.75 for 2 pieces
Credit cards: Yes
Cuisine: Japanese

Serving: L, D
Handicap Access: Yes

An iron teapot with green tea would be an aromatic accompaniment to the exceptionally fresh sushi and sashimi at Hamachi House, perhaps the suzuki or striped sea bass or hotate, a scallop. Rolls come in extravagant combinations and classic simplicity. But fans of noodle dishes, tempura, and yakitori also have pleanty of choices from the long menu at this restaurant, Halifax's best for fresh sushi. The same company also owns **Hamachi Steakhouse Bar & Grill** (902-422-1600) at 1477 Lower Water Street, and **Hamachi Grill and Sushi House** (902-444-4688) at 644 Portland Street, in Dartmouth.

ONYX

902-428-5680
onyxdining.com
5680 Spring Garden Rd., Halifax,
Open: Mon.–Sat. 4:30 PM–2 AM; kitchen open Mon.–Wed. till 11 PM, Thurs.–Sat. till 1 AM.
Price: Fixed price, $46 for three courses, $37 for two courses
Credit cards: Yes
Cuisine: International fine dining
Serving: D
Handicap Access: Yes
Special Features: Sheer curtains separate tables, and the bar glows

To begin with, you can consider a whole menu of mojitos, like a bellini version with muddled ripe peaches and a little peach schnapps, Piper-Heidsieck Champagne, and cherry brandy; or one called the Aphrodisiac with strawberries and mint. Or just skip the cocktails for a bottle of Thirty Bench Riesling, from the Niagara peninsula in Ontario; it will be poured in the right varietal Riedel glass. Roasted squab might come with foie gras and oven-dried figs along with a first course of gazpacho with

poached shrimp, or grilled octopus with lemon and lime corn and tomatillo salsa. The herb-crusted rack of lamb is an Onyx and Nova Scotia specialty with a sauce made with Périgord truffles. End with a fruit napoleon made with house-made marshmallow layered with almond filo and passion fruit Bavarian cream.

SEVEN STEAK AND SEAFOOD

902-444-4777
sevenwinebar.com
1579 Grafton St., Halifax
Open: Mon.–Sat.
at 4, Sun. at 5
Price: Entrées $30 to $45
Credit cards: Yes
Cuisine: International and Maritime, with a focus on local ingredients
Serving: D
Handicap Access: Yes
Special Features: Inventive small plates served in the lounge

One of the city's best wine lists is in this restaurant; come here for one of the 30 wines offered by the glass, perhaps Rosenblum Cellars Vintner's Cuvée Zinfandel from California. The Nova Scotia wineries are certainly represented, with Jöst Eagle Tree Muscat sometimes available by the glass. But since drinking without eating is only half the fun, you can consider fine dining off a full menu in the restaurant or trying small plates in the lounge. On a full menu, an appetizer of seared Brier Island scallops was accompanied by green peas and prosciutto tortellini ($15), and the foie gras came with a savory apple tart ($21). Steaks are available with a choice of sauces like foie gras jus or truffled hollandaise, mushroom sides (some from the forest nearby), or compound butters like Blue Benedictine (made with a Quebec blue cheese).

Things get exciting with the small-plates menu here, with dishes like grilled short ribs with chipotle, corn, and smoked bacon, or the foie gras and chicken corn dogs.

Cafes and Bistros

Thriving ethnic eateries fill this little city, and various interests support a vegetarian association (halifaxvegetarians.blog spot.com), a little and a big coffee roaster, and belly dancing, to name just a few.

✪ CHABAA THAI

902-406-3008
1546 Queen St., Halifax
Open: Mon.–Sat. lunch 12–2:30 PM, dinner 5–10 PM
Price: Lunch $8.50, dinner entrees $10 to $15
Credit cards: Yes
Cuisine: Thai
Serving: L, D
Handicap Access: Yes, with elevator

The name means hibiscus in Thai, and artificial ones decorate the modern dining rooms with big windows. This recommended Thai restaurant uses all the Thai classics in its meals, from lime juice and lemongrass to fish sauce and shrimp paste. An appetizer of fried Thai crispy rice features rice with ground pork, coconut milk, coriander, peanuts, and chilies. A mango salad with shallots, chilies, and mint with lime juice, or a shredded green papaya salad with long beans, would be cool on a hot day. Lemongrass pork with tamarind or spicy seafood noodles with squid, mussels, and shrimp are two possibilities for dinner.

CHIVE'S CANADIAN BISTRO

902-420-9626
chives.ca
1537 Barrington St., Halifax
Open: Daily for dinner 5 PM to last seating at 9:30 PM
Price: $20 to $25
Credit cards: Yes
Cuisine: Italian and Maritime

A table in the casual bistro Chives in downtown Halifax

Serving: D
Handicap Access: No
Special features: Private dining room, tasting menus

Co-owner and pastry chef Darren Lewis and chef and proprietor M. Craig Flinn opened this bistro in December 2001. They like to show off the province's best, and they might be offering a risotto that does just that for lobster, scallops, and Indian Point mussels. Pork loin stuffed with apple and maple sausage with a side of carrot and rutabaga "smash" are on one menu, along with Swiss chard and asparagus with pan-fried haddock. These meals, off Chive's seasonal menus from the farms of Nova Scotia, will stick to your ribs.

ECONOMY SHOE SHOP

902-423-7463
economyshoeshop.ca
1661–1663 Argyle St., Halifax

Open: Daily 10 AM–2:30 AM
Price: $6 to $25
Credit cards: Yes
Cuisine: Maritime with Asian diversions
Serving: L, D, Sun. brunch
Handicap Access: At the Backstage door,
with accessible bathrooms
Special Features: Charming, imaginative
décor; no reservations

Started in 1995 as a little spot to enjoy a
beer, this multi-roomed restaurant wears
an odd neon sign that reads ECONOMY SHOE
SHOP. "The coolest place in town for a
drink," is one local's judgment, even
though he deplores the service. The bar,
with no TV or video gaming machines, was
the beginning of the business—leading to
other rooms: Backstage, dominated by a
"tree"; The Belgian Bar, devoted to beer and
achieving a light-filled plant paradise even
in dark winter; and The Diamond, with a
jukebox devoted to the best Nova Scotia
music. The Italian hot sausage pizza would
go perfectly with beer, but the jumbo Thai
shrimp pasta dish might be just as good
with a dry white wine from Nova Scotia,
Grand Pré's L'Acadie Blanc. You can order
from the tapas or appetizer menu until 1:45
AM, and that includes the mini Thai chicken
spring rolls and baked goat cheese on garlic
toast.

ITALIAN MARKET
902-455-6124
italianmarket.ca
6061 Young St., Halifax
Open: Mon.–Fri. 8 AM–7 PM, Sat. 9 AM–7 PM,
Sun. 11 AM–6 PM
Price: $7 to $11
Credit cards: Yes
Cuisine: Italian
Serving: L, D
Handicap Access: Yes
Special Features: Also a take-out lunch hot
spot, and market for all Italian specialty
foods

The bakery might be the downfall of an
innocent visitor who was hoping simply to
pick up one of the prepared salads to eat in
the café or take out. It displays its beautifully iced concoctions and its fruit tarts in a
glass case. They are as alluring as a movie
star. Braised beef ribs with peppers and
onions would be another kind of meal,
tempting in the chilly weather, as would be
the chicken souvlaki with tatziki or the eggplant au gratin. The market has daily specials too, of both pasta and prepared salads.
A big slice of pizza is just $3.95.

IT'S ALL GREEK TO ME
902-406-3737
allgreektome.com
6196 Quinpool Rd., Halifax
Open: Mon.–Sat. 11 AM–10 PM
Price: $14 to $26
Credit cards: Yes
Cuisine: Greek
Serving: L, D
Handicap Access: No
Special Features: A patio with awnings dur-
ing good weather, Greek music, reserva-
tions recommended (often booked solid)

Halifax enjoys an abundance of good Greek
cooking. Greeks are often the owners of
restaurants that have been serving fried
fish for generations. But at It's All Greek To
Me, opened in September 2007, customers
can taste Greek cuisine as compelling as
Italian or Middle Eastern. Skewers of
grilled meat are cooked after marinating in
lemon juice and olive oil and come with
roasted potatoes and Greek salad, with its
mouthwatering feta adding the perfect
tanginess to cucumbers, tomatoes, and
crunchy lettuce. Who wants to resist a
starter of grilled loukaniko, the garlicky
Greek sausage, or a marinated and grilled
octopus salad, with a glass of Boutari wine?
Simmered greens with olive oil and lemon
called horta could be paired with a plate of
the feta, and they would be put together just

as they should be. Beware the specialty loukoumathes, fried dough with vanilla ice cream in the center and honey or chocolate sauce on top.

✪ JANE'S ON THE COMMON
902-431-5683
janesonthecommon.com
2394 Robie St., Halifax
Open: Lunch Tues.–Fri. 11 AM–2:30 PM; dinner Tues.–Thurs. and Sun. 5–9 PM, Fri.–Sat. 5–10 PM; brunch Sat.–Sun. 9:30 AM–2:30 PM; closed Mon.
Price: $15 to $19
Credit cards: Yes
Cuisine: Comfort food with style, some French, Indian influences
Serving: Brunch, L, D
Handicap Access: One step up at front door, with accessible washrooms
Special Features: Reservations not accepted

This is the place everyone tells you to visit, and a glance at the easy-on-the-wallet menu tells why. White bean cassoulet with duck confit holds Sweet Williams Sausage, made by a local sausage maker and sold at the Saturday Farmers' Market in Halifax— "A beautiful homemade sausage," said Jane Wright, the owner. Madras vegetable curry takes you for a journey if you want to leave behind the indigenous pleasures, but sesame-crusted salmon with a soy, maple, and lemon glaze highlights the best of what is nearby. The Indian Point mussels bring both the near and far together with a Thai red coconut curry sauce. Opened in late 2003, this small neighborhood bistro has been consistently successful with its mix of straightforward informality and just enough pizzazz. Wright said farewell to the politically active first stage of her life and embarked on a career feeding customers satisfying, not overly rich meals that they might like to enjoy a few times a week. It's a policy that has earned her an established place among the city's best-loved restaurants.

MCKELVIE'S
902-421-6161
mckelvies.ca
1680 Lower Water St., Halifax
Open: Mon.–Sat. from 11:30 AM, Sun. from 4:30 PM
Price: $18 to $27, higher for lobster
Credit cards: Yes
Cuisine: Seafood
Serving: L, D
Handicap Access: Yes
Special Features: Outdoor seating in good weather

McKelvie's, a recommended seafood place, is set inside old Fire Station No. 4, with floor-to-ceiling windows. Lobster holds top billing on the menu, steamed, served with steaks, or stir-fried with cashews and pineapple. But the rest of the sea is presented on plates here, like the Digby scallops, salmon, and haddock gratin, or a crab bisque. Mussels are steamed with parsley and garlic butter, and Colville Cove oysters from Prince Edward Island can be enjoyed either raw on the half shell or baked à la Rockfeller with spinach, bacon, and Parmesan. There are steaks, chicken, and salads as well. "We're famous for our bread— bannock, originally an Indian dish. Our version has raisons, whole wheat flour, oats, bran, and no yeast," said manager Glorianne Young. You can also buy the bannock mix here.

NEW FORTUNE
902-431-7575
480 Parkland Dr., Clayton Park West, Halifax
Open: Mon.–Thurs., 11 AM–10 PM, Fri.–Sat. 11 AM–11 PM, Sun. 3–10 PM
Price: Entrées $8 to $16
Credit cards: Yes
Cuisine: Vietnamese and Asian
Serving: L, D

Making stock from its carcasses and bones, the Vietnamese owner of New Fortune makes excellent Pho, with tender rare beef or chicken, or seafood. Vietnamese hot and sour soup is served with rice or vermicelli; jack fruit juice or a mango shake will appeal to a fruit lover. Braised lemongrass beef or chicken with rice or vermicelli, or Chinese classics like Szechuan fried shrimp, are all fine resources for a visitor ready to try something different. On weekends you can try the Vietnamese pancakes.

SAEGE BISTRO
902-429-1882
saege.ca
5883 Spring Garden Rd., Halifax
Open: Tues.–Fri. 11:30 AM–10 PM, Sat.–Sun. 8 AM–10 PM, closed Mon.
Price: $15 to $25
Credit cards: Yes
Cuisine: Maritime, Italian, and Asian
Serving: B, L, D
Handicap Access: Yes

Geir Simensen, owner of Saege Bistro and Scanway Catering, added an upscale bistro to this neighborhood in 2005 when most of the other places to eat were very simple; the 'ae' in Saege is a single letter in Norwegian. Seared scallops might come with Oulton Farm smoked bacon from Windsor, and carrot tarragon sauce—unless you opted to try a Maritime fettuccine of lobster, shrimp, and scallops, mixed up with noodles, broccolini, and roasted garlic cream. One pizza features barbequed chicken and roasted red peppers, or mushrooms with pesto and arugula. On Wednesday nights you can try that pizza or one of the pasta dishes for just $10—and Simensen plans to sustain that deal into 2009. Fish Friday offers a shallow-fried beer-battered fish and oven-baked fish coated with a partly whole-grain and sunflower-seed crust (there's no deep frying here), served with grilled Yukon Gold potatoes and cucumber salad.

SWEET BASIL BISTRO
902-425-2133
scanwaycatering.com/SweetBasil
1866 Upper Water St., Halifax
Open: Daily, lunch from 11:30 AM, dinner from 5 PM; brunch Sat.–Sun. 10 AM–to 3 PM
Price: $14 for pizza to $24
Credit cards: Yes
Cuisine: Eclectic
Serving: L, D
Handicap Access: No
Special Features: Outdoor patio

In the middle of Historic Properties with its fine shopping is a refuge for weary consumers, or just footsore waterfront walkers—Sweet Basil Bistro. Thirty-five seats inside and 25 seats on the patio in this historic building have been rejuvenating customers since the early 1990s. This Scanway Catering property, also owner of Saege Bistro mentioned above and the Cheapside Café (see the Art Gallery of Nova Scotia in the Culture section below) serves an eclectic menu here with haddock and preserved lemon, or salmon with sweet basil and mango, or a steak with brandy cream. Among the appealing pasta dishes is a whole-wheat spaghetti dish with grilled chicken and Asiago. But you are not really supposed to omit dessert, and the list, which includes warm apple cake, will make sure that you don't.

WHET CAFÉ AT FRED SALON, BEAUTY ART FOOD
902-423-5400
fredsalon.ca
2606 Agricola St., Halifax
Open: Tues.–Sat. from 10 AM
Price: Lunch $7 to $11.50
Credit cards: Yes
Cuisine: Casual and upscale lunch
Serving: B, L
Handicap Access: Yes
Special Features: Art gallery featuring local and Canadian artists, hairstyle salon

Lunch at Fred is not to be missed. This hybrid business combines Whet Café with an art gallery and a hair salon. An all-day breakfast starts with a croissant, and lunch includes organic salads, soups, and tempting cupcakes. Enjoy a glass of wine with the panini, as you sit in your white chair in the open space of the café, after a visit to the glowing deep pink washroom. You are feeling more beautiful already. The business is located just a few blocks north of Citadel Hill down Robie Street and one block to the right.

THE WOODEN MONKEY

902-444-3844
thewoodenmonkey.ca
1685 Argyle St., Halifax
Open: Sun.–Thurs. 11:30 AM–10 PM, Fri.–Sat. 11:30 AM–11 PM
Price: $17 to $18.75
Credit cards: Yes
Cuisine: Vegan and classic locally sourced meat and seafood
Serving: L, D
Handicap Access: Yes, in new place
Special Features: Sidewalk dining

The description on the wall sums it up. The Wooden Monkey is "striving to offer locally grown and organic food." But no one here will give you any attitude. You'll have the best of both worlds, enjoying delicious food and feeling just a little smug about it. If you want a vegan meal, it's here. But the lamburger, made with local lamb, is resplendent with local flavor inside its chewy bun, with an herbed goat cheese. The rosti, spears of highly seasoned potatoes (local, of course), are too good—because you won't be able to stop eating them. The house salad that I ordered could not have been better, with tender early summer greens perfectly dressed in a light rice-vinegar dressing, with pumpkin seeds and raisins to add texture and interest. Start with an organic screwdriver and then try the local wines. The Gaspereau Lucie Kuhlmann, a slightly sour red, needed the lamb to keep in bounds. The funky interior with bead curtains and a restrained use of monkey statues makes this place as comfortable as your best friend's house.

Pizza, Pasta, and Diners

ARMVIEW RESTAURANT

902-455-4395
thearmview.com
7156 Chebucto Rd., Halifax
Open: Mon.–Wed. 11 AM–midnight, Thurs.–Sun. 8:30 AM–midnight
Price: Entrées $9 to $16
Credit cards: Yes
Cuisine: Comfort diner food with regional inspiration
Serving: B, L, D
Handicap Access: No
Special Features: Outside patio, with a bar DJs every Fri. night, occasional live jazz or acoustic music

Eighty percent of the food served here is classic, untouched diner food, like club sandwiches and hot burgers. "We make everything here," said George Kapetanakis, one of the owners. Twenty percent of the menu changes seasonally. In August a halibut burger and a warm Chilean salad with chilies, and chorizo and chicken with a balsamic glaze were specials.

The lamb burger is made with free-range Nova Scotia lamb. An emu burger made with Nova Scotia–raised emu is "actually delicious," Kapetanakis said. Bison, boar, and other unusual meats are also served in burgers. But you will always find a classic made with local beef, "cooked with love." At breakfast, customers like the eggs Benedict with sliced chorizo, red onion, and red pepper.

✪ COASTAL COFFEE

902-405-4022
thecoastal.ca
2731 Robie St., Halifax
Open: Tues.–Fri.
8 AM–3 PM, breakfast till 2, lunch till 3; Sat. 8 AM–3 PM, breakfast all day; Sun. 10–3, breakfast all day; closed Mon.
Price: $6 to $10
Credit cards: Yes
Cuisine: Casual fare with Tex-Mex and

Asian influences
Serving: B, L
Handicap Access: Yes
Special Features: Wi-Fi, coffee from Laughing Whale Coffee Roasters in Lunenburg, organic Fair Trade beans

Mark Giffin, the chef of fine-dining spot Bish for six years before he opened this place of his own in June 2008, is now in the business of making the perfect hamburger. Giffin said he hand-forms the patty—it's not a premade frozen patty. "At this price point, we're doing it pretty much by hand," Giffin said, and that includes the house sausage. Tex-Mex and Asian flavors are featured on the breakfast and lunch menus, and if the dishes sound exalted, the atmosphere is intentionally relaxed and low-key. For breakfast dishes, consider the Huevos Pedro, a frittato of chorizo, goat cheese, grilled peppers, and Papas Bravas; or the Zurich, a french-toasted croissant stuffed with marzipan, white chocolate, and mocha Nutella sauce. Besides that perfect burger in the changing menu, there might be beef and mango sate with peanut sauce and glass-noodle salad. Muffins, scones (sometimes made with Toblerone chocolate), and oatcakes go right with the micro-roastery coffee from Lunenburg or a fantastic hot chocolate.

IL MERCATO HALIFAX

902-422-2866
il-mercato.ca
5650 Spring Rd., Halifax
Open: Mon.–Sat. 11 AM–11 PM
Price: pizza and entrées $13 to $23
Credit cards: Yes
Cuisine: Italian
Serving: L, D
Handicap Access: Yes

Popular for its pasta and gelato, Il Mercato also makes pizza, from the basic classic with buffalo mozzarella, basil, and tomato to heartier versions with salami or house sausage. Main courses like grilled rack of lamb are other temptations on the menu, as are focaccia sandwiches. A pasta dish might be spaghettini with grilled vegetables, tomato, and artichokes with ricotta, or linguine with sautéed shrimp and romesco sauce. A selection of gelati is another summertime attraction.

✪ MORRIS EAST

902-444-7663
morriseast.com
5212 Morris St. (corner of Barrington), Halifax
Open: Lunch Tues.–Sat. 11:30 AM–2:30 PM; dinner Tues.–Thurs. 5–9 PM, Fri.–Sat. 5–10 PM, Sun. 5–9 PM, except last Sun. of the month, when restaurant hosts a supperclub, dinner by reservation only; no reservations at other times
Price: Pizza $13 to $17
Credit cards: Yes
Cuisine: Inventive and Italian
Serving: L, D
Handicap Access: Yes, a new installation
Special Features: Wood-fired over burning apple wood from Annapolis Valley

Peach and prosciutto with rosemary aioli, goat cheese, and charred shallots? Count me in, especially since I can order the pizza here on white, whole-wheat, or gluten-free (with a surcharge) dough. There is a genius at work thinking these things up, like the beet green pesto, with cherries, caramelized onion, arugula, and Ketch Harbour bresaola (salt-cured beef). The salads—of shaved fennel and grapefruit with coriander, for example, or watercress and oven-dried tomatoes—are equally appetizing, and so is the goat cheese soufflé. Promise the little ones a wood-fired s'more, and linger on with the strawberry and rhubarb shortcake with vanilla gelato.

PIZZARIA AMANO

902-423-6266
pizzariaamano.ca

1477 Lower Water St., Halifax
At Bishop's Landing
Open: Mon.–Sat. 11:30 AM–10 PM
Price: $13 to $15, but you may add sides or
contorni for $6
Credit cards: Yes
Cuisine: Italian
Serving: L, D
Handicap Access: Yes, the women's (but
really unisex) bathroom is accessible

Classic Italian thin-crust pizza with three or
four ingredients or less allows the crust to
survive as a crisp perfect counterpoint to the
creamy flavors on top of it; Amano's
reminds one Haligonian of the kind of pizza
made in Italy—and the real reason the dish
became a world-wide institution. Adventurous diners will jump to try the "Fichi,"
with fig confit, arugula, prosciutto, and bocconcini on top, or the "Tartufato," with wild
mushrooms, buffalo mozzarella, and a touch
of béchamel. But the $13 "Margherita," with
fresh mozzarella, basil, and tomato sauce, is
all anyone really needs in life. Eggplant
Parmesan to start, braised pork or baked
fish to continue, are also on the menu.

DARTMOUTH AND OUTER AREAS

CELTIC CORNER
902-464-0764
celticcorner.ca
69 Alderney Dr., Dartmouth
Open: Sun.–Thurs. 11 AM–midnight,
kitchen 11:30 AM–10 PM; Fri.–Sat. 11 AM–
1 AM, kitchen 11:30 AM–11 PM
Price: $8 to $15
Credit cards: Yes
Cuisine: Irish, and eastern Atlantic coast
Serving: L, D
Handicap Access: Yes
Special Features: Traditional music

From shepherd's pie to steak and kidney
pie to fisherman's pie, from pasta to barbequed ribs, the cuisine here is eclectic and
friendly. With exposed brick and lace cur-

tains on the front windows, the interior is
just as congenial. A few little rooms, each
holding a table for a private party, are in the
back, but the long, red bench seat is ready
for the social crowds who assemble to listen
to traditional music, fiddling, and singing
by local talent, played six nights a week (no
cover charge). At 5 PM on Sunday, a Cape
Breton ceilidh, or house party, starts up.
Local brews from Rickard's, Propeller,
Garrison, and Keith's breweries.

JOHN'S LUNCH FISH AND CHIPS
902-469-3074
johnslunch.com
352 Pleasant St., Dartmouth
Open: Mon.–Sat. 10 AM–9 PM, Sun.
11 AM–9 PM
Price: $2.35 to $14.50
Credit cards: Cash only, but there's a debit
ATM with a fee
Cuisine: Seafood
Serving: L, D
Handicap Access: No
Special Features: Local devotion

Take the Woodside ferry to take-out or eat
in at this little diner with big servings.
Fried clams are a specialty, and if you eat
here you can enjoy them at the counter or in
a booth. Most of John's Lunch's surfaces
have endured since 1969, leaned on by customers eager to raise another forkful of
fried haddock from a clean kitchen run by
co-owners Fotis Fatouris and Stratos Baltas,
who started off as employees. The calamari
is their Greek addition to a classic fish-and-
chips menu, but the liver with bacon or
onions has been on the menu forever.

KABABJI, AUTHENTIC
LEBANESE CUISINE
902-468-555
kababji.ca
202 Brownlow Ave., Dartmouth
Open: Mon.–Tues. 11 AM–4 PM, Wed. 11 AM–
8 PM, Fri.–Sat. 11 AM–9 PM, closed Sun.

HUBBARDS

SHORE CLUB

902-857-9555

lobstersupper.com

250 Shore Club Rd., Hubbards

Open: Early June–early Oct.,
Wed.–Sun. 4–8 pm; Sat.–Sun. only
in part of May

Price: in 2008, $27 to $39, for a
small to large lobster plus

Credit cards: Yes

Cuisine: Lobster

Serving: D

Handicap Access: Yes

Special Features: Saturday night
dances 9:30 to 1:30 with live music,
rock, clues, Zydeco, swing and more

The captain pointing the way stands outside of the Shore Club in Hubbards.

An institution since 1946, the Shore Club is a supper and dance club. Its meals and entertainment are a summertime excursion that locals look forward to, and some of them buy the ticket books for discounts for repeat visits. Don't miss what Prince Charles and Lady Diana enjoyed in 1983—the fresh boiled lobster, all-you-can-eat salad bar (served from a dory), unlimited fresh mussels, dessert, and coffee and tea. Those rare lobster-haters can get a steak, chicken, or vegetarian meal ($22.75), and the kids' menu with a hot dog, macaroni and cheese or grilled cheese is $6.96.

Gallant's Canteen (no phone), 226 Shore Club Rd. just past the entrance to Hubbard's Beach Campground. Open May 10 through mid to late Sept., 9 am–9 pm, with weekend breakfast until 11 am. No credit cards, and take-out only. You'll find "the best fish and chips" here, according to locals, at $6.75 for two pieces of fish. Kids swarm around this place like bees, but the owner doesn't let them get away with a thing.

Hubbards Beach Campground & Cottages (902-857-9460; hubbardsbeach.com), 226 Shore Club Rd. With spaces for campers, tents, RVs, and cabins for rent by the night or week, this campground by the beach and near Halifax is easy to get to and popular. The simple cabins close to the road are spartan but clean, with a shellacked pine table, mismatched chairs, a tiny kitchen with a modern fridge. Outside, yellow lawn chairs are placed by a tire rim for an evening fire. Three waterview cabins hold six. The beach is free to campers who walk the short distance from the campground. Rates for cabins range from $120 to $135 a night.

Price: $25 per person for minimum of 2, assorted mezze, platters $15 to $15
Credit cards: Yes
Cuisine: Lebanese
Serving: L, D
Handicap Access: Yes
Special Features: Belly dancing on Saturday nights

This restaurant is in the Burnside area (across the McKay Bridge, off Exit 3). Inside its double-height room hung with red-orange lights, brown-toned photographs show scenes from Lebanon. A bowl of the fatoosh salad doesn't include broken, toasted flatbread, but the chunks of cucumber, tomato, and red peppers mixed with chopped mint and parsley in a lemon juice dressing are utterly wonderful. A huge pita wrap stuffed with kefte, spiced beef meatballs, with tahini sauce and more chopped tomato and parley and mint, is even better. The only drawback I discovered was how messy and hard to eat it was, an argument for ordering one of the many platters instead.

RHUBARB GRILL & CAFE
902-821-3500
rhubarbgrill.com

8650 Peggy's Cove Rd., Indian Harbour
Open: Daily in summer 5–9:30 PM; call for off-season hours
Price: $18 to $29
Credit cards: Yes
Cuisine: Nova Scotian classics with Asian influences
Serving: L, D
Handicap Access: Yes
Special Features: Outside patio seating, early-bird menu for folks seated before 5:30

Priding itself on fresh and straightforward food, Rhubarb Grill served a salad with local lettuces, herbs, and flowers with julienned sugar beet, carrot, and celery, in 2008. Rhubarb and raspberry yogurt dressing and berries topped it off. Thai mussels came in a red curry sauce with coconut cream.

The scallops came glazed in rhubarb and tamarind, and long-line halibut was seared and accompanied by mango-strawberry salsa. Wild mushroom tofu ragout topped with chèvre makes this place a find for vegetarians, but the Angus beef filet with Stilton would woo any of the rest of us. Finish up, perhaps, with the fiery and fragrant ginger cake.

FOOD PURVEYORS

Bakeries
Julien's French Pastry Shop (902-455-9717; juliens.ca) 5517 Young St., Halifax, in the Hydrostone Market. The favored source of good bread for good restaurants' sandwiches, Julien's Pastry Shop lets you sample the breads fresh. Rye bread, almond croissants, and pain au chocolate, fruit tarts, and far more are the ultimate pick-me-up on the waterfront. Also in Chester.

Cafés and Coffee Shops
Barrington Street Cafe (902-422-5651; justuscoffee.com/barrington.aspx), 1678 Barrington St., Halifax. Open Mon.–Tues. 7:30 AM–5:30 PM, Wed.–Fri. 7:30 AM–7 PM, Sat. 9 AM–5:30 PM, Sun. 10AM–5 PM. Featuring Nova Scotia's own Just Us coffee (and free Wi-Fi), the café offers a lunch of vegetable pakora or chicken samosa, among other things.

Ciboulette Café (902-423-5282; ciboulette.ca), 1541 Barrington St., Halifax, next door to Chives on Barrington St. Open Mon.–Fri. 7 AM–5 PM. The chocolate-toffee scones would be the carrot on the stick that leads us inside, but the breakfast biscuit with local sausage, egg, cheddar, and tomato on a Chives buttermilk biscuit ($4.50) could turn into a regular habit. Fair Trade Organic Coffee is served, and the lunch possibilities are fascinating. This business can also cater a lunch or breakfast for six or more.

Coburg Coffee House (902-429-2326), 6085 Coburg Rd., Halifax. A popular place for students.

✪Java Blend Coffee Roasters (902-423-6944; javablendcoffee.com), 6027 North St., Halifax. Phenomenal coffee that's roasted right at the café, Java Blend uses beans that are Fair Trade Certified. It's also a member of the Cup of Excellence Program, an organization that sources out the best coffees from producing countries and then ships them to the members who win bids on the supply: they get to roast the best beans in the world. With one shipment that arrived from El Salvador, Java Blend won the bid on its favorite of 25 coffees that had already been chosen by Cup of Excellence from 300 to 500 samples. Winning coffee-bean farmers see prices that are four to a hundred times the price within the Fair Trade Coop. A "drip station" brews up a cup at a time in about a minute. Muffins, pastries, and Wi-Fi. Jim Dikaios is in charge.

King of Donair is famous for having introduced Nova Scotia to its now-beloved Donair, a Lebanese-style pita stuffed with spiced, sliced ground beef that is doused with a sweet sauce made with evaporated milk, sugar, garlic powder, and white vinegar. The business makes pizzas and salads if you want to persuade a reluctant friend to visit, but the pocket of spiced meat with onion and tomatoes—a whole pound of it for $9.99, or a regular quarter-pound for $3.99—should be sampled. Its five locations are: 6420 Quinpool Rd., Halifax (902-421-0000); 278 Lacewood Dr., Clayton Park (902-445-0000); 668 Sackville Dr., Lower Sackville (902-865-0000); 378 Herring Cove Rd., Spryfield (902477-7111); and 451 Windmill Rd., Dartmouth (902-461-8888).

Spring Garden Just Us! Café (902-423-0856; justuscoffee.com/springgarden.aspx), 5896 Spring Garden Rd., Halifax (near Halifax Public Gardens). Open Mon.–Fri. 7:30 AM–9 PM, Sat.–Sun. 8:30 AM–7:30 PM. Featuring Nova Scotia's premium quality, Fair Trade coffee from Just Us! (and free Wi-Fi), inside an old building. Samosas, parathas, vegan or organic free-range meat soup of the day, and grilled panini.

Tea and Treasures (902-823-1908; users.eastlink.ca/~teaandtreasures/), 8369 Peggy's Cove Rd., Indian Harbour. Wonderful baked goods and apple pie spring directly into a local fan's mind at his café. Fish and chips, soups, straightforward sandwiches for lunch, and nightly specials for dinner.

Uncommon Grounds (902-446-9115; coffeesoldhere.com), at the corner of Argyle and Sackville in downtown Halifax, and also located at 1030 South Park St. (902-431-3101) and 1801 Hollis St. & Duke St., at Upper Water St. (902-404-3117). This business is a distributor of Nova Coffee. Another outpost sells invigorating cups of coffee inside Horticultural Hall in the **Halifax Public Gardens.**

Cabin Coffee (902-422-8130), 1554 Hollis St., Halifax.Open Mon.–Fri. 6:30 AM–8 PM (till 6 PM in the off-season), Sat. 7:30 AM–6 PM, Sun. 9 AM–5 PM. This cozy refuge from modern times is recommended for breakfast, especially for the "breakfast bun" on a bagel or scone with a fried egg with cheese or bacon or ham inside. Oatmeal or bagels with cream cheese are easy to digest in the comfortable leather upholstered chairs and couch amid the log walls, a fireplace with a wooden moose head over it, and a canoe hanging over the tables. Sandwiches for lunch and dinner, like clubs, BLTs, and tuna melts.

Farmers' Markets
The Saturday Morning Farmers' Market in Halifax, 1496 Lower Water St., Brewery Market, Halifax (Apr.–Dec., 7 AM–1 PM, Jan.–Mar., 8 AM–1 PM) is also a crafts boutique with international take-out food and fresh-baked bread. Musicians add to the pleasure, and fresh produce is still the raison d'être. Try to find John Brett if you can, to buy some of his hard cider and excellent sweet cider. Ted Hutton of Hutton's Family Farm, who can also be found here, supplies a lot of produce to Jane's On the Common. "It's a very magical market," said Jane Wright, owner of that neighborhood bistro.

French Fries
The chip wagon that has been parked the longest near the Public Library on Spring Garden Road —since 1977—is owned by Nancy and Bob True and called **Bud the Spud's**. Their homemade French fries are always delicious.

Gourmet and Deli Markets
Jane's Next Door, beside the restaurant Jane's on the Common (902-431-5683; janeson thecommon.com), 2398 Robie St., Halifax. Open: Tues.–Fri. 8 AM–8 PM, Sat. 8 AM–6 PM. Muffins, croissants, and pecan sticky buns are made here. The panini might be filled with roasted vegetables and goat cheese, or curried chicken or roast beef. Visitors with kitchen privileges can heat up the house soups or the fish pie held in the freezer. A perfect place to put together a lunch for picnicking on nearby Citadel Hill. Julien's Bakery provides the bread.

Bud and Nancy True sell fries on Spring Garden Road at their mobile business, Bud The Spud.

Mid-East Food Centre (902-492-0958), 2595 Agricola St., Halifax. Open weekdays 9 AM–7 PM, Sat. 9 AM–6 PM, closed Sun. With a store and a café (which closes around 6 or 6:30), you can sample the hummus first; or you can try samosa, pita wrap, shrawmas (a pita wrap stuffed with vegetables, halal chicken, beef, and garlic sauce), rice dishes, and many other Lebanese dishes such as falafels, bryani rice, and stuffed grape leaves. To-go containers and combination plates are available. The tabouleh, made fresh twice a day, is chockful of parsley—"You should see how many orders of parsley come in here every day," said Erin Smith-Burton, kitchen worker and server.

Pete's Frootique (902-425-5700; petesfrootique.com) 1515 Dresden Row, Halifax. Open Mon.–Fri. 8 AM–8 PM, Sat.–Sun. 8 AM–6 PM. Inside a 26,000-square-foot space are amazing groceries perfect for hotel visits, with a salad bar and delicatessen full of pre-pared meals you can enjoy, or a take-out selection that offers hot meals, cold salads, or sliced-up fruit to go. A second location is at (902-835-4997), 1595 Bedford Hwy., Sunnyside Mall, Bedford, open Mon.–Fri. 8 AM–9 PM, Sat.–Sun. 8 AM–to 6 PM. In Bedford you will also find a selection of wine from around the world.

Ice Cream and Candy

Dio Mio Gelato International Café (902-492-3467), 65-5670 Spring Garden Rd., Halifax. Also at Dartmouth Crossing, 21 Logiealmond Close, Dartmouth. Open Mon.–Fri. 8 AM–9 PM, Sat.–Sun. 12–6 PM. Bagels, sandwiches and salads, fajitas, and more, but also a destination for dessert. Rosewater mint gelato is sometimes one, and so is the brownie sundae. Gelato comes in fifty or so flavors, stracciotella, vanilla with chocolate shaving, or a peppermint version, is well loved; peanut butter and jelly.

Freak Lunchbox (902-420-9151; freaklunchbox.com—but it's just one page with music), 1473 Barrington St., Halifax and also (902-405-4052), 1595 Bedford Hwy. at the Sunnyside Mall. This is the place to take the kids, where everyone is wowed by the sugar, and the colors bedazzle your eyes. Pez collectors beware.

Sugah! (902-421-6079, 866-440-7867; sugah.ca), On the Boardwalk at Bishop's Landing, 1479 Lower Water St., Halifax. Open in summer daily 10 AM–9 PM. Chocolates, brittle, chocolate bars, toffee, and chocolate clusters and fudge are the staples. When you order ice cream in one of four flavors, it can be "hand-paddled" together with whatever you want to add in, like a log of that fudge—it turns into ribbons as it gets mushed into the ice cream—or hazelnut crunch, or rum cake, another specialty. Mango, guava, or pas-sion fruit lollipops are another possibility, perhaps best enjoyed outside of the ice cream. Sugah! has another location in Horticultural Hall in the **Halifax Public Gardens**, where you can also find **Uncommon Grounds**, for coffee and tea.

Microbreweries and Pubs

This section owes a large debt to the investigative work of Bob Connon, a Wolfville author who wrote the excellent guide to finding good ale in the Maritimes, *Sociable, The Elbow Bender's Guide to Maritime Pubs,* a must read for anyone in Nova Scotia who loves a good pub.

The best microbrews and Nova Scotia beers today have garnered many awards, and two to make sure to try are the Propeller IPA Extra Special Bitter, winner of a gold medal at the World Beer Championships in Chicago in 2006 and 2007, and Garrison IPA, which won Canadian Beer of the Year in 2007.

"Taverns came into existence in Nova Scotia in the late 1940s," said Connon, when I

Ice cream is sold at Sugah! inside Horticultural Hall in Halifax Public Gardens.

asked about the history of the pubs, and when women began to visit them—because his book mentioned that they were excluded in the first decades.

In New York City, Connon told me, women didn't go into taverns until Prohibition, when they began to visit speakeasies; they were likely the bohemians and intellectuals. When Connon lived in Ireland, women patronized the lounge and not the public bar, with its sawdust on the floor; they were also served only a half-pint or "glass" of beer. My Irish friend Kate O'Halloran confirmed that it was considered coarse for a woman to drink an entire pint—even into the 1980s. Up until 1972 Nova Scotia taverns would not serve women, Connon said.

Connon said, and writes in his book's introduction, that women brewed the beer in the 13th century and ran the ale houses in England; hence the name Alewives. The business turned into a man's world by the 18th century with the addition of hops, a preservative that allowed transportation of beer. Originally a local pub brewed its own beer of necessity, but with hops and the railroad, beer became an industry.

The Granite Brewery (902-422-4954; granitebrewery.ca), 1662 Barrington St., Halifax. Open daily from 11 AM. The first in Nova Scotia to start up a microbrewery, Kevin Keefe is the original talent behind the award-winning ales at The Granite Brewery. Any self-respecting ale-lover will visit this pub to taste its own Peculiar, based on a historic English version, or the Best Bitter, Best Bitter Special, or India Pale Ale. You can also taste them at The Henry House, next in the listings. An Asian stir-fry is a lighter choice for dinner, but the traditional steaks, barbequed ribs, lamb curry, and fish and chips are all available.

The Henry House (902-423-5660; henryhouse.ca), 1222 Barrington St., Halifax. Open 11:30 AM daily; Mon.–Wed. and Sun., kitchen closes at 10 PM; Thurs.–Sat., kitchen closes at midnight. Serving six Granite House–brewed ales, including Best Bitter and Peculiar—"A dark malty brew full in taste with a sweet/dry finish," the Web site describes it. Other Nova Scotian draft ciders, cream ale, and IPA, and single-malt whiskeys. Fishcakes, house-made beans, and chicken and leek pie are on the menu, with a proper bread pudding for dessert. All can be enjoyed within the ironstone and granite walls of this 1834 building, once the home of Confederation father William Alexander Henry. Celtic music on Saturday nights.

The Lower Deck (902-425-1501; lowerdeck.ca), Historic Properties, 1869 Upper Water St., Halifax. Open daily at 11:30 AM, kitchen open till 10 PM. Serving Alexander Keith's ales and providing live entertainment every night, The Lower Deck is a summer desti-nation—for a drink on the patio, where you can watch the ships sail by—and a winter refuge. Bangers and mash, Thai salmon, and fried scallops with chipotle tartar sauce and chips are on the menu. **The Beer Market** upstairs serves slightly more upscale menu items and a full range of cocktails.

Maxwell's Plum (902-423-5090; themaxwellsplum.com), 1600 Grafton St., Halifax. Open daily at 11 AM. This pub boasts that it serves 60 types of draft beer. Every night there are specials, including the 60-ounce pitchers. Garrison Brown, Keith's Red, and Propeller Extra Special Bitter are a few possibilities from the drink list, a feature that will attract the true beer tourist, along with young students that are Maxwell's Plum's core cus-tomers. Bar food.

O'Carroll's Restaurant & Irish Pub (902-423-4405; ocarrolls.com), 1860 Upper Water St., Halifax. Open daily at 11 AM. If you want to be able to enjoy your pint of Guinness, this and the following pub, The Old Triangle, are the places to go. According to pub expert Bob Connon (see the introduction to this section), a proper Guiness should be poured and allowed to settle for five minutes, before the glass is topped off. That endows the pint with a creamy head, giving a rich mouthfeel to the first sips. You will also see bubbles traveling down the inside the glass, a function of the nitrogen gas used for carbonation. Sleeman's Honey Brown, O'Carroll's Amber Ale, Propeller Seasonal brews served. Oysters on the helf shell and Saganaki cheese (a fried Greek cheese) add panache to the menu, which proceeds to a lobster sandwich or a lamb burger or steak and kidney pie. Entertainment every night.

The Old Triangle Irish Ale House (902-492-4900; oldtriangle.com), 5136 Prince St., Halifax. Open Mon.–Fri. at 11 AM, Sat.–Sun. at 11:30 AM. This is the place for the proper Guinness (see above) with the creamy head, or Nova Scotia's own Propeller Stout, among several other local brews. Bob Connon said this popular pub has many comfortable spaces and places to retreat to. Opened by Irish musicians in 2000, The Old Triangle emphasizes "music for the soul." Live entertainment every night and Irish dancing on Sunday at 2 PM.

Rogue's Roost (902-492-2337; roguesroost.ca), 5435 Spring Garden Rd., Halifax. Open Mon.–Sat. at 11 AM, Sun. at noon. Rogue's Roost is a microbrewery and sells its own Red Ale, Cream Ale, Oatmeal Stout, and IPA. The long pub-food menu lists poutine, deep fried pepperoni, and house hummus to start, and a BBQ burger or veggie burger to continue. With an outdoor patio and windows over Spring Garden Road, the space is bright. One seasonal ale, Weisen, is a summer-wheat ale with a bright fruity, banana aftertaste and a popular choice on a hot day. In the deep of winter, Russian Imperial Stout with a higher alcohol content, from 7 to 7.9 percent, has a heavier, richer flavor than the oatmeal stout, and it's likely on draft beginning in December. Entertainment on the weekends.

The Split Crow (902-422-4366; splitcrow.com), 1855 Granville St., Halifax. Open daily at 11 AM. Keith's IPA and Molson on draft, to name just two. This popular institution opened in 1979, taking the name of Nova Scotia's first tavern, opened in 1749. But the Monte Cristo on the breakfast menu is thoroughly up to date, made of french toast layered with ham and Swiss cheese. The crab dip for dinner combines red crab and roasted sweet red peppers. Salads, sandwiches, and pizza. Live entertainment, including many Maritime musicians, every night and on Saturday at 3 PM.

The Victory Arms in the Lord Nelson Hotel (902-423-6331; lordnelsonhotel.com), 1515 South Park St., Halifax. The older version of this hotel's pub was the LBR (now the nearby Oasis), which stood for Lady's Beverage Room. Since women were excluded from taverns in Nova Scotia until the early 1970s, the hotel did business under another name and did not admit unaccompanied men.

Today's pub serves locally brewed beers and also has a good wine list, with its menu of fish and chips or shepherd's pie, or more upscale plates like sea bass with kaffir lime and chili and steak frites. Settle into an upholstered booth in the dark and luxurious surroundings, and raise a glass to the victorious admiral, Lord Nelson.

IN ENFIELD

Curly Portable's Pub & Grub (902-883-8273; curlyportables.com), 450 Hwy. 2, Enfield. (Exits 7 off Hwy. 102, right on Hwy. 2) Open for dining 11 AM–9 PM. Casual standards and steak are on the menu at this bike-friendly pub with an outdoor patio, inside air-conditioning, and live music on Saturday night.

CULTURE

Churches

CHRIST CHURCH

902-466-4270
christchurchdartmouth.ns.ca
61 Dundas St., Dartmouth, NS B2Y 4H5

Look up at the top of Christ Church, the oldest church in Dartmouth, to see the weather-vane of Halley's Comet.

ST. MARY'S BASILICA

902-423-4116
stmarysbasilica.ns.ca
1508 Barrington St., Halifax, NS B3J 1Z3

Built in 1820, this Gothic Revival cathedral is made of ironstone, with a sandstone façade. Shipwrights built the enormous roof, never before attempted in Halifax, in the style of a ship's hull. In 1860 the windows were altered to achieve a more uniform Gothic style, but all of the original stained glass was destroyed in the Halifax Explosion of 1917; the windows were replaced with windows made by the German company of Franz Meyer.

ST. PAUL'S CHURCH

902-429-2240
stpaulshalifax.com
1749 Argyle St., Halifax, NS B3J 3K4

St. Paul's Church is the oldest building in the city, built in 1750, one year after the city was founded. Its original timbers came from Boston. From 1787 to 1865 the church was the Maritime Provinces' cathedral. Memorial tablets recite the names of historical figures, and the "Explosion Window" in the upper level, west wall, third from the back of the church, memorializes the devastation of the Halifax Explosion in 1917, when the church's vestry was an emergency hospital.

Galleries

ANNA LEONOWENS GALLERY, NOVA SCOTIA COLLEGE OF ART & DESIGN

902-494-8223
nscad.ns.ca/students/gallery
1891 Granville St., Halifax
Mail: 5163 Duke St., Halifax, NS B3J 3J6
Open: Tues.–Fri. 11 AM–5 PM, Sat. noon–4 PM; opening receptions Mon. 5:30–7 PM
Admission: Free

More than 100 exhibitions are shown here every year, with student work, faculty work, and visiting artists' work among them, in three public galleries. The gallery is in a pedestrian mall and attracts many visitors.

ART GALLERY OF NOVA SCOTIA

902-424-7542
artgalleryofnovascotia.ca
1723 Hollis St., P.O. Box 2262, Halifax, NS B3J 3C8
Open: Daily 10 AM–5 PM, Thurs. 10 AM–9 PM

Dedicated to art by artists from Nova Scotia and Canada, this gallery holds many charms of the province. One favorite of a new Halifax resident, retiree Nora McKay from Montreal, is in the Quebec Room, where paintings by Jean Paul Lemieux (1904–1990) are displayed. His stark landscapes, infused with austerity, reveal memories of the past—on a sled in a winter scene, for example.

Another artist whose actual home, a tiny one-room house that became her most charming canvas, is on display here, is Maud Lewis (1903–1970). Her folk art displays a charm and joie de vivre that, considering her straitened circumstances, aroused in me a sense of gratitude for the courage she conveys.

The **Cheapside Café** (902-425-4494), open daily 10 AM–5 PM, Thurs. till 8 PM, Sun. 11 AM–5 PM, with lunch from 11:30 to 2:30, is managed by Scanway Caterers, whose other businesses include Saege Bistro and Sweet Basil Bistro, described in the Restaurants section above. The café menu offers Thai chicken salad with peanut sauce, a classic Caesar, and a phyllo strudel with wild mushrooms and chèvre; there are tortes, cakes, and tarts for dessert, with organic Fair Trade coffee served.

DALHOUSIE ARTS CENTRE & GALLERY

902-494-2403 (front desk), 902-494-2195 (main office)
artgallery.dal.ca
6101 University Ave., Halifax, NS BH 3J5
Open: Tues.–Sun. 11AM–5 PM
Admission: Free

The oldest art gallery in Halifax is the Dalhousie Art Gallery, part of Dalhousie University, where you can find exhibits, lectures, films, and artists' lectures. The Permanent Collection amassed over the years encompasses more than 1,000 works, from the first donation, a print of an engraving by John James Audubon, to a mixed-media-on-paper image called *Dress #6* by Susan Wood. Exhibitions explore contemporary issues like animal and human interactions, and an early European exploration of Labrador.

DEGARTHE GALLERY AND THE DEGARTHE MONUMENT

902-823-2256
109 Peggy's Point Rd., Peggy's Cove, NS B3Z 3S1
Open: July–Aug., daily 9 AM–7 PM; May, June, and Oct., daily 9 AM–5 PM
Admission: Adults $2, children under 12 free.

Run by the Visitor's Information Centre across the parking lot, this gallery, an addition to the artist's former home, can be opened by request after 4:30, when it is usually locked. Displaying 65 paintings by marine landscape artist and sculptor William E. deGarthe, donated by his wife in 1993, the gallery achieves the wishes of the artist (1907–1983) to share his vision with Nova Scotia. Born in Finland, deGarthe came to Canada in 1926. He taught at the Nova Scotia College of Art and started deGarthe Advertising Art in Halifax. In

The weeping beech behind this fountain in Halifax Public Gardens made a cool hideaway.

front of the deGarthe's house is a 100-foot-long, 30-meter granite carving of 32 fishermen and their families, under the outspread wings of St. Elmo, patron saint of fishermen, and also Peggy of Peggy's Cove. Work, bounty, and grace characterize the three parts of the unfinished work.

MOUNT ST. VINCENT UNIVERSITY ART GALLERY

902-457-6160
msvuart.ca
166 Bedford Hwy., Bedford, NS B3M 2J6
Open: Tues.–Fri. 11 AM–5 PM, Sat.–Sun. 1–5 PM
Admission: Free

Exhibitions focus on the work of Nova Scotia artists and develop themes under study at the university. Student shows, and a collection that includes ceramic work by Alice Hagen, displayed on campus.

Gardens

HALIFAX PUBLIC GARDENS

902-490-4000
halifaxpublicgardens.ca
Spring Garden Rd. at South Park St.
Open: Early May–Oct. daily 8 AM to dusk
Admission: Free

This Victorian landscape of 17 manicured acres or 7 hectares has been flourishing in the middle of Halifax since 1867. Sketching under a weeping beech, letting your toddler amble after the tame ducks, listening to a man in a kilt give a tour—recreation and self-improvement were never so pleasurable as during the odd hour you might spend here, in the most beautiful public garden I've seen. Formal beds of impeccable annuals, flourishing perennials, and landscaping with large trees and graceful shrubs surround an ornate central gazebo, which shelters bands that play free concerts on summer Sundays at 2 PM. A pond, of course, and an enclosure for an irascible swan or two, surrounded by arching pathways, provide enough room if you need to get away, as I did, from a film crew setting up to film *HMS Sea Wolf*, based on a story by Jack London, with Tim Roth and Ned Campbell.

Historic Buildings, Ships, and Sites

BLUENOSE II

902-634-1963
bluenose.ns.ca
Based in Lunenburg, NS
Open: Hours change every summer, check Web site for schedule

This reproduction of the victorious racing champion and fishing schooner *Bluenose* arrives in Halifax for visits every year. Depending on its schedule the ship docks in Halifax for one or more visits in the summer, when it opens its decks for visitors. The original ship was built to show off fishing schooners' speed and strength, after Nova Scotian fishermen grew disgusted with the inability of the World Cup racing sailboats to weather strong winds and harsh weather. It won a fishing schooner race every year from 1921 to 1938 as well as many other competitions, and it is now honored by being depicted on the back of the Canadian dime.

THE HALIFAX CITADEL NATIONAL HISTORIC SITE AND ARMY MUSEUM
Citadel 902-426-5080, Museum 902-422-5979
pc.gc.ca, search National Historic Sites
5425 Sackville St., P.O. Box 9080, Station A, Halifax, NS B3K 5M7
Open: Citadel Hill open year-round except Christmas Day; Museum open May 15–Oct. 15, daily 9 AM–5 PM
Admission: Peak season (June to Sept.) adults $11.70, seniors $10.05, children 6–16 $5.80; shoulder season (May 7–31, Sept. 16–Oct. 31) adults $7.80, seniors $6.55, children $3.90

Citadel Hill earned its fame as one of the largest British fortresses in North America when it was built soon after the settlement of Halifax, in 1749. The noon gun has been fired ever since, and you'll hear it best on Citadel Hill. The fantastic view overlooking the harbor made this spot the prized resource of a nation in regular battle with France. Today visitors can conquer hunger with a picnic on the sloping hillside around the star-shaped fort. The private museum, part of the Organization of Military Museums of Canada, exhibits more than 70,000 artifacts from the British and Canadian military on the second floor of the Cavalier Building. In that three-story building, areas that used to be barracks are now restored and on display, as is a soldier's library. A coffee bar is ready with refreshments. The musketry gallery, which surrounds the perimeter of the fort, is fascinating, but now open only in a small section. Nevertheless it gives a visitor an idea of what the fort was first like.

HMCS SACKVILLE
In summer, 902-429-2132, in winter, 902-427-2837
hmcssackville-cnmt.ns.ca
P.O. Box 99000 Station Forces, Halifax, NS B3K 5X5
Open: End of June–mid-Sept., daily 10 AM–5 PM
Admission: Adults $4, seniors 55 and older and children 12–19 $2, children under 12 free

HMCS *Sackville* is Canada's Naval Memorial, the last of 120 Canadian World War II convoy escort corvettes. In that war this corvette was credited with destroying a German U-boat and doing damage to others as it safeguarded Allied convoys. Today it's docked next door to the Maritime Museum of the Atlantic, on the Halifax waterfront, and is open for tours. In a shed on the wharf is a gift shop with T-shirts, mugs, and more with the ship depicted on them. The *Sackville* sometimes hosts private functions; on the evening of Canada Day in 2008, it had been boarded and taken possession of by people wearing black T-shirts with the word *Euroband.* The ship's trustees meet on the ship every Friday at lunchtime in an off-limits area.

THE PEACE PAVILION
On the Dartmouth waterfront in Ferry Terminal Park
Open: Always
Admission: Free

This triangular structure symbolizing peace, unity, order, and equality holds stone and bricks from around the world, including a heavy hunk of the Berlin Wall, torn down in 1989.

Shubenacadie Canal
shubie.chebucto.org

Located at Prince Albert Road and Pleasant Street in Dartmouth, inside a small park where the Star Manufacturing buildings used to stand, is a buried turbine room, one part of work done in the 1860s on a waterway that bisected the province of Nova Scotia. The turbine room powered a sled that moved up an inclined plane or marine railroad, which hauled boats up a slope to the next part of the canal.

The turbine chamber is an arched stone chamber made with hand-carved stone. An open house in 2007 held by Shubenacadie Canal Commission, after archeological work done by the Cultural Resource Management Group, publicized the workmanship and elegance of what had been sitting for decades below the surface.

The waterway was originally a route used by Mi'kmaq to cross Nova Scotia from the Bay of Fundy to the Atlantic coast, and it involved a few portages or treks across land carrying canoes. European settlers first attempted in the 1820s to construct a canal navigable by boat, utilizing 17 expensive stone locks, but in 1831 the Shubenacadie Canal Company ran out of money after building only 13 of those 17 locks.

In 1853, The Inland Navigation Company formed and redesigned the canal with a shallower draft and fewer locks as well as the inclined plane or marine railroad, with tracks powered by the turbine room. The canal operated for only nine years—shipping pieces of railroad track, among other goods— before the railroad system superseded it, especially effectively in 1870 when it built low, fixed railroad bridges that would not allow ships to pass underneath.

Someday the links in the Canal Greenway will stretch across the province from Dartmouth to the Bay of Fundy. But this is still in the planning stage. Lock 1 is already fully restored and visible in Dartmouth. Locks 2 and 3 are visible at Shubie Park, which stretches from Lake Banook to Lake Micmac (see Shubie Park below, under "Parks" in the Recreation section below for more information).

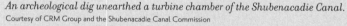

An archeological dig unearthed a turbine chamber of the Shubenacadie Canal.
Courtesy of CRM Group and the Shubenacadie Canal Commission

PROVINCE HOUSE
To book a tour, 902-424-4661
gov.ns.ca/legislature/visitor_info
1726 Hollis St., Halifax, NS B3J 2Y3
Open: July–Aug., Mon.–Fri. 9 AM–5 PM, Sat.–Sun. and holidays 10 AM–4 PM; rest of the year, weekdays 9 AM–to 4 PM.
Admission: Free

Since February 1818, Nova Scotia's elected legislature has been meeting in Province House, a monument to Palladian-style architecture. Nova Scotia's first elected government in 1758 had no permanent meeting place. But British Governor Sir John Wentworth required a beautiful residence, and it was built over seven years beginning in 1800. Costs rose, and despite controversy over the extravagance, the province paid them. After Wentworth moved out of his old house, he gave the plot of land it stood on to the province as a site for its own "home." Up it went from 1811 to 1818, built of sandstone from Wallace, Nova Scotia. Inside the elegant symmetrical façade there are intricate plasterwork and acanthus leaf–topped columns. The library first housed the Supreme Court of Nova Scotia. A fine brochure about the history and architecture is available at the site. This is the second-oldest building still being used as an assembly building in Canada.

YORK REDOUBT, A HISTORIC SITE OF CANADA
902-426-5080
pp.gc.ca
Purcell's Cove Rd. (off Rte. 253), Halifax
Mail: York Redoubt National Historic Site, P.O. Box 9080, Station A, Halifax NS B3K 5M7
Open: May 15–Aug., 9 AM–8 PM; Sept., 9 AM–7 PM; Oct., 9 AM–6 PM
Admission: Free

The York Redoubt was the center of Halifax defense during World War II, when a net was strung across the mouth of the bay to snag enemy submarines. But its existence began with a military battery built in 1793 to defend the harbor and bombard any French ships hoping to take the prize of Halifax from Britain. The area is now open to the public, who can enjoy the magnificent views of the harbor and the Atlantic, and there are many trails and mature trees. Part of the Halifax Defense Complex.

Interpretive Centers

FISHERMAN'S COVE MARINE INTERPRETIVE CENTRE
902-465-6093
fishermanscove.ns.ca
30 Government Wharf Rd., Eastern Passage, NS B3G 1M7
Open: Call for hours
Admission: $1

With fish tanks and detailed descriptions of marine life, this building holds the story of the marine life that you might also encounter while walking the oceanside boardwalk in Fisherman's Cove, with its charming galleries and shops, or on a whale-watching excursion from the dock, or taking a short boat ride to McNab's Island (see "Parks" in the Recreation section below). Children's activities.

Libraries

HALIFAX PUBLIC LIBRARIES
902-490-5744
halifaxpubliclibraries.ca
60 Alderney Dr., Dartmouth, NS B2Y 4P8
Main branch in Halifax: Spring Garden Road Memorial Library, 902-490-5700, 5381
Spring Garden Rd.
Open: Hours vary by season and location
Admission: Free

Fourteen branches and one mobile library offer the local population and visitors more
than a million items, from books to CDs and DVDs. Wi-Fi and a computer are available at
all branches. Visitors who present a picture ID can get a special card that allows them to
take out two items at a time. Many programs—including story hours for children—are
offered, and all are accessible by clicking the Programs tab at the top right of the library's
home page.

KILLAM MEMORIAL LIBRARY AT DALHOUSIE UNIVERSITY
902-494-3601
library.dal.ca/killam/
6225 University Ave., Halifax, NS B3H 4H8
Open: Mon.–Thurs. 8 AM—9 PM, Fri. 9 AM—6 PM, Sat.–Sun. 1—5 PM
Admission: Free

With more than 500,000 books and periodicals, this is the largest academic library in
Atlantic Canada, built for $7.3 million and finished in 1971. Most of its patrons are some
of the 8,000 undergraduates at Dalhousie University, which also has four other libraries
devoted to design, technology, law, pharmacy, and health sciences. A glass roof covers the
courtyard, which now contains green plants year-round and a Second Cup coffee shop.

PATRICK POWER LIBRARY, SAINT MARY'S UNIVERSITY
902-420-5547, information desk 902-420-5544
stmarys.ca/administration/library/
5932 Inglis St., Halifax, NS B3H 3C3
Open: Hours vary depending on time of year
Admission: Free

Supporting university student and faculty research and located in the city's South End, this
is a small library with great staff and a limited number of computers available to the public
for research purposes. Construction of "The Atrium," an open-area teaching and learning
space, including a computer commons, study rooms, classroom, offices, and a coffee shop
adjoining the library, is projected to be completed by September 2009.

UNIVERSITY OF KING'S COLLEGE LIBRARY
902-422-1271
ukings.ca/kings_2859.html
6350 Coburg St., Halifax, NS B3H 2A1

Open: Hours vary
Admission: Free

This library holds a venerable as well as a modern collection, with books in classics and other studies filling shelves since 1802. In the 1800s the collection was expanded with natural-history specimens and historical artifacts; the new library building, finished in 1989, presents the past in an updated structure. In special collections (by appointment only in summer) there are incunabula (15th-century printed books) and medieval and renaissance manuscripts. Some pieces from the Weldon Collection of 17th- and 18th-century Chinese porcelain are on display in the foyer.

Lighthouses

Sambro Lighthouse, Sambro. The oldest operating lighthouse in North America, built in 1759. The lighthouse is made of stone covered with wood shingles to protect the mortar; it's painted white with three red stripes to make it stand out in snowstorms.

Museums

BLACK CULTURAL CENTRE FOR NOVA SCOTIA
902-434-6223, 800-465-0767
bccns.com
1149 Main St., Dartmouth, Nova Scotia B2Z 1A8
Open: June–Aug., Mon.–Fri. 9 AM–5 PM, Sat. 10 AM–3 PM; rest of the year Mon.–Fri. 9 AM–5 PM, closed Sat.–Sun.
Admission: Adults $6, students and seniors $4, families of two adults and up to three children $20, children 5 and under and all members free

This center was built in 1983 to provide a place for music, plays, workshops, and lectures about the history of the African Canadians who have been part of eaastern Canada for centuries. Some of the first were slaves brought into Quebec by French colonists. Later, American exiles who had fought for Great Britain during the American Revolution arrived here, hoping for the freedom they had been promised in return for their service. But in Nova Scotia they faced an established slave trade and prejudice; losing claims on land, many were forced to labor on public projects. As many as 1,190 men and women took the 15 ships that left Halifax in 1792 for Sierra Leone. Between 1813 and 1815 more black refugees from the United States settled in the Maritimes, and after 1833, when slavery was abolished in the British Empire, many American blacks escaped slavery and found their way here through the Underground Railroad. Many black Canadians can trace their ancestry back to the Underground Railroad.

BURKE-GAFFNEY OBSERVATORY
Department of Astronomy and Physics
902-420-5828, information line 902-496-8257
smu.ca/academic/science/ap/bgo.html
Saint Mary's University, Halifax, NS B3H 3C3
Tours: On clear nights only, every Sat. June.–Sept.; rest of the year, 1st and 3rd Sat. of each month.
Admission: Free

Named in honor of the Reverend M. W. Burke-Gaffney, the university's beloved astrono-mer who died in 1979, and built with an anonymous donation, the Ealing 41-centimeter diameter Cassegrain reflecting telescope is set on the top of 22-story Loyola Residence Tower. Tours of the telescope are offered, and updated schedules are available on the information line. The tours are free and offered on clear nights only. The decision to offer the tour is made by 6 PM on Saturday and recorded on the information line. When the night skies are clear, visitors can view the moon, the planets, and other celestial wonders.

COLE HARBOUR HERITAGE FARM AND MUSEUM
902-434-0222
coleharbourfarmmuseum.ca
471 Poplar Dr., Dartmouth, NS, B2W 4L2
Open: May 15–Oct. 15, Mon.–Sat. 10 AM–4 PM, Sun. 12–4 PM; off-season by appointment
Admission: By donation only

Set near a marsh and nature walk, this old farm and its barns might harbor goats, pigs, chickens, and ducklings, depending on who can loan some animals and the equipment of another place in time. There are barns, exhibits, a large garden, a picnic area, and a walk-ing trail to a neighboring lake. The era represented here spans the 1760s to the 1960s, because in the 1960s this was still a pig and market-produce farm. Guided tours are offered by appointment only. Giles House is one of the oldest structures in Cole Harbour, with period furniture; the the history of the Babes-in-the-Wood cradle (owned by two lit-tle girls who wandered into the woods in Dartmouth and were found embracing, frozen to death) is a story that has resounded in folklore ever since.

The Rose & Kettle Tea Room offers a cup of tea and scones and lunches, and events like a strawberry social the first Saturday in July, a rhubarb festival in June, and harvest dinners held in October can be found at the Web site.

DISCOVERY CENTRE
902-492-4422
discoverycentre.ns.ca
1593 Barrington St., Halifax, NS B3J 1Z7
Open: Mon.–Sat. 10 AM–5 PM, Sun. 1–5 PM
Admission: Adults $7.50, children 2-18 $5, students with ID $6, seniors $6.50

Opened in 1990, the Discovery Centre brings its science know-how to the schools of Nova Scotia during the school year, offers science day camps in the summer, and feeds the curiosity of visitors throughout the year with exhibits and experiments open to all. The Ames Room gives us a chance to finally walk away from our shadows, while the Room for Small Wonders lets our toddlers walk away from us—for a few minutes of play with floating Ping-Pong balls. Changing exhibits have included the Lego secrets of the pharaohs. There is a chemistry set in the center's store just waiting for you.

EVERGREEN HOUSE AND QUAKER WHALER HOUSE
902-464-2300
dartmouthheritagemuseum.ns.ca
Evergreen House: 26 Newcastle St., Dartmouth

Quaker Whaler House: Ochterloney St., Dartmouth
Mail: Dartmouth Heritage Museum, Evergreen House, 26 Newcastle St., Dartmouth, NS
B2Y 3M5
Open: June–Aug., Tues.–Sun. 10 AM–5 PM, except closed for lunch Sat.–Sun. 1–2 PM, closed
Mon.; Sept.–May, closed Sun. and Mon.
Admission: Adults $2 per house, children 12 and under free

Evergreen House, built by Judge Alexander James in 1867 and furnished in the style of
that period, is the present site of an exhibition gallery, a reference library with 14,000
photographs, and a gift shop with items for sale like a CD of traditional folk songs about
the sea, or a cross-stitch kit. Victorian-era events occur through the summer, perhaps a
Victorian picnic. Quaker Whaler House is older, built in 1785, and one of the oldest houses
in the metropolitan area. Its first owner, William Ray, was a cooper and a Quaker, one of
a group that worked at the whaling industry and arrived here from Nantucket Island,
Massachusetts. Guides dressed in Quaker clothes gives tours through the house and herb
and vegetable raised-bed gardens, and children can check out the dress-up trunk. Craft
demonstrations are offered over the summer, perhaps quilting, coopering, and Ukrainian
egg dying. Both houses are run by the Dartmouth Heritage Museum Complex.

MARITIME COMMAND MUSEUM
902-721-8250
users.pspmembers.com/marcommuseum
Admiralty House, P.O. Box 99000, Station Forces, Halifax, NS B3K 5X5
Open: Mon.–Fri. 9:30 AM–3:30 PM
Admission: Donation only

The 1819 Georgian stone mansion that holds this military museum was originally the summer residence of the North Atlantic Station Admiral. In 1974 it opened as a museum, and
today it houses model ships and almost everything that once voyaged in the ships themselves, from a sailor's uniform to ships' bells. The largest of 55 museums operated by
Canada's Department of National Defense, it still resounds with the sounds of former garden parties and balls held here for the British Navy and Canadian Maritime Forces, when
formally attired guests wandered in today's 30 rooms of artifacts. The front parlor and
reading room host parties today.

The headquarters for Maritime Command is also located on this base, as is the NATO
Training Facility, where you may see many soldiers here from around the world. A separate
gate leads to the museum. The 100th anniversary of the Canadian Navy will come in 2010,
when renovations and new exhibits will celebrate the year.

MARITIME MUSEUM OF THE ATLANTIC
902-424-7490
maritime.museum.gov.ns.ca
1675 Lower Water St., Halifax, NS B3J 1S3
Open: June–Sept., daily 9:30 AM–5:30 PM, Tues. till 8 PM; May–Oct., same hours but opens
at 1 PM on Sun.; Nov.–Apr., shorter hours and closed Mon.
Admission: May to October, adults $8.75, seniors $7.75, children $4.75; less off-season.

From the shoes of an unknown child from the *Titanic* to an old ship chandlery, the Maritime Museum shows off most of its more than 24,000 artifacts. CSS *Acadia,* Canada's first hydrographic vessel, is located dockside by the Maritime Museum of the Atlantic. A ship's carpenter's shop exhibits the tools of the trade, including carving tools. Sailor's souvenirs, along with the essential sextants, telescopes, and charts that helped the officers plot the course, are all on view. More than 300 ship portraits please the gaze of any admirer of the historic shipbuilding trade. In the summer you can take a 15-minute virtual visit to the shipwrecked *Titanic,* but that wreck is only one of 5,000 near the coast, and many others are described and illustrated. A kiosk in the Shipwreck Exhibit lets you find the sites of some of these wrecks and might feed your fantasies, if you've ever imagined yourself on the hunt for salvage.

NOVA SCOTIA MUSEUM OF NATURAL HISTORY

902-424-7353
museum.gov.ns.ca/mnh
1747 Summer St., Halifax, NS B3H 3A6
Open: June–Oct. 15, Mon., Tues., Thurs.–Sat. 9 AM–5 PM, Wed. 9 AM–8 PM, Sun. 12–5 PM;
Oct. 16–May, Tues. & Thurs.–Sat. 9:30 AM–5 PM, Wed. 9:30 AM–8 PM (free after 5),
Sun. 1–5 PM, closed Mon.
Admission: Adults $5.75, seniors 65 and older $5.25, children 6–17 $3.75, 5 and under free
(Consider buying a pass here for all 27 Nova Scotia Museums.)

A wonderful place for an amateur naturalist to start a visit to Nova Scotia, this museum can introduce you to the flora and fauna of the land and sea in Atlantic Canada, like the wild horses on Sable Island, which presides over the treacherous southwest of the province where the sea is nicknamed Graveyard of the Atlantic.

PIER 21, CANADA'S IMMIGRATION MUSEUM

902-425-7770
pier21.ca
1055 Marginal Rd., Halifax, NS B3H 4P6
Open: May–Nov., daily 9:30 AM–5:30 PM, with Research Centre closing at 5 from Oct.;
end of Nov.–Mar., Tues.–Sat. 10 AM–5 PM (extra hours during Mar. break); Apr., Mon.–
Sat. 10 AM–5 PM.
Admission: Adults $8.50, seniors 60 and older $7.50, students $6, children 6–16 $5;
family rates available

Set inside an original immigration shed, the last to survive in Canada, this museum invites visitors to use their Pier 21 "passport" to travel through a virtual immigration, or to ride a simulated train car to Vancouver, or listen to emotional accounts from those who were immigrants or soldiers or soldiers' wives here, among the 1.5 million whose lives began a Canadian chapter when they arrived in this building between 1928 and 1971.

The Research Centre holds records of some of those who came through the building, and each era has a different story to tell, like that of 3,000 children who were evacuated from Great Britain when the bombs were falling during World War II. Estonians fleeing Russia, Dutch toting cheeses they watched be confiscated, and Hungarian refugees from the 1956 revolution were some of the other newcomers.

SCOTT MANOR HOUSE MUSEUM

902-832-2336
www.scottmanorhouse.ca
15 Fort Sackville Rd., Bedford, Nova Scotia B4A 2G6
Open: July–Aug., daily 1–4 PM; off-season by appointment
Admission: Free
Handicapped accessible on first floor

This two-story, gambrel-roofed house was built by Irishman Joseph Scott on land given to him by the British king in 1749. Two mortarless chimney bases here survived both the Halifax and Magazine Hill Explosions, one reason why the house remained an admirable private property until 1992. It's next door to the site of Fort Sackville, which protected Halifax in its early days, and is now a Provincial and Municipal Heritage Property. An annual Graveyard Walk is scheduled in mid-September.

Best of all, for some of us, is the tea served in the Tea Room during the hours the building is open, with jam, lemonade, and in-season raspberries from the property itself. Tea and oatcakes were $2.50 in 2008, berries and ice cream $3.50, and all the profits support the house and its events.

UNIACKE ESTATE MUSEUM PARK

902-866-0032
uniacke.museum.gov.ns.ca
758 Hwy. 1, Mount Uniacke, NS B0N 1Z0
Open: House, June–mid-Oct., Mon.–Sat. 9:30 AM–5:30 PM, Sun. 11 AM–to 5:30 PM; trails open year-round, dawn to dusk.
Admission: Adults $3.25, seniors and children 7–17 $2.25

Seven walking trails offer the alternative of a long hike before or after or instead of a visit inside Attorney General Richard John Uniacke's fine house. Built between 1813 and 1815, the house contains fine Wedgwood china, old portraits, and English mahogany furnishings, some by George Adams, a London cabinetmaker. Many of the original furnishings are still here, and the building has not been modernized. Portraits of the Botineau family, done by Robert Feke in 1748, are another feature. An archeological dig unearthed parts of a haha, a retaining wall built into a ditch that allowed the eye to look out from a house and its garden without the obstruction of a fence, and yet kept the sheep or cattle out of the grounds. You can learn about this elegant landscaping trick on the Lake Martha Loop Trail, one of the seven maintained for walking. In the basement of the house is the Post Road Tea Room, where pie, tea biscuits, shortbread cookies, old-fashioned candy like jawbreakers, and gifts are for sale.

Nightlife

Many pubs listed in the end of the Restaurants section above offer live entertainment. Music festivals are listed under "Seasonal Events," below.

Theater

ALDERNEY LANDING

902-461-8401
alderneylanding.com/theatre/theatre.html

Alderney Landing Cultural Convention Centre, next to Dartmouth Ferry Terminal.
Mail: P.O. Box 725, Dartmouth, NS B2Y 3Z3
Open: Schedule available on the Web site
Admission: Varies according to the event; adult tickets from $20 to $110

Offering a children's theater camp in the summer, this convention center and theater also
hosts concerts and performances year-round.

DARTMOUTH PLAYERS

902-465-7529
dartmouthplayers.ns.ca
Theater: 33 Crichton Ave., Dartmouth
Mail: 23 Wildwood Blvd., Dartmouth, NS B2W 2L7

Performing since 1987 in a theater at the Crichton Avenue Community Centre, this amateur community-theater group presents four shows every year; it has been presenting
plays every year since 1957.

NEPTUNE THEATRE

902-429-7070, 800-565-7345
neptunetheatre.com
1593 Argyle St., Halifax, NS B3J 2B2
Open: Box office hours Mon.–Fri. 9 AM–5 PM, Sat. 12–5 PM.
Admission: Adults $15 to $58, senior discount 10 percent, students 20 percent

Opening night for live drama at Neptune Theatre came July 1, 1963, but both before and
after that date, the fortunes of this spot have been in the hands of muses of drama. In the
1920s performers offered vaudeville, and customers watched movies through the 30s,
40s, and 50s. After a splendid beginning, the new Neptune Theatre suffered from poor
ticket sales in the late 1960s, but the theater had the support of the province from its
beginning and it weathered that storm. Indeed, when the old building's limitations and
deterioration forced an opportunity to build something big with a campaign that started
in 1989, government and private donations undertook the challenge, opening the modern
57,000-square-foot theater in 1997. From April to May in 2009, Disney's *High School
Musical* will be performed here.

SHAKESPEARE BY THE SEA

902-422-0295
shakespearebythesea.ca
5799 Charles St., Halifax, NS B3K 1K7
Open: July–Aug.
Admission: By donation, suggested $15 per person (chair rental $2)

This outdoor summer theater was started in 1994 to offer affordable and professional
theater to Nova Scotians and its visitors. Performances are staged in Point Pleasant Park's
Cambridge Battery, a 12-minute walk from the parking lot at the Tower Road entrance to
the park (see Point Pleasant Park under "Parks" in the Recreation section below). When it
rains, performances are held in the more limited space at SBTS's headquarters in the
lower parking lot of Point Pleasant Park (seats are available on a first-come, first-served

basis). In 2008 the season began July 1, with 7 P.M. shows Tuesday to Sunday and 1 P.M. matinees Saturday and Sunday. William Shakespeare's tragedy, *Othello,* and comedy, *A Midsummer Night's Dream,* were performed. *Cinderelly*—"the fairy tale country and western musical"—was a third production.

THEATRE ARTS GUILD
902-477-2663
tagtheatre.com
Open: Sept.–July
Pond Playhouse Theatre, 6 Parkhill Rd. (off Purcell's Cove Rd.), Jollimore
Mail: Theatre Arts Guild, 287 Lacewood Dr., Unit 103, Suite 412, Halifax, NS B3M 3Y7
Admission: Prices vary according to productions

With a season of five productions that runs from September to July, the Theatre Arts Guild is Canada's oldest community theater. During World War II the guild presented entertainment for troops stationed in the city. Today performances are held in a former church owned by the guild since 1966. *Marie Antoinette: the Colour of Flesh,* by Joel Gross, will be the summer production here in 2009.

Dinner Theaters

GRAFTON STREET DINNER THEATRE
902-425-1961
graftonstdinnertheatre.com
1741 Grafton St., Halifax, NS B3J 2W1
Open: Three to six performances a week year-round starting at 6:45 PM
Admission: In 2008, adults $36.24 plus tax, children 12 and under $17.69
Handicapped accessible

Started in 1987, Grafton Street Dinner Theatre blends improv, stand-up comedy, and music to recreate a year in the history of the province, using original scripts. In 2008 the menu started off with seafood chowder or vegetable soup, then headed into steak or chicken, fish, or a vegetarian pasta dish, and ended with cheesecake, berry crumble, or apple crisp.

PETRIE'S HALIFAX FEAST DINNER THEATRE
902-420-1840
feastdinnertheatre.com
Maritime Centre, 5188 Salter St., Halifax, NS B3J 2T3
Open: Schedule varies
Admission: For a show and dinner in 2008, adult $48.25 (tax included), children 12 and under $24.13.

Four shows are performed every year, all written by owner and artistic director Jim Petrie. His *Cape Breton Idle* shows I, II and III, full of Cape Breton music and characters, have been a hit. This is Halifax's oldest dinner theater, started in the mid-1980s. Nine entrées include glazed salmon, seafood casserole, and roast loin of pork.

This ornate gazebo is at the center of Halifax Public Gardens, where free concerts are held in the summer.

Seasonal Events

May
Bluenose International Marathon May 16–18

June
Bedford Days (bedforddays.ca). Family events, fireworks.
Free concerts through the summer starting June 15, at the bandstand in the Halifax Public Gardens.
Greek Fest (902-479-1271; greekfest.org). Mid-June. Saint George Greek Orthodox Church, 38 Purcell's Cove Rd., Halifax.
Jeux de l'Acadie, a sports competition for 11- to 16-year-old Francophone participants from the Atlantic Maritimes, held in Halifax in 2008, may return in the future.
Nova Scotia Multicultural Festival (902-425-4200; multifest.ca), 2 Ochterloney St., Dartmouth. Global food fair, performers, children's tent.
Nova Scotia Multicultural Festival, Dartmouth waterfront. Food fair with offerings from all over the world.

July
Alexander Keith's Natal Day Festivities (natalday.org), end of July to beginning of August, Halifax.
Atlantic Jazz Festival, mid-July, Halifax.

Highland Games and Scottish Festival, Dartmouth Common (near the Angust L. MacDonald Bridge), Dartmouth.

Maritime Old Time Fiddling Contest, Dartmouth.

Nova Scotia International Tattoo, July 1–8, Halifax Metro Centre, a huge indoor performances featuring more than 2,000 military and civilian performers, Halifax.

Pacafiesta & The Atlantics International Fibre Fiesta (pacafiesta.com), Exhibition Park, Halifax. Spinners and weavers at work and great food and wine.

Pride Festival, mid-July, Halifax.

August

Atlantic Fringe Festival, end of Aug., beginning of Sept., Halifax.

Halifax Antique Car Show.

Halifax International Busker Festival (buskers.ca).

September

Atlantic Film Festival, Halifax.

Great Atlantic Blues and Beyond Festival, Halifax.

October

Halifax Pop Explosion Music, Art, and Culture Festival, mid-Oct., Halifax.

RECREATION

Beaches

Bayswater Beach Provincial Park (902-902-662-3030; novascotiaparks.ca), Bayswater. Twenty kilometers or 12 miles south of Hwy. 103, Exit 7, west of Halifax. Supervised white sand ocean beach in July and August. Open mid-May to mid-October. A memorial here commemorates the 229 passengers and crew who died offshore in SwissAir Flight 111 in 1998. A second memorial is located at Whaleback on Route 333 near Peggy's Cove.

Crystal Crescent Beach Provincial Park (novascotiaparks.ca), Rte. 349, Cape Sambro, 18 miles south of Halifax. Boardwalks offer easy passage to two of three white sand beaches located in the mouth of Halifax Harbour. The trail head of a hike to Pennant Point 6 miles each way, is also here. Open May 20 to October 10.

Jerry Lawrence Provincial Park (novascotiaparks.ca; 902-662-3030), Timberlea. Twenty-five kilometers or 15.5 miles west of Halifax off Hwy. 103. This park was renamed in 2007 after an activist radio talk-show host and cabinet minister who made sure a person in a wheelchair could go fishing, roll along the trails, pull right up to a picnic spot, and get inside the washroom. Fishing in the stocked waters of Round Lake and unsupervised swimming at a different location.

Laurie Provincial Park (902-662-3030; novascotiaparks.ca), Grand Lake. Located at the edge of Shubenacadie Grand Lake, this park offers a camping area, swimming, and fishing. Open June 17 to September 5.

Lawrencetown Beach (902-662-3030; novascotiaparks.ca), Lawrencetown. The destination of area and visiting surfers who are eager to catch the highest waves, Lawrencetown Beach Provincial Park presents 1.5 kilometers or 1 mile of sand beach. Lifeguards, canteen, showers, flush toilets, and boardwalks for a quiet visit. The **September Storm Classic** (surfns.com) gives professional surfers a chance to compete—for $10,000 in 2008. In early to mid-June the **Cyclesmith Duathlon** (cyclesmith.ca), a race that sandwiches 34 kilometers of biking in between 5K and 6K runs, has most often been held at Lawrencetown Beach since 1989 (close to Halifax, and listed both here and in the section on the Eastern Shore, below).

MacCormacks Beach (902-662-3030; novascotiaparks.ca), Fisherman's Cove. The views of Lawlor's and Devil's islands and Halifax Harbour make this a fine picnic spot. Boardwalk.

Oakfield Provincial Park (902-662-3030; novascotiaparks.ca), Rte. 2, Grand Lake. Thirteen kilometers or 8 miles north of Hwy. 102, Exit 5A. Small beach and lots of places to picnic, hard-surface trails, and a wheelchair-accessible boat launch.

Porter's Lake Provincial Park (902-827-2250; novascotiaparks.ca), West Porter Lake Rd. Four and a half kilometers or 2.8 miles south of Hwy. 107, Exit 19. Located beside a 24-kilometer lake, Porter Lake Park has camping, either drive-up or canoe-in, and unsupervised swimming.

Rainbow Haven Beach Park (902-662-3030; novascotiaparks.ca), 2248 Cow Bay Rd., Cow Bay, on the Eastern Shore. Supervised swimming in July and August, and heavy surf that makes this a favorite spot for surfers. The beach of sand and cobblestone is set at the mouth of Cole Harbour, and the park offers boardwalks, changing house, showers, and a canteen. Open mid-May to mid-October. (See also **Point Pleasant Park** below, under "Parks.")

Bicycling

For bike rentals, **Idealbikes** (902-444-1678; idealbikes.ca), Barrington St., Halifax, is the only company in town that rents bikes—exclusively second-hand bikes, maintained at a high level. The rental bikes are the same as those that are for sale. You can rent a high-end machine, although over a tag value of $500 the rental fee is $50 for one day or $150 for a week. Modestly priced bikes rent for $25 a day and $75 a week. Dave Schuhlein, owner, started this business in a basement room in North Halifax and worked with local kids to keep them in legal bicycles; read the Web-site story about the troubled end to the tale. **Puddle and Sea Adventures** (902-858-3030, 877-777-5699; puddleandseaadventures .com), in Hubbards, rents bicyles. Use these numbers for reservations for bike rentals. Free delivery to the Halifax area. **Train Station Bike and Bean** (902-820-3400), 5401 St. Margarets Bay Rd., Tantallon, is on the Rails to Trails with 40 kilometers or 25 miles of traffic-free riding. A café is open with coffee, panini, salads, sandwiches, and soups. A full-service bike shop here does repairs, and there is a shop for accessories. At **Freewheeling Adventures** (800-672-0775; freewheeling.ca), 2070 Hwy. 329, Hubbards, bike rentals can be delivered to you for a fee, but are free to Halifax, Peggy's Cove, or Chester, if the rental is over $300. This long-standing company offers international tours that could involve biking, or kayaking, or both. In Atlantic Canada, bike tours wind along the Southern Shore, or climb up and down the challenging Cabot Trail on Cape Breton Island.

For new bike sales, repairs, and accessories, the area has two large businesses among its many bike shops. **Bicycles Plus** (902-832-1700; bicyclesplus.ca), 1519 Bedford Hwy., Bedford, on the way in from the airport, is run by Barry Misener and hosts bike clubs as well as selling them and repairing them, with clothes and accessories also for sale. **CycleSmith** (902-425-1756; cyclesmith.ca), 6112 Quinpool Rd., Halifax, and (902-434-1756), 114 Woodlawn Rd., Dartmouth, NS B2W 2S7, is the biggest bike store in Nova Scotia.

Halifax Coalition, a local activist group, hosts mass rides (a link is on bicycle.ns.ca).

Atlantic Canada Cycling (atlanticcanada cycling.com) is a rich resource of information about routes in Nova Scotia. A 10-day tour of the province gets folks around much of the coastline.

Bird Watching

Canadian Birding (902-852-2077; maybank.tripod.com/cb/canbird-ns.htm), Whites Lake. When requested, the expert who runs this business can get you to spectacular birding sites. Blake Maybank is the author of *The Birding Sites of Nova Scotia,* the bible of birders (at amazon.com). A detailed Web site, birdingtheamericas.com, can get you to this book online. Depending on the time of year and what clients want to see, a custom tour is arranged. Nova Scotia has an incredible autumn seabird migration. Beauty is another rated quality in Maybank's guide.

Cole Harbour, Chezzetcook Inlet, Petpeswick Inlet, and Musquodoboit Harbour are nearby areas that attract huge flocks of migrating birds, especially black ducks and Canadian geese. The Eastern Shore is a place that goldeneyes and scaup stay for the winter, and piping plovers and eagles are also visitors.

Boating

Murphy's On The Water (902-420-1015; murphysonthewater.com), 1751 Lower Water St., Halifax. Located on the Halifax Waterfront, next to Cable Wharf, Murphy's offers many ways to tour the harbor and the city. The two-masted, 75-foot ketch *Mar* leaves the dock through the afternoon for a "pirate cruise." *Mar* takes a cocktail cruise, party cruise, and moonlight cruise at 10:30 PM on Friday and Saturday nights only. *Halligonian III* offers four nature and whale-watching cruises a day, and the *Harbour Queen I* takes passengers on dinner and dancing cruises. The *Harbour Hopper* (902-490-8687) is an amphibious vehicle that tours land and sea with a 55-minute narration about the city and its history. A tour to Peggy's Cove takes 2.5 hours and can bring whale and dolphin sightings. Deep-sea fishing and *Theodore II,* a tugboat and character in a children's program, are also parts of this busy business. Tickets range from $20 to $70 for adults, depending on the trip you choose to take, less for seniors and children.

Silva (902-429-0151; tallshipsilva.com), Halifax Waterfront. Tall Ship *Silva* is a three-masted 130-foot schooner that sets sail for a tour of Halifax Harbour at 12 noon, 2 PM, and 4 PM, May through Oct. A late-night party cruise with open-air dancing to a DJ's music sails at 10:30 PM on Thursday, Friday, and Saturday nights ($20). Drinks are served on board from the licensed bar. Passengers are invited to haul on the lines with the crew or steer from the helm, and a junior sailor program enlists children for pay in chocolate gold coins. Narrative of the sights and history provided. Admission: Adult $19.95, seniors or students $18.95, children $13.95.

Brewery

Alexander Keith's Nova Scotia Brewery (902-455-1474, 877-612-1820; keiths.ca), 1496 Lower Water St., Halifax. Open June–Oct., Mon.–Sat. 12–8 PM, Sun. 12–5 PM; Nov.–Apr. Fri. 5–8 PM, Sat. 12–8 PM, Sun. 12–5 PM; May, Sun.–Thurs. 12–5 PM, Fri.–Sat. 12–8 PM. When you tour this brewery, you will encounter the costumes, stories, and songs typical of 1863, when the brewery was in full steam. You could try to pick up a jig, or after learning about fermenting the ale and its ingredients, consider a career as a brewer yourself. Of course tasting the ale is very essential to the experience, but children who don't are well entertained for the 55 minutes the tour lasts. Alexander Keith started the brewery in 1820 when he found himself in a town full of soldiers and sailors. They proved to have a great thirst for his India Pale Ale, made with good barley malt and flavored with hops. Gift shop with beer and more. Admission: Adult $15.95; student, senior, and military $13.95, children $6.95.

Camping

Shubie Campground (902-435-8328, 800-440-8450; shubiecampground.com), 54 Locks Rd. off Rte. 318, Dartmouth. (Mail: P.O. Box 36058, 5675 Spring Garden Rd., Halifax, NS B3J 3S9). Located in Shubie Park between Lake Micmac and Lake Charles in Dartmouth, this is the only campground inside the city limits (the Halifax Regional Municipality, which owns this campground, contains Dartmouth, Bedford, and other areas as well as Halifax). It has a new store and canteen, the picnic tables are recent replacements, and the washrooms and laundry facilities are too. You can opt to stay inside the Shubie Yurt, or in your own tent or RV. Thirty-three unserviced sites are $26.77 a night, the yurt is $52.21, and 67 RV and motorized camper sites with water and electricity range from $32 to $40.

Casinos

Casino Nova Scotia (902-425-7777, 888-642-6376; casinonovascotia.com), 1983 Upper Water St., Halifax. Open daily 10 AM–4 AM. With more than 700 slot machines in its 34,000 square feet, you will find 750 ways to gamble along with dining and free live entertainment. (Visitors must be 19 years of age or older.) Low rates for hotel rooms are sometimes available.

Family Fun

Atlantic Playland (902-865-1025; playland.ns.ca), 1200 Lucasville Rd., Hammonds Plains. Open Mid-June–Sept. 1, daily 10 AM–6 PM. Entertainment park with waterslides, rides and arcades, and bumper cars. A 30-horse antique carousel is the ticket for the toddler you are traveling with. The Gravity House will twist your mind, or at least your sense of balance. Admission with tickets to each attraction; one ticket $1.05, book of 20, $18.95, book of 50, $39.95. "Super bracelets" for unlimited use of the water slides and rides: for individuals 48-inches tall and taller, $20.95; under 48 inches, $16.50, plus tax.

Ferries

The Dartmouth Ferry (902-490-4000; halifax.ca/metrotransit) Metro Transit, Halifax Regional Municipality, 200 Ilsey Ave., the oldest continuous salt-water passenger ferry service in North America, has taken folks across Halifax Harbour since 1752. Today it travels to two places on the Dartmouth side, Woodside and Dartmouth Waterfront Park. It's still a pleasanter way to cross the water than in your car on either of the two bridges that were built to do the same thing. Park and Ride lots, some with fee, allow you to leave your car behind. The Dartmouth Ferry leaves every 15 minutes during commuter hours and midday, every 30 minutes otherwise and in the evening until 11:30 on weekdays, and every 30 minutes on weekends. The Woodside Ferry leaves every half hour in the morning and late afternoon on weekdays, with no service on weekends. One-way adult ticket $2, children 5–15 and seniors 65 and older $1.40, and it includes a transfer to take a bus on the other side.

Fishing

Murphy's On The Water (902-420-1015; murphysonthewater.com), 1751 Lower Water St., Halifax. Located on the Halifax Waterfront, next to Cable Wharf, Murphy's on the Water offers four-hour deep-sea fishing trips.

Fitness Center

Cole Harbour Place (902-464-5100; coleharbourplace.com), 51 Forest Hills Pkwy., Darmouth. A bright, sunny pool complex that includes water slides with lots of twists and turns, and squash courts. A day pass for an adult is $6.

Golf

Ashburn Golf & Country Club (902-443-8260; ashburngolfclub.com). Two golf courses run by this private club hold distinct challenges, and the newer Ashburn course slides through trees and lakes. The first golf course opened in 1923. Views of Halifax are a feature of the old course, at 3250 Joseph Howe Dr., Halifax. The new course is at 60 Golf Club Rd., Windsor Junction, and has a new clubhouse.

Glen Arbour Golf Course (902-832-2963; glenarbour.com), Clubhouse Ln., Hammond's Plains. Beautifully maintained, with 90 sand bunkers and water features throughout, this course has views of three lakes. A handsome clubhouse holds a lounge that opens daily at 11 AM, and a pro shop.

Granite Springs Golf Club (902-852-4653; granitespringsgolf.com), 4441 Prospect Rd., Bayside. Hills, ocean views, and many course challenges 15 minutes from Halifax, with full services.

The Links at Penn Hills (902-758-1406 for pro shop; linksatpennhills.com), P.O. Box 219, 14049 Hwy. 215 (Exit 10 off Hwy. 102), Shubenacadie. Set along the Shubenacadie River and its tidal river dike lands, The Links at Penn Hills is recently opened and is arranged according to a modern design by Les Furber. Its setting inspired a bookish Haligonian to think how much the golfers must enjoy walking the greens. The new clubhouse enjoys great river views.

There are more than a dozen local golf courses, and they can be found at http://www.halifaxinfo.com/recreation.php.

Hiking

From Dartmouth past Lake Banook to Shubie Park and as far as Fletcher Lake, off the Waverly Road, Route 318, there is a good fitness trail. See Shubie Park under "Parks," below.

Sir Sanford Fleming Park, near Herring Cove, holds 95 acres, with walking trails and a tower called The Dingle, built in 1912 in honor of 150 years of representative government in Nova Scotia. A 10-story climb inside the tower rewards you with views of the Northwest Arm. You can also visit a salt-water beach and playground here.

Horseback Riding

Hatfield Farm (902-835-5676; hatfieldfarm.com), 1840 Hammonds Plains Rd.,
Hammonds Plains. Trail rides, pony rides, riding lessons, and playgrounds. Ride to
Fort Clayton and camp out overnight under the stars, or just sit on a pony for a few min-
utes, if you are new to this kind of thing.

Isner Stables Limited (902-477-5043; isnerstables.com), 1060 Old Sambro Rd.,
Harrietsfield. Offering wagon and sleigh rides, trail rides, and pony rides, Isner Stables
is located amid woods, water, and pastures, making for a pretty journey however you go.
The stable is 9.5 kilometers or 6 miles from Halifax's Armdale Rotary.

Kayaking and Canoeing

Capt. Canoe (902-827-3933; captcanoe.com), Lawrencetown Beach 5336 Hwy. 207,
Dartmouth. Located on a canal that accesses Porter's Lake or the Halifax Harbour.
Renting canoes and kayaks with all the gear for day trips. This business is a 30- to
40-minute drive from Shubie Park.

East Coast Outfitters (902-852-2567, 877-852-2567; eastcoastoutfitters.net), 2017 Lower
Prospect Rd., Lower Prospect, 25 to 30 minutes from Halifax on Rte. 333. A second
location is at 617 Main St., Mahone Bay. Rentals of single and double sea kayaks and
canoes. No delivery. Offers training classes and guided single and group tours, or you
can take off on your own exploration of the bay and coastline alongside the business.

Freewheeling Adventures (800-672-0775; freewheeling.ca), 2070 Hwy. 319, Hubbards.
Kayaks rentals can be delivered to you for a fee, but are free to Halifax, Peggy's Cove, or
Chester, if the rental is over $300. A skills assessment is necessary before the kayaks
can be rented. This company, started in 1987, offers tours that could involve biking, or
kayaking, or both, in Atlantic Canada. Kayak tours wind along the Southern Shore. A
kayak bike and hike tour in Cape Breton has received great reviews from the clients.

Sea Sun Kayak School (902-850-7732, 866-775-2925; paddlenovascotia.com), Shining
Waters Marina, Peggy's Cove Rd., Peggy's Cove. A 20-minute drive from Halifax west on
Hwy. 103. Rents single and double kayaks, and offers guided tours, a sunset trip. An
apple orchard, hot showers,

Motorcycling

Every Thursday night is Bike Night in Halifax, with free parking in certain areas of Cable
Wharf from 5:30 PM to midnight.

Parks

Halifax Public Gardens, next to the Citadel in central Halifax. Open from 2nd weekend in
May to 1st weekend of Nov., closed for the winter. This Victorian landscape of 17 manicured acres has been flourishing in the middle of Halifax since 1867. The garden is a
National Historic Site and is considered the finest example of Victorian public gardens
in North America. Even so, Hurricane Juan, in late September 2003, showed little
mercy, destroying 25 percent of the garden's trees. A multi-million dollar restoration
followed, with much of it paid for by public donation, because this garden in the heart
of the city is as vital to many of the people who live here and arrive for "soul work" every
day of the week during the growing season. The restoration included additional work to
improve aspects of the gardens that had grown somewhat tired. The renovated

Horticultural Hall, along the south side of the park and now a visitor's center, coffee house, and ice cream stand, was where the Nova Scotia Horticultural Society met to "discuss the noble pursuits of horticulture," according to Halifax Municipality planning manager Peter Bigelow. That was the group that decided to establish the public gardens in order to demonstrate ornamental planting. Although many of the garden's older specimens might no longer be considered unusual, all are still informative. A Pinatum, displaying pines from around the world, and Griffin's Pond are features to study and admire. May is spectacular, and fall is also beautiful, but formal flower beds assure colorful bloom any day you can visit.

The garden grounds are located on the Halifax Common, granted in 1763 to the people of Halifax—and across the street are playgrounds perfect for little children, along with hospitals and churches. All are set at the side of Citadel Hill.

Hemlock Ravine Park (novatrails.com/halifax/parks). A 197-acre wilderness with trails that once held the "lovenest" of Prince Edward and his mistress, Julie St. Laurent, on property earlier owned by John Wentworth, Nova Scotia lieutenant governor in the late 1700s. It's now owned and maintained by the municipality. But still on private property, and visible, is the Rotunda, built at the same time as the heart-shaped pond called Julie's Pond in the Park. Five trails weave through the wilderness, with the ravine trail most challenging, especially after rain.

MacCormacks Beach Park. Next to Fisherman's Cove, with boardwalks and clear views of Eastern Passage, Lawlor's Island, Devil's Island, and Halifax Harbor.

MacNab's and Lawlor Islands Provincial Park (902-662-3030; novascotiaparks.ca), at the mouth of Halifax Harbour. A visit is a 25-minute boat trip away. MacNab's Island is the destination, because Lawlor Island is a wildlife area closed to the public. But MacNab's, with its hikes, beaches, and history, has plenty to offer for a day trip and a picnic basket. The visitor information centers at Historic Properties or at Eastern Passage can help you find a boat to take you there.

Point Pleasant Park (open from dawn to midnight) lies at the southernmost tip of downtown Halifax, facing down the mouth of Halifax Harbour and out to sea. That strategic location has endowed its edges with many forts and fortifications, and among the earliest is the Prince of Wales Tower, a Martello tower built by the Duke of Kent, Queen Victoria's father, who was stationed here in 1796. **Prince of Wales Tower National Historic Site of Canada** is open July and August. The tower was built in 1796–97 to protect British forces from the French navy. Fort Ogilvie, built in 1862, was later the site of the city's World War I and II defenses. (Open July–Aug. daily, 10 AM–6 PM; call 902-422-5979 for Sept. hours).

Almost 70,000 of Point Pleasant's trees were blown down by Hurricane Juan in the early morning hours of September 29, 2003. "The eye of the storm came right through the city," said Peter Bigelow, manager of real property planning and the task-force leader for Hurricane Juan restoration for the Halifax Regional Municipality. "And the hurricane had some of its most dramatic impact in the park."

Some of the destruction actually uncovered some aboriginal sites 2,200 years old, and also traces of earlier European settlement, which are on display with interpretive materials installed in 2008.

As for the reforestation, Bigelow said it was for the most part in nature's hands. The parkland is regenerating itself with the seedlings of a natural Acadian forest, including sugar maple, red maple, pine, fir, oak, and hemlock.

"We've planted 70,000 trees in the last two years, but nature does far more than that," he said. The beautiful location has 3 kilometers of shoreline, with picnic areas and some public swimming spots. Locals and visitors alike came come here to walk, or to jog, or to explore—and to see a play in the summer (see Shakespeare By the Sea, in the Culture section above).

If you wish to stay late, remember to park in the upper parking lot off Tower Road and not in the lower parking lot, which closes at 8 PM.

Shubie Park (902-462-1826; novascotiaparks.ca), 54 Locks Rd. (off Rte. 318), Dartmouth. Trails and seasonal boat tours are part of Shubie Park's many charms. This park also holds the city's only campground, for both tents and RVs (listed under "Camping," above). Exhibits on the Shubenacadie Canal System are on display at the Fairbanks Centre, at 54 Locks Road, where there is also a public washroom.

The park is set at the southern end of an aboriginal water route that European settlers carved, in two separate attempts, into a canal across the province to the Bay of Fundy. Irish and French immigrant workers dug the canal system, Scotsmen fitted the stones, and British soldiers oversaw it all. The route connected across the province; but after 10 years, when the railway arrived, it was abandoned (see more about the Shubenacadie Canal under "Historic Buildings, Ships, and Sites" in the Culture section above). In the late 1970s and early 1980s, some of the canal's locks were restored. Plans to route the Trans Canada Trail will make this canal system part of a trail that leads to the Pacific Ocean.

South of the park is Lake Micmac, and south of that, Lake Banook, near downtown Dartmouth, where world-championship rowing races take place. Residents take advantage of the many boat clubs everywhere on the lakes, and their children are in boat clubs ever summer, learning to canoe and paddle and swim. Visitors can rent canoes and kayaks and get to know the lakes and canal from the water.

Running

Point Pleasant Park, listed under "Parks" above, is an excellent park for runners.

Tours

Grey Line Sightseeing (902-425-9999, 800-565-7173; ambassatours.com), 2631 King St., Halifax. Ticket Booth is on the Halifax Waterfront next to the Maritime Museum of the Atlantic. A city tour on one of the double decker Grey Line red buses will give you the lay of the land in three hours, including stops at the Halifax Public Gardens and the Citadel (the tour ticket includes admission). Other tours go to Peggy's Cove, adding Keith's Brewery, a great interactive tour, or Lunenburg and Mahone Bay.

Haunted Hike of Halifax (902-495-6450; hauntedhikeofhalifax.bravehost.com), Halifax. Offered nightly June 15–Sept. 15 at 8:30 PM, and Sept. 15–Oct. 31 at 7 PM. Offered nightly June 15–Sept. 15 at 8:30 PM, and Sept. 15–Oct. 31 at 7 PM. May be offered earlier in the year depending on weather. The tour starts at Robbie Burns Memorial in Victoria Park, across from the main gate to the Halifax Public Gardens, and ends at Murphy's on the Waterfront. Guides in period costume detail the horrific story of the 1917 Halifax Explosion as you wind through the Old Burying Grounds. Also offered is a **Historical Walk** of the waterfront, leaving from Bishop's Landing, Lower Water Street, daily from June 15 to September 15 at 2 PM, reservations unnecessary.

The Harbour Hopper, an amphibious vehicle, is described under "Boating," above.

SHOPPING

Antiques

ABC: Antiques, Books & Collectibles (902-826-1128; abcantiques.ca), 12723 Peggy's Cove Rd., Tantallon. Furniture, glass, and ceramics are some of the items in this collection that includes "a little bit of everything," according to Joselle Barrington, who runs ABC with her husband Parker. Local interest books too.

Finer Things Antiques (902-456-1412; finerthingsantiques.com), 2797 Agricola St., Halifax. Formal and primitive furniture, hooked rugs and folk art, and nautical finds in 1,700 square feet of space. There are 15 dealers here covering the history of manufactured and handmade objects.

McLellan Antiques & Restoration (902-455-4545; 3.ns.sympatico.ca/jimmclellan/mclellan.html), 2738 Agricola St., Halifax. Antique furniture in pine and formal, 1920s mahogany, old lighting, clocks, and phonographs.

Bookstores

Back Pages (902-423-4750), 1526 Queen St., Halifax. Winter hours Mon.–Sat. 9:30 AM–5:30 PM, Sun. 12–5 PM; call for spring to fall hours. Opened in 1979, Back Pages is owned by Michael Norris, who sells secondhand books, constantly changing in inventory. "There's always something coming out of the woodwork worth reading," Norris said.

Books Galore and More (902-826-1565), St. Margaret's Bay Rd., Upper Tantallon. Used CDs, used paperbacks, and hardcover nonfiction.

Dartmouth Book Exchange (902-435-1207; dartmouthbookexchange.ca), 1187 Cole Harbor Rd., Dartmouth. Open Mon.–Fri. 10 AM–8 PM, Sat. 10 AM–6 PM, Sun. 11 AM–5 PM. Fiction, science fiction and fantasy, religious, self-help, children's room, and best-selling paperbacks priced at 3 for $12; if you bring them back to exchange, you receive a $2 store credit for each one. Wade and Amy McIsaac have been in charge since 2000.

Dust Jacket Books and Treasures (902-492-0666; dustjacket.com), 1505 Barrington St. Maritime Centre, Halifax. Open Mon.–Fri. 10 AM–4 PM. A large collection of used and rare books, with records, and a few antiques. Chris Cooper often has a strong selection of Maritime history, gardening, military, nautical, crafts, cooking, and children's books.

John W. Doull, Bookseller (902-429-1652; doullbooks.com), 1684 Barrington St., Halifax. Open Mon.–Tues. 9 AM–6 PM, Wed.–Fri. 9:30 AM–9 PM, Sat. 10 AM–9 PM. Specializing in literature, history, Atlantic provinces, nautical and scholarly works, with 35,000 in stock. One of them was a signed edition of *Image Maker* by James Merrill, printed by Sea Cliff Press in 1986.

The Jade W (902-423-5233; thejadeW.com), 5233 Prince St., Halifax. Open Mon.–Sat. 10 AM–6 PM. New and secondhand books in a two-floor shop that sells children's books, travel writing, Canadian fiction and nonfiction, to mention a few categories. Women's studies is another. The stock here is split with the nearby bookstore above, John Doull, Bookseller—he gets all the nautical books to sell, and Sydney Hansen keeps the children's books. They share cookbooks. Ask, and if one or the other of them can help you, they will let you know.

The Last Word Bookstore (902-423-2932), 2160 Windsor St., Halifax. Open Mon.–Sat. 10 AM–6 PM, Fri. till 9 PM; June–Oct., also open Sun. 12–6 PM. A small collection of secondhand and rare books focused on history and literature.

Old Fezziwig's Books and Baubles (902-883-1335; oldfezziwigs.tripod.com), 296 Hwy. 214, Unit 14, Elmsdale. This store, convenient to the airport, sells used books, paperbacks, fantasy and science fiction, fiction, history, children's gaming cards and sports cards. CDs and DVDs are also stocked, as are books about Nova Scotia from Glen Margaret Publishing.

Schooner Books (902-423-8419; schoonerbooks.com), 5378 Inglis St., Halifax. Open Mon.–Thurs. and Sat. 9:30 AM–5:30 PM, Fri. 9:30 AM–6 PM. Lots of Canadian books, maps, engravings, and art. In business since 1975, in a blue Victorian building within walking distance of the universities, Schooner Books is skilled at finding exactly what the varied clientele are searching for, with a particular emphasis on Atlantic provinces history and literature—a catalogue usually appears a few times a year about these offerings. Vintage photographs reveal the world that used to circulate around the Maritimes.

Woozles (902-423-7626, 800-966-0537; woozles.com), 1533 Birmingham St., Halifax. Open Mon.–Thurs. and Sat. 9:30 AM–5:30 PM, Fri. 9:30 AM–9 PM, Sun. 11 AM–to 5 PM. Canada's oldest children's bookstore, Woozles started selling books to kids in 1978, and now it's selling books to those kids' kids. Inside a house that has had two additions, this bookstore has room for every kind of kid book from wordless to pictureless, as well as the question, Is this the oldest children's bookstore in North America? Drop by to see if they have found out.

Crystal

Nova Scotian Crystal (902- 492-0416, 888-977-2797; novascotiancrystal.com), 5080 George St., Halifax. Open Mon.–Fri. 9 AM–6 PM, Sat.–Sun. 10 AM–5 PM. You can see the open oven to heat the glass and the glassblowers molding their pieces when you visit this artisan shop on the Halifax Waterfront. Craftsmen brought the skills with them from Ireland in 1996 and built a business that now uses Nova Scotia as its inspiration—and is the only crystal maker in the nation. The pattern named after the *Titanic*, which sunk off the coast of Nova Scotia, is complex and ornate, and "The Citadel" shows off multiple points. Best of all is to get one in your hand and feel the heft and strength of it.

Galleries

Argyle Fine Art (902-425-9456; argylefa.com), 1869 Upper Water St., Halifax. Open most of the year, Mon.–Thurs. 10 AM–6 PM, Fri. 10 AM–8 PM, Sat. 10 AM–6 PM, Sun. 12–6 PM. Representing Simone LaBuschangne, from Lunenburg, and other local or Nova Scotian established and emerging artists working in an array of styles and mediums.

Gift and Specialty Shops

The Bay Hammock Company (902-820-3045, 888-820-3045; bayhammocks.com), 11452 Peggy's Cove Rd., Seabright. Local workers make the hammocks by hand. They are guaranteed for five years. The best hammocks are made of rope—also made here from scratch. Custom sizes are sold at no extra cost, and the hammocks are also shipped in Canada and in the U.S.A. free of charge, or were in the summer of 2008.

Shopping Areas and Malls

Barrington Place Specialty Shops
(902-429-3660), 1903 Barrington
St., Halifax. Open Mon.–Sat. 9:30
AM–6 PM, Sun. 11 AM–to 5 PM. Thirty
shops carry the latest looks, and **7th
Avenue Boutique** (902-422-8827;
7thavenue.ca), Barrington Place
Shops Lower Level, carries them new
and secondhand for a little mercy on
the price.

Historic Properties (902-429-0530;
historicproperties.ca), 1869 Upper
Water St., Halifax. Near the Halifax
Ferry Terminal). Three restored

*Yarn jellyfish swim in the window of The Loop
in Halifax.*

blocks on the waterfront with shops, cafes, and boardwalks, this area has won awards
for the preservation and revitalizing of a district of Halifax waterfront that the city wears
today like a jewel. Inside the area are seven national historic sites, including the
Privateer's Wharf that held the spoils of privateers, ships commissioned by the British
navy to seize the ships of the enemy and its allies. **Spiro's** (Open daily 10 AM–8 PM) is a
traditional men's barbershop here for 30 years where you could get an historical rundown better than the ones on some of the tour boats'.

Hydrostone Market (hydrostonemarket.ca). Directions from the Web site: "From downtown Halifax, take Barrington Street or Gottingen Street northwards and turn left on
Young Street." Built after the city was in a shambles following the Halifax Explosion of
1917, and made with a concrete block called hydrostone, this neighborhood was
designed as an English garden suburb. Today it is teeming with shops and places to eat.
Rejuvention—of your manicure—can be arranged at **Chrysalis Spa & Skin Care Centre**
(902-446-3929; chrysalisspa.com), 5521 Young St. **Bogside Gallery** (902-453-3063),
5527 Young St., sells Atlantic Canadian artisans' crafts. **Julien's French Bakery**, listed
under "Bakeries" in the Food Purveyors section above, is its own destination.

Spring Garden Road (902-423-3751; springgardenroad.com), Spring Garden Area
Business Association, 5670 Spring Garden Rd., Suite 610, Halifax, NS B3J 1H6. Nine
blocks of pedestrian paradise center on Spring Garden Road, with cafes, shops, and
people watching. Clothes shops, coffee houses, and beautiful architecture line the
streets in this area near the Citadel and Halifax Public Gardens.

Yarn

The Loop (902-429-5667; theloophalifax.ca), 1547 Barrington St., Halifax. Yarns of all
descriptions, with many from Canadian sources, fill the wall shelves of this fine knit-
ting store. Upstairs is a link with the next door café, **Ciboulette**, so you could easily get
a start on your next project with the help of a fine cup of coffee and scone.

THE EASTERN SHORE

Northeast of the city of Halifax is a quiet coastline of fishing villages, and a second section of this chapter focuses on its small inns and enchanting living museums. The towns stretch south to north on a five-hour-long drive, on the rough, curvy road that hugs the coastline. Several re-creations of historical places include one in Jeddore Oyster Pond, where a tiny house holds the **Fisherman's Life Museum,** once the home of a 19th-century fisherman, his wife, and their 13 daughters. A sunny bedroom added on in 1933 was built for a daughter ill with tuberculosis—who lived to be 83.

Driving north along Nova Scotia's Atlantic Coast leads you into curvy, rough roads that can seem endless on a foggy night. But interludes make the long journey wonderful, like the ring-necked pheasant with his tail feathers erect who crossed the road ahead, or the sea otter gulping fresh perch in the water, just in front of the ramp for the ferry to Isaac's Harbour across Country Harbour River, where roseate terns flew past and absorbed every moment before the ferry's arrival.

LODGING

SOUTH END OF THE EASTERN SHORE

LISCOMBE LODGE
902-779-2307, 800-665-6343
signatureresorts.com
Liscomb Mills, NS B0J 2A0
Open: Mid-May–late Oct.

Price: $140 to $155, includes buffet breakfast
Credit cards: Yes
Handicapped Access: Yes, two rooms in lodge and two chalets
Special Features: Wi-Fi, indoor pool, tennis, hiking trails

With 17 private "chalets," 5 four-bedroom cottages, each with a stone fireplace, and 30

The fishing boats are docked up the shore from Canso village in this working harbor.

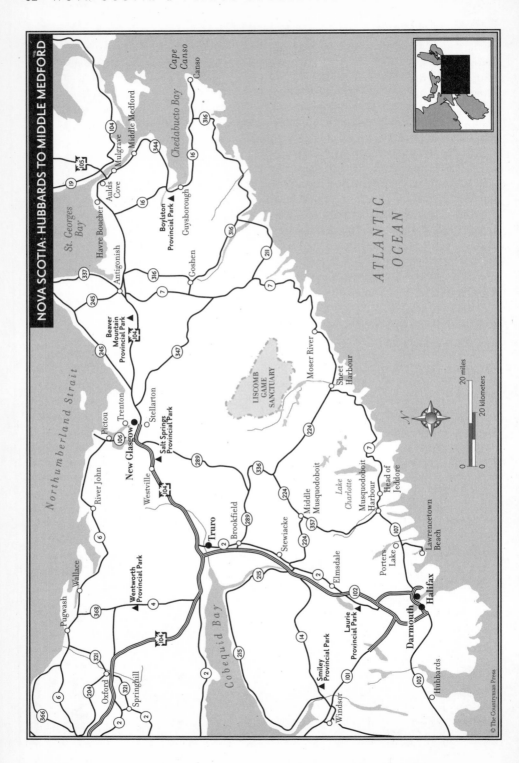

NOVA SCOTIA: HUBBARDS TO MIDDLE MEDFORD

lodge rooms, this large hotel is now owned by the provincial government and run by Newcastle Resort, which is carrying on a tradition that began in 1960.

Dinner is served in the Riverside Room, with a view of Liscomb River and a fireplace at one end. Planked salmon is another tradition here, cooked over an open fire. And before you dine, there could be a river tour on the lodge's 12-passenger boat. After dinner there might be a movie to watch, on the lawn outside. For a fee, your children can enjoy a campfire cookout, bonfire, and storytelling.

SALMON RIVER HOUSE COUNTRY INN

Adrien Blanchette and Elisabeth Schwarzer, innkeepers
902-889-3353, 800-565-3353
salmonriverhouse.com
9931 Hwy. 7 (Marine Dr.), Salmon River Bridge, NS B0J 1P0
Price: $108 to $144
Credit cards: Yes
Handicapped Access: Yes, one first-floor room
Special Features: Wi-Fi, restaurant with deck and river view

The Salmon River House started as a bed and breakfast in 1920, under the name, Jeddore Hotel. Today it is the area's best restaurant (see the review in the Restaurants section below) and a casual, fun place to stay. Hints of tradition are stationed at every corner in the many rooms, from the "bistro," a place for guests to sit and have a drink, to the old-fashioned furniture. If some of the rooms seem a little dated, with 1970s furnishings, everything is in good condition, and well kept.

A large soaking tub enhances the Captain's Room, a handicapped-accessible first-floor room. Other rooms have acrylic surround showers that are very good looking. The Hideaway is in the back of the second floor, and it enjoys both privacy and a view of the wide river where there is fishing when the mackerel or other fish are running. Canoes are available, and guests can also scale a steep hill on the side of the river to explore some of the inn's 50 acres, which include a pond.

SHERBROOKE AND NORTH

SEAWIND LANDING COUNTRY INN

Ann Marie and David de Jongh, innkeepers
800-563-4667
seawindlanding.com
159 Wharf Rd., Charlos Cove, RR #2, Larry's River, NS B0H 1T0
Price: $95 to $169
Credit cards: Yes
Handicapped Access: One unit
Special Features: Dinner served 6–9 P.M. daily, entrées $23 to $25

The seclusion of the Eastern Shore is perfect by the time you have arrived at Charlos Cove in Larry's River (and watch out for the left turn if you are heading north to Canso!). SeaWind Landing takes advantage of all that the landscape has to offer, with its 25 acres bordered by quiet beaches and woven with walking trails. With a GPS system in a rental car, you can plot your course here without a glitch, but expect a rough road on your way here.

The de Jonghs relocated here from Alberta in 2008, with a stint in Toronto and Edmonton before that. "We sold our house, we quit our jobs, we sold most of our belongings, and ended up in a village of 104 people," said David de Jongh.

The existing staff all stayed on, and de Jongh lauds his "phenomenally talented chef"—serving dishes like local cod almondine, scallops in Vermouth sauce, salmon served poached or cedar-planked, pork tenderloin with apple-brandy sauce. Otherwise, a meal is at least a half hour's drive.

Of 14 rooms, all with private bath, 6 are in the main building. The Captain's

Quarters has a window seat. A minute's walk away is Land's End, a building at the end of the peninsula, which has a high-peaked roof and contains 8 rooms all with sea views.

SHERBROOKE VILLAGE INN

Carol and Rennie Beaver, innkeepers
902-522-2235, 866-522-3818
sherbrookevillageinn.ca
7975 Hwy. 7, P.O. Box 40, Sherbrooke, NS
B0J 3C0
Price: $80 to $140
Credit cards: Yes
Handicapped Access: No
Special Features: Wi-Fi, 10 percent senior discount, pets welcome with $10 fee, breakfast served at the restaurant

With a variety of units, including 12 motel-like rooms with king-size beds or two double beds, 3 cottages, a house, a suite, and two efficiencies, all with private baths and cable TV, Sherbrooke Village Inn allows a traveler to find the right room. People with sensitivities to chemicals will appreciate the use of scentless, green cleaning products, but the intense smells of cleaning products and room deodorizers can be an issue for anyone. "We're in a setting that includes a pond," within walking distance of the historic village and shops. Canoes can access the ocean in a two-minute drive.

CANSO

THE LAST PORT MOTEL & RESTAURANT

Mary Jean and Fred Hanhams, owners
902-366-2400
10 Hwy. 16, RR #1, Canso, NS B0H 1H0
Open: Year-round
Price: $65
Credit cards: Yes
Handicapped Access: Yes
Special Features: Wi-Fi, but it may not work in your room—try the restaurant

This modest motel surprises with its tiled bathrooms, comfortable beds, and squeaky clean rooms, renovated and up to date. The restaurant is another pleasure, open from 7 AM until 10 PM in summer (8 AM to 8 PM off-season), a wonderful favor when you discover, as I did, that the 85-mile road to Canso from Sherbrooke is the twistiest, turniest thicket ever devised by a rocky coastline. The only peaceful part is crossing a river on a ferry (every 15 minutes July and August). What a relief it is to finally arrive, turn past the little lighthouses at the entrance, and relax. Bright rooms with floral coverlets on the double beds have TVs and solid wood furniture. The restaurant opens for breakfast (not included) at 7 AM, and the Number 3 ($7) eggs with sausage, reveals the hand of a perfectionist, the yolks still runny and the white still tender. Now that you are rested, you can contemplate a hike on a walking trail or a picnic on a beach, after you take the short boat ride and tour of Grassy Island Museum (see below).

✪ WHITMAN WHARF BED & BREAKFAST

Elizabeth and John Measures, innkeepers
902-366-2450, 888-728-2424
whitemanwharf.com
1309 Union St., Canso, NS B0H 1H0
Open: May–Oct., with the possibility of off-season
Price: $79 to $95
Credit cards: Yes
Handicapped Access: None
Special Features: Wi-Fi, Garden House for enjoying a take out meal, folk art for sale

The flavorful, full-bodied coffee is the tip-off that the innkeepers at Whitman Wharf know exactly what they are doing. This B&B rents three bedrooms, all comfortable and well appointed, with the one drawback that guests must share a bathroom. The bath holds a wide, modern tub with several steps to reach its capacious depths, and thick, large towels are piled on the shelf for a luxurious drying session.

Elizabeth Measures makes her own soaps and bath salts, which stock the bathroom and can be bought here—there are hundreds of roses in the rose soap, she said, contained in the essential oil she uses. The Dovecote has a tiny sitting area from which to gaze at the sea, and Lavender Fields has its own cedar closet. All three rooms have deep, springy, high-quality mattresses and box springs. Breakfast always includes fruit: it could be a crêpe with fruit or a waffle piled with fruit or a mini-quiche. In this most easterly point of North America, birding is supreme, and the Measures can accommodate guests with guides and tips for the best birding spots. Start with a trip to the top of Whitman House Museum next door, where the Widow's Walk give a perfect view.

GUYSBOROUGH

DESBARRES MANOR INN

902-533-2099
desbarresmanor.com
90 Church St., Guysborough, NS B0H 1N0
Open: May–Oct.
Price: $149 to $259
Credit cards: Yes
Handicapped Access: None
Special Features: Wi-Fi, fine dining

This 1837 mansion was the home of Supreme Court Justice W. F. DesBarres, and the present-day innkeepers have pulled out the stops to recreate the early splendor. Original art, 600-thread-count sheets and perfect beds work with the modern amenities to invite relaxation. Breakfast, afternoon tea, and handmade truffles are part of the experience, and the rate. The Williams Room is perfect for a couple who like to relax together in a big tub, or sleep in a four-poster bed near a gas fireplace. Antiques scattered among the rooms

include a Duncan Fife parlor table. A cocktail is available in the Parlour Room, and the next morning there will be a full breakfast that might involve apple and cheddar crêpes or banana-bread french toast.

RESTAURANTS

SOUTH END OF THE EASTERN SHORE

THE LOBSTER SHACK RESTAURANT AT SALMON RIVER HOUSE

Adrien Blanchette and Elisabeth Schwarzer
902-889-3353, 800-565-3353
salmonriverhouse.com
9931 Hwy. 7 (Marine Dr.), Salmon River Bridge
Open: May–Oct. daily
Price: $6 to $55 for a 2-pound lobster
Credit cards: Yes
Cuisine: Seafood, Maritime classics, and German and French dishes
Serving: L, D
Handicap Access: Yes
Special Features: Eastern Shore Pirate Festival in mid-Sept.

The dark wood booths and casual atmosphere are friendly and welcoming at this multi-roomed restaurant, reliable for a lobster dinner, with mussels, potato salad, and dessert. It's also a place to turn to for a respite from seafood, with German dishes (under the direction of one of the owners, Elisabeth Schwarzer) such as Salmon River House schnitzel. Seafood pasta, sautéed Digby scallops, and fish and chips along with crêpes, quiche, and baked camembert. You can sit in the "bistro" for a glass of Stutz hard apple cider and enjoy a view of the wide river from the dining room, perhaps catching a glimpse of someone fishing for sea turtle or mackerel. If you drop by in mid-September, the pirates will be coming ashore and drinking grog at the next table.

It doesn't look exciting, but on a stretch of country road in Moser River Trail Stop's good food is welcome.

TRAIL STOP

902-347-2602

trailstop.ca

Marine Dr., Hwy. 7 (just east of Moser River Bridge), Moser River

Open: In summer, Mon.–Thurs. 12–8 PM, Fri.–Sat. 10 AM–10 PM, Sun. 10 AM–8 PM.

Price: $2.25 to $9

Credit cards: No

Cuisine: Fresh, local when available

Serving: B, L, D

Handicap Access: No

This isn't exactly a restaurant, but it deserves as much attention as one because good food on this stretch of Nova Scotia's coast can be hard to find. Battered and fried mushrooms, excellent battered fried haddock (bought in Tangier), mussels from Ship Harbour—if it's growing anywhere near, Gail Martin will buy it and serve it. The Truckers Breakfast, has three eggs laid by her own chickens, sausage, bacon, and ham, hashbrowns, toast, juice, and coffee— for $7.50. It's almost enough to make you move next door.

SHERBROOKE AND NORTH

MAIN STREET CAFÉ

902-522-2848

17 Main St., Sherbrooke

Open: May–Sept., daily 8 AM–9 PM

Price: $8 to $15

Credit cards: Yes

Cuisine: Casual Maritime

Serving: B, L, D

Handicap Access: Ramp, but washrooms are not accessible

Special Features: Patio with four tables

Eric and Connie Nauffts run this café and bistro, bakery, and pizzeria, which serves seafood. Fried clams come from local clam flats and are especially popular.

GUYSBOROUGH

DAYS GONE BY BAKERY

902-533-2762
daysgoneby.ca
143 Main St., Guysborough
Open: In summer, daily Mon.–Fri. 7 PM–
7 PM, Sat. 8 AM–7 PM, Sun.–8 PM
Price: $9 to $13
Credit cards: Yes
Cuisine: Comfort food
Serving: B, L, D
Handicap Access: No
Special Features: Gift shop

This shop combines a bakery, café, and antiques and gift shop. The bakery is busy making lemon bread, ginger snaps, macaroon brownies, and cinnamon rolls. You can pick up a package of something for the rest of the drive. In the café, haddock, turkey, and spaghetti with meat sauce are some of the dinner items, but don't look for fried fish, because nothing is deep fried in the kitchen. For breakfast you can enjoy the french toast made with the bakery's own multigrain bread, and what's more, it is served all day. Wine and beer available.

DESBARRES MANOR INN

902-533-2099
desbarresmanor.com
90 Church St., Guysborough
Open: May–Oct., daily 6 AM–8 PM
Price: $28 to $32
Credit cards: Yes
Cuisine: Contemporary Canadian fine dining
Serving: L, D
Handicap Access: No
Special Features: Fireplace in the dining room, outside deck, organic vegetable garden, wine dinners, and cooking classes

Carrot bisque with vanilla honey and mint starts a certain kind of dinner off right— and DeBarres Manor is intent on making the evening thoroughly enjoyable. Next could be a pheasant breast with spiced apple glaze, or rack of lamb with a raspberry demiglace. A dessert of vanilla cake with strawberries and lemon curd acknowledges the power of tradition. Three entrées are offered every night, and they change daily. Smoked Atlantic salmon bread pudding is an invention of the chef, Shaun Zwarun, shared on the Web site. Award-winning Zwaren, a native of Glace Bay, might use Screech, Newfoundland's rum, and truffles with scallops, or stuff from the garden to showcase local lobster mushrooms, or Aspy Bay oysters. Elegant, dark wood chairs make the dining room distinctive. A wide range of wines.

✪ THE RARE BIRD PUB

902-533-2128
rarebirdpub.com
80 Main St., Guysborough
Open: June–mid-Oct., daily from 11 AM
Price: $12 to $19
Credit cards: Yes
Cuisine: Wood-fired oven pizza, seafood
Serving: L, D
Handicap Access: Yes
Special Features: Waterfront patio, marina if arriving by boat

The home of microbrewery, Chedabucto Brewing Company, follows this town's heritage—which, its Web site reports, included a commercial brewery in 1659. On tap at the pub only are Willy's Highland Ale, Rare Bird Ale, light and fresh tasting, and Beachcomber Blonde, all with no additives or sugars. The spacious, chic dining room offers a Sunday brunch of steak and eggs or crab omelets. Cream and sherry go into the Chedabucto Bay seafood chowder, mussels and spring rolls are among the appetizers, and there is a particularly appealing Rueben among the sandwiches, with house sauerkraut. Fried local clams, fish cakes and beans, meatloaf and gravy share the dinner menu.

Food Purveyors

Coffee Shops

Village Coffee Grind (902-522-2217), 27 Main St., Sherbrooke. Open Mon.–Fri. 9 AM–8 PM, Sat. 10 AM–6 PM, Sun. 11 AM–6 PM. Breakfast of toast and bagels; lunch and dinner include soups, sandwiches, and pasta salads. Of course a variety of coffees is always available.

Meat, Fish, Poultry

Smoked Fish from J. Willy Krauch & Sons (902-772-2188; willykrauch@ns.sympatico.ca), Hwy. 7, Tangier. Open Mon.–Fri. 8 AM–6 PM, Sat.–Sun. 10 AM–6 PM. World famous, this smokehouse sells to the aficionados in New York City. You can get your lox from the source, or try some of the other delicacies, like smoked mackerel—a fish jammed with healthy Omega-3s—or smoked eel. If you aren't staying at a place that would make these treats appropriate, you can taste them here and choose something to be shipped to arrive when you're back home.

Culture

Galleries

See "Galleries" in the Shopping section below.

Historic Buildings, Ships, and Sites

ACADIAN HOUSE MUSEUM AND LA CUISINE DE BRIGITTE

902-827-5992 (in season), 902-827-2248 (off-season)
E-mail: sa.lowe@ns.sympatico.ca
79 Hill Rd., West Chezzetcook, NS B0J 1N0
Open: July–Aug., Tues.–Sun. 10 AM–4:30 PM
Admission: Free

A scale-model display of the Acadian community from around 1900, and panels about clamming and schooner building are displayed in this house museum devoted to presenting the heritage of local Acadians. Men from the area learned the trade of brick building in New Hampshire and returned to build a brickyard in the mid-1800s that operated for more than 50 years. In the small tearoom called La Cuisine de Brigitte, you can sometimes enjoy fricot aux coques, clam stew. On Sunday lunch always presents traditional Acadian dishes, perhaps fishcakes and baked beans, with a dessert of gingerbread with lemon or brown-sugar sauce.

CANSO ISLANDS AND GRASSY ISLAND FORT

902-366-3136 (summer), 902-295-2069 (off-season)
parkscanada.gc.ca
Union St., Canso
Mail: P.O. Box 159, Baddeck, NS B0E 1B0
Open: June 1–Sept. 15, 10 AM–6 PM

AFRIKAN CANADIAN HERITAGE AND FRIENDSHIP CENTER
902-533-4006
Chedabucto Place
27 Green St., Guysborough, NS B0H IN
Open: During the school year
Admission: Free

The first settlements of free blacks in Nova Scotia, outside of Halifax, were in Country Harbour, Upper Big Tracadie, Sunnyville, and elsewhere. A ship of 226 black loyalists, who had fought with Britain against American revolutionaries, in part to gain their freedom from slavery, arrived in Chedabucto Bay in June 1784. The history of their experience here is portrayed in photographs and publications. The first winter was brutal, with supplies stolen by a mutinous crew, and the means of hunting denied to the black settlers, who were not permitted to own guns.

From the distribution of land to the sharing of supplies, blacks came up short. British promises were broken, and the whites in the area were prejudiced and resentful. Nevertheless, the community of Lincolnville was settled and survives to to this day.

A plaque in Country Harbour describes the black communities that once were settled in the area.

Admission: Suggested admission only, including the boat trip
Handicapped accessible Visitor's Centre

The grassy, windswept island just 15 minutes from shore by boat was once thronged with New Englanders, who spent their summer drying the codfish so abundant here. In the 1730s, thousands of tough fishermen hauled in the cod on their schooners each summer and laid out 8 million to dry on the "flakes," long tables of rough wood, still roughly visible on the island, before packing them up to sell in Europe and America.

But all that abundance was inevitably disputed. The French and the English had been fishing here since the beginning of the 1600s. Between 1713 and 1720 the English threw out the French and built a fort that the British then refused to man. In 1744 the French got back at them, attacking the island and burning the buildings. All the while smuggling had kept some of them in touch with each other.

New Englanders attacked and overran nearby Louisburg in 1745, but they didn't return to Canso.

Archeological digs have uncovered part of an exploded shell from a French ship's gun and the broken plates and cups of these inhabitants. The Visitor's Centre holds some of these artifacts, as well as dioramas of an officer's study, a tavern, and a merchant's parlor. A short video introduces visitors to the area and its history.

COMMERCIAL CABLE HERITAGE SITE
902-533-4433
ccrsociety.ca
Hazel Hill, Canso, NS

This large, shuttered, and disintegrating brick building was once the telegram-transmitting facility of Commercial Cable, started in 1884. Fundraising is ongoing to restore the building. A plaque in a neighboring park tells the story of the arrival in the secluded Canso area of a regiment of sophisticated engineers. Along with the telegraph office and 20 family homes, the new village at Hazel Hill included a cricket pitch. Before it began operating, the Anglo-American Telegraph Company charged huge fees for telegrams, and an American newspaper owner, dependent on the telegraph for news, decided to break that monopoly. He and his partners came up with the money for the new telegraph company, but it was the English who had made and laid the transatlantic cable and created on Hazel Hill a British "fiefdom" that had little to do with the surrounding people. In 1927 Commercial Cable was sold to International Telephone and Telegraph, ITT, which was sold to Western Union in 1988. The Canso Station stopped working in 1962.

MEMORY LANE HERITAGE VILLAGE

902-845-1937, 877-287-0697
heritagevillage.ca
Lake Charlotte, NS
Open: Mid-June–mid-Oct., daily 11 AM–4 PM
Admission: With a meal, adults $12, children 7–17 and seniors 60 and over $11

The era presented in this village, the 1940s, is certainly within memory for many of us, yet still a pleasure to relive. Volunteers might show you how to recognize gold, or how to cut pulpwood by hand, or do laundry with a ringer. The old cars and trucks drive among relocated buildings from the surrounding communities, barns, a boat shop, a one-room schoolhouse, and a village garage among them. There are farm animals, period bicycles for visitors to ride, and a pump organ that you can play. Homemade brown bread is always for sale.

Eat at a replica of a 1940s Cookhouse, open daily from 11:30 AM to 3:30 PM, and enjoy baked beans for (in 2008) $8 per person.

Filling up the 1948 International pickup truck at Memory Lane Heritage Village
Courtesy of the Lake Charlotte Area Heritage Society

One of the painted stones in the monument to Acadian history in Larry's River called Parc de nos Ancestres

PARC DE NOS ANCESTRES
902-525-2074, Jude Avery, president
La Société des Acadiens de la Région de Tor Baie
Tor Bay Acadian Society
Rte. 316, Larry's River (across from L'Église Saint Pierre, St. Peter's Church, NS)
Open: Always
Admission: Free

Large, flat-faced boulders stand in an arch at this roadside monument, each with brilliantly colored historical scenes painted by Monica Duersch and Charlotte Pitts. The park is laid out like an anchor, the symbol of the people it commemorates, Acadians who refused to leave and stood their ground, like an anchor with a good hold, when the British were expelling the other Acadians on the Nova Scotia farmlands.

This community represents the smallest part of L'Acadie. "We come from a batch of families who were kept prisoners of war during the expulsion," Jude Avery, president of the society, said; 2,000 were kept on Georges Island near Halifax. Next, their ancestors went to Chezzicook, only to be uprooted again. They planted themselves on Tor Bay and refused to leave. The Acadian descendents honor the story of their past with these painted stones, each detailed scene telling a chapter of their history of the French in the New World. La Société des Acadiens de la Région de Tor Baie also hosts Festival Savalette, started in 2005, on the second weekend of August.

PRINCE HENRY SINCLAIR MONUMENT
902-647-4016
sinclair.quarterman.org/sinclair/phssna.html
Rte. 16, Halfway Cove, NS
Open: Always
Admission: Free

The Prince Henry Sinclair expedition arrived here in 1398, the story goes, a century before Christopher Columbus, and the Prince Henry Sinclair Society erected this monument in

1996 to tell us about it. The 15-ton granite boulder has a black-granite plaque that describes the history. Sinclair was an admiral who became Lord Chief Justice of Scotland. The society believes he sailed with the Venetian Zeno family and that he also arrived in Massachusetts in 1399. Large-log picnic tables nearby allow you to enjoy lunch at this historic location.

Lighthouses

PORT BICKERTON LIGHTHOUSE AND
NOVA SCOTIA LIGHTHOUSE INTERPRETIVE CENTRE
902-364-2000
nslps.com
640 Lighthouse Rd., Port Bickerton, NS

This point was settled in the 1840s, after fishermen first settled the island just offshore. In 1901 the first of three lighthouses was built. Today the functional lighthouse is a small white building on the point, and the second light, built in 1930, is the Interpretive Centre. It is set on a bluff on the west side of Barachois Head.

Museums and Living History Attractions

CANSO MUSEUM, WHITMAN HOUSE
guysboroughcountyheritage.ca.
902-366-2170
1297 Union St., Canso, NS B0H 1H0
Open: June–Sept., daily 9 AM–5 PM
Admission: Free

Built in 1885, Whitman House has windows that are amber in their upper panes—to create sunny light, according to one historian writing on the Web site. Owner and shipowner C. H. Whitman entertained in his double parlor and lived here until 1932. The town bought the building in 1974 to create a museum inside it. Period furniture, art, and photos are inside; up top, you can visit a widow's walk and enjoy the view. The defunct fish plant was being dismantled in the summer of 2008, to transform the Canso waterfront and beautify the village. This house is also the area Visitors' Centre, with brochures and informative staff.

FISHERMAN'S LIFE MUSEUM
902-889-2053
museum.gov.ns.ca/flm/
58 Navy Pool Loop, Jeddore Oyster Pond, NS B0J 1W0
Open: June–Oct., Mon.-Sat. 9:30 AM–5:30 PM, Sun. 1–5:30 PM
Admission: Adults $3.25, seniors 65 and older and children 6–17 $2.25

This utterly charming museum is part of the Nova Scotia Museum complex, 24 different sites around the province that bring the past back to life. On my visit to this tiny house—complete with kittens playing in the barn and a lamb and its ewe in their pen—the kitchen wood stove was lit and the women had used it to bake cookies for Canada Day. Wearing aprons and dresses they had made them-selves, these guides know as much as there is to know of the history of the house, par-ticularly the years between 1900 and 1920, and of its owners Ervin and Ethelda Myers, a fisherman and his wife, and their 14 daughters, one of whom died in infancy. You can see how it might have been possi-ble for them to squeeze inside, upstairs, in the three small bedrooms, when each bed held several children. Quilts, fine-knit coverlets, furniture, and hooked rugs all come from that era—as the three surviving daughters made sure. While Myers rowed his dory five miles down the river to fish, his wife and daughters picked berries and grew the vegetables that stocked the root cellar and fed them through the winter.

Guide Linda Fahie knows the history at Fisherman's Life Museum in Jeddore Oyster Pond.

GOLDENVILLE GOLD MINING INTERPRETIVE CENTRE

902-522-4653
Hwy. 7, Goldenville, NS (3 kilometers or 1.8 miles west of Sherbrooke Village)
Open: June–Sept., daily 9:30 AM–5:30 PM
Admission: Adult $2.50, children $1

The Nova Scotia gold rush started in 1860, when a farmer in Musquodoboit found gold in a quartz boulder. Within a short time buildings and a new settlement were established in Goldenville, and the mining that ran from 1861 to 1942 became the source of more than 200,000 ounces of gold. That was by far the largest amount of gold refined in any area in Nova Scotia. Old mining towns have today shrunk to tiny outposts, and some no longer exist. But a visitor to this museum can see the faces of their inhabitants in photographs, research family names in genealogical records, or hear recorded interviews with miners. Mining tools are on display; gold panning and tours of the mining areas are offered.

OUT OF THE FOG MUSEUM

902-358 2108
guysboroughcountyheritage.ca
Hwy. 316, Halfway Cove, NS
Open: June 20–Sept. 20
Admission: Free

This museum is run by the Keepers of the Beacons, a group of people who maintain the automated Queensport Lighthouse on Rook Island at the mouth of Queensport Harbour. They have collected artifacts that help describe how keepers lived in isolated lighthouses before the days of automation. The Queensport Lighthouse is visible from the picnic park nearby.

SHERBROOKE VILLAGE

902-522-2400
sherbrookevillage.ca
P.O. Box 295, Sherbrooke, NS BoJ 3Co
Open: June 1–Oct. 15, daily 9:30 AM–5 PM
Admission: Adults $10, seniors $8, children $4.25, 6 and younger free

Everyday people at Sherbrooke Village, wearing the clothes of their ancestors, are undertaking the work of the past; they do this on schedule at 10:30 and 11:30 AM and at 2 and 3 PM. The blacksmith hammers a fiery red piece of metal into shape, while at Cumminger House melted fat and beeswax is poured into candlestick molds. Handcream is a favorite souvenir, and you can watch it being compounded of mineral oil, borax, and rosewater. Flax processing for linen thread, a printing press, wood turning, and more keep the industrious crew busy.

Music

Chedabucto Place Performance Center (902-533-2015; connectwithourenergy.com), 27 Green St., Guysborough. Events year-round include ceilidhs, famous musicians, and theater.

Courthouse Concerts are hosted by Sherbrooke Village (902-522-2400; sherbrooke village.ca), weekly or more often through the summer and into the fall. The Web site will take you to an updated schedule.

Nightlife

The Rare Bird Pub (902-533-2128; rarebirdpub.com), 80 Main St., Guysborough, NS BoH 1No. On summer Wednesdays, The Rare Bird Pub holds a community ceilidh, or house party. Live entertainment starts at 9 PM when it is offered; check the Web site for the schedule.

Theater

MULGRAVE ROAD THEATRE

902-533-2092
mulgraveroad.ca
68 Main St., P.O. Box 219, Guysborough, NS BoH 1No
Open: Year-round
Admission: Ticket price varies

Mulgrave Road Theatre produces original plays with wide-ranging and compelling subject matter. A writer-in-residence program brings Canadians to the area to spend two or three weeks at work on a project, finishing with a public reading. Play scripts are considered for production, and the artistic director also commissions plays about specific subjects. Emmy Alcorn, a well-known performer and playwright who is the present artistic director, wrote the production *Spin,* about gambling, which toured Nova Scotia after it was presented in 2005. "Typically, the theatre produces two new plays per year, for a two-day run in Guysborough, followed by a tour through Nova Scotia. Occasionally the theatre tours outside of the region on a national and international basis," Alcorn said. Mulgrave Road Theatre was founded in Guysborough County in 1977. A festival weekend is held annually at end of July.

Seasonal Events

July

The Stan Rogers Folk Festival, Canso. First weekend in July. This hugely popular festival brings together songwriters and performers from around the world to play on seven stages and celebrate the memory of song writer Stan Rogers. Rogers loved to spend time on the Eastern Shore and wrote "The Jeannie C. Guysborough Train" and "Fogarty's Cove" inspired by the region. Workshops in folk music, crafter's village, and more than 600 volunteers to make things go smoothly.

August

Canso Regatta Week with races on final weekend, third week of August.

Festival Savalette, hosted by La Société des Acadiens de la Région de Tor Baie, The Tor Bay Acadian Society, on the second weekend of August (902-525-2074, Jude Avery, president). There's a Friday concert at **Chedabucto Place Performance Center** in Guysborough and a beach bonfire with musicians and songs. Saturday brings a miniature boat race on the river, and there's a dance at the Community Center, Larry's River Saturday evening.

Clam Harbour Beach Sandcastle Contest

Clam Harbour Beach Provincial Park is 84 kilometers or 52 miles from Dartmouth, south of Route 7, on the Eastern Shore. With hundreds of competitors and thousands watching, this annual contest is a fabulous day on the beach. Scheduled on a Sunday in the middle of August, the contest offers a fine reason to enjoy a picnic on the top of a bluff overlooking the sea, or time on the wide sandy beach itself. Children compete for their own prizes. There are changing rooms, showers, a canteen, and supervised swimming on the weekends.

September

Pirates Festival Around September 19, International "Talk Like A Pirate Day," Salmon River House Innkeeper Adrien Blanchette holds his own Pirates' Festival. His staff will be in full regalia, and swaggering pirates will crowd the public rooms.

RECREATION

Beaches

Black Duck Cove Provincial Day Park, Rte. 16, Canso. With a wheelchair-accessible, white sandy beach, and a beautiful boardwalk, this is a perfect destination for families with small children. The shallow, protected water is warm. Visitors could also try their hand at digging clams. The trail here is also recommended.

Lawrencetown Beach (902-662-3030; novascotiaparks.ca), Lawrencetown. The destination of area and visiting surfers who are eager to catch the highest waves, Lawrencetown Beach Provincial Park presents 1.5 kilometers or 1 mile of sand beach. Lifeguards, canteen, showers, flush toilets, and boardwalks for a quiet visit. The **September Storm**

Classic (surfns.com) gives professional surfers a chance to compete—for $10,000 in 2008. In early to mid-June the Cyclesmith Duathlon (cyclesmith.ca), a race that sandwiches 34 kilometers of biking in between 5K and 6K runs, has most often been held at Lawrencetown Beach since 1989 (close to Halifax, and listed both here and in the Halifax section).

Martinique Beach Provincial Park, East Petpeswick Rd., 11 kilometers or 7 miles south of Musquodoboit Harbour. Boardwalks, beach, and picnic area in both open and wooded areas behind the dunes.

Taylor Head Provincial Park (902-772-2218 mid-May–mid-Oct., or 902-885-2377; parks.gov.ns.ca), on Rte. 7 east of Spry Bay. "The most beautiful beach in Nova Scotia" according to Adrien Blanchette, owner of Salmon River House. Certainly there are 16 kilometers or 10 miles of coastline inside this 6.5-kilometer or 4-mile peninsula. The work of eons of accumulating sand and silt created its unusual volcano-like formations, called sand volcanos. The rise of the sea, after the glacier on top of this land melted, drowned a forest here and continues to eat at the shore. Peat bogs and fresh-water marshes grow pitcher plants and black crowberry, sustaining a wide variety of birds and other wildlife. Parking is by Psyche Cove, with trails in two directions. Call for a brochure with a trail map.

Camping

Seabreeze Campground & Cottages (902-366-2352), 230 Fox Island Main Rd., Canso. Ann Marie Rhynold is your host at this tidy campground 10 kilometers or 6 miles from Canso, and she offers both housekeeping cottages and an RV for rent. Washrooms, playgrounds, a camp store, and lobster pound.366-2206

Golf

Osprey Shores Golf Resort (902-533-3904, 800-909-3904; ospreyshoreresort.com), 119 Ferry Ln., Guysborough. The spectacular views from this golf course and the pine, balsam, and fir forests bordering the greens make this a lovely course. The Clubhouse at the end of the ninth green serves "light fare." The resort also holds accommodations, 10 renovated rooms with many amenities ($109 to $129 a night, depending on the season).

River Oaks Golf Club (902-384-2033; riveroaksgolfclub.com), Hwy. 357, Meagher's Grant. A 27-hole golf course that includes an eight-unit motel with an outdoor pool and a restaurant.

Hiking

Chapel Gully Trail, Canso. A 10-kilometer or 6-mile hiking trail that includes picnic tables for a snack or lunch, and takes hikers through jack pine forest and mudflats where, depending on the season, many birds can be spotted. Arrive during spring or fall migration for the greatest number. A 139-foot bridge crosses the Chapel Gully, and elsewhere tidal floats take you across the muck.

Kayaking

Coastal Adventures (877-404-2774; coastaladventures.com), P.O. Box 77, Tangier, NS B0J 3H0. This company runs kayaking tours all over the Maritimes. Trips can be as long as eight days; they explore many of the coastal regions, with camping in coves by night or settling in at a bed & breakfast being two of the options. The Eastern Shore Archipelago gets folks out to the islands in this isolated area. All-women tours are offered too, and no experience is necessary. If you want to bone up on your skills, however, sea kayaking instruction is given at the Sea Kayaking School.

SHOPPING

Galleries

Barry Colpitts (902-772-2090), 15359 Hwy. 7, East Ship Harbour. Near Black Sheep Gallery is the home of Barry Colpitts, a folk artist. The house makes a startling appearance at the side of the road and proclaims just that. Exterior walls are decorated with carved painted signs and carvings, including one for Jesus. Visitors are welcome.

Black Sheep Gallery (902-889-5012; lighthouse.ca), 1689 West Jeddore Rd., West Jeddore Village. Open June–mid-Sept., daily 11 AM–4 PM, or by chance or appointment. This old fish store is the source and destination for much of the best folk art made in Nova Scotia.

Leather Goods

Cobbler's Awl (902-533-3054), RR #2, Boylston. Paul Marcella makes leather purses, briefcases, belts, custom moccasins, and more. Open by appointment or chance.

Specialty Shops

The Bat House (902-845-2458), 888 West Ship Harbour Rd., Lake Charlotte. Keith Kerr would be happy to help you select one of his handmade bat houses, to naturally reduce the population of mosquitoes in your yard.

Completely rebuilt after a fire, St. John's Anglican Church shows off its pristine Carpenter's Gothic architecture.

4

THE SOUTHEASTERN COAST AND YARMOUTH

Art and Industry on a Historic Coast

This chapter travels south through Chester, a treasure trove of art galleries, to picturesque Mahone Bay, famous for its three churches reflected in the water. A pewter factory is a good tour in that town.

Lunenburg, the home port for *Bluenose II*, is a microcosm of another century, the era of shipbuilding, but it still gets most of its living from the sea. Swiss Germans were invited by the British to settle Nova Scotia—and founded the city of Lunenburg in 1753.

Port Medway's Long Cove, its lighthouse and rocks with crashing waves, are distillations of this scenic coastline, as is Western Head near Liverpool, with its exposed lighthouse and violent surf. Vogler's Cove is a pristine inlet with boxy houses set with precision on green grass.

Some of the dozens of idyllic fishing villages that line the coastline fill this chapter with favorite places for beaches and seafood, including Anglophile Shelburne, with its living museum, dory builders, and barrel makers.

But when you reach the area round Yarmouth, arrival port for the Maine ferry called The CAT, you are also in the middle of the French shore, with museums, restaurants, and long, peaceful beaches. Your first encounter with rappie pie, an Acadian specialty in this area, might be your last. But it's easy to develop a taste for the ultrasmooth potato and meat or clam dish that has fed locals on the holidays for generations.

Since this chapter embraces such a long stretch of coastline, it is divided into three sections.

CHESTER, LUNENBURG, AND MAHONE BAY TO PORT L'HERBERT

Traveling between Lunenburg and LaHave on the coast you can get out of the car for five minutes while enjoying a quick cable ferry passage for $5 (in 2008) across the mouth of the LaHave River. The crossing can save 45 minutes in driving time for a driver who wants to stay on the twisting and turning coastline connecting Routes 332 and 331.

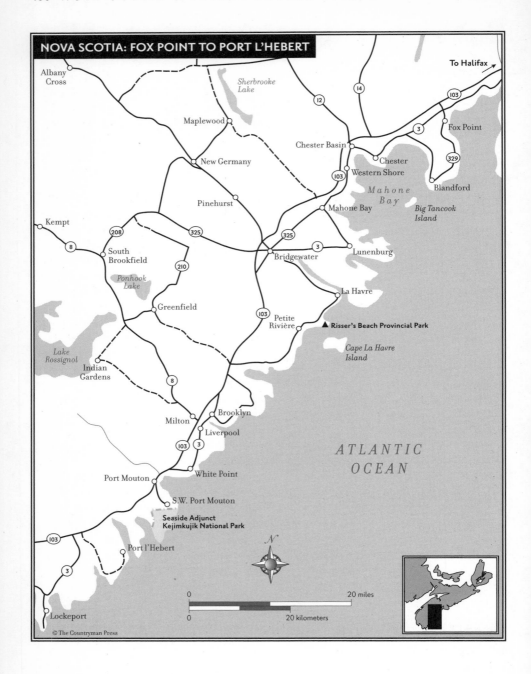

LODGING

ASHLEA HOUSE BED & BREAKFAST

Lynn and John Gillard, innkeepers
902-634-7150, 866-634-7150
ashleahouse.com
42 Falkland St., Lunenburg, NS B0J 2C0
Price: $90 to $185
Credit cards: Yes
Handicapped Access: None
Special Features: Wi-Fi, outside deck and gazebo

Ashlea House has the colorful history of a life of adventure—from its beginnings in fine circumstances, when shipbuilding and the sea supported all of Lunenburg, to its days of poverty, first as a boarding house and then as a brothel. Just as it was about to be condemned and destroyed, a local man rescued it, tearing wallboard out and uncovering the enormous pocket doors and finely carved moldings of the double front parlor, where today the Gillards host a New Year's Eve party—all guests invited.

Today, too, you can find a spot at the dining room table that stretches down the long formal room with plenty of room for 14; Nova Scotia baked beans, with local molasses and free-range pork, might be part of your meal. A cupola seat at the top of the house looks out over the top of the next-door foundry toward the sea. Each room is decorated in its own style, with local ash flooring in West Mount from nearby Buddhist Wind Horse Farm.

BAYVIEW PINES

Chris and Joanna Grimley, innkeepers
902-624-9970, 866-624-9970
bayviewpines.com
678 Oakland Rd., Mahone Bay, NS B0J 2E0
Turn off Rte. 103 toward the ocean just north of Mahone Bay
Price: $90 to $150
Credit cards: Yes
Handicapped Access: None
Special Features: Walking trails, small beach with a place to launch boats

Away from the center of town and situated on the sea, Bayview Pines has pleasant accommodations that include sunny bedrooms (some ground floor), with ocean views, and two apartments with a dining and sitting area. The beautiful setting on the water is at Indian Point, on 14 acres of pasture. Rooms 5 and 6 share a deck with views of the water, and folks traveling together like to take them both. Except for Rooms 3 and 9, which are apartments with kitchens, a full breakfast is included in the rates. Date muffins and homemade preserves and marmalade might accompany that meal, along with bacon and eggs or french toast. Walking trails cover a kilometer on this property, and there's a longer 5K trail that goes through the woods to a Rails-To-Trails and back.

EDGEWATER BED AND BREAKFAST AND SEA LOFT COTTAGE

Susan and Paul Seltzer, innkeepers
902-624-9382, 866-816-8688
bbcanada.com/edgewater
44 Mader's Cove Rd., RR #1, Mahone Bay, NS B0J 2E0
A right turn just south of Mahone Bay on Hwy. 3
Price: $110 to $225 for cottage
Credit cards: Yes
Handicapped Access: None
Special Features: Wi-Fi

A Yamaha studio grand piano sits in the common space of this B&B, available for guests to play, perhaps at the same time that the waterfall feature on the back of the fireplace is running, filling the sunny space with the tranquil sound of water. Susan and Paul Seltzer rent three rooms in the main house, each one bright with pale-painted beaded board and light-colored bedding. In

The view from a room at the Lunenburg Arms shows off a ship in the harbor and the golf course across the water.

Room 1 two seats in front of the window enjoy a sea view. But views of the sea are available from the porch, with its comfortable lawn chairs, and from the cottage's second-floor deck and front deck too. You can look forward to the platter of fresh fruit served every morning at breakfast, as well as crêpes, for example, and Fair Trade coffee.

1880 KAULBACH HOUSE

David and Jenny Hook, innkeepers
902-640-3036, 800-568-8818
kaulbachhouse.com
75 Pelham St., P.O. Box 1348, Lunenburg, NS B0J 2C0
Price: $99 to $169
Credit cards: Yes
Handicapped Access: None
Special Features: Wi-Fi

Owners David and Jenny Hook took on the work of innkeeping in 2007, after arriving from the United Kingdom. Their blue and white dining room is an oasis of cool formality, with an array of elegant porcelain soup tureen and casserole lids forming an original decoration on the wall. Six bedrooms each have their own bathroom and a TV and DVD player. The Ruby Room wraps a queen-size bed in ruby walls, and Land & Sea has two twin beds for travelers like a parent and child who prefer to sleep in the same room.

1826 MAPLEBIRD HOUSE

Susie Scott and Barry Chapell, innkeepers
902-634-3863, 888-395-3863
maplebirdhouse.ca
36 Pelham St., P.O. Box 278, Lunenburg, NS B0J 2C0
Open: Jan.–Oct.
Price: $85 to $110

Credit cards: Yes
Handicapped Access: None
Special Features: Wi-Fi, outdoor pool

Four bedrooms with queen-size beds are on offer at this 1826 former farmhouse with 60-year-old roses blooming in the back yard. You will be able to learn about the unique architectural feature, the Lunenburg bump, in the front of the house, but if you're not in a particularly studious frame of mind, you can go for a swim in the pool instead, or sit on the swing on the veranda. Count on the charms of an old house that will let you experience history as you climb to your bedroom. This house has been a B&B since 1991, and since 1998 it has been in the hands of Susie Scott and Barry Chapell. Fruit crêpes, french toast and sausage, mushroom and cheese omelets, are some of the dishes that you might find waiting for you, if you spent the night.

✪ LUNENBURG ARMS

902-640-4041, 1-800-679-4950
lunenburgarms.com
94 Pelham St., Lunenburg, NS B02 2C0
Price: $109 to $199
Credit cards: Yes
Handicapped Access: Yes
Special Features: Wi-Fi, spa, Tin Fish restaurant, pets allowed

The amenities at Lunenburg Arms make it the most luxurious lodging in town. A view of the harbor adds to a room's charm on the side of the inn that looks over the tops of the downhill buildings toward the docks, and across the blue water to nearby Island Golf Course. When it comes time to luxuriate inside, however, the large spa tub, double shower, and cushy capacious beds made up with the silkiest linens make it impossible not to feel superbly well cared for. Among all the beds I had a chance to try out during my Maritime travels, the one at Lunenburg Arms was the best.

LUNENBURG INN

Donna and Deryl Rideout, innkeepers
800-565-3963
lunenburginn.com
26 Dufferin St., P.O. Box 1407, Lunenburg, NS B0J 2C0
Price: $85 to $180
Credit cards: Yes
Handicapped Access: None
Special Features: Wi-Fi

Five guest rooms and two suites have an old-fashioned décor, with brass or painted iron beds and antique bureaus and chairs. The Demone Suite is named after former innkeepers who were in charge here from 1939 to 1979, when the building was called the Hillside Hotel. It takes up the whole third floor with its bedroom, living room, with refrigerator and microwave oven, and bathroom with separate shower. Back in the old days the inn had one bathroom only, for all of its 13 rooms—the one located today inside the Ada Mary Knickle Room. Now each room comes with its own, thank heaven. Freshly squeezed lemonade and fresh-baked cookies are available each afternoon, and the breakfast included in the rates might involve fruits, coffee and juice, and a hot dish like baked eggs, or perhaps whole-wheat toast with yogurt and stewed rhubarb.

✪ 1775 SOLOMON HOUSE BED & BREAKFAST

Janet and George Palmer, innkeepers
902-634-3477
bbcanada.com/5511.html
69 Townsend St., P.O. Box 681, Lunenburg, NS B0J 2C0
Price: $85 to $115
Credit cards: Yes
Handicapped Access: None
Special Features: History

This house is one of the oldest in town, with paneling and crooked corners that attest to the passage of time. It was built by Heinrich Koch, who opened the town's first sawmill. Every square inch also charms those who revel in history, like innkeepers Janet and George Palmer, who have managed to put private baths inside the two front rooms and provide an unshared bathroom for the third room in the back of the house. The original open fireplace faces the dining room table, and on another wall Janet Palmer has arranged her collection of old china on open shelves. She will serve her guests breakfasts with her own cashew granola, made with the fine dried cranberries of a local supplier, and perhaps a frittata with gruyère or crème brûlée french toast. Her old quilt collection adds elegance to the rooms, and inside the Solomon room one is tucked inside an antique child's bed. That same room has a view of the town's extraordinary St. John's Anglican Church, completely rebuilt after a destructive fire in 2002.

THREE THISTLES BED AND BREAKFAST

Phyllis Wiseman, innkeeper
902-624-0517
three-thistles.com
389 Main St., Mahone Bay, NS B0J 2E0
Price: $90 to $125
Credit cards: Yes, Visa and Mastercard
Handicapped Access: None
Special Features: Wi-Fi, organic ingredients at breakfast, green cleansers, yoga studio and classes available, Spanish spoken

Along with three bright bedrooms with private washrooms, you can also rent the loft apartment over the yoga studio, with its small kitchen, dining area, sitting area, and bed for $125 to $150 depending on the season (breakfast not included). Beach Rose, on the first floor of the house, a parsonage built in 1890 by St. John's Lutheran Church, has a gleaming brass bed set on hardwood floors. Upstairs, Chanterelle and Silver Birch are equally bright rooms with quilts

and a rocking chair. Throughout the house, there are dispensers of fragrance-free shampoo, body wash made by Downeast, Kiss My Face hand lotion, and individual soaps made by a local woman. Three people are available to give massages at the studio, and another can arrive for spa services. Gardens are growing wider in the back of the property, with a new pond. "I envisioned this house as a healing place," said Phyllis Wiseman.

WHITE POINT BEACH RESORT

800-565-5068
whitepoint.com
White Point Beach, NS B0T 1G0
Price: $129 to $315
Credit cards: Yes
Handicapped Access: Yes
Special Features: Wi-Fi, beach, saltwater pools and restaurant, spa with massage and body treatments, nightly entertainment in summer

This 1928 resort is a family favorite with various recreation programs, tennis courts, an indoor pool and hot tub, and an outdoor pool, available in warm weather. Kayaks, canoes, bicycles, and surfboards are for rent. Wet suits and boogie boards for body surfing are also for rent. A nine-hole golf course competes with the tennis courts for the guests' attention, and both benefit from the availability of babysitting services. Pine headboards furnish some of the 15 rooms in the main lodge, each with a private balcony. Lodge rooms, also with private balconies, typically have double beds. In the Ocean Lodge facing the beach, there are eight rooms around a rustic living room with a stone fireplace. Oceanfront cottages are furnished with upholstered chairs, some with a fireplace and others with a woodstove, and other cottages have views of the tidal lake. Three-bedroom Tide Watch Cottage is the fanciest one here, with hardwood floors, two fireplaces, and great views. In high season some of the cottages require a minimum seven-day stay.

RESTAURANTS

BEST COAST COFFEE GALLERY

902-935-2031
7070 Hwy. 331 (Lighthouse Dr.), Broad Cove
Open: Mid-June–mid-Oct. or Canadian Thanksgiving, Tues.–Sun. 9:30 AM–4 PM, closed Mon.
Price: $15 to $25
Credit cards: No; cash or check only
Cuisine: Imaginative and inventive
Serving: L, D
Handicap Access: No
Special Features: Art gallery

Pasta (or rice) night on Tuesday till 8 PM offers a pasta dinner with homemade focaccia, salad, and desert for $15. Friday-night dinners, up to $25, have a set menu and are offered by reservation only. The Friday menu starts with soup or salad or an hors d'oeurvre, like a tomato and cheese tart. Then might come braided salmon (formed in a circle) filled with prawns and black Thai rice. A palate-cleanser sorbet arrives next, perhaps basil-lime or mango-thyme. Desserts have been panna cotta with mango sauce or a raspberry coulis. Owner Wendy Michiner said that one of the sandwiches available for lunch is made with caramelized apple and shrimp, and the soup might be pumpkin spice or yam, coconut, and ginger.

THE CHEESECAKE GALLERY AND BISTRO

902-624-0579
533 Main St., Mahone Bay
Open: Daily 11 AM–8 PM; closed Jan.
Price: $8 to $24
Credit cards: Yes
Cuisine: Casual continental
Serving: L, D
Handicap Access: Ramp, but no accessible washrooms
Special Features: Local art on the walls, wine bar

A wonderful menu makes up for the initial confusion of the name—this is a place that serves lunch and dinner as well as cheesecake. Seafood chowder, steak with caramelized onion with blue cheese, and chicken and shrimp curry pasta are some highlights of the menu. Pan-fried haddock is "kept simple," said Esther Bourgelis, owner with Robyn Graham since the Cheesecake Gallery opened in 2003.

✪ FLEUR DE SEL

902-640-2121. 877-723-7258
Fleurdesel.net
53 Montague St., Lunenburg
Open: May–New Year's Eve, lunch in season
Price: $24 to $36
Credit cards: Yes
Cuisine: French
Serving: L, D
Handicap Access: No
Special Features: Tasting menu

With an ambitious menu, Fleur de Sel is shooting for the stars. The butter-yellow walls, glossy woodwork, and silky smooth white linens in this house on Montague Street create a luminous stage for the square and rectangular white plates that flow out of the kitchen. Meals might start with an amuse-bouche of thin rings of local calamari and tomato salad. The Domaine de Pré New York Muscat smells like mint and tastes of apricot and peach. A plate of smoked salmon with two little buckwheat blini stinted on the crème fraîche and New Brunswick sturgeon caviar, but was excellent nonetheless. Orange and tarragon sorbet tasted like crushed ice with herbal syrup. A veal tasting plate excelled with its veal sweetbreads and a cabbage-leaf-wrapped mélange of veal and Swiss chard with a parsnip puree. But a veal loin arrived raw and, even reworked by the kitchen when I expressed discontent, remained disagreeable. A couple from the United Kingdom who were seated nearby loved the Digby scallops and thin-sliced duck. And once I moved on past the main course, there was only pleasure waiting in the little profiteroles with bittersweet chili-sparked chocolate and the creamiest vanilla ice cream. Meringue kisses and weensy madeleines arrived with the tab.

THE KIWI CAFÉ

902-275-1492
kiwicafechester.com
19 Pleasant St., Chester
Open: Daily 8:30 AM–4 PM
Price: $4 to $18 for a lobster roll
Credit cards: Yes
Cuisine: Inventive, casual international
Serving: B, L
Handicap Access: Ramp, but no accessible washroom
Special Features: Australian hospitality

A Kiwi breakfast burrito holds scrambled eggs, cheddar, avocado, and salsa in a whole-wheat wrap, and eggs Benedict can come with smoked salmon. The ABC at lunch spells out apple, bacon, cheddar and Dijon mustard, grilled on LaHave Bakery cracked wheat and flax bread. Nova Scotian smoked salmon is on another baked item from LaHave—a bagel—served with cream cheese, red onions, and capers. Fish cakes are accompanied by mango salsa and a mesclun salad. The Java Blend coffee is wonderful.

THE KNOT PUB

902-634-3334
4 Dufferin St., Lunenburg
Open: Daily 10 AM–late
Price: $7 to $17
Credit cards: Yes
Cuisine: Maritime classics and more
Serving: L, D
Handicap Access: No
Special Features: Local brews from Keith's, Propeller, and Moosehead; live music in the off-season; Thursday-night Trivia contests

Inside a shingled, vine-covered house, through a dark passageway, are the cozy upholstered booths, oak paneling, and oak tables of the dark, cool Knot Pub. Knots are displayed, and rope is hung in huge loops outside the entrance, in small decorative frames around the dart boards and everywhere in between. The menu advises caution navigating across the multilevel floor, but however nautical, the Knot is not really pitching from side to side. Opened in 1988, this beloved pub celebrates a seagoing heritage with its unique décor and with its substantial meals, like chili with cheddar. Knockwurst and kraut honors the 1,500 Germans who cleared the land for this port in 1753. Fish and chips, mussels, scallops wrapped in bacon, and much more.

LAHAVE BAKERY

902-688-2908
Rte. 331, LaHave
(Small bakery at 3 Edgewater St., Mahone Bay)
Open: In summer, 8:30 AM–6:30 PM; in winter, 9 AM–4:30 PM, Sun. brunch 9 AM–2 PM
Price: $4 to $6
Credit cards: Yes
Cuisine: "Everything is made here"
Serving: Brunch, L
Handicap Access: No
Special Features: Picnic tables at the side of the building with water view, at the mouth of LaHave River

Lunches are served at this bakery, with homemade soups, sandwiches, and pizza—some with fresh vegetables, depending on what is ready in owner Gael Watson's garden. One August pizza was made with hot peppers and spinach, and another with chopped basil and fresh tomato with Parmesan. Soups are all made from scratch, like a smoked salmon chowder made with salmon from Willy Krauch on the Eastern Shore.

Greek pizza, pepperoni, and cheese are always served. For breakfast you can find bagels, blueberry cinnamon rolls, muffins, and scones, but egg dishes are served only on Sundays. The bakery's seed, potato, and 12-grain breads receive a slow rise to bring out their flavors. A farmer's market is held in the parking lot in the summer, Saturday 9 AM to 1 PM. A second location is a small bakery at 3 Edgewater St., in Mahone Bay, NS, 902-624-1420.

MAGNOLIA'S GRILL

902-634-3287
128 Montague St., Lunenburg
Open: In summer, Mon.–Sat. 11:30 AM–10 PM; Mar.–June & Sept.–Oct., till 9 PM; closed Nov.–Feb.
Price: $9 to $24
Credit cards: Yes
Cuisine: Eclectic, with Cajun and traditional Lunenburg dishes
Serving: L, D
Handicap Access: Yes
Special Features: No reservations, outdoor patio

Owner Nancy Lohnes said that three perennial draws on her menu are the three different mussel dishes (the mussels are from Mahone Bay): plain with white wine; with coconut curry; and provençal with tomato and Pernod. Among the menu's many salads, grilled asparagus with goat cheese and a balsamic reduction is a standout. The onion soup is exceptional—perhaps because the kitchen uses really good sherry; "We've had people come back over and over for it," Lohnes said. Fresh scallops are served pan-fried in butter with a little lemon juice. "We don't want to mess with them at all." Halibut, swordfish steaks on the barbecue,

sesame peanut noodles, lobster linguine, and rib eye are more reasons to dine here. Opened in 1988, this place sustains its good reputation and enjoys deserved popularity. Black and white tiles on the floor, cream-paint beaded-board booths, and dozens of framed photographs create a charming décor, all centered on a back wall covered with the world's currencies.

RUM RUNNER INN

902-634-9200, 888-778-6786
rumrunnerinn.com
66 Montague St., Lunenburg
Open: Daily 11 AM–9 PM
Price: $13 to $26
Credit cards: Yes
Cuisine: Continental, with pasta and lobster
Serving: L, D
Handicap Access: No
Special Features: Outside deck on waterfront

Konrad Haumering and his wife Cammy Tibbo run this restaurant, bringing international experience to the lunch and dinner menus. You could splurge on classic lobster Thermidor, sauced with cream and cognac and topped with cheese. Or you could try a modest, appetizing dish of pasta with Gorgonzola and mushrooms. The chef also offers pork schnitzel, roast lamb, and chicken curry. Fish and chips, creamed lobster with rice, and steamed mussels are served for lunch. With any meal, a seat on the deck will offer a glorious view of the waterfront.

SALT SHAKER DELI

902-640-3434
saltshakerdeli.com/
124 Montague St., Lunenburg
Open: Daily 11 AM–9 PM
Price: $7 to $13
Credit Cards: Yes
Cuisine: Imaginative sandwiches and pizza

Serving: L, D
Handicapped Access: Yes, large doors on washrooms, but no wall bars
Special features: Deck overlooking waterfront, across the street from the *Bluenose II* when it's in port

The owners of formal Fleur de Sel also own this deli, where the food is made from scratch. Thin-crust or deep-dish pizza are offered with toppings that range from mushroom with Brie to the "Meat Lovers" with pepperoni, bacon, sausage, ground beef and mozzarella and cheddar cheese. Roasted garlic and cream is the most popular of the nine possible styles for an $8 pound of Indian Point mussels, but Portuguese style with sausage or creamy Madras curry sound inspired. A pint of Propeller draft beer and a pound of the mussels was just $10 in 2008.

SEASIDE SHANTY RESTAURANT

902-275-2246
seasideshanty.com
5315 Hwy. 3, Chester Basin
Open: May–Oct.; in July–Aug., 11:30 AM–9 PM daily; otherwise open till 8 PM
Price: $8 to $19
Credit cards: Yes
Cuisine: Seafood and casual standards
Serving: L, D
Handicap Access: Yes
Special Features: Excellent chowder

Although this roadside restaurant is small and quiet on the outside, it holds a treasure worth seeking out. Owner Gillian McKenzie has perfected her menu, creating examples of seaside classics that have visitors raving and local young people willing to go out on a limb. A man heard on CBC declared the chowder at Seaside Shanty the second best

The excellent chowder at Seaside Shanty in Chester Basin should not be missed.

in the whole world—after a three-year search. Lobster and seafood chowder is the most expensive ($17.95), but even the fish chowder ($9.25) will deliver. Smoked ribs and knockwurst provide excellent dinners for anyone not eager to try the cioppino or seafood crêpes for a main course. The blueberry grunt—blueberries with scones baked on top, served with whipped cream—is a traditional dessert.

TIN FISH AT THE LUNENBURG ARMS

At the Lunenburg Arms Hotel
eden.travel/
94 Pelham St., Lunenburg
Open: Daily
Price: $14 to $22
Credit cards: Yes
Cuisine: Regional standards with German flavor
Serving: B, L, D
Handicap Access: Yes
Special Features: Local ingredients

Tin Fish inside the Lunenburg Arms presents a bouquet of colors to a visitor's first glimpse, with a turquoise bar with black trim, violet walls, mustard-yellow walls, lime, purple, and red walls. As for the food: Indian Point mussels are in a starter, with roasted garlic, oregano, and toasted chili ($7). The Lunenburg sausage and pudding ($14)—a kind of blood pudding or pâté made of spicy sausage—comes with sauerkraut and shows off the area's Germanic roots. Annapolis Valley pork tenderloin takes advantage of local Stutz hard cider, organic apricots, and honey mustard ($21), and Digby scallops are elaborated on with rum and maple cream and sweet-potato fries.

TRATTORIA DELLA NONNA

902-640-3112
nonnadining.ca
9 King St., Lunenburg
Open: Lunch Tues.–Fri. from 11:30 AM; dinner Tues.–Sun. from 5 PM; Sun. brunch from 10:30 AM
Price: $12 to $26
Credit cards: Yes
Cuisine: Italian
Serving: Brunch, L, D
Handicap Access: No
Special Features: Italian coffees with liqueurs

The stuccoed walls and stairs ornamented with iron scrollwork surround black tables set with deep gold runners; in the morning the staff polishes everything at each setting, making sure every surface gleams. This highly recommended restaurant makes wood-fired oven pizza like the Toscana ($13) with eggplant, zucchini, pepper, caramelized onion, and gorgonzola. Indian Point mussels are part of the linguini puttanesca—with capers, black olives, anchovies, chili, and roasted tomatoes. A carbonara "di pesce" turns the old pancetta and eggs classic into an original showcase for scallops and prawns. Grilled salmon, seared New York strip sirloin, and a rack of lamb display the Italian know-how in cooking meat. Try the Negroni, an Italian cocktail that exploits aromatic Campari, and depend on it, the coffee will be perfetto. Torta al formaggio, a ricotta cheese cake with Marsala-soaked fruit, is a destination in itself.

FOOD PURVEYORS

Bakeries

Julien's French Bakery (902-275-2324; juliens.ca), 43 Queen St., Chester. Lobster sandwiches, four ounces of lobster on slices of fresh bread, regularly fly out the door. You can also enjoy a glass of wine on the deck outside, or stop in for a breakfast of pain au chocolate and café au lait in the morning.

Cafés and Coffee Shops

✪ **The Biscuit Eater Books and Café** (902-624-2665; biscuiteater.ca), 16 Orchard St., Mahone. The excellent fare served here is "not to be missed," as a local resident put it. That's because owners Alden Darville and Dawn Higgins are able to translate their obsessions with local and high-quality food into a delicious menu. Even with the choice of only one sandwich for lunch, ham and cheese with mild mustard on a croissant (because of Monday and Tuesday's limited menu), I was thoroughly content. Goddess of Mercy oolong ($2.20 for a small pot) was an excellent tea, chosen from among dozens. Orange and peppercorn teacake and cookies and other cakes beckon from the display case. Those extraordinary "biscuits"—not scones because they are made with buttermilk without eggs or butter—are exceptional. The kitchen uses Red Fife heritage wheat, an organic flour from Speedwell Flour Mill. Red-topped pedestal tables on a two-level deck outside are set under a grape arbor amid flowers. Inside, the umber and gold rooms are well thought out, with plugs for computer users and upholstered chairs for relaxation.

Gourmet Shop at the Lanes Privateer Inn (902-354-3456; lanesprivateerinn.com), 27–33 Bristol Ave., Liverpool. A fire warms up one spot in this shop, and the chocolate cake will warm up the rest of you. Next to Snug Harbour Books (see under "Books" in the Shopping section of this chapter), so you can choose a read to kindle your imagination. You can sit at a table in the bookstore for table service.

Historic Grounds Coffee House (902-634-9995; historicgrounds.com), 100 Montague St., Lunenburg. Open in summer Mon.–Fri. 7:30 AM–5 PM, Sat.–Sun. 8:30 AM–to 5 PM; winter closing at 4 PM and opening later on weekends. Great coffee that's locally roasted is the first draw, but the courtesy of an outlet for your laptop's plug is another, and the fresh pastries and lunches of soup and sandwiches round out the services.

Gourmet and Deli Markets

Kiwi Too (902-275-2570; kiwicafechester.com), 15 Pleasant St., Chester. Open daily 10 AM–4 PM; accessible earlier when the café is open at 8:30. Prepared meals; soups like squash, apple and brie, or Hungarian mushroom; supplies and more. Nova Scotian Propeller Beer and Jöst Winery are some of the esteemed labels, and Ran-Cher Acres goat's-milk cheeses and yogurt are wonderful. You could also pick up dried galangal and kaffir lime leaves.

Lunenburg Country Store (902-640-3443; lunenburgstore@eastlink.ca), 139 Montague St., Lunenburg. Open Mon.–Sat. 7 AM–9 PM, Sun. 12–7 PM. This is every hungry traveler's finest resource, with freshly baked bread, locally grown produce, and the freshest

Adams and Knickle scallops, arriving on the coast a block or so away. John and Lynn Gillard opened the store in the spring of 2008, and they like to call it the farmers' market for the other six days of the week, when the farmers' market isn't operating. Crab or Canadian pea-meal bacon goes into the hot sandwiches ($7.99), the soup is fresh, and beer and other things to drink are in abundant variety on the shelves, as are cheeses, smoked Nova Scotia salmon, and snacks.

Lobster Suppers

Lobster Suppers at Petite Rivière Fire Hall (902-688-2356), on the River Road in Petite Rivière. Usually the first weekend in August, this lobster supper started in 2007. "Barring anything unforeseen it will become an annual thing," said Dawn Teal, president of the Lady's Auxiliary of the Petite Rivière Volunteer Fire Department. With a 1¼-pound lobster, fresh rolls, salads, strawberry shortcake, one glass of wine, and more, this was $35 in 2008. An open bar offered extra drinks at two seatings, 5:30 and 7 PM.

Microbreweries and Pubs

The Mersey House (902-354-4000; merseyhouse.com), 149 Main St., Liverpool. Open daily at 11 AM, this pub it serves as a live entertainment center; offering live music every weekend and as often as five nights a week in summer (for further details, see the entry under "Music" in the Culture section below). Pub food includes the Snacker, with nachos, onion rings, potato skins, and chicken fingers for $15. Meat loaf, fish and chips, and lasagna are on the main menu.

The River Pub (902-543-1100), 750 King St., Bridgewater. An outside patio takes advantage of the river views, easy on the eye while you drink River Pub Ale from Propeller Brewery. Seafood and more on the pub food menu.

Wineries

Lunenburg County Winery (902-644-2415; canada-wine.com), RR #3, Lunenburg County, NS B0J 2E0 (Hwy. 103, Exit 11 and 24 kilometers or 15 miles inland to Newburne). Open spring and summer daily 9 AM–9 PM, rest of year 9 AM–5 PM except Sun. Before sampling the wine, you'll find that this 100-acre commercial blueberry farm is a fun place for U-Pick raspberries, from mid-July to mid-August, and U-Pick blueberries from August to October. Picnic tables are available to enjoy a meal. Heather Sanft, an owner, said, "The winery makes wines with all the fruits that grow in the province." All wines are made with 100 percent Nova Scotia fruit, and the winery is known for its blueberry wines; pear, strawberry, peach, apple, and elderberry are more of the fruits used. "We start with maple in the spring, and then rhubarb," Sanft said. Sanft, an exceptional basketmaker, sometimes gives basket classes and workshops in woven fences, another fascinating feature on the grounds of the winery.

Petite Rivière Vineyards (902-693-3033; petiteriviere wines.ca), 1300 Italy Cross Rd., Crousetown, Petite Rivière. (Mail: 180 Dufferin St., Bridgwater, NS B4V 2G7.) Open July–Sept., Thurs.–Sun. 12–5 PM; Oct.–Dec., Sat.–Sun. 12–5 PM. "Côtes de LaHave" is the appellation of this area, with poor rocky soils (according to the winery) and a long growing season combining into a perfect place for grapes.

CULTURE

Churches

ST. JOHN'S ANGLICAN CHURCH
902-634-4994
stjohnslunenburg.org
81 Cumberland St., Lunenburg, NS B0J 2C0

Walk up the hill from the harbor to encounter a spectacle of perfectly turned out Carpenters Gothic in this rebuilt church. Burned almost to the ground in November 2001, this historic church was rebuilt exactly as it had stood before the fire, and today it is a pristine example the indigenous wood version of the stone Gothic-Revival architecture that swept the Western world in the mid to late 1800s. The church began in a meeting house in 1753 and was enlarged and "beautified" in the 1870s. Elaborate chimes, cast in West Troy, New York and presented to the church in 1902, were restored after the fire by a company in Ohio. Stained-glass windows given to the church over the last 150 years were also restored following the fire, and they are now in place. Visitors are welcome, and guides and pamphlets are available.

Galleries

CHESTER ART CENTRE
902-275-5789
chesterartcentre.com
60 Queen St., P.O. Box 654, Chester, NS B0J 1J0

The Chester Art Centre sponsors the three-day Chester Art Fair with local artists, exhibitions, and talks. It also houses an exhibition space and studios for classes for both adults and children.

LUNENBURG ART GALLERY
902-640-4044
lunenburgartgallery.com
79–81 Pelham St., P.O. Box 1418, Lunenburg, NS B0J 2C0
Open: April–Oct., Tues.–Sat. 10 AM–5 PM, Sun. 1–5 PM

Run by the local nonprofit, the Lunenburg Art Gallery Society, this gallery exhibits local, provincial, and international artists inside its old building on Pelham Street. The Wet Paint Sale, a two-day event at the end of July, has more than 60 artists painting in the open air around town, doing work you are welcome to buy at a silent auction later that day.

Historic Buildings, Ships, and Sites

BLUENOSE II
902-634-1963
bluenose.ns.ca
121 Bluenose Dr., P.O. Box 1963, Lunenburg, NS B0J 2C0
Open: Schedule varies every year; check Web site

Admission: Adults 13 and older $40, children 3–12 $25 (75 people can take the cruise at one time).

Bluenose II is a 1963 reproduction—made at the same Lunenburg shipbuilder by some of the same shipwrights—of the first *Bluenose* built in 1921. The original sailing ship fished on the George's Banks during the year and earned Nova Scotia glory every fall from 1921 to 1938, when she won a race for fishing schooners initiated by the *Halifax Herald*. You will find an image of the original on one side of the Canadian dime. Today *Bluenose II* is the sailing ambassador for Nova Scotia and every summer travels around Atlantic Canada, visiting ports and opening her decks for the curious. She always attends the annual Dory Races in Gloucester, Massachusetts; otherwise the summer schedule depends on events and invitations. *Bluenose II* will be part of the Tall Ships flotilla in 2009. In July, two-hour cruises are offered out of Lunenburg, and they can be enjoyed whenever the boat is in port (check the Web site for an up-to-date schedule) in good weather.

Living Museum and Economuseum/Économusée

AMOS PEWTER
902-624-9547, 800-565-3369
amospewter.com
589 Main St., Mahone Bay, NS BoJ 2Eo
Open: July–Aug., Mon.–Sat. 9 AM–6 PM, Sun. 10 AM–5:30 PM; May–June & Sept.–Dec., Mon.–Sat. 9 AM–5:30 PM; Jan.–Apr., Mon.–Sat. 9 AM–5 PM
Admission: Free

Watch the craftsmen and women fashion vases and jewelry out of pewter, demonstrating a craft that has been practiced in this business since 1974. They work in what was an old empty boat-building shop. The Économusée group presents artisans at work around the Maritimes, Quebec, and other countries; the businesses that participate support themselves with the sales of their crafts. In this case, pewter jewelry or cups or vases will be that much more meaningful to a buyer who has seen them made. Antique pewter is on display.

ROSS FARM
877-689-2210
museum.gov.ns.ca/rfm/
4568 Hwy. 12, RR #2, New Ross, NS BoJ 2Mo
Open: May–Oct., daily 9:30 AM–5:30 PM; Nov.–Apr., Wed.–Sun. 9:30 AM–4:30 PM
Admission: Adults $6, seniors 65 and older $5, children 6–17 $2

Oxen, work horses, Berkshire pigs, silver-gray Dorking chickens, and sheep share the barns and fields with visitors, who can encounter a farm like those that filled the hillsides of Nova Scotia more than a century ago. The acreage occupied by the Ross Farm is land given originally to Captain William Ross's family by the governor of Nova Scotia in 1816; land grants to British soldiers, some of whom had fought in the Napoleonic wars, brought the ancestors of many of the local people to this part of Nova Scotia. Rose Bank cottage on the farm housed five generations of the Ross family. Hat-making, quilting, hand-cutting the hay, and snowshoe-making are some of the activities a visitor might be able to watch.

Lighthouses

PORT MEDWAY LIGHTHOUSE PARK
Long Cove Rd., Port Medway, NS B0J 2T0

With a park, interpretive panels, and grass, this is a perfect spot for a a bit of history and a picnic, east of Liverpool and up the coast from Medway Head.

Museums

FISHERIES MUSEUM OF THE ATLANTIC
902-634-4794, 866-579-4909
museum.gov.ns.ca/fma/
68 Bluenose Dr., Lunenburg, NS B0J 2C0
Open: July–Aug., daily 9:30 AM–5:30 PM except Tues.–Sat. till 7 PM; May–June & Sept.–Oct., daily 9:30 AM–5:30 PM; Jan.–mid-May, Mon.–Fri. 9:30 AM–4 PM
Admission: In season, adults $10, seniors $7, children 6–17 $3; off-season, $4 for everyone, children free

Eleven saltwater tanks and three freshwater tanks compose the aquarium, and the waters are full of life, with starfish ready to be touched and other sea creatures a little more shy. *Bluenose II*, which is part of this museum when it is in port, is the subject of an exhibit of artifacts. Go below deck in the *Theresa E. Connor*, which spent 25 years taking dory fishermen out to the fishing grounds. *Cape Sable* is a steel trawler like the ones that replaced dory fishing. Inside the old scallop-shucking house are photographs and other memorabilia about the scallop industry, still one of Nova Scotia's most famous.

FORT POINT MUSEUM
902-688-1632
fortpointmuseum.com
Fort Point Rd. (off Rte. 331), P.O. Box 99, LaHave, NS B0R 1C0
Open: June–Sept., 10 AM–5 PM
Admission: Free

Located at the site of the Fort Sainte Marie de Grace, which was destroyed in a fire in 1654, this museum also honors the original lighthouse, inside the building that was earlier the last lighthouse keeper's home. An automatic light was installed in the 1950s, but the new lighthouse structure is an homage to the first lighthouse. A French garden holds flowers and herbs typical of 17th-century gardens, and apple trees on the land are grafts of some of the old trees. Champlain roses bloom here, named after Samuel de Champlain, who mapped this region in 1604. The river beach offers unsupervised swimming, and picnicking is popular on the 3.5 acres of grounds.

LAHAVE ISLANDS MARINE MUSEUM
902-688-2973
users.auracom.com/limms/
100 LaHave Islands Rd., P.O. Box 69, LaHave, NS B0R 1C0
Open: June–Sept. 1, daily 10 AM–5 PM
Admission: Free

This museum inside an old church holds the story of the fishing community that once flourished in the region. Rum barrels, a nine-pointed star fish, a rosary "found in the mouth of a codfish by a seven-year-old island resident," according to the Web site, and more artifacts of the past are on display. A dory belonging to a local teenager who drowned was donated by his mother, and it is now filled with things that would have been used in a fishing vessel. Charm is the right word for these things, which reach back into local history and the lore of the sea.

MAHONE BAY SETTLERS MUSEUM

902-624-6263
settlersmuseum.ns.ca
578 Main St., Mahone Bay, NS B0J 2E0
Open: June–Aug., Tues.–Sat. 10 AM–5 PM, Sun. 1–5 PM
Admission: Free

Run by the Founder's Society, this museum opened in 1988 and houses a collection of ceramics owned by the Nova Scotia Museum. Lustreware, porcelain, creamware, Wedgwood bowls, and willowware are part of the local Inglis/Quinlan Collection, and selected pieces are on exhibit every year. A walking-tour map of Mahone Bay is available at the museum, and an introduction to some of the more interesting structures and their local architecture is another draw. An exhibit about the history of the town's ship-building industry is open by appointment or on special weekends.

PERKINS HOUSE MUSEUM

902-354-4058
perkins.museum.gov.ns.ca
105 Main St., P.O. Box 1078, Liverpool, NS B0T 1K0
Open: June–mid-Oct., Mon.–Sat. 9:30 AM–5:30 PM, Sun. 1–5:30 PM
Admission: Adults, children 6–17, and seniors 65 and older, $2

The history at this museum comes from an original source, the owner Simeon Perkin's meticulous diary (kept from 1760 to 1812), which includes the building of his house now the museum. Smallpox inoculation, with a cut and an "infected thread," was an ordeal, but everyone in his family survived. Join in a game of lawn bowls and pall mall, which is like croquet, every day of good weather from 10 AM to 3 PM. Children's events are held regularly. In 2009, ghosts (something like a hologram) will be interacting with visitors, and they will certainly include Mr. Perkins himself. Perkins House Museum is next door to Queens County Museum, below.

QUEENS COUNTY MUSEUM

902-354-4058
queenscountymuseum.com
109 Main St., P.O. Box 1078, Liverpool, NS B0T 1K0
Open: June–mid-Oct., Mon.–Sat. 9:30 AM–5:30 PM, Sun. 1–5:30 PM; Oct. 16–May 30, Mon.–Sat. 9 AM–5 PM,
Admission: Adults, children 6–17 and seniors 65 and older $2; may increase in 2009

Queens County Museum is next door to Perkins House Museum, above. It holds an exhibit that shows off Liverpool's major role in privateering, when ships with the British king's letter of marque could attack and take possession of enemy ships, keeping both ships and cargo for their own use—with a share going to the king, of course. There's a model of the *Liverpool Packet,* which captured 50 American ships during the War of 1812, despite a brief spell in American hands. Period weapons and a copy of the letter of marque to the owner of the *Liverpool Packet* are also on display.

THE ROSSIGNOL CULTURAL CENTRE
902-354-3067
rossignolculturalcentre.com
205 Church St., Liverpool, NS B0T 1K0
Open: Mid-May–mid-Oct., Mon.–Sat. 10 AM–5:30 PM; July–Aug., also open Sun. 12–5:30 PM
Admission: Adults $4, children and seniors $3, children under 6 free (also good for the Sherman Hines Museum of Photography, a two-minute walk away)

Who could pass up the exhibits at the Museum of the Outhouse? It has its own Web site, outhousemuseum.com, a wall of outhouse models, outhouse humor, outhouse postcards, outhouse books, and outhouse photos. The museum followed a natural progression, after Sherman Hines, a local photographer, started taking photographs of local outhouses—to "document" them. He published books of his outhouse photos. Then in 1980 Hines started buying actual outhouses. Two outhouses inside and six outside are part of the fascinating display.

Also at the Rossignol Cultural Centre are folk art, wildlife art, hunting, fishing, Mi'kmaq history, and more.

SHERMAN HINES MUSEUM OF PHOTOGRAPHY
902-354-2667
shermanhinesphotographymuseum.com
The Town Hall, 219 Main St., Liverpool, NS B0T 1K0
Open: Mid-May–mid-Oct., Mon.–Sat. 10 AM–5:30 PM; July–Aug., also open Sun. 12–5:30 PM
Admission: Adult, $4, children and seniors $3, children under 6 free (also good for the Rossignol Cultural Centre, a two-minute walk away)

Photography from the beginning to its contemporary best. Sherman Hines, a well-known Nova Scotia photographer, is represented here with rare prints. A collection of stereo views take a viewer fishing, traveling, and even into comedy. The display of a Victorian photography studio contains the backgrounds and photographic equipment used at the time.

WILE CARDING MILL MUSEUM
902-543-8233
museum.gov.ns.ca/wcm/
242 Victoria Rd., Bridgewater
Mail: c/o DesBrisay Museum, 60 Pleasant St., Bridgewater, NS B4V 3X9
Open: June–Sept., Mon.–Sat. 9:30 AM–5:30 PM, Sun. 1–5:30 PM
Admission: Adults $3.50, seniors 65 and older $2.25, children 6–17 $2

If you could find a place to do a week's work in one hour, as this mill did for Nova Scotians from 1860 to 1968, wouldn't it be wonderful? The river and the invention of a carding machine changed the rhythm of lives in Bridgewater. Women ran this mill, which sometimes operated 24 hours a day, preparing wool for bedding and for spinning. Demonstrations, held on special days, teach you how to spin wool with a hand spindle, or quilt or hook rugs.

Music

CHESTER BANDSTAND CONCERTS
Chester, NS

Concerts on Sunday evenings at changing dates during the summer, with music played by the Chester Brass Band.

CHESTER PLAYHOUSE
902-275-3933, 800-363-7529
chesterplayhouse.ns.ca
22 Pleasant St., P.O. Box 293, Chester, NS BoJ 1Jo

The Summer Night Music series presents musicians from the Maritimes and visitors like Maria Osende performing flamenco dance.

LUNENBURG HERITAGE BANDSTAND SUMMER CONCERTS
902-634-3498
lunenburgheritagesociety.ca
125 Pelham St., PO Box 674, Lunenburg, NS BoJ 2Co

A summerlong (June through September) series of concerts by a variety of groups, at a bandstand at the junction of Cumberland and King streets, next to the Town Hall in Lunenburg. The bandstand was re-created in 1987 after the 1889 original. Concerts are sponsored by the Lunenburg Heritage Society; see their Web site for the complete schedule.

THE MERSEY HOUSE
902-354-4000
merseyhouse.com
149 Main St., Liverpool, NS BoT 1Ko
Live entertainment on weekends year-round, more in summer
Admission: Cover charge varies

This pub was named Nova Scotia Music Venue of the Year in 2006; it serves as a live entertainment center, has a 100-seat theater, and even a recording studio. Live music, as often as five nights a week in summer, ranges from acoustic and rock roots to Maritime music, but there is no heavy metal. Just about everybody who is important in the Maritimes has played here, said the owner, Michael Loveridge. The Web site listings are linked to artists' home pages, and you can sample their music online.

MUSIC AT THE THREE CHURCHES
902-531-2248
threechurches.com
P.O. Box 391, Mahone Bay, NS BoJ 2Eo

Summer concert series
Admission: Adults $15, children 12 and under free

Classical music, by choirs, soloists, trios, and duos, is presented in five concerts each summer, each performed at one of the town's three picturesque churches, Trinity United Church, St. James Anglican Church, and St. John's Lutheran Church.

MUSIQUE ROYALE
902-634-9994
musiqueroyale.com
St. John's Episcopal Church, 64 Townsend St., Lunenburg, NS BoJ 2Co
Apr.–Sept. season
Admission: Varies

Musique Royale is a summertime concert series presenting early music from Nova Scotia's musical heritage. From its home base at St. John's Anglican Church in Lunenburg, Musique Royale brings performances of early and traditional music to historically and culturally significant venues throughout the province.

Theater

CHESTER PLAYHOUSE
902-275-3933, 800-363-7529
chesterplayhouse.ns.ca
22 Pleasant St., Chester, NS BoJ 1Jo
Open: July–Sept.
Admission: Varies

With seats for 176 today, the playhouse has been filled since 1987 during the Chester Summer Theatre season. In addition to its own Chester Playhouse Productions, the theater hosts a variety of events (music, dance, etc.) with performers from around Canada.

Seasonal Events

May
Mahone Bay/ Indian Point Mussel Festival (mahonebay.com), Mahone Bay.

July
Boxwood Festival and Workshop (902-634-9994; boxwood.org), St. John's Anglican Church, Lunenburg. Final week of July. A weeklong festival with performances of folk, baroque, and renaissance music and dance, with classes and workshops offered.
Paint Mahone Bay (902-624-6263; settlersmuseum.ns.ca/events/pmb/). Artists paint the town and its views, and there are children's painting events and an art exhibition and sale.

Late July/early August
Classic Boat Festival (902-624-0348; mahonebayclassicboatfestival.org), P.O. Box 609, Mahone Bay, NS BoJ 2Eo. Workshops, races—with some captains looking for crew—and a street dance.

August
Chester Art Fair, Chester, at the Chester Art Centre, 60 Queen St.
Nova Scotia Folk Art Festival (902-640-2113; nsfolkartfestival.com), Lunenburg.
Sponsored by the Lunenburg Heritage Society, the festival in the Lunenburg Memorial
Arena, Green Street, exhibits and sells art by the best folk artists in the province.

August
Acadian Mi'kmaq Festival, Fort Point Museum (902-688-1632; fortpointmuseum.com),
Off Rte. 331, LaHave. Late August

September
The LaHave River Folk Festival, Fort Point Museum (902-688-1632; fortpointmu-
seum.com), off Rte. 331, LaHave. Early September
Mahone Bay Scarecrow Festival and Antique Fair, Mahone Bay. Late September to early
October

November–December
Father Christmas Festival, Mahone Bay.

RECREATION

Beaches
Beach Meadows Beach, Brooklyn Shore Rd., Beach Meadows. Off Hwy. 103, east of Liverpool. Elevated boardwalk, sandy beach, and great, long walks.
Carter's Beach, S.W. Port Mouton. Six kilometers or 3.7 miles from the Port Mouton exit
on Hwy. 103.
Cherry Hill and Broad Cove Beach, Henry Conrad Rd., Cherry Hill. A favorite spot for
surfers who arrive with the big autumn and winter swells, beside Cherry Hill Studio, a
glassworks.
Green Bay Beach, near Petite Rivière. Perhaps one of the most important reasons to visit
this beach is the take-out spot, **MacLeod's** (902-935-2031), Shore Road off Green Bay
Road, with its esteemed onion rings and burgers. It's open from July 1 to Labour Day,
daily 1–9 PM.
Hirtle Beach, Rte. 332, Kingsburg. Two miles of white sand beaches are a favorite resource
of body surfers and kite flyers.
Risser's Beach Provincial Park (902-688-2034; parks.gov.ns.ca), Rte. 331, Petite Rivière.
Twenty-four kilometers or 15 miles south of Bridgewater. With camping, trails, a canteen, and supervised white sand beaches that are 1,000 meters or 3,300 feet long. A
salt-marsh trail on an elevated boardwalk takes visitors through this habitat, flows into
the salt marsh, is "one of only two rivers in the world where the Atlantic whitefish is
found," according the Nova Scotia Provincial Parks brochure.
Second Peninsula Provincial Park (902-662-3030; parks.gov.ns.ca), Rte. 3, Lunenburg.
Ten kilometers or 7 miles south of Hwy. 103, at Exit 10. Open May 20–Oct. 10. The cob-
ble beach is accessed from a wooded picnic area with water views.

Bicycling

East Coast Outfitters (902-624-0334, 877-852-2567; eastcoastoutfitters.net), 617 Main St., Mahone Bay. A second location is at Lower Prospect Road, Lower Prospect. Bike rentals and tours.

Lunenburg Bike Barn (902-634-3426), 579 Blue Rocks Rd., Lunenburg. Renting quality hybrid bikes, tandem road bikes by the day, half day or week. Repairs, parts, and accessories.

Bird Watching

National Migratory Bird Sanctuary, Head of Port Joli Harbour. An observation site that looks into the sanctuary is located on the St. Catharines River Road. Eel grass and tidal mudflats attract American black duck, green-winged teal, terns, and the endangered piping plover, as well as many other migratory birds.

Camping

RayPort Campground (902-627-2678; rayport.ca), RR #2 Martin's River, NS B0J 2E0. The campground lies beside Martin's River, close to Mahone Bay, with 60 sites with services and 10 without. Wi-Fi, camp store, free cable TV connections, swimming pool, and Washer Tournaments—with a portable game of horseshoes that most folks in RVs bring with them. Trout fishing (get your Nova Scotia fishing license about a kilometer or .62 miles away) is good at Martin's River, and old logging roads leading away from the campground are good hiking trails. Ten percent senior citizen discount.

Fishing

Lobstermen Tours (902-634-3434, 877-500-3434; lobstermentours.com), leaving from near the Fisheries Museum of the Atlantic on the Lunenburg Waterfront, from June to September daily, weather permitting. A working lobster boat takes as many as 30 people out to pull some traps and teach passengers how lobstering works and how lobsters live.

Lunenburg Ocean Adventures (902-634-4833; lunenburgoceanadventures.com), Railway Wharf, Lunenburg Waterfront. Captain William Flower offers fishing charters, shark fishing, and diving at the Saguenay wreck or Bill's Bluff on his 42-foot boat.

Hiking

Chester Connection Trail & Aspotogan Trail (902-275-3490; district.chester.ns.ca), Municipality of Chester, Recreation and Parks Department, 151 King St., P.O. Box 369, Chester, NS B0J 1J0. Following the old railway route from Halifax to the South Shore from Hubbards to Martin's River, these two trails total 47 kilometers or 29 miles and can be used for hiking, skiing, snowmobiling, and snowshoeing. A trail map is available from Chester Recreation and Parks Department. Parking areas are frequent along the trail, and the Gold River Bridge near Chester Basin, spanning 367 feet, is one highlight.

Liverpool Harbour Trail Loop, Liverpool. A 3.5-kilometer or 2-mile walk across a railway trestle bridge and along the water in Privateer Park can be enjoyed by wheelchair users and bicyclists as well as walkers.

Trot In Time Buggy Rides bring the sights of Lunenburg into the right perspective.

Horse-drawn Buggy Rides

Trot in Time Buggy Rides (902-634-8917; trotintime.ca), Bluenose Dr. on the Waterfront
in Lunenburg. Operating from May to mid-October 9:30 AM to half an hour before
dusk, weather permitting, blankets available in cool weather. Run by Basil Oickle,
whose knowledge spans decades of a life spent in Lunenburg County. His tours and his
drivers are set to the pace of his horses (meet them on the Web site) and wind among
the houses of historic Lunenburg. Adults $20, children 5–12 $8, under 5 free.

Kayaking and Canoeing

East Coast Outfitters (902-624-0334, 877-852-2567; eastcoastoutfitters.net), 617 Main
St., Mahone Bay. A second location is at Lower Prospect Rd., Lower Prospect. Rentals of
single and double sea kayaks and canoes. No delivery. Offers training classes and
guided single and group tours, or you can take off on your own exploration of the bay
and coastline alongside the business.

Parks

Kejimkujik National Park Seaside Adjunct (902-682-2772) Located 25 kilometers or
15.5 miles south of Liverpool, off St. Catharines River Rd. A long section of the coastline
accessible by hiking, this area is separate from the main inland Kejimkujik National
Park. It features Harbour Rocks Trail and Port Joli Head Trail, both of which take you to
the coast and its rocky inlets and white sand beaches. The Seaside Adjunct covers 363
square kilometers, or 140 square miles, and is a main nesting area for the endangered

piping plover (leashes are required for dogs). During the piping plovers' nesting period, from April to August, part of St. Catharines River Beach is closed.

Ovens Natural Park (902-766-4621; ovenspark.com), Riverport. Admission: Adult $8, seniors 65 and older and children 5–11 $4. Privately owned by the Chapin family, Ovens Natural Park offers visitors a hike along cliffs to view sea caves called ovens, and several look-out points with views of Lunenburg Harbour. The caves were deepened by gold-mining operations, which in the 1861 gold rush turned the area into a busy town. A small museum about the gold rush, and gold pans for rent, educate visitors about that time and its labors. A concrete staircase takes hikers to a balcony inside Cannon Cave, where you can hear its natural booming caused by ocean waves. Camping, a swimming pool, and a restaurant are on the property, with nightly musical entertainment.

Port L'Herbert Pocket Wilderness, Port L'Herbert. A park with 150 acres and trails that go along the the ocean, in an area once inhabited in summer by Mi'kmaq.

Thomas Raddall Provincial Park (902-683-2664; novascotiaparks,ca), Port Joli Harbour. Open mid-May–mid-Oct. Mink and snowshoe hare live here, and bears and moose inhabit the bogs on the 678 hectares, or 1,675 acres, of this park named for a popular Nova Scotia author. Shell middens, the refuse piles of the original Mi'kmaq inhabitants, demonstrate the people's affection for the area as a summer retreat 2,500 years ago. Eleven kilometers or 7.5 miles of trails, with viewing platforms to bird-watch, camping with one 13-site walk-in area, and unsupervised swimming.

Whale Watching

Lunenburg Whale Watching (902-527-7175, 902-634-7127; whalewatchingnovascotia .com), P.O. Box 11, Lunenburg, NS B0J 2C0. Open May through October, whale- and bird-watching tours leave from the Fisheries Museum Wharf on the Lunenburg Waterfront four times daily. Harbour Tours are given on days too rough for a journey offshore. The 45-foot boat is wheelchair accessible, and can carry 46 people. You might see fin, pilot, humpback or minke whales; also dolphins and seals, Atlantic puffins, Manx shearwaters, roseate terns, phalaropes, and much more.

SHOPPING

Antiques

Joy of Antiques (902-688-1578), 15 River Rd., RR #1, Petite Rivière. Pine country furniture, Persian carpets, and unique furnishings.

Birds

For the Birds Nature Shop (902-624-0784; forthebirdsnatureshop.com), 647 Main St., Mahone Bay. Binoculars, books, an Audubon bird call and more for bird lovers.

Bookstores

Carousel Bookstore (902- 543-1434), 527 King St., Bridgewater. Open Mon.–Sat. 10 AM–5 PM, Fri. 10 AM–8 PM, and during the summer Sun. 12–4 PM. With a deep discount, books at Carousel cover fiction, nonfiction, and everything in between.

E.J.'s Fantastic Fiction (902-527-0404), 192 North St., Bridgewater. Open Tues.–Fri. 9 AM–6 PM, Sat. 10 AM–4 PM. Paperback fiction, romance, science fiction, mystery, and more with a 50 percent discount, and good-quality hardcovers $5.

Elizabeth's Books (902-634-8149), 134 Montague St., Lunenburg. Open year-round, daily 3–9 PM. Chris Webb sells both used and rare books in paperback and hardcover covering a wide range of subjects, with a section devoted to nautical books.

Snug Harbour Books at the Lanes Privateer Inn (902-354-3456; lanesprivateerinn.com), 27–33 Bristol Ave., Liverpool. Maritime books and bestsellers. Coffee and more are served inside the book shop from the next door Gourmet Shop.

The Biscuit Eater Books and Café (902-624-2665; biscuiteater.ca), 16 Orchard St., Mahone Bay. Open in summer daily 8:30 AM–5:30 PM; winter Wed.–Sun. 8:30 AM–4 PM. Both new and used books are for sale in a wide ranging selection. See also under "Coffee Shops" in the Food Purveyors section above.

Wells Books (902-356-3131; wellsbooks.com), 226 Main St., Liverpool. Open in summer daily 10 AM–4:30 PM, winter 10 AM–4 PM. Jeri Bass sells antiquarian books and ephemera.

Follow the sign to The Maritime Painted Saltbox Gallery in Petite Rivière, for folk art, fine art, and furniture.

Galleries

Anderson, Gallery of Contemporary Photography (902-640-3400; www.andersonmontague.com), 160 Montague St., Lunenburg. Open May–mid-June, Mon.–Sat. 11 AM–5 PM, Sun. 12–5 PM; June 15–Sept., Mon.–Sat. 10 AM–5 PM, Sun. 12–5 PM. Call or check the Web site for off-season hours. Amazing contemporary photography is presented in an old 1884 warehouse on the waterfront. The spacious renovated building holds the gallery on the second floor, and on the ground floor a bookstore with cards with photographic images. Books are on many subjects, but all are chosen because of the fine photographic images inside.

Black Duck Gallery (902-634-3190; blackduck.ca), 8 Pelham St., Lunenburg. The gallery is open from mid-April to December, representing local artists. The shop is open July–Aug., Mon.–Sat. 9 AM–8 PM, Sun. 1–5 PM.; Jan.–Apr., Mon.–Sat. 10 AM–5:30 PM; May–Dec., Mon.–Sat. 10 AM–5 PM, Sun. 1–5:30 PM. Fisherman knit sweaters, wools, fine housewares, toys, and jewelry.

The Clever Hen Pottery (902-273-2251), 117 Hwy. 14, Chester. Lyrical whimsy—or whimsical lyrics—arise from the story-telling teapots with rolling wheels and legs.

Houston North Gallery (902-634-8869; Houston-north-gallery.ns.ca), 110 Montague St., Lunenburg. Inuit art, folk art, and Nova Scotian artists.

Jim Smith—Fine Studio Pottery (902-275-3272; jimsmithstudio.ca), corner of Water and Duke sts. on Front Harbour, Chester. Open July—Aug., Mon.—Sat 9 AM—8 PM, Sun. 1—5 PM. Off-season call ahead. Beautifully decorated faience and elaborate urns, pitchers, platters and bowls. Jim Smith is a member of the Royal Canadian Academy of the Arts.

The Maritime Painted Saltbox Gallery (902-693-1544), www.paintedsaltbox.com), 265 River Rd., Petite Rivière. Artists Tom Always and Peter Blais are the masterminds behind the array of art, furniture, folk art, and more, which they sell in their renovated barn and coop beside their house. The painted and stained furniture would be not be out of place in the most elegant house, and the paintings of seaside scenes are brilliantly colored and charming. Humorous metal cut-out chickens and a charismatic rooster sit in the coop, presiding over walls full of morality lessons illustrated with whimsy.

Moorings (902-624-6208; mooringsgallery.com), 575 Main St., Mahone Bay. Representing unique fiber artists, painters, ceramicists, and jewelers, Moorings is a gallery sure to have something fascinating on exhibit. One artist, Louise Lortie, who with Elaine Schuller is "Fibre Ensemble," began her career crocheting bikinis for her Barbie doll. Another, Teresa Bergen, sculpts intriguingly active performers you can't forget.

Moxie the Gallery (902-530-3060; moxiethegallery.com), 619 Main St., Mahone Bay. Contemporary art from Atlantic Canada artists. Drawing, photos, printmaking, and cards.

North Shore Canadian Art (902-634-1903; degarthe.com), 8 Linden Ave., Lunenburg. This gallery sells paintings and other art made from 1860 to 1970, and in particular work by Nova Scotia artist William deGarthe. The art for sale is called "Historically Important Canadian Art" and selected for its value as an investment as well as its importance as art.

Nova Scotia Folk Art, 788 Back Rd., Vogler's Cove. With a skinny wooden man holding flags at the bottom of the driveway, outfitted in blue and red with white polka dots, Reynolds Aulenback announces his craftwork. He uses hand tools to carve little people and animals.

Nova Terra Cotta Pottery (902-634-8902; joanbruneau.com), 10 Dufferin St., Lunenburg. Organic curves and deep-hued glazes are signatures of the ceramic work by Joan Bruneau. Beaded jewelry by Chris Marin and landscapes by Scott MacLeod.

Out of Hand (902-634-3499) 135 Montague St., Lunenburg. Marja Moed represents many different artists and craftspeople, with jewelry, ceramics, painting, woodwork, paintings, glass, paper-mache, and pewter among the work for sale. Atlantic Provinces craftspeople include Kathi Peterson, who makes Puffer Bellies, carved wood, whimsical fish, mermaids, and mirror frames.

Peer Gallery (902-640-3131; peer-gallery.com), 167 Lincoln St., Lunenburg. An artists' cooperative gallery representing 12 Nova Scotia artists who are all well known in the province. Woodturning, printmaking, painting and drawing, and more.

Quartet Gallery (902-634-4110), 144 Lincoln St., Lunenburg. Closed Wed. This small cooperative represents four excellent acrylic/oil artists who paint landscape, animals, seascape, portraits, and more as their subjects.

The Spotted Frog Folk Art Gallery (902-634-1976; spottedfrog.ca), 125 Montague St., Lunenburg. Meg Hatton runs this charming shop where a black crow carved by B. Nangler was $200 in 2008. Maud Lewis prints are sold here too, and many other artists are represented.

Spruce Top Rug Hooking Gallery (902-624-9312; sprucetoprughookingstudio.com), 255 West Main St., Mahone Bay. Open year-round, Mon. and Wed.–Sat. 10 AM–4 PM, Sun. 12–4 PM. Spruce Top exhibits and sells hooked rugs and teaches people how to make them. The company can also execute a commission, or sell you a kit to make your own hooked rug.

Glass

Chez Glass Lass (902-275-5545; kilnart.com), 63 Duke St., Chester, and **Sharon McNamara, et al** (902-275-9100; kilnart.com), 65 Duke St., Chester. Neighboring businesses owned by Sharon McNamara and Paul Palango. McNamara and Palango make unusual glass dinnerware, mirrors, picture frames, trays, and more, with pulverized stained glass fused in the kiln in extraordinary patterns and designs. The second business features the designs of other craftspeople as well.

Quilts

Quilts by the Sea (902-634-4203; quiltsbythesea.com), 34 Linden Ave., Lunenburg. Nova Scotia and Maritime quilts.

Skateboards

Homegrown Skateboards (902-688-1180; homegrownskateboards.com), Building 3421 (3rd floor of LaHave Bakery), Rte. 331, LaHave. Jesse Watson and his skateboarding staff are making skateboards in this workshop, pressing, shaping, and silk-screening each "deck" or skateboard body here. They are made with East Coast rockmaple. Clothing, custom designs, and more.

SHELBURNE TO PORT LA TOUR

LODGING

ABOVE STUDIO 14

Mary Lou Keith, innkeeper
902-875-1333
studio14.ns.ca
14 George St., Shelburne, NS B0T 1W0
Price: $85
Credit cards: No, cash or checks only
Handicapped Access: None
Special Features: Wi-Fi

A two-bedroom housekeeping apartment in the top floor of an 1875 house, with low ceilings, in the middle of Shelburne's Historic District, Above Studio 14 also has a balcony over a large yard with a garden. This is a favorite place for return visitors, having a great living room and dining room, with a view of the water down the street and a park all located near the Osprey Performing Arts Centre. One bedroom with a queen-size bed, one with a double and a

The Gracie George Room at the Cooper's Inn in Shelburne

twin, are both full of light; their beds have fiberbed and featherbeds on top of the mattresses. The barbeque is available for use by guests.

THE COOPER'S INN

Paul and Pat Dewar
902-875-4656, 800-688-2011
thecoopersinn.com
36 Dock St. at Mason Ln., P.O. Box 959, Shelburne, NS B0T 1W0
Take Exits 25 or 26 off Hwy. 103
Price: $100 to $185
Credit cards: Yes
Handicapped Access: No
Special Features: Wi-Fi, in-room wine, chocolates, coffee and tea, some 32-inch LCD TVs

When I arrived, Paul and Pat Dewar were finishing installing some modern windows at their old inn. The back of the inn, with three modern rooms, was originally a

cooper's shop. Today barrels are still pieced together across the street.

But Cooper's Inn is dedicated to the more comfortable arts of hospitality. The George Gracie Room is named after the original owner, a British loyalist who arrived after the American Revolution and built the house. The bedside tables and the table at the end of the four-poster king-size bed were made by Paul Dewar himself; the small complimentary bottle of Jöst Contessa Red was made in Malagash.

Another resident also has the welfare of the guests in mind—her tall, slender, and erect figure has been glimpsed, by three guests, engaged in housekeeping in her late-1700s dress. When guests congratulate Pat Dewar on being up at 3 A.M. baking bread, she declines the compliment. She says the smell of baking bread is just another one of the resident ghost Mrs. Crowell's personal attentions to the guests.

MACKENZIE'S MOTEL AND COTTAGES

Jim Goodick and Sandra Downey, owners
902-875-2847, 866-875-0740
mackenzies.ca
260 Water St., Sherburne, NS B0T 1W0
Price: $75 to $150
Credit cards: Yes
Handicapped Access: Yes, 1 two-bedroom cottage
Special Features: Wi-Fi, heated pool, free continental breakfast, CAA/AAA discount

Six motel units, 3 one-bedroom and 3 two-bedroom cottages, and two suites each with a fireplace and whirlpool bath make up the wide range of accommodations at Mac-Kenzie's. The pine-paneled cottages have fully equipped kitchens, and the two-bedroom cottages have a patio with a barbeque. MacKenzie's is exceptionally well regarded by guests, who extol the cleanliness of the place. Continental breakfast includes juices, breads, bagels, cold and hot cereal, fruit, and muffins. The motel is completely nonsmoking, and natural cleaners are used in the rooms.

THE MILLSTONES BED & BREAKFAST

Nancie Smith and Darlene Williams, innkeepers
902-875-4525, 866-240-9110
millstonesbedandbreakfast.com
2 Falls Lane, Shelburne, NS B0T 1W0
Exit 26 from Hwy. 103
Price: $90 to $140
Credit cards: Yes
Handicapped Access: None
Special Features: Wi-Fi, wood stove in cushy living room

Darlene Williams and Nancie Smith bought this B&B in 2005, and they keep it shining. Their rooms are named after plants that grow in the area; the Trailing Ivy, for example, the smallest room, is a charmer with pale green walls and a pot of ivy being trained around the window. The rooms are set under the slanting walls of the eaves, but feel roomy nonetheless, and the one suite available has its own entrance. A rushing river borders one side of the property, and across the street the Islands Provincial Park offers trails that many visitors like to hit after too long inside their cars, hiking the 3 kilometers or 1.8 miles to the beach. Taz, the friendliest dog, is in residence.

RESTAURANTS

✪ CHARLOTTE LANE

902-875-3314
charlottellane.ca
13 Charlotte Ln., Shelburne
Open: Lunch Tues.–Sat., 11:30 AM–2:30 PM; soup and dessert 2:30–5 PM; dinner 5–8 PM; closed Sun.–Mon.
Price: $20 to $29
Credit cards: Yes
Cuisine: British classics and Italian and Maritime dishes
Serving: L, D
Handicap Access: Yes
Special Features: Gift shop in the front of the house, dinner reservations recommended

Charlotte Lane won the Taste of Nova Scotia 1999 Restaurant of the Year Award. Seafood crêpe casserole, and lobster and scallops brandy gratin with Monterey and cheddar cheese are two of the seafood dinners you might find at Charlotte Lane, the well-loved restaurant in Shelburne. The garlic scallop linguine, and pork tenderloin Zurich with rosti potatoes in a Port and mushroom sauce are two good entrées. With a dessert of sticky toffee pudding or spiced apple cake and a sampler of three Nova Scotia dessert wines for $10.95, a meal in this mustard-brown shingled house is a worthy goal. There's an extensive wine list.

LOTHAR'S

902-875-3697
lothars-cafe.com
149 Water St., Shelburne

Open: Thurs.–Sat. 11:30 AM–2 PM and 5–8 PM; Sun. 11 AM–2 PM and 5–8 PM; closed Tues.–Wed.
Price: $14 to $26
Credit cards: Yes
Cuisine: German and classic
Serving: L, D, Sun. Brunch
Handicap Access: Yes
Special Features: Jaeger Schnitzel and more from Germany

An excellent lunch of haddock fish cakes and four of this restaurant's salads persuaded me there was an utterly reliable hand in the kitchen. The fish cakes were crisp on the outside and full of fish inside with a touch of green onion. The salads, a mesclun mix with pungent, creamy dressing, cucumbers, creamy German potato salad, and a tart red cabbage slaw were complemented by the chow or stewed green tomatoes with a touch of sugar and clove. Dinners are more elegant, with braised lamb shanks, prawn fettuccini, European potato crêpes, and paprika schnitzel vying for your attention. The simple dining room holds unique wrought-iron coat racks shaped like cursive Ls, and the sturdy oak tables are set on iron pedestals.

FOOD PURVEYORS

Coffee Shops
The Bean Dock (902-875-1302), RR1 Site 2 Box 16, Shelburne. Open Mon.–Fri. 8:30 AM–4 PM, Sat. 10 AM–4 PM; closed Sun. Monique Fillmore owns this charming little coffee shop, with fresh-baked temptations like rhubarb tarts. Lunch could be a chicken burger or a cup of house-made soup or the excellent seafood chowder.

A cannon marks the site of the Port La Tour Fort Saint-Louis.

CULTURE

Churches

THE STONE CHURCH
Clark's Harbour, Cape Sable Island, NS

A 3-foot-thick, hand-cut granite foundation and cobblestone walls hold up the Stone Church, built in ten years starting in 1921 by Thomas Doucette. Inside, handsome woodwork adorns the walls.

Historic Buildings and Sites

PORT LA TOUR FORT SAINT-LOUIS
Port La Tour, NS

Lamont and Betty Lovitt shared land and mowed the path to this squat tower that commemorates the early Acadian outpost on the waterfront. According to the plaque, when Charles la Tour tried to get his son Claude to give in to the Scotsmen with whom he traveled here, his son refused, Charles ended up needing to take refuge with Claude to be protected from the Scotsmen's wrath. Isn't it curious that descendents of an English settler, named Lovitt, should have been the caretakers of this French site? A small cannon protects the coastline.

Lighthouses

WEST BACCARO LIGHTHOUSE
In a small park next to the lighthouse in West Baccaro is the site of a memorial to District 8 Fishermen, with a list of names of men who died pursuing the ancient risky work of finding a living from the sea.

Museums

BLACK LOYALIST HERITAGE SITE AND OLD SCHOOLHOUSE MUSEUM
902-875-1310
blackloyalist.com
98 Old Birchtown Rd., Birchtown
Mail: P.O. Box 1194, Shelburne, NS B0T 1W0
Open: July–Aug., Tues.–Sun. 10 AM–5 PM
Admission: Adults $2.50

The black loyalists who joined British forces to fight in the American Revolution in exchange for their freedom settled around the world, after the war had made them unwelcome in the new United States. Many came to Shelburne, where 2,500 were then settled in Birchtown. Despite a promise of land, however, very few received any—only 189 family

The Old Birchtown School Black Loyalist Heritage Site honors blacks who arrived in Shelburne after the American Revolution.

heads out of a total of 649. The first school for the children of the black loyalists was a seg-regated school started in 1785 by Stephen Blucke. In 1787, Blucke had 36 students in the Birchtown school. The schoolhouse that houses the museum was built in the 1830s. Panels about slavery and the suffering of the early black population are inside, along with arti-facts. A trail and the Black Loyalist Monument are just down the Birchtown Road from the museum. The site is at what is believed to be the original burial ground of the black loyal-ists, is always open.

THE DORY STORE MUSEUM
902-875-3219
museum.gov.ns.ca/dory
11 Dock St., P.O. Box 39, Shelburne, NS B0T 1W0
Open: June–Sept., daily 9:30 AM–5:30 PM
Admission: Adults $3, or for all four museums in complex $8, under 16 and Sun. morning free

There may still be a dory-maker at work inside this 1880 dory shop, which once sheltered a business that made thousands of the sturdy boats for the Grand Banks fishery—and if not, you can watch one at work on a video. For years, a man could fish from a dory with a baited hook and hand line and catch fish after fish. With the invention of long lines, with many baited hooks, fishermen decided to carry dories out to sea on schooners, nesting as many as 14 into each other on deck and deploying their crews across the rich waters to haul in a bigger catch. Canadian and American captains bought their dories in Shelburne, where shipbuilder Isaac Crowell had come up with a cheaper way to make the curved wood planks on the sides of the charming boats.

MUIR-COX SHIPYARD
902-875-3219
historicshelburne.com/muircox.htm
Dock St., P.O. 39, Shelburne, NS B0T 1W0
Open: June–Sept., daily 9:30 AM–5:30 PM
Admission: Adults $3, or for all four museums in complex $8, under 16 and Sun. morning free

This shipyard has been operating almost every year since the 1820s, making it one of the oldest continually running yards in North America. The Yacht Shed, reopened in 2001, builds custom wooden boats. In the Interpretive Centre you can learn about local ship-building, and begin to see the bristling masts of the historic harbor, once full of fishing schooners and some square-rigged barques, all built here.

ROSS-THOMSON HOUSE AND STORE MUSEUM
902-875-3219
museum.gov.ns.ca/rth
Charlotte St., P.O. Box 39, Shelburne, NS B0T 1W0
Open: June–mid-Oct., daily 9:30 AM–5:30 PM
Admission: Adults $3, or for all four museums in complex $8; under 16 and Sun. morning free

In 1785, if your grocery list had included a barrel of flour, this would have been the right place to come. Once serving the needs of 10,000 inhabitants (twice the population of Halifax then), the stock of the store was typical of the 1780s, when Shelburne had just swelled with newcomers who had pledged their loyalty to the British crown and who were no longer welcome in what had become, after the American Revolution, the United States of America. The store owners, brothers George and Robert Ross, were loyalists themselves with a West Indies trade, bringing salt, tobacco, and molasses to Shelburne, after selling cargos of pine boards and pickled herring. The Ross-Thomson House is furnished in the formal, somewhat austere style of the era.

THE SHELBURNE COUNTY MUSEUM
902-875-3219
historicshelburne.com/scm.htm
20 Dock St., P.O. Box 39, Shelburne, NS B0T 1W0
Open: June–Oct. 15, daily 9:30 AM–5:30 PM; mid-Oct.–Dec., 10 AM–12 noon and 2–5 PM (check for changing schedule)
Admission: Adults $3, or for all four museums in complex $8, under 16 and Sun. morning free

One of the oldest fire pumpers is on permanent exhibit here, along with exhibits about shipbuilding and Shelburne loyalists. Microfilms of 18th- to 20th-century newspapers and court records, and Shelburne County family records are among the resources.

Theater

OSPREY ARTS CENTRE
ospreyartscentre.com
902-875-2359
107 Water St., P.O. Box 193, Shelburne, NS B0T 1W0
Open: Events schedule varies
Admission: Ticket prices vary

Holding more than 60 events every year, The Osprey Arts Centre has a 190-seat theater, an outdoor amphitheater, and an art gallery. It was opened in 2003 after the renovation of a shipbuilding structure. Check the schedule for showings of exceptional movies, concerts, and gallery openings.

Seasonal Events

May
Loyalist Landing Celebration (loyalitsatShelburne.com), Shelburne.

June
Shelburne County Lobster Festival (shelburnenovascotia/lobsterfest), Shelburne.

August
Annual Kitchen Party at the Osprey Arts Centre (902-875-2359; ospreyarts.com), 107 Water St., Shelburne.
March to Birchtown (902-875-1310; blackloyalist.com).

September

Shelburne Harbour Whirligig and Weathervane Festival (whirligigfestival.com),
Shelburne.

November

A Loyalist Christmas (loyalistsatShelburne.com), Shelburne.

December

New Year's Eve Ball, at the Osprey Arts Centre (902-875-2359; ospreyarts.com), 107 Water
St., Shelburne.

RECREATION

Parks

The Islands Provincial Park (902-875-4304; novascotiaparks.ca), Shelburne Harbour.
Nova Scotia's oldest camping park, The Islands was opened more than 50 years ago. It's
easy to see why people have always wanted to camp along the harbor here, with its view
of the Shelburne waterfront. An old administration building, made of red spruce logs,
holds the staff and a stone fireplace. Boulders on the property were left behind by the
melting glaciers, and the roads bend around them. Visitors can hike the now defunct
railway route, 2 kilometers or 1.2 miles into Shelburne, or take a longer hike west to
Birchtown and the Black Loyalist Heritage Site. The Picnic Park, on a second island, is
just a short walk out of the camping area. The park was the site of a quarry of granite

James Mackay, the force behind Timber Art, works on a sculpture.

called Scotia Grey that was used in the building of both the *Halifax Herald* Building in Halifax and St. Bernard's Church on the French shore.

Shopping

Bookstores

The Whirligig—Books, Collectibles, Memorabilia (902-875-1117; thewhirligigbook shop.com), 135 Water St., Shelburne. New and used books make this an essential stop; the collectible Hardy Boys and other children's series are abundant on the shelves, but so are the latest thrillers. Whirligigs, a local specialty, are whizzing in the doorway.

Gift and Specialty Shops

Timber Art (902-875-6388; mackaycarvings.com), Water St., Shelburne. James Mackay is the artist with the chainsaw who created the two sculptures at MacKenzie's Motel and Cottages. He can carve you an eagle with a fish in its talons for $600; his work can be seen at the cooperidge on Water Street across from Cooper's Inn. He himself can be seen there too, with his earphones in place, smoothing those eagle's wings.

Tottie's Crafts (902-875-2584), 24 Dock St., Shelburne. Pottery and jewelry, quilts, and baby sweaters are all made by Maritimes artisans. Wool hats, paintings, and more are part of the fine selection. No tax is charged on the sales, because the profits all go to the Shelburne Museum complex.

Clark's Harbour, Yarmouth, and the French Shore

Lodging

Clark's Harbor

OCEAN TIDE BED & BREAKFAST
Heather Mundell, innkeeper
902-745-0429
oceantidebandb.com
2804 Main St., P.O. Box 467, Clark's Harbour, Cape Sable Island NS B0W 1P0
Price: $45 to $90
Credit cards: Cash or checks only
Handicapped Access: None

One of the upstairs rooms has its own bathroom, but Room 2 comes with the use of the bathroom downstairs through the kitchen—not an appealing prospect if you need to go in and out during the breakfast hour. But the bed is comfortable, and the accommodations are spotless. In quiet Clark's Harbor, this is the only place to stay, and the owner will go out of her way to make things as pleasant as possible. Eggs over easy, bacon, fresh-made biscuits, and local jam provide a good breakfast.

Yarmouth and the French Shore

AUBERGE CHEZ CHRISTOPHE GUEST HOUSE
902-837-5817
chezchristophe.ca
2655 Rte. 1, Grosses-Coques, NS B0W 1M0
Price: $50 to $85
Credit Cards: Yes
Handicapped Access: No
Special Features: Wi-Fi, restaurant Chez Christophe across the street

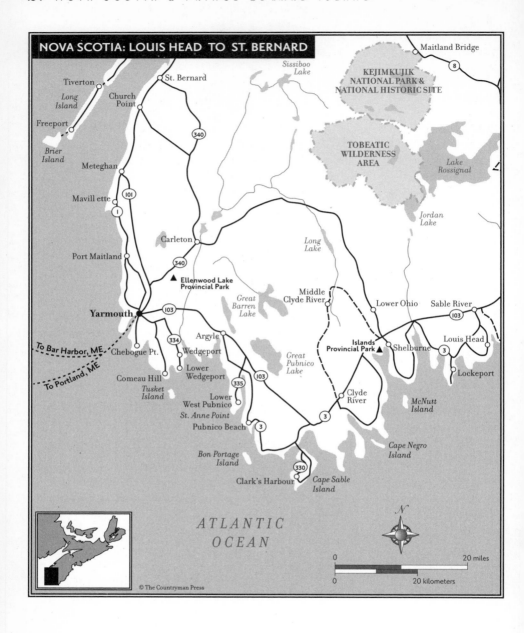

NOVA SCOTIA: LOUIS HEAD TO ST. BERNARD

Maitland Bridge

8

Sissiboo Lake

KEJIMKUJIK NATIONAL PARK & NATIONAL HISTORIC SITE

Tiverton

St. Bernard

Long Island

Church Point

Freeport

340

TOBEATIC WILDERNESS AREA

Lake Rossignal

Brier Island

Meteghan

101

Mavill ette

1

Jordan Lake

Carleton

Long Lake

340

Port Maitland

Ellenwood Lake Provincial Park

Great Barren Lake

Middle Clyde River

Lower Ohio

Sable River

103

Yarmouth

103

Louis Head

To Bar Harbor, ME

334

Argyle

Islands Provincial Park

Shelburne

3

Chebogue Pt.

Wedgeport

Great Pubnico Lake

Lockeport

To Portland, ME

Comeau Hill

Lower Wedgeport

335

103

Clyde River

McNutt Island

Tusket Island

Lower West Pubnico

St. Anne Point

3

Pubnico Beach

3

Cape Negro Island

Bon Portage Island

330

Clark's Harbour

Cape Sable Island

ATLANTIC OCEAN

N

0   20 miles

0   20 kilometers

© The Countryman Press

Simple, handsomely furnished rooms in this clean, white-painted house share a bathroom. Guests staying in one of the five bedrooms also can make use of the full-sized kitchen and a living room. The location—in the middle of the French Shore—seems like a new country, and beautiful beaches are a short drive away.

GUEST LOVITT HOUSE

Bruce and Twyla Rogers
902-742-0372, 866-742-0372
guestlovitt.ca
12 Parade St., Yarmouth, NS B5A 3A4
Price: $129 to $199
Credit cards: Yes
Handicapped Access: None
Special Features: Wi-Fi, phone, TV, DVD

Bruce and Twyla Rogers have poured their hearts and souls into this Victorian, and it wears their work with pride. Guest-Lovitt Room 1 is comfortable and its amenities elegant, with the big, wide bed foremost among them. In the back of the house is a room with its own private deck and a hot tub that overlooks the gardens. A private bath is part of each room. After you take a tour of the finest properties in the area in

Room 1 at Guest Lovitt House shows off historic elegance.

the B&B's Model T Ford, either room would be a fine place for a nap. Breakfast is served at the dining room table in the formal dining room, and complimentary wine is generously poured in the parlor in the evening. The house boasts a matched set of gothic Victorian carved-wood furniture. The widow's walk is set up with a little table and two chairs for a cup of tea at sunset.

LAKELAWN MOTEL

Cheryl MacAvoy, innkeeper
877-664-0664
lakelawnmotel.com
641 Main St., Yarmouth, NS B5A 1K2
Price: $59 to $99
Credit cards: Yes
Handicapped Access: No
Special Features: Cable TV, Wi-Fi planned.

This simple motel offers the traveler on a budget a clean place to stay with a private bath. The main house was built in 1864. Built since then as part of the property are the 26 units of the motel with parking in front. Four B&B rooms, furnished with antiques, all with private baths, have TVs and offer a breakfast: fresh fruit, yogurt, fresh-baked muffins, and a choice of a hot main dish. A smaller breakfast with bagels, muffins, toasts, and cereal is available to other guests who must pay extra.

MACKINNON-CANN INN

Michael Tavares and Neil Hisgen, innkeepers
902-742-9900
mackinnoncanninn.com
27 Willow St., Yarmouth, NS B5A 1V2
Price: $128 to $180
Credit cards: Yes
Handicapped Access: Yes
Special Features: Wi-Fi, DVD, heated bathroom flooring

Before this 1887 house could be demolished, it was rescued and revived as an inn.

It is a fine example of Italianate Victorian, one of the popular styles of the best houses in Yarmouth. There are four parlors, and the seven guest suites are each decorated in the style of another era. The 60s Room is furnished with Danish modern pieces intended to transport you to *The Dick Van Dyke Show*. All seven rooms have private baths, and some are whirlpools.

MURRAY MANOR B&B

Brenda Atwood, innkeeper
902-742-9625, 877-742-9629
murraymanor.com
225 Main St., Yarmouth, NS B5A 1C6
Price: $95 to $139
Credit cards: Yes
Handicapped Access: None
Special Features: Gardens

Murray Manor B&B, a Regency-style house with gothic influences, was built around 1825. The bedrooms have prayer windows—and you must kneel down to look out of them. The white and turquoise Brier Island Room has the feel of a summer escape and a window on the garden; this is the inn's one accommodation with a private bathroom. In another room, the Cape Forchu, two rocking chairs offer quick relaxation after a day of exploring the area.

A bed and breakfast for the past 25 years, this property stands one block up the hill from the ferry dock in Yarmouth, where the CAT arrives in season from Portland and Bar Harbor. Around 33,000 square feet of beautiful lawn hold flowers and trees and a hedge, all enclosed by the original stone wall.

RESTAURANTS

CHEZ BRUNO'S BISTRO

902-742-0031
chezbrunocafe.com
222 Main St., Yarmouth
Open: Tues.–Sun. 11 AM–7 PM, later on weekends; Mon. 11 AM–3 PM only.
Price: $10 to $32
Credit cards: Yes
Cuisine: Continental and Maritime
Serving: L, D
Handicap Access: Yes

Rack of lamb is one dinner favorite here; another is free-range chicken, which might be served with sautéed mushrooms and cream, or baked with tomato sauce and Parmesan and mozzarella and served over linguine. A special of salmon in puff pastry with dill sauce, lobster linguine, and haddock with shrimp provençal are possible seafood dishes. Escargots bourguignon with garlic butter are always on the menu, and usually fried calamari is too. Depending on the temperature outside, Hoegaarden , one of the good Belgian beers, might be a good choice with lamb. Chef/owner Bruno Sieberath is Belgian and has been here since 2003, after arriving on the south shore following years working on cruise ships and for the enormous Canadian Pacific hotel company.

MACKINNON-CANN INN

902-742-9900
mackinnoncanninn.com
27 Willow St., Yarmouth
Open: 5:30–9 PM, reservations required
Price: $19 to $27
Credit cards: Yes
Cuisine: Continental
Serving: D
Handicap Access: Yes
Special Features: The restaurant is in an elegant ballroom

Neil Hisgen was in charge of this dining room during 2007 and 2008; he is well known for his pecan pie, made with a little bourbon and drizzled with caramel sauce. "I believe in comfort food," Hisgen said. Another worthy main dish is Nova Scotia haddock, lightly breaded and pan fried—the fish arrives fresh off the boat, delivered by

Try the Rappie Pie—at least the little taste provided for free—at Chez Christophe in Grosse Coques.

the local fisherman he works with. A café outside, set in a garden, is in the planning stages and expected to open in the summer of 2009. Hisgen calls himself a very good cook but not a chef, and he said that a culinary institute graduate will be the chef in 2009.

ORGANIC GARDEN CAFE
902-637-3948
3644 Hwy. 103, Barrington Passage
Open: Mon.–Sat. 9 AM–6 PM, Fri. 9 AM–8 PM.
Price: $5 to $10
Credit cards: Yes
Cuisine: Organic with Mexican, Asian, and French influences
Serving: B, L, D
Handicap Access: Yes
Special Features: Local produce from Pubnico and Annapolis Valley, in season

This organic restaurant is a resource for travelers and locals alike. A picnic lunch might center on a chicken panini made with spinach, tomato, cucumber, and various cheeses. The many vegetarian meals include four vegetarian wraps and salads like the cranberry walnut salad. French onion soup is popular, and so is the grilled

Greek bagel sandwich, stuffed with feta, cucumber, olives, and lettuce. A special of fettucine Alfredo, or salmon with rice and asparagus, is geared toward dinner, for take-out or eat-in.

Gluten-free and dairy-free items are available, including smoothies. More than 30 smoothies and fresh-squeezed juices are sold. Not licensed.

✪ RESTAURANT CHEZ CHRISTOPHE
902-837-5817
chezchristophe.ca
2655 Rte. 1, Grosses-Coques
Mail: P.O. Box 61 Church Point, NS B0W 1M0
Open: Tues.–Sun.; breakfast 6–9 AM; lunch 11:30 AM–2 PM; dinner 4:30–8 PM.
Price: $7 to $15
Credit cards: Yes
Cuisine: Acadien
Serving: L, D
Handicap Access: No
Special Features: Bilingual waitstaff

Chef/owner Paul Comeau is cooking in the back of this 1837 house, which his own great-great grandfather built. The four charming small rooms in the front are filled with tables, and the place is typically jammed. The lunch rush, when I arrived on July 1, looked overwhelming to me, but the servers said that sometimes there are 20 at the door. "And they don't take No," one server said. (The wait staff veers back and forth from Acadian French to English, and so do the customers.)

The best rappie pie, or pâté à la râpure, an Acadian specialty, is made in this kitchen, but this unusual dish can be strange to palates not used to its texture. Chez Christophe, therefore, serves anyone who has never had it just a little taste, before taking an order for a whole meal. The server said 95 percent of those who try it first do not order it. The "pie" is really a casserole made with shredded potato cooked with chicken broth and beaten into an ultrasmooth or gluelike consistency. Shredded chicken or clams is combined with the potato mixture, and it is baked until it has a golden brown crust. I loved it.

But pan-fried scallops, roast pork, haddock, chicken soup with dumplings, and other dishes are fine alternatives on the appetizing menu. Save room—though it will be a challenge—for the pies: cherry, apple, apple caramel, blueberry, and strawberry rhubarb or apple crisp. The strawberry shortcake in a small glass dish is made with chopped strawberries saturating a tender tea biscuit with their fragrant juice. Topped with heavenly whipped cream, this was the best strawberry shortcake I encountered in Nova Scotia.

RUDDERS SEAFOOD RESTAURANT & BREW PUB

902-742-7050
ruddersbrewpub.com
96 Water St., Yarmouth
Open: Open daily at 11 AM and through the evening
Price: $5 to $27
Credit cards: Yes
Cuisine: Maritime seafood, pub food
Serving: L, D
Handicap Access: Yes, from the sidewalk
Special Features: Waterfront deck, microbrewery, 12-slip dock for boating customers, live entertainment

Rudders is convenient to The CAT, which is lucky, because the food on The CAT isn't all that convenient, or good, for its travelers. Recommendations I received from locals proved to be completely reliable. Excellent fried calamari ($7.99) was made with squid that came from Digby; it was served with Thai sauce, a chili-flake sauce that it sweetened exactly enough. A 10-ounce glass of the Yarmouth Town Brown with its balanced bitterness was a perfect accompaniment. Rudder's Red has two kinds of hops infusing its bright flavor, and a 64-ounce pitcher is $13.95. The deck, with umbrella tables overlooking the water, can be packed, and the open, raftered room inside, including the four wooden booths on the street side of the dining room, is often full too.

FOOD PURVEYORS

Meat, Fish, Poultry

Sea View Take Out, aka West Head Take Out, 902-745-1322, 81 Boundary Rd. (West Head Rd.), Clark's Harbor. Open for summer season only. This tiny outpost, across the street from a fish and lobster-packing plant, sells its seafood platter for $11.50 ($13 with tax). On the day I visited, the scallops and shrimp were juicy and the haddock presentable, but the clams seemed a little over the hill. "The bottom's a little greasy," the order person told a customer when she handed him his brown paper bag, "So don't set it on your lap." Chicken poutine and hamburg poutine (both $6.95 before tax) and a cup of gravy ($1) were also listed on the outside of the little building, but I didn't dare. Most people drive away with their order and eat it somewhere else.

CULTURE

Churches

STE-ANNE CHURCH AND CHAPEL SITE
Rte. 3, Ste-Anne-du-Ruisseau, NS
Open: Self-guided tours May–mid-Oct., daily 9 AM–5 PM
Admission: Free

The handsome 1900 church features oil paintings and stained-glass windows. A mile from the church is the site of the original chapel of this parish on Rocco Point, with a replica of the original chapel, built in 1784, next to an old cemetery. Rocco Point was first settled in 1767 by Acadians returning from an exile imposed on them by the British, and the chapel was shared with local Mi'kmaqs. A trail is located at the chapel site.

SAINT BERNARD'S CHURCH
902-837-5687
baiestemarie.com
Rte. 1, St. Bernard, NS

The largest church on the French shore, this church was built between 1910 and 1942—with a single row of granite blocks each year—using granite quarried from nearby Shelburne and hauled by train over 120 miles. Each block was cut by hand. The 3-foot-thick walls are held together with hand-forged iron rivets. Clear windows endow the spacious interior with a rare elegance. The church hosts concerts every summer in a series called Musique St. Bernard (see "Music," below).

SAINTE MARIE CHURCH
902-769-2832
baiesaintemarie.com/ste-marie
Rte. 1, Church Point
Open: Year-round for services; museum open with guided bilingual tours available mid-May–mid-Oct., 9 AM–5 PM
Admission: Donations, minimum $2 recommended

St. Mary's Church in Church Point is the largest church made of wood in North America.

The largest wooden church in North America rose up in this parish over the years between 1903 and 1905. The steeple is 56.4 meters or 185 feet tall—and would have been taller but for a lightning strike in 1914, when it was set on fire. Rain that immediately followed put out the fire, which parishioners saw as the protection of the Virgin Mary. Tall columns supporting the arched roof are solid tree trunks covered in plaster. The magnificent stained-glass windows were shipped from France packed between bags of molasses to keep them from breaking. The altar, also from France, was brought here by a cousin of a customs official—evading duty tax, my guide mentioned, because that captain was usually a rumrunner and his cousin never checked his cargo. A collection of statues of the Madonna in the exhibit rooms is a fascinating tour of the world on a few shelves. Pastor Edgar Mvubu, Congo-born, was in charge of the parish in 2008.

Galleries

ART GALLERY OF NOVA SCOTIA, YARMOUTH

902-749-2248
artgalleryofnovascotia.ca/en/yarmouth
341 Main St., P.O. Box 246, Yarmouth, NS B5A 4B2
Open: Mid-May—mid-Oct., daily 10 AM—5 PM; July—Aug., Thurs. till 8 PM; off-season Fri.—Sun. 12—5 PM.
Admission: Adults $5, seniors 60 and older $4, children 6—17 $2

Located in a former Royal Bank building, this western branch of the Art Gallery of Nova Scotia (in Halifax) was opened to make art more accessible in the province. Changing exhibitions bring a range of talent to the gallery, from plates by Walter Ostrom, a famed "master of maiolica," to pieces from the gallery's collection in Halifax. A 2008 show featured landscapes of the south shore, depicting all the variations of light and weather that arrive here. Workshops and school programs are often offered.

Historic Buildings and Sites

ARGYLE TOWNSHIP COURT HOUSE & ARCHIVES

902-648-2493
argylecourthouse.com
Rte. 3, Tusket, NS
Open: July—Aug., daily 9 AM—5 PM; May—June and Sept.—Oct., Mon.—Fri. 8:30 AM—4:30 PM; museum closed off-season, archives open year-round
Admission: Adults and seniors $2, children under 12 free

Canada's oldest court house and jail was built in 1804, and the first court session was held in 1805. This court saw a lot of bootleggers, who could pay $50 fine or spend three months in jail after they were convicted. Stubborn Sylvan LeFave, aka Blind Punch, was imprisoned six separate times for bootlegging in 1899, 1901, 1904, 1909, 1911, and 1913. The court reporter's desk and plain wood benches in the upstairs court room give a sense of the austerity of another time. Downstairs, six cells have been restored; they contain the cots the prisoners would sleep on. In the debtor's cell are bowls and other accessories. One cell is inhabited—by a dummy.

NEW FRANCE

Rte. 340 (17 miles inland from Weymouth, NS)

The remains of this once-thriving community are all that a visitor can see today. Founded by the Stehelin family from France, the town had electricity at the same time as Digby. From 1895 to 1912 it was the center of a lumber business that shipped boards on a short railroad to Weymouth to be exported. The Stehelins lived in an elaborate mansion, and elsewhere buildings housed a cookhouse for loggers, a chapel, a mill, a wine cellar, and lodging. Though the lumber business faded, and the town was abandoned, the town and its founders live on in the establishment of Université Ste-Anne.

Lighthouses

CAPE SABLE LIGHTHOUSE

At the end of The Hawk, southernmost tip of Cape Sable Island

This tall, automated lighthouse built in 1924 replaced the original lighthouse built in 1861. The fixed red light of the first lighthouse was kept going by John H. Doane. It was first erected after a ship, the *Hungarian*, smashed up on an offshore ledge.

CAPE FORCHU LIGHTHOUSE

902-742-4522
nslps.com
1856 Cape Forchu Rd., Yarmouth, NS
Open: Late May (or when The CAT begins service)–mid-Oct., Mon.–Sat. 11 AM–5 PM, Sun. 8:30 AM–to 5 PM
Admission: Free, donations accepted

This 1963 lighthouse stands on a narrow cape that extends like two prongs of a fork into the sea. The red and white vertical stripes make a distinctive pattern for ferry-goers entering the harbor at Yarmouth, and the light itself is visible for 22 miles. The lighthouse is owned by Yarmouth and run by the Friends of Yarmouth Light Society; its resident lightkeepers left in 1993, the last of any still caring for lighthouses in Nova Scotia. A small museum and gift shop are now installed in the keeper's house. A tearoom and restaurant serves fish chowder, seafood, picnic lunches packed in a returnable basket, and more. Breakfast is served Sunday starting at 8:30.

Museums and Living Museums

ARCHELAUS SMITH MUSEUM

902-745-3361
archelaus.org
915 Hwy. 330, Centreville, Cape Sable Island, NS
Mail: c/o Bryant Newell, P.O. Box 190, Clark's Harbour, NS B0W 1P0
Open: Mid-June–Aug., sometimes later in Sept., Mon.–Sat. 9:30 AM–5:30 PM, Sun. 1:30–5:30 PM
Admission: Free

Archelaus Smith, an early resident on Cape Sable Island, is also the name of a museum exhibiting fishing artifacts and genealogy records of the local, preloyalist fishing community. Smith was a local magistrate, surveyor, and pastor when no other was available. According to the Web site of the Archelaus Smith Historical Society, "Almost everyone on Cape Sable Island can trace their ancestry to Archelaus and his wife, Elizabeth."

BANGOR SAWMILL MUSEUM

877-462-5273
cardcity.com/mill
728 Maza Rd., Bangor, NS
Open: July–Aug., Tues.–Sun. 10:30 AM–4:30 PM
Admission: Adults $3

This water-powered sawmill from the 19th century was once one of many on the rivers of Nova Scotia, where the logs from inland woods, formed into booms, floated down to them through the summer season. It was built in the 1880s to replace the second mill on this site to be destroyed by fire, and it operated for 100 years. Blades with replacable teeth cut the logs into boards, and the boards built the towns and churches of the surrounding communities; other lumber was exported from the wharf in Yarmouth.

BARRINGTON WOOLEN MILL MUSEUM

902-637-2185
museum.gov.ns.ca/bwm
2368 Hwy. 3, Barrington, NS B0W 1E0
Open: June–Sept., Mon.–Sat. 10 AM–6 PM, Sun. 1–6 PM
Admission: Adults, children 6–17 and seniors 65 and older $3

Dressed like the mill workers of the late 1800s, guides at this woolen mill will help you understand how this 1882 factory worked. The community operated it, using the power of the water wheel to transform raw wool into cloth, thus relieving the local women from the hand washing, spinning, and weaving they had spent so much of their lives doing before it was built. The most yarn and cloth for blankets and clothing was made here in the first decade of the 1900s; but the mill operated up until 1962, when it was turned into a museum. A gift shop sells hand-knit socks, mittens, and hats, and natural-dyed wool hand-spun by the guides.

FIREFIGHTERS' MUSEUM OF NOVA SCOTIA

902-742-5525
museum.gov.ns.ca/fm
451 Main St., Yarmouth, NS B5A 1G9
Open: July–Aug., Mon.–Sat. 9 AM–9 PM, Sun. 10 AM–5 PM; June and Sept. Mon.–Sat. 9 AM–5 PM; Oct.–May, Mon.–Fri. 9 AM–4 PM, Sat. 1–4 PM
Admission: Adults $3, seniors 75 and older $2.50, children 6–17 $1.50

Nova Scotia is "a province made of wood," and firefighting has been needed from the beginning of European settlement. From a horse-drawn steam engine, the Amoskeag Steamer made in 1863 to a 1922 Model T Hose Truck, the engines that have fought fires in Canada are here and on display. With communities under constant threat of fire, these inventions helped many survive. Children can put on a firefighter's helmet and take the wheel of the 1933 Chevrolet Bickle Pumper. Handicapped accessible.

HISTORIC ACADIAN VILLAGE
LE VILLAGE HISTORIQUE ACADIEN DE LA NOUVELLE-ÉCOSSE
902-762-2530
museum.gov.ns.ca./av/
Rte. 335, West Pubnico
Mail: P.O. Box 70, Lower West Pubnico, NS B0W 2C0
Open: June–mid-Oct., daily 9 AM–5 PM
Admission: Adults $4, seniors 65 and older, $3.50, students 18 and younger, $2, children 6 and younger free.

Acadians have lived in West Pubnico since 1653, the year Sieur Philippe Mius-d'Entremont arrived to found the town. The Historic Acadian Village, with its Acadian houses, wharf, and walks set on a 17-acre point of land, was built beginning in 1997 with local contributions of buildings, money, and labor, and with government support. Open since 1999, the village presents Acadian-speaking citizens busy in the old ways of life, fishing and farming. View a blacksmith shop, salt-marsh haystack, the fish shed, and the Charles Duon and Maximin d'Entremont houses.

MUSÉE ACADIEN
902-762-3380
museeacadien.com
Rte. 335, West Pubnico, NS B0W 3S0
Open: mid-June–mid-Sept., Mon.–Sat. 9 AM–5 PM, Sun. 12:30–4:30 PM
Admission: Adults $3, children 12 and under free

Opened in 1979, this museum shows visitors the life of French settlers in the area in the 1700s and 1800s. French settlers here built the aboiteaux, wooden pipes with a moving door—open to let rain out, closed to keep salt water away—that drained salt marshes inside earthen dikes, and one example was found in 1990 when boards were seen sticking out of a salt marsh on Double Island, also called Île-de-Grave. That aboiteau is now on exhibit at the museum. More than 300 cameras give a glimpse into another development—the history of photography. Different examples from a family-owned collection of hand-carved birds by the late Richard d'Entremont, beautifully painted in precise detail, is exhibited here every year.

OLD MEETINGHOUSE MUSEUM
902-637-2185
museum.gov.ns.ca/omh/
2408 Hwy. 3, Barrington, NS B0W 1E0
Open: June–Sept., Mon.–Sat. 9:30 AM–5:30 PM, Sun. 1–5:30 PM
Admission: Adults, seniors and children 6–17 $3

Built to house all the religious worship practiced in the area, the Old Meeting House was the center of the town in 1765. Fifty Cape Cod families settled here and built it together to have a place to meet and do the business of the town. The building became neglected when

Seal Island Light Museum in Barrington is lighted every year on Christmas.

churches were built and a local courthouse went up, leaving it without a purpose. But today the Cape Sable Historical Society manages the building and oversees exhibits. The old graveyard next door holds headstones for the original settlers. A church service is held here the first Sunday in August, led by a different denomination every year.

SEAL ISLAND LIGHTHOUSE MUSEUM

902-637-2185
2410 Hwy. 3, Barrington, NS B0W 1E0
Open: June–Sept., Mon.–Sat. 9:30 AM–5:30 PM, Sun. 1–5:30 PM
Admission: Adults, children, and seniors $3, under 5 free

Visitors can climb five stories to the cast-iron lantern on top of this reconstruction and touch the Fresnel lens. That top structure, the original lantern from the Seal Island Lighthouse, was supposed to go to Ottawa, but the locals protested so loudly it was taken by helicopter to Barrington instead. The lens is lighted for Christmas. In the museum, the stories of Cable Sable Lighthouse, as well as the lighthouses on Bon Portage and Seal Island, are told. An ice cream and snack bar in front of the museum is ready to reward you when you come back down.

WEDGEPORT SPORT TUNA FISHING MUSEUM

902-663-4345
wedgeporttunamuseum.com
57 Tuna Wharf Rd., P.O. Box 488, Lower Wedgeport, NS B0W 2B0
Open: June and Aug., daily 10 AM–6 PM; Sept.–May, Mon.–Fri. 9 AM–4 PM
Admission: Adults $2, children 12 and under free

This museum opened in 1996 to present the memorabilia of the 1930s when this town stood at the pinnacle of tuna sport fishing. Tuna tournaments are still held every summer in mid-August, but Ernest Hemingway isn't participating. After all, he wouldn't be able to reel in an 800-pound tuna these days. The heaviest catch at the 2007 tournament were two tuna that together weighed 707 pounds.

Wedgeport was settled by Acadians who had been deported and returned to Nova Scotia from around Boston, and Acadian history is also presented in the museum.

W. LAURENCE SWEENEY FISHERIES MUSEUM

902-742-4357
sweeneyfisheriesmuseum.ca
112 Water St., Yarmouth, NS B5A 1L5
Open: May–Oct., Sat.–Sun. 10 AM–6 PM
Admission: Call for current prices

This museum is a replica of a fishing wharf, with fishing, processing and repair sheds, and a coastal freighter, a 1/3-scale model, you can explore. The galley and the sleeping quarters give a clear picture of life on the ship. The site once held a large fish-processing plant owned by W. Laurence Sweeney; his son and two daughters have put together the museum, re-creating the world their father ran. Fishing boats owned by the plant, some of the 80 built or contracted for over the years, brought in swordfish killed by harpoon darts—harpoons are on display in the fishing stores—and their holds were also full of cod and haddock caught with long lines, fishing lines that dangled many baited hooks. Wheelchair accessible.

YARMOUTH COUNTY MUSEUM

902-742-5539
yarmouthcountymuseum.ednet.ns.ca
22 Collins St., Yarmouth, NS B5A 3C8
Open: Mid-May–mid-Oct., daily 9 AM–5 PM, archives closed Sun.; off-season Tues.–Sat. 1–5 PM
Admission: Adults $3, seniors 65 and older $2.50, students $1; $1 extra to enter the other properties, open only mid-May–mid-Oct.

An 1800 Acadian loom, a child's room full of antique toys, and an oil portrait of the ship *Souvenir*, painted in 1875 by Belgian Jean Loos, are among the excellent artifacts collected at this museum, run by the Yarmouth County Historical Society. There's also a large costume collection. The society also runs the **Pelton-Fuller House,** 20 Collins St. (next door to the Yarmouth County Museum), summer home of the man who made a fortune with the Fuller Brush Company. The house has a collection of antique glass and silver as well as fine furniture. At another property, the **Killam Brothers Shipping Office,** 90 Water St., there is a noteworthy double stand-up desk so worn that the cash drawer has grooves.

Music

MUSIQUE DE LA BAIE, ACADIAN KITCHEN PARTIES
902-837-7100, 877-462-5273
Municipality of Clare, NS
Open: Evenings in July and Aug.
Admission: Free with meal at venue

Acadian kitchen parties with entertainment by musicians are scheduled Monday through Friday for the two months of summer, and they take place at restaurants in the municipality of Clare.

MUSIQUE ST. BERNARD
902-638-8288
St. Bernard Church, Old Rte. 1 (Exit 28 off Rte. 101), St. Bernard, County of Clare, NS E0W 2M0
Open: Series runs in June and Sept.
Admission: Adults $15, students and children $5

This classical-music series, with some concerts of folk and music from other countries, is a draw for people in the whole region, who drive here from Yarmouth to the south and Wolfville to the north. At least half of the concerts are choral music. The concerts enjoy beautiful acoustics in this historic church (see above under Churches.)

Seasonal Events

June
Annual Tern Festival (museeacadien.ca), at the Acadian Village, Le Village Acadien, West Pubnico.
Rhubarb Festival (museeacadien.ca), at the Acadian Village, Le Village Acadien, West Pubnico.
Yarmouth and Acadian Shores Lobster Festival, Yarmouth.

July
Festival Acadien de Clare, Municipality of Clare. Look for the quilt exhibit at the church in Saulnierville.
Nova Scotia Marathon and Half-Marathon (barringtonmunicipality.com), Barrington.
Quilt Expo and Sale (museeacadien.ca), at the Acadian Village, Le Village Acadien, West Pubnico.

August
Clare Bluegrass Festival (clarebluegrass.org), Saulnierville.
Expo-Couverte géante, Giant quilt Expo, Église Sacré-Coeur (902-769-2113), Saulnierville.
Historical Reenactment Camp, Yarmouth.
Wedgeport Tuna Tournament, Wedgeport.

September
Beausoleil Music Festival, Quinan.

October
Haunted Village (museeacadien.ca), at the Historic Acadian Village, Le Village Acadien, West Pubnico.

RECREATION

Beaches
Mavillette Beach State Park (902-424-5937; novascotiaparks.ca), Mavillette. The best-loved beach of the area is this 1.5-kilometer or 1-mile sand beach with a dune carpeted with marram grass. A large sand flat is exposed at low tide, and observation platforms overlook the salt marsh for visitors to bird-watch—perhaps seeing willets or sharp-tailed sparrows. Changing rooms, boardwalk, and fresh water taps.
Port Maitland Provincial Park (902-424-5937; novascotiaparks.ca), Port Maitland. Picnic tables and a long, sandy beach bordered by shallow tidal estuaries.

Bird Watching
Cape Sable The site of migratory birds feeding by the thousands, Cape Sable is the southernmost point of Nova Scotia. Drive past stunted spruce hung with lichen, through this skinned land battered by the sea to the **Hawk Point Flats** in spring and fall to see the thousands of migrating birds that use this area for a staging point, before another long leg of their journey. The Brant, which has a similar appearance to the Canadian goose and breeds in the Arctic, is one of the most unusual bird species to pass through here.

This fishing boat has retired off Hawk Point Flats, where migratory birds can be seen every spring and fall by the thousands.

Golf

Clare Golf & Country Club (902-769-2124; claregolf.ca), 423 P. F. Comeau Rd.,
Comeauville. An 18-hole course on St. Mary's Bay, with a restaurant specializing in
Acadian dishes.

West Pubnico Golf and Country Club (902-762-2007), Greenwood Rd., Pubnico. Usually
open March to November, this 18-hole course features an island green at the 15th hole.

Yarmouth Links (902-742-2161), at corner of Kempt and Forbes sts, in the south end of
Yarmouth. Part of the Yarmouth Golf and Curling Club, this is an 18-hole links-style
course.

Parks

Ellenwood Lake Provincial Park (902-761-2400; novascotiaparks.ca), Deerfield.
Swimming in this warm lake is a favorite summer recreation for locals, and lifeguards
are on duty. Fishermen come here for the pickerel and trout (online fishing licenses are
available at gov.ns.ca/fish/), and canoeing is great. Several rare plants grow on the
rocky shore that visitors are asked to leave undisturbed: pink coreopsis, Plymouth gen-
tian, and water pennywort. Wooded campsites have their own beach (unsupervised).
A trail winds through the woods.

Joseph and Marie Dugas Park (902-424-5937; novascotiaparks.ca), Belliveau Cove.
Next to the Information Centre is this lighthouse and park that leads to a 5-kilometer or
3-mile walk and informational panels about local birds and wildlife, ending at an old
Acadian cemetery.

Sand Hills Provincial Park (902-424-5937; novascotiaparks.ca), Villagedale. Changing
rooms and picnic tables are amenities next to the 2.5-kilometer or 1.5-mile white sand
beach, and the entrance is located at the border of Coffinscroft and Villagedale.

Smuggler's Cove Provincial Park (902-424-5937; novascotiaparks.ca), Meteghan. Now
with viewing platforms and steps to the beach, this spot was long a favorite of rumrun-
ners during Prohibition.

SHOPPING

Blacksmiths

Clare Blacksmithing (902-769-2516; fundyarts.com), 143 Lower Mill Rd., Concession.
Decorative wrought-iron fences, gates, door hardware, brackets, and metal sculptures.

Bookstores

Librairie Sigogne, Université Sainte-Anne (902-769-3562), Pointe-de-l'Église, Church
Point. This campus store sells French children's books, novels, and Acadian history
books, CDs of French music, and more.

Galleries

La galerie Comeau (902-769-2896; lagaleriecomeau.com), 761 Comeauville,
Saulnierville. Paintings of the landscape, and abstracts and prints, by Denise Comeau,
with a focus on the Acadian region of Clare.

Gift and Specialty Shops

Hands On Crafts (902-742-3515; handsoncerafts.ca), 314 Main St., Yarmouth. All Nova Scotia—made crafts are sold at this shop, along with yarn and rug-hooking supplies.

The Yarmouth Wool Shoppe (902-742-2255), 352 Main St., Yarmouth. The 100-plus selection of clan tartans is sure to thrill a Scottish heart, and Nova Scotia tartan is made up in kilts, shawl, throws, and more. Inuit carvings, celtic jewelry, wool yarns, and a huge array of hats—Balmoral to safari—are also on the shelves. Open till 9 PM on Friday.

Glass

Sous Le Soleil (902-769-0861; jayleblanc.ca), 131 Cottreau Rd., Little Brook. Jay LeBlanc makes stained-glass pieces with shells and stone, copper wire, and small gaps; the pieces resemble abstract mosaics and are full of vitality.

A re-creation of an Acadian House, Annapolis Royal Historic Gardens

DIGBY AND ANNAPOLIS ROYAL TO WOLFVILLE

The Fertile Valley

In 1604 the French established Port Royal, near today's Port Annapolis, in what they called Acadie, Acadia. The original buildings were destroyed in 1613. The Habitation, at Port-Royal National Historic Site, is a replica of the first settlement based on duplicates of the plans; the staff wears historic costumes at this popular tourist site.

In 1755 and for several years afterward, about 10,000 French settlers were expelled from Nova Scotia by British authorities who believed this action would stop dissension against their rule. This chapter of suffering—many Acadians died in the ships taking them away—is now commemorated at Grand-Pré National Historic site near Wolfville.

The Evangeline Trail is the provincial name for the route hugging this coastline and passing through its friendly towns. Annapolis Royal features the spectacular Historic Gardens full of roses, and north in the smooth, green land are grown stupendous crops of apples. Digby is famous for its scallops and large scallop fleet. At the end of Digby Neck several whale-watching companies operate tour boats through the summer.

Farther up the coast, Halls Harbour is a fine place to witness the world's highest tides, especially while dining on a lobster at its famous lobster pound. Cape Split's "hell-hole," a long hike to the sea, displays the powers of three tidal currents intersecting.

ANNAPOLIS ROYAL, DIGBY, AND THE SOUTHWEST BEACHES

LODGING

ANNAPOLIS ROYAL

DRAGONFLY INN
Cori Horton, innkeeper
902-532-7936, 877-943-2378
dragonflyinn.ca

124 Victoria St., P.O. Box 715, Annapolis Royal, NS B0S 1A0
Open: Apr.–Nov., closed Dec.–Mar.
Price: $69 to $139
Credit cards: Yes
Handicapped Access: Yes, Room 9
Special Features: Wi-Fi, AC, down duvets, pets allowed in some rooms

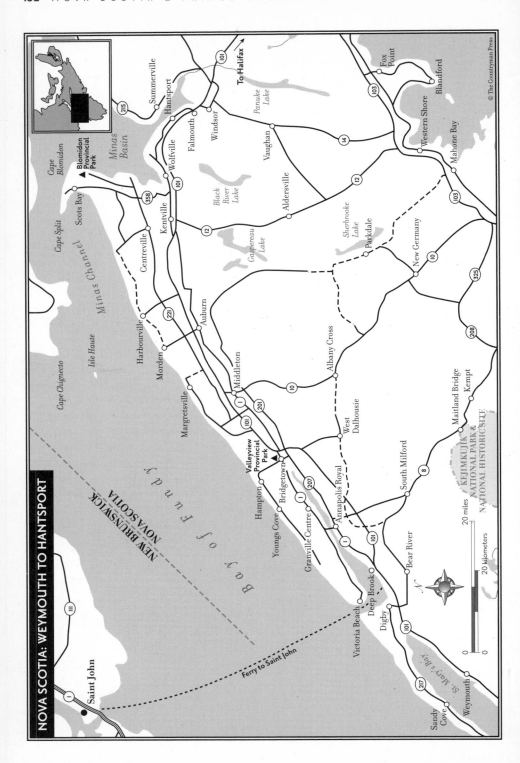

NOVA SCOTIA: WEYMOUTH TO HANTSPORT

© The Countryman Press

Bed-and-breakfast rooms are inside the main house, while six rooms, in multiple shades of red, with a continental breakfast served in a buffet from July to September, are rented for a lower rate in the coach house. Everywhere a love of deep color and engaging art reigns, along with the comfort of feather beds, the availability of great coffee, and the expert advice of Cori Horton, who provides all her guests with a detailed rundown of the best local restaurants. Breakfast at either eight or nine o'clock might be french toast with organic maple syrup or fresh berry muffins. Cookies arrive in your room in the evening. Tiled baths inside the main house are in an array of colors and textures.

GARRISON HOUSE

902-532-5750
garrisonhouse.ca
350 St. George St., Annapolis Royal, NS BoS 1Ao
Price: $69 to $149
Credit cards: Yes
Handicapped Access: No
Special Features: A ghost of a young girl named Emily

With seven rooms available, Garrison House has earned its reputation for comfort and hospitality (see the review in the Restaurants section, below). Each room has its own private bath with Italian tile and antique furniture. A canopied double bed in Room 3 is in a cozy room with a tile-floor bathroom. Garrison House Room 1 has a couple of wingback chairs to relax in after your long exploration of nearby Annapolis Royal Historic Gardens; you can sip a cup of tea provided by the host, if you request it. Next door is the Fort Anne Historic Site, another long day's worth of exploration. Although the building was first called The Temperance Hotel, you can enjoy a glass or bottle of wine from the restaurant.

HILLSDALE HOUSE

902-532-2345
hillsdalehouseinn.ca
519 St. George St., Annapolis Royal, NS BoS 1Ao
Price: $79 to $149
Credit cards: Yes
Handicapped Access: Limited, ground-floor room, no accessible bathroom
Special Features: Wi-Fi, picnic lunches available, croquet, bocce, horseshoe pit, pets welcome

With 13 rooms in the main inn and in the attached carriage house, formal parlors and 12 acres of lawn, gardens, and trees, Hillsdale House is an established presence among luxury inns. Climb the two wooden steps into the four-poster canopy bed in Room 1, where Queen Victoria's grandson, later George V, is reported to have spent a night in 1884. Today, you will have the advantage of a flat-screen television. Seating on the grounds and the veranda, and a good breakfast, along with the lawn games and a glass of wine or cocktail in the evening at this Italianate 1859 inn, all show the benefit of the hospitality practiced here.

QUEEN ANNE INN

902-532-7850, 877-536-0403
queenanneinn.ns.ca
494 Upper St. George St., Annapolis Royal, NS BoS 1Ao
Price: $99 to $209
Credit cards: Yes
Handicapped Access: Yes, in carriage house

Ten rooms in the main inn and four in the carriage house are all air-conditioned, the better to let you appreciate the antiques and pretty details. Room 8, with its carved wood bedstead and Victorian-style upholstered chair, is a study in comfort. The carriage-house rooms, for example Room 11, are more rustic in style, with exposed beams and paler wood floors. With 600 square feet on two levels, Room 11 has enough room for a family. Feather beds, bath salts, and other perks outfit all the rooms.

DIGBY

THE BREAKERS BED & BREAKFAST

Greg and Betty Cook, innkeepers
902-245-4643, 866-333-5773
thebreakersbb.com
5 Water St., Digby, NS B0V 1A0
Price: $125 to $139
Credit cards: Yes
Handicapped Access: None
Special Features: Wi-Fi

Close to Digby's little downtown, The Breakers is open year-round (but off-season reservations are required) and nicely situated for exploring Digby Neck, one of the most scenic spots in Nova Scotia. The granola served at breakfast, in a room of early pine furniture, is also sold for a snack on your day trip—but try to make a meal at Lavena's Catch (reviewed in the Restaurant section below) part of the journey. The Neoclassical mid-1800s house holds three rooms with all the amenities, including reading and writing areas and of course private baths. Each room is ornately

The East Room at Montegue Row B&B, in Digby

decorated, with floral or elaborate wallpaper, old lamps, and dark wood furniture.

DIGBY PINES GOLF RESORT AND SPA

902-245-2511, 800-667-4637
signatureresorts.com
103 Shore Rd., P.O. Box 70, Digby, NS B0V 1A0
Open: Mid-May—mid-Oct.
Price: $160 to $175
Credit cards: Yes
Handicapped Access: Limited
Special Features: Wi-Fi, outdoor pool, spa, tennis, walking trails, pub, restaurant, and bar

Seventy-eight rooms, 30 cottages with fireplaces, and six housekeeping suites are all set close to the 18-hole golf course that attracts many of the guests to a vacation here. Children's programs may help the whole family enjoy their stay if both parents want to be on the links. Guests can also match wits with the giant outdoor chess set, or while away the afternoon playing croquet.

❂ MONTAGUE ROW BED AND BREAKFAST

Heather Jenkins, innkeeper
902-245-6039, 866-905-7755
montaguerow.com
66 Montague Row, P.O. Box 1411, Digby, NS B0V 1A0
Open: May—Oct.
Price: $70 to $120
Credit cards: Yes
Handicapped Access: None
Special Features: Wi-Fi

Heather Jenkins spent some of her previous life in the Middle East, as the inlaid chess set and brass trays reveal; in one of the bedrooms, the East Room, a wide flat basket like a platter, in warm, earthy colors hangs on the pale mustard walls. Affixed to the wall at the head of the bed are two old doors, polished and glowing with their handsome stained wood. Out the two windows is the view of the channel and of Digby Neck, the tongue of land that reaches out and to the south, providing Digby with its famous protected waters and scallop fishing fleet. The South Suite is larger and also eclectically decorated.

Breakfast in her formal dining room might be tender scrambled eggs, bacon, and whole-wheat toast with homemade strawberry preserves. The coup de grace is the just-squeezed orange juice, perfection in a glass.

THISTLE DOWN COUNTRY INN

902-245-4490, 800-565-8081
thistledown.ns.ca
98 Montague Row, P.O. Box 508, Digby, NS
B0V 1A0
Open: May–Oct.
Price: $75 to $130
Credit cards: Yes
Handicapped Access: None
Special Features: Wi-Fi, pets allowed

The view of the Digby Harbor is one of the virtues of Thistledown Inn, with its bright rooms, some outfitted with fringed curtains and four-poster beds. The 12 different rooms all have air-conditioning and private baths, and the parlor in the 1904 house is outfitted with antiques. A scallop omelet might be for breakfast. The inn is within a short walk of the small village of Digby and its working waterfront.

RESTAURANTS

ANNAPOLIS ROYAL

CAFÉ COMPOSÉ

902-532-1251
235 St. George St., Annapolis Royal
Open: 11:30 AM–2 PM and 5–8 PM, except Wed. and Sun closed for lunch; closed mid-Nov.–mid-Apr.
Price: $17 to $24

Credit cards: Yes
Cuisine: Austrian
Serving: L, D
Handicap Access: No

With the best ambiance in town, according to an enthusiastic patron, Café Composé is a small but consistent restaurant that is perfect for lunch. Nothing served is deep fried, and everything is cooked from scratch using some organic ingredients. Pan-fried salmon or haddock comes with white wine parsley sauce, a shrimp skewer, and seasonal vegetables and roasted garlic potatoes. The schnitzel is made with sirloin pork steak, roasted garlic potatoes, and carrots, Brussels sprouts, zucchini. Linzertorte, apple strudel—warmed—with vanilla ice cream, are desserts. Gruener Veltliner, a white wine, and Zweigelt, a red wine, both from Austria, are perfect with the meals.

GARRISON HOUSE

902-532-5750
garrisonhouse.ca
350 St. George St., Annapolis Royal
Open: Mid-May–Oct., daily 5–9 PM
Price: $16 to $29
Credit cards: Yes
Cuisine: Continental with Asian and Cajun influences
Serving: D
Handicap Access: No

The good reputation of this dining room makes it a magnet for hungry travelers. Local wild mushroom soup or a salad made with local greens could precede a main course of Vietnamese coconut milk shrimp and chicken curry, or a dish of hot, spicy jambalaya. Someone less intrigued by Asian or Cajun cuisine could enjoy the poached salmon with a bourbon and maple glaze, or Digby scallops cooked with roasted garlic, basil, and sun-dried tomatoes. The plates will not stint on the fresh vegetable side dishes, and the wine list features Nova Scotian wines along with international labels.

GERMAN BAKERY & GARDEN CAFE

902-532-1990
441 St. George St., Annapolis Royal
Open: Mid-May–mid-Oct., daily 8 AM–6 PM
Price: $5 to $6
Credit cards: No
Cuisine: German
Serving: L, D
Handicap Access: Yes
Special Features: Covered outdoor café and terrace

You can access this outdoor café from either the street or the Annapolis Royal Historic Gardens next door. During the morning and mid-afternoon, who could resist the apple strudel, or the Danishes made with blueberries, cherries, apples or chocolate? For a more substantial meal, the café serves schnitzel, ham, tuna and chicken or roast beef sandwiches on its own white or whole wheat bread, or a seven-grain Kaiser roll. Pizza, a daily soup, and two salads are also on the short menu.

LEO'S CAFE

902-532-7424
222 St. George St., Annapolis Royal
Open: Mon.–Sat. 9 AM–4 PM
Price: $5 to $10
Credit cards: Yes
Cuisine: Soups, salads, and sandwiches
Serving: L
Handicap Access: No
Special Features: Outside deck for good-weather dining

The fresh salads, fresh-baked bread, and everything else are made here. Paula Buxton, trained at the Culinary Institute of America in Hyde Park, New York, makes a mile-high lemon-meringue pie that amazes on sight. The large sandwiches are made to order with freshly cut bread and as much local produce as possible. The popular veggie sandwich is made with a spread of ground sunflower seeds. Soups change

daily; one was Thai pineapple chicken soup. "I have about 150 soups; I try to do what's in season." Buxton said. Blueberry season brings blueberry sour cream pie, enormous blueberry muffins, and a two-crust blueberry pie.

✪ QUEEN ANNE INN

902-532-7850, 877-536-0403
queenanneinn.ns.ca
494 Upper St. George St., Annapolis Royal
Open: Tues.–Sat. at 6 PM
Price: $15 to $24
Credit cards: Yes
Cuisine: Seafood
Serving: D
Handicap Access: No
Special Features: Dinner served on the deck on weekends in good weather

The 14-foot high ceilings of this elegant inn endow the dining room with a special elegance, but what's on the plates keeps locals eager to return. Grilled sweet and spicy shrimp salad and lobster Waldorf salad are two things found on one summer menu; pot stickers and mussels with coconut cream are two starters. Greg Pyle, the owner of the inn, has sought out sustainable seafood to serve on his menu, so you can be confident your dinner isn't depleting the oceans. Blackened Arctic char, Cajun style, might come with roasted potatoes. Lovers of lobster can taste it three ways: curried, creamed, or steamed. Vegetable stew and vegetable stir-fry cater to vegetarians, the stew made with a yogurt and mustard sauce.

Digby

ED'S TAKEOUT

902-245-2071
424 Hwy. 303, Digby NS B0V 1A0
Open: May–Sept., 11 AM–9 PM; closing earlier off-season and end of Dec.–Apr.
Price: $6 to $20
Credit cards: Yes

Carla Crowell is the manager at Ed's Take-Out, Digby.

Cuisine: Seafood and burgers
Serving: L, D
Handicap Access: No
Special Features: Free fries if you buy a specially marked yellow or orange gumball from the machine

In business for more than 40 years, Ed's Takeout is respected near and far for its high-quality deep-fried seafood. When I dropped in, Carla Crowell, manager for seven years, was getting things organized for another busy day. "We cook by sound," Crowell said. "They make a lot of noise in the fryer. The sound changes when they're ready." Since she does everything in the kitchen, including changing the oil every two days, she has learned to keep track with expert ears. Tartar sauce is made in-house. The clams come from South Shore diggers. Onion rings, poutine, a double burger, clam roll, scallop roll, and a seafood platter are a few highlights of the basic menu.

FUNDY RESTAURANT
902-245-4950, 866-445-4950
fundyrestaurant.com
34 Water St., Digby
Open: June–Aug., daily 8 AM–10 PM; off-season, daily 11 AM–8 PM
Price: $17 to $28

Credit cards: Yes
Cuisine: Seafood, pasta, and steak
Serving: B, L, D
Handicap Access: Yes
Special Features: Two waterside decks

The 11-pound lobster in the tank was on offer to anyone with $215 or so who wanted to eat it. Yes, the texture is a little tougher with such a large lobster, the polite host said, but it tastes like lobster.

Well, the scallops are much better. Try them with bacon as an appetizer. If you use the appetizer as a main course (skipping the baked potato or rice in the dinner, as I did), you will be getting just as many. Nevertheless I wanted the scallops pan-seared with garlic butter, not with bacon,

A dinner out at Fundy Restaurant, on the upper deck, in Digby

and I wanted a Greek salad on the side ($1.50 extra) instead of the potato or rice. These made an excellent supper, the scallops cooked precisely to translucency, still tender and utterly fresh.

Solomon Gundy is pickled herring, made in a plant just south of town in Saulnierville and worth tasting. The two decks fill up with Fundy's customers, and with a glass border around the top deck, the view and the action on the wharf are fun to watch.

FREEPORT

✪ LAVENA'S CATCH CAFE

902-839-2517
15 Hwy. 217, Freeport, on Digby Neck
Open: Mid-May—mid-Oct., daily 11 AM—8 PM; off-season, weekends only 4—9 PM
Price: $7 to $14
Credit cards: Yes
Cuisine: Seafood, but no deep frying

Serving: L, D
Handicap Access: Yes
Special Features: Outdoor seating, local musicians offer monthly entertainment in summer, biweekly in winter.

Set on a hill, Lavena's Catch Café is one of those places everyone knows about and loves to come to. A small or large bowl of chowder or a plate of Solomon Gundy, the region's excellent pickled herring, makes a perfect start to a meal. "Just Scallops" is a favorite main course, pan-seared or oven-baked, but they also come wrapped in bacon, in a haddock and scallop sampler. Try the egg tart for dessert—with vinegar, sugar, and vanilla beaten and cooked in a pastry shell. "We sell thousands of those in a season," said owner and cook Lavena Crocker; her aunt does the baking. The luscious lemon pie or ice-cream sundae are excellent alternatives for dessert.

CULTURE

Art

THE REPLICA OF THE MAUD LEWIS HOUSE

902-245-2631
11585 Hwy. 217, Digby, NS B0V 1A0
Open: Daylight hours
Admission: $2 or by donation

The right turn off the road south on Digby Neck is sometimes hard to spot, but this little house, down a dirt road, is a wonderful monument to the narrow life of folk artist and heroine Maud Lewis, who lived nearby in Marshalltown until her death in 1970. Her original house, considered a work of folk art in itself, is now on display at the Art Gallery of Nova Scotia in Halifax. This replica is faithful to every detail, from the flower-painted windows and stove to the brightly colored door. What's more, you

The replica of the Maud Lewis House on Digby Neck presents her desk, cot, and reproductions of her painting all over the inside and outside of the house.

can go inside and climb the little staircase to see the cramped loft above, where Maud Lewis slept until her bad arthritis kept her downstairs on a couch.

Cultural Center

BEAR RIVER FIRST NATIONS HERITAGE & CULTURAL CENTER
902-467-0301
bearriverculturalcenter.com
194 Reservation Rd., P.O. Box 210, Bear River, NS B0S 1B0
Open: July–late Aug., Wed.–Sun. 9 AM–8 PM
Admission: $5, free for children 3 or younger

The Mi'kmaw (the correct pronunciation of Mi'kmaq in that language) heritage, culture, and spirit are the subjects of this center, with exhibits of the land's first inhabitants' tools and artifacts, some as old as 2,000 years, and demonstrations of songs and dance. Stories are told by a video and by the guides. A birchbark canoe completed in 2002 is modeled on the canoes that brought Mi'kmaw guides and hunters through the area for centuries. Guided walks on the Medicine Trail and "the medicines of the forest" are offered for $5. Bear River First Nation is one of 13 native communities in Nova Scotia.

Galleries

ARTsPLACE
902-532-7069, 800-228-4492
arcac.ca
396 St. George St., Annapolis Royal, NS
Open: Check exhibition schedule
Admission: Free

The Annapolis Region Community Arts Council founded in 1982 sponsors exhibitions of Nova Scotia artists, workshops, classes, and concerts. Its August fundraiser, Paint The Town, brings more than 80 artist to town to create works that are sold to benefit the organization.

Gardens

ANNAPOLIS ROYAL HISTORIC GARDENS
902-532-7018
historicgardens.com
441 St. George St., Annapolis Royal, NS B0S 1A0
Open: July–Aug., 8 AM–dusk; May–June and Sept.–Oct., 9 AM–5 PM
Admission: Adults $8.50, students and seniors 60 and older $7.50, children under 6 free

The formal and historic gardens of Annapolis Royal Historic Gardens are laid out close to the gardens' entrance. A 17th-century knot-garden, and an 18th-century garden that might have been planted at the time of the original British governor, are two pleasures to encounter on a walk. Farther away lies a replica Acadian house with an exterior bread oven and thatched roof. When you walk out on the top of the dike, re-created by machinery, the peace and tranquility of the area are like a balm. An example of the boiteau used by Acadians to drain the salt marsh is situated inside the garden. These wood-framed pipes with gates that shut out salt water and allowed fresh water to drain created the farms that made Acadians prosperous and envied. Magnificent roses, a heath and a daylily collection are other highlights. See **German Bakery and Garden Café** below for a description of the garden café.

Historic Buildings, Districts, and Sites

ANNAPOLIS ROYAL HISTORIC DISTRICT TOURS
902-532-3035
tourannapolisroyal.com
P.O. Box 659, Annapolis Royal, NS B0S 1A0
Open: Different tours listed in description below.
Admission: Adults $7, children 13 to 18 $3, 12 and under $1

The 131 registered historic properties of this small community, with less than 500 residents, make it the largest historic district in Canada. The Historical Association of Annapolis Royal offers several different guided tours of the historic district and sites, included evening, candlelight graveyard tours, given Sunday, Tuesday, Wednesday and Thursday at 9:30 PM at the Fort Anne National Historic Site, rain or shine (so to speak). National Historic District tours are offered Monday, Wednesday, and Thursday at 2 PM, starting at the Annapolis Royal lighthouse. Acadian Heritage tours are given Tuesday and Thursday at 2 PM, also at the Annapolis Royal lighthouse, when your guide can tell the story of his own ancestors' deportation and teach you a step or two of an Acadian dance.

FORT ANNE NATIONAL HISTORIC SITE
902-532-2397, in season only
parkscanada.qc.ca/fortanne
St. George St., P.O. Box 9, Annapolis, NS B0S 1A0
Open: Mid-May—mid-Oct.
Admission: Adults $3.90, children 6–16 $1.90 and seniors 65 and older $3.40

A tapestry depicting 400 years of history, woven by more than 100 people over four years, hangs in the Officers' Quarters Museum; it measures 18 feet long by 8 feet high. Military historians will want to examine the Vauban earthworks around the fort. Battles fought here between the French founders and the British endow the very earth with historic interest. The French arrived in 1604 and built the first fortifications of their capital of Acadia; they were taken over by the British in the 1620s, but they reverted to the French in the 1630s. The earthworks visible today were constructed after 1702. In 1710 the War of Spanish Succession put the fort back into British hands, after a seven-day siege. Thereafter, despite repeated attempts by the French to win it back, it remained in British hands and was the site of the deportation of Acadians from the area in 1755.

KEJIMKUJIK NATIONAL PARK & HISTORIC SITE
902-682-2772
pc.gc.ca/pn-np/ns/kejimkujik/
P.O. Box 236, Maitland Bridge, Annapolis County, NS B0T 1B0
Open: Mid-June—Labour Day, 8:30 AM–8 PM; Labour Day—mid-June, 8:30 AM–4:30 PM
Admission: Adults $5.80, seniors 65 and older $4.90, children 6–16 $2.90

A rental concession at Jakes Landing inside this park rents canoes, bicycles, and more. This inland park, the only one in the Maritimes, is full of canoe routes, portages, and trails that bring visitors up close to the wildlife of the region (like loons and barred owls) and the scenic beauty of the woods. Scallop-edged water pennywort, a threatened species, may be encountered at the edge of the waterways. Petroglyphs made by Mi'kmaq who lived here in the 18th and 19th centuries show fishing and hunting scenes. The areas where they are found are closed, but they can be seen during guided walks given by park interpreters. When Europeans arrived, they mined gold in three places inside the park, but there wasn't much gold in the ore. The area worked best as a sports destination, when Kedge Lodge was built and guides took sportsmen fishing and hunting.

PORT-ROYAL NATIONAL HISTORIC SITE

Mid-May–mid-Oct. 902-532-2898, off-season 902-532-2321
pc.gc.ca/lhn-nhs/ns/portroyal/
P.O. Box 9, Annapolis Royal, NS B0S 1A0
Open: July–Aug., daily 9 AM–6 PM; mid-May–June and Sept.–mid-Oct., daily 9 AM–5:30 PM
Admission: Adults $3.90, children 6–16 $1.90 and seniors 65 and older $3.40

At this reconstructed 17th-century site, costumed interpreters will show you how the days passed, scything hay or cultivating herbs, when the French were in charge of Acadia. That place started here with the arrival in the area of a Frenchman named Pierre Dugua de Monts in 1604. Although battles and a fickle government left his fur monopoly in tatters, his son remained to establish a life. The Order of Good Cheer, a club with a regular dinner meeting, set in motion a culture of resourceful fine dining, based on wild birds, moose, caribou, beaver, otter, raccoon, and other game. Pumpkin soup, steamed eel, and marzipan tarts might all have shown up at the table.

SINCLAIR INN NATIONAL HISTORIC SITE

902-532-7754
annapolisheritagesociety.com
230 St. George St., Annapolis Royal
Mail: 136 St. George St., P.O. Box 503, Annapolis Royal, NS B0S 1A0
Open: June–Aug., daily 9 AM–5 PM; Sept., Mon.–Fri. 9 AM–5 PM, Sat. 1–4 PM
Admission: Free

Built in 1710, Sinclair Inn shows off Acadian building techniques: clay walls made of a mixture of marsh grass and clay, mortice and tenon joints, and wood pins fastening the corners of the frame, made with hand-hewn rafters. In 1738 the building became a Masonic Lodge, the first in Canada.

Museums

BEAR RIVER HERITAGE MUSEUM

902-467-3809
1890 Clementsvale Rd., Bear River, NS B0S 1B0
Open: July–Sept., Mon.–Sat. 9:30 AM–4:30 PM, Sun. 1:30–4:30 PM
Admission: Free

Opened in 1983, Bear River Heritage Museum holds artifacts about life in the area since it was settled by Europeans and a large collection of military memorabilia.

HMCS/CFB CORNWALLIS MILITARY MUSEUM
902-638-3118
cornwallismuseum.ca
Hwy. 1, 726 Broadway, Clementsport, NS B0S 1E0
Open: End of June–Aug. Wed.–Mon. 10:30 AM–5 PM; to mid-Sept., 1:30–5 PM
Admission: Adults $3, children under 15 $1

Originally the Canadian Naval training base for World War II sailors, when as many as 11,000 people were working here, this facility became a center for the army, navy, and air force when the Canada's three military branches were unified. It closed in 1995, and has been transformed into an industrial park. The museum, inside the former St. George's Protestant church, holds donated artifacts and exhibits of all branches. The base is named after Edward Cornwallis, the founder of Halifax and Nova Scotia's governor from 1749 to 1752.

NORTH HILLS MUSEUM
902-532-2168
museum.gov.ns.ca/nhm/
5065 Granville Rd., Granville Ferry, NS
Mail: 136 St. George St., P.O. Box 503, Annapolis Royal, NS B0S 1A0
Open: June–mid-Oct., Mon.–Sat. 9:30 AM–5:30 PM, Sun. 1–5:30 PM
Admission: Adults $3, children 6–17 $2, seniors 65 and older $2

The old Rumsey Farm became the location of a vast collection of Georgian English ceramics, silver, and furniture, under the ownership of Robert Patterson. In 1974 he left the house and its contents to the province, which now opens it as a museum with the help of the Annapolis Heritage Society. Guide Bruce Gurnham called this one of the premier collections of Georgian art in Canada. It includes paintings by Thomas Buttersworth and Spaniard Francesco de Zurbarán, done from 1713 to 1830, when four king Georges reigned in England. In the guest book one visitor wrote, "Fascinating look at the highly cultured tastes of an eclectic collector."

O'DELL HOUSE MUSEUM
902-532-7754
annapolisheritagesociety.com
136 St. George St., P.O. Box 503, Annapolis Royal, NS B0S 1A0
Open: Late May–early Sept., daily 9 AM–5 PM; off-season, Mon.–Fri. 1–4 PM, but call ahead to confirm
Admission: Adults $3, seniors and children 6–17 $2

The destination for the stagecoach, and a longtime tavern, the O'Dell House Museum presents the interior of a late-Victorian house on the first floor, and exhibits on the second. The dining room is set for company, and in the parlor a Victorian grapeback sofa and chairs declare the accumulated wealth of the residents, who used most of the house as a tavern and inn. Corey O'Dell, the first tavern-keeper and owner, had been a rider in 1849 for the short-lived Pony Express, which took dispatches off ships in Halifax Harbour and rode them as fast as a horse could go to the ferry in Annapolis Royal, to get them to a telegraph office in New Brunswick—a system that was used during the first year of business for Associated Press, or AP.

TUPPERVILLE SCHOOLHOUSE MUSEUM
902-665-2427
auracom.com/tuppervillemuseum
2663 Rte. 201, Tupperville, NS
Mail: RR #3, Bridgetown, NS B0S 1C0
Open: Mid-May–early Sept., 10 AM–6 PM
Admission: Free

This 1869 or 1870 building, moved to its present location and active as a schoolhouse until 1970, gives children and teachers a vivid grasp of the way things were. There are lots of interesting items, among them a leather strap—not the school's original, but another one that was brought from Port Lorne Country School; after all, the item was in wide use for years and not rare. Examples of schoolwork make the past—and the children hunched over their desks—easy to imagine. A 100-year-old teacher's desk, the school bell, and carvings by Mi'kmaq Louis Jeremy, a much-admired local artisan, are a few of the charming details a visitor encounters here.

Music

MUSIC IN THE GARDENS
Annapolis Royal Historic Gardens
902-532-7018
historicgardens.com
441 St. George St., P.O. Box 278, Annapolis Royal, NS B0S 1A0
Open: Schedule varies
Admission: Varies

A concert series held in the summer months, Music in the Gardens includes classical, jazz, vocalists, and more. Call to confirm that any given event is in fact taking place.

Power Plant

TIDAL POWER PLANT
902-532-5454
tradeannapolis.com
236 Prince Albert Rd., P.O. Box 2, Annapolis Royal, NS B0S 1A0
Open: Mid-May–Sept. or later; Nova Scotia Power must permit the tours
Admission: Adults $4, must be 16 and older to go on the belowground tour

North America's only tidal power plant is located in Annapolis Royal, where you can be sure that the technology is a focus of much attention. The Straflo Turbine generates as much as 30 million kilowatt-hours a year. (Tours were canceled because of maintenance for most of the summer in 2008.) An exhibit upstairs in the Visitor's Information Centre, which conducts tours when Nova Scotia Power allows them, describes the generation of power. A traveler can call Nova Scotia Power, at 902-532-2306, and company representatives may be able to offer tours when the Visitor's Information Centre here is closed, from October to mid-May.

Theater

KING'S THEATRE
902-532-5466 for events, 902-532-7704
kingstheatre.ca
209 St. George St., P.O. Box 161, Annapolis Royal, NS BoS 1Ao
Open: Year-round
Admission: Varies according to events

A theater that shows movies and presents live performances of dance, music, and stage productions, King's Theatre also houses an art gallery, open May to October. The 1921 theater was on its last legs in the early 1980s, when it was sold at a sheriff's sale; but the Annapolis Royal Development Commission bought it and renovated it, bringing the building back to life. It's now run by the King's Theatre Society. A children's theater workshop is held in the summer. Eight 10-minute plays are performed during the King's Shorts Festival in mid-June.

Seasonal Events

May
Annapolis Valley Apple Blossom Festival (902-678-8322; appleblossom.com), Kentville.

July
Bear River Cherry Carnival (902-467-3633), Bear River.
Granville Ferry Annual Pig Roast (902-532-0901), Granville Ferry.

August
Annapolis Royal & Area Natal Days (902-526-0279; annapolisroyal.com), Annapolis Royal.
Digby Scallop Days (digbyscallopdays.com), Digby. Parades, scallop-shucking contest, recycled raft race, and more.
Military Encampment (902-532-2321; pc.gc.ca/fortanne), Fort Anne, Annapolis Royal.
Paint the Town (902-532-7069; arcac.ca), ARTsPLACE, Annapolis Royal.

September
Annual Ox Pull & Supper (902-467-3818), The George Allen Park & Forester's Hall, Clementsvale.

December
Silver Bells New Year's Eve Gala (902-532-7018; historicgardens.com), Annapolis Royal.

RECREATION

Amusement Parks

Upper Clements Parks (902-532-7557, 888-248-4567; upperclementspark.com), Hwy. 1, Upper Clements. Open Admission $8, seniors 65 and older $5, children 2 and under free. Tickets for rides $3, book of 10 $27 (all plus tax). Bumper boats and bumper cars, kiddie rides and rides on a rollercoaster, waterslide, and Rock-O-Planes. The Wildlife Park takes an hour to tour; it holds great horned owls, emus, black bears, caribou, foxes, beavers, the little Sable Island wild horses, and more.

Golf

Annapolis Royal Golf and Country Club (902-532-2064; annapolisroyalgolf.com), Rte. 1, Annapolis Royal. A restaurant, The 19th Hole, serves lunch and supper, and the Arthur Kennedy Restaurant is for fine dining. Tee times required on weekends only. A swimming pool is also available. There are terrific views of Annapolis Basin and the National Historic Site of Fort Anne.

Pines Resort Golf Course (902- 800-667-4637; digbypines.ca/pines_golf.html), Digby. Designed by Sir Stanley Thompson, this 18-hole par 71 course lies on the Bay of Fundy. The challenging course holds pine trees, a winding brook and ponds, and a hole that goes into a gorge. An avid Nova Scotian golfer calls this the best course in western Nova Scotia.

Hiking

Balancing Rock, near Tiverton on Digby Neck. An eroded rock that appears to be balancing, called (not surprisingly) Balancing Rock, is worth finding on the coastline.

Delap's Cove Wilderness Trail (902-532-2334; annapoliscounty.ns.ca), Annapolis County Recreation Department, Annapolis Royal, NS B0S 1A0. Views of the Bay of Fundy north of Annapolis Royal and the site of an abandoned town from as early as 1800, a black loyalist settlement, are alongside the trail system here. Bohaker, Charles, and the Shore Road trails take in a waterfall and the tides of the bay.

Whale Watching

For more detail about the ferries mentioned below, see "By Ferry" in Chapter Two, *Transportation.*

Brier Island Whale and Seabird Cruises (902-839-2995, 800-656-3660; brierisland whalewatch.com), 223 Water St., Westport. Two boats operate giving tours for this company, with five departures daily in season. The business operates out of Westport, on the last island at the end of Digby Neck, two ferry rides removed from the mainland. Captain Harold Graham has been working with whales for more than 20 years. Shelley Barnaby, an experienced naturalist, narrates during the cruises, which are three to five hours long and require a minimum of 10 people. Dress warmly.

Mariner Cruises (902-839-2346, 800-239-2189; novascotiawhalewatching.ca), Westport. This business, like the one above, operates out of Westport, on the last island at the end of Digby Neck, two ferry rides from the mainland. Cruises pass by Peter's Island Bird Sanctuary and include descriptions of the area's geology and history. In the spring,

166 NOVA SCOTIA & PRINCE EDWARD ISLAND

finback and minke whales and harbour porpoises are the first to show up in the Bay of Fundy; later on, humpback whales and white-sided dolphins join them. Cruises are two to five hours long. Dress warmly.

Ocean Explorations (902-839-2417, 877-654-2341; oceanexplorations.ca), Tiverton. Tim Goodwin, the owner and a biologist, has been taking visitors whale watching for more than 20 years. Right whales, an endangered species, are sighted in the summer, as are puffins and seals. His trips leave from Tiverton, near the ferry wharf, which is where your car will be delivered by the Tiverton ferry. Departures depend on reservations and when that ferry arrives, and trips last between two and two and a half hours. Warm clothes are a must, no matter what the time of year.

Shopping

Antiques

Far-Fetched Antiques & Art Gallery (902-532-0179; fairtrading.com), 27 Church St., Annapolis Royal. The owners travel for six months of the years, and bring back to Nova Scotia the best paintings and furniture and other art objects they encounter for sale in Asia. According to one local, visitors to town may arrive just in order to shop here; shipping to eastern Canada and the United States can be arranged.

Bookstores

Bear River Bargains + Books (902-467-0908), Main St., Bear River. Used books and old postcards, 19th- and 20th-century newspapers, magazines, maps, pamphlets and memorabilia.

Crooked Timber Books (902-245-1283; crookedtimber.com), 17 Water St., P.O. Box 2170, Digby. Bill Schrank sells a wide variety of books about history and economics, as well as fiction, mysteries, and cookbooks. A special focus on Irish literature, poetry, history, and drama.

Endless Shores Books (902-665-2029), 160 South St., Bridgetown. A coffee shop is a plus here, while browsing the collection of books covering all subjects—"Used books for the whole family," Lewis Falls calls his selection.

Crafts

Lucky Rabbit (902-532-0928; luckyrabbitpottery.ca), 15 Church St., Annapolis. Open May–Oct. Utterly delightful pottery—consider the golden squirrel on the back of the smiling jaguar, on the lid of a jar—fills this studio with bright colors like a coral orange, and the presence of fish and flowers and bees and more that are precise and yet full of whimsy complete the experience.

Gifts and Accessories

Flight of Fancy (902-467-4171), Main St., Bear River. Open mid-May–Dec. 24. Inside a village on a tidal river, this shop sells work by Nova Scotia artisans including burl turnings, jewelry, pottery, Mi'kmaq crafts, bone and antler sculpture, and Maritime books.

The Blomidon Inn in Wolfville

Grand Pré and Wolfville Area

Lodging

BLOMIDON INN

800-565-2291
blomidon.ns.ca
195 Main St., Wolfville, NS B4P 1C3
Price: $99 to $269
Credit cards: Yes
Handicapped Access: Yes, one unit
Special Features: High-speed Internet (plug-in), AC, dining room, gardens, tennis

The elaborately carved four-poster in which I slept so soundly, in "Cape Split" (all the rooms are named and not numbered) had two little steps for climbing up to its high mattress. Perhaps it was that sense of climbing away from it all that made resting here so easy. An alcove bed in the same room would be perfect for a smaller child. The Jacuzzi in the bathroom was another route to relaxation, but best of all was one detail not always attended to—the thickest, softest towels you'll ever encounter in an inn. Blomidon Inn was built by a sea captain and shipbuilder who bought the land for $1,400 and made his money when trade between the New World and the old depended on his sailing ships. The inn's 29 units all have private bathrooms; two suites and a cottage in the 4 acres of gardens that surround the inn are among the accommodations that offer a fireplace. Two front parlors hold comfortable Victorian furniture to relax in, with a cup of tea. The next-door gift shop sells ornate iron planters outside its doors and hats, art, and gardening accessories within.

THE DELFT HOUSE B&B
Ray and Debra Ridley, innkeepers
902-678-4333, 866-851-4333
delfthaus.com
1942 Hwy. 359, Centreville, NS B0P 1J0
Price: $115 to $139
Credit cards: Yes
Handicapped Access: Limited
Special Features: Wi-Fi, mountain bikes free to use, laundry facilities

Four-poster beds and private baths are the foundations of the high-quality hospitality here, along with the hosts' detailed suggestions for days of exploration and a massage in the therapy room available if you walked too far out during low tide. The Daffodil Room is a suite with a commodious place to relax or read, and the Orchid Room with handsome dark-wood furniture holds a little foot stool beside the Victorian-style chairs. Breakfast might be stuffed french toast and fruit, or local eggs and bacon, and Debra Ridley's own whole-grain molasses and honey bread comes with damson plum jam or strawberry jam made in this kitchen with fresh fruit.

✪ EVANGELINE INN AND MOTEL
The Sterling Family, innkeepers
902-542-2703, 888-542-2703
evangeline.ns.ca
11668 Hwy. 1, P.O. Box 4, Grand Pré, NS B0P 1M0
Price: Inn rooms $95 to $115, motel $75 to $95
Credit cards: Yes

Handicapped Access: Yes
Special Features: Wi-Fi, indoor pool

In the inn, once the home of Sir Robert Borden, Canadian statesman and prime minister from 1911 to 1920, you can stay in one of five rooms with private baths, three with private entrances. Each room comes with breakfast in the beloved café next door included in the rate. Some inn rooms hold twin wingback chairs for relaxing in. The 1950s-style motel, now completely updated, has 18 rooms, each with private bath, air-conditioning, and cable TV (no pets allowed).

THE OLDE LANTERN INN & VINEYARD
Alan Connor, innkeeper
902-542-1389, 877-965-3845
oldlanterninn.com
11575 Hwy. 1, Grand Pré, NS B0P 1M0
Price: $89 to $139
Credit cards: Yes
Handicapped Access: Yes or None, or Limited
Special Features: Wi-Fi, Vineyard

The slippery-soft, high-threadcount sheets, the soft towels, the Jacuzzi bath, and the shower and the LCD television combine to pamper a visitor—who will hardly need the spa services on top of all that. A view of the vineyard from the windows of L'Acadie Blanc, named after an indigenous Nova Scotia grape, would be a fine thing during harvest season. A finished-wood paneled ceiling is an intriguing feature of another room, Vineyard, which has a gas fireplace flanked by wingback chairs and a four-poster bed. A shrimp, ham, and cheese omelet might be for breakfast. The Domaine de Grand Pré Winery and its restaurant, Le Caveau, are next door.

ROSELAWN COTTAGES AND EFFICIENCY UNITS
Lisa Peters, innkeeper
902-542-3420, 866-710-5900

roselawnlodging.ca
32 Main St., Wolfville, NS B4P 1B7
Price: $85 to $160
Credit cards: Yes
Handicapped Access: None
Special Features: Wi-Fi, pets allowed, outdoor pool, tennis court

A family business for more than 25 years, Roselawn has a mix of accommodations, all of them likely to appeal to a budget-minded traveler. Cabin 6, with white interior walls and pretty taupe curtains, has a large window overlooking the lawn and its apple trees, plus an acrylic sink bath in good condition. Cabins 1 to 4 are beside the pool, swings, and a slide. Unit 306, in the efficiency motel units building located at the rear of the grounds, is plain but well maintained. The kitchen, along with the laundry facilities, makes it a good base for a long stay in the area.

TATTINGSTONE INN

Betsy Harwood, innkeeper
902-542-7696, 800 565-7696
tattingstone.ns.ca
620 Main St., Wolfville, NS B4P 1E8
Price: $98 to $178
Credit cards: Yes
Handicapped Access: No
Special Features: Wi-Fi, AC

Ten rooms all display the sleek formality of this elegant house, decorated with antiques like Sheffield silver from the collection of the innkeeper, Betsy Harwood. Room 3 has a four-poster bed and a blue sofa. Tiled bathroom floors add to the impression of solidity and quality workmanship that pervades the rooms. This is not the place for someone seeking a warm and fuzzy style of hospitality, although everyone I encountered was gracious and polite. But if a certain kind of formality appeals to you, you will have a perfect fit here.

VICTORIA'S HISTORIC INN

Sherrie Cryan, innkeeper
902-542-5744, 800-556-5744
victoriashistoricinn.com
600 Main St., Wolfville, NS B4P 1E8
Price: $118 to $245
Credit cards: Yes
Handicapped Access: No
Special Features: Wi-Fi

A fortune made shipping the area's iconic Gravenstein apples to Europe built this house, when "Apple Baron" William Henry Chase could afford the embellishments of Italian-tiled fireplaces and an 8-foot by 6-foot stained-glass window. Later a maternity home for unwed service women, and still later student housing, it has been an inn since 1947. The present owners added fireplaces and bathrooms with whirlpool tubs. Nice rooms are now available for a night's stay in the main inn, and seven more are in the carriage house. The extravagant Chase Suite, with two rooms, is on the inn's second floor and holds an armoire owned by the Chase family.

RESTAURANTS

ACTONS GRILL & CAFE

902-542-7525
Actons.hub.org
406 Main St., Wolfville
Open: Daily, lunch 11:30 AM–2 PM, dinner from 5 PM
Price: $16 to $26
Credit cards: Yes
Cuisine: Italian and Maritime, with Thai
Serving: L, D
Handicap Access: No

Crab and whiskey bisque is a specialty of Acton's, a handsome restaurant on Wolfville's Main Street. The assortment of salads, from smoked salad and asparagus to beef tenderloin salad with leeks, is particularly appealing. Sautéed shrimp and rice noodles are flavored with a soy glaze for a small dish or appetizer. The chicken liver pâté with pear compote and the crab cakes are two other appealing choices. Roasted rack of lamb might come with roasted parsnips, and the beef tenderloin on one menu was accompanied by a gorgonzola sauce.

BLOMIDON INN
800-565-2291
blomidon.ns.ca
195 Main St., Wolfville
Open: Daily, lunch 11:30 AM–2 PM, dinner 5:30–9:30 PM
Price: $19 to $50
Credit cards: Yes
Cuisine: Continental
Serving: L, D
Handicap Access: Ramp to dining room from back parking lot; call ahead for seating
Special Features: Outside patio dining

From scallops in apple and sherry cream, to grilled portobello mushroom on rice with a roasted red pepper puree, to the filet of prime Maritime beef with Madagascar pepper sauce and two lobster tails, the dinners at Blomidon Inn have a wide range. Jerk pork with roasted red pepper puree and pineapple salsa, or a ragout of caribou, are other adventures on the menu.

✪ EVANGELINE CAFE
Sterling Family, innkeepers
902- 888-542-2703
evangeline.ns.ca
11668 Hwy. 1, Grand Pré
Open: Mon.–Sat. 8 AM–7 PM, Sun. 9 AM–7 PM
Price: $4 to $10
Credit cards: Yes
Cuisine: High-quality diner standards and more
Serving: B, L, D

Handicap Access: Yes
Special Features: Air-conditioning in one dining room, screened porch

The Sterling family has owned this café for more than 50 years—which is why the locals call it "Sterling's." But by that name or as Evangeline Café, this is the place for excellent, seasonal fruit pies and shortcakes, and it offers a proper excuse to indulge in a tender, light tea biscuit. The fish chowder is made with a flavorful milk broth and lots of fresh fish. Salads—like the spinach salad with red onion, mushrooms, bacon, sliced egg, and mozzarella—and sandwiches and burgers are additional lunch choices. For dessert at lunch or an early supper, try the butterscotch, lemon meringue, apple, or blueberry pie. In strawberry season, when I had the good luck to drop in, there's strawberry glazed pie, strawberry rhubarb pie, and strawberry shortcake.

HALLS HARBOUR LOBSTER POUND & RESTAURANT
902-679-5299
hallsharbourlobster.ns.ca
1157 West Halls Harbour Rd., Rte. 359, Centreville
Open: July–Aug., daily 11:30 AM–9 PM; May–June and Sept.–mid-Oct., daily 12–7 PM
Price: $10 to $28
Credit cards: Yes
Cuisine:
Serving: L, D
Handicap Access: Yes
Special Features: A walkout on the boardwalk

Pick your own lobster from the tank and carry it in a basin to be cooked, at Halls Harbour Lobster Pound & Restaurant. You won't have to pick the strawberries for your dessert, but in season you can count on them being flavorful and, despite the canned whipped "cream," making a great shortcake. Lobster rolls, fried scallops, and clams and burgers are other selections you could try here. Indoor and outdoor seating, all with a view of the inside harbor with its rising and lowering tides.

RESTAURANT LE CAVEAU, DOMAINE DE GRAND PRÉ

902-542-1753
grandprewines.com
11611 Hwy. 1, Grand Pré
Open: Lunch 11:30 AM–2 PM, dinner from 5 PM
Price: $23 to $29
Credit cards: Yes
Cuisine: Maritime and international
Serving: L, D
Handicap Access: Yes, but call in advance so the driveway can be opened to a vehicle

The décor suggests a wine cellar with rough walls and windows with elegant curved tops, but the meals are full of sunlight, from the fresh local greens and spiced pecans for a salad or the warm Stilton tart, to the Moroccan chicken with toasted cashews, dates, and couscous. Quail is grilled and flanked by turnip puree and sauced with a reduction of Stutz hard apple cider. The lobster is poached in butter and served with risotto and chervil pesto. A final delight lies in an Eton Mess of folded-together whipped cream, broken meringue, and berries.

✪ TEMPEST

902-542-0588, 866-542-0588
tempest.ca
117 Front St., Wolfville
Open: Mid-May–Oct., Tues.–Sun., lunch 11:30 AM–2 PM, dinner 5:30–9 PM, till 10 PM Fri.–Sat.; closed Mar.–Apr., but check for new schedules
Price: $19 to $31
Credit cards: Yes
Cuisine: "World Cuisine" according to the card
Serving: L, D
Handicap Access: Yes
Special Features: Locally sourced meat, potatoes, and much else

The vineyard at Domaine de Grand Pré

A cooling Campari Crush, a cocktail made of Campari, gin, red grapefruit juice, and lime, set things into gear nicely for me on a hot evening. A simple salad—really a mountain of assorted greens—showed off local farmers who devised the combination of bitter, spicy, and mild lettuces with a touch of genius. Rib eye from a large nearby farm, cooked medium rare, held all the virtues of beef, with rich flavor and a rim of melting fat. The crisp frites or fries were the best of all that I tried in Nova Scotia and Prince Edward Island—no small number considering the central role of the potato in this region. Crispy French bread with some whole-grain flour and smooth butter went well with the Malbec that perfectly matched the beef. And the slightly rough textures of the perfect panna cotta was exactly matched with rhubarb-cranberry compote and a little cone of rhubarb leather.

My server, Sara Munroe was a tranquil woman with an exceptional flair, and she set me to thinking about how to be exactly yourself and yet completely responsive with the public. Not many of us can begin to achieve this, as she did.

The menu boasts that the finnan haddie and chorizo chowder is its signature—reason enough to taste it. Owned and run by chef Michael Howell, Tempest deserves the accolades thrown around Howell's neck like flowery leis.

VEGETARIAN LUNCHBOX
902-542-1887
420 Main St., Wolfville
Open: Daily 9 AM–5 PM, till later Thurs.–Fri.
Price: $5 to $6
Credit cards: Yes
Cuisine: Organic and natural
Serving: B, L

All-day breakfast, and the egg and veggie wrap, are among the pleasures for diners at this entirely vegetarian restaurant that opened in August 2007. Owner Janet Harnum serves a popular hummus wrap and roasted vegetable panini for lunch. The small, attractive café is also a perfect spot for coffee.

FOOD PURVEYORS

Cafés and Coffee Shops
Grand Pré Café (902-542-7474; justuscoffee.com/Grandpre), 11865 Hwy. 1, Grand Pré (Exit 10 off Hwy. 101). Open Mon.–Fri. 7:30 AM–6 PM, Sat. 9 AM–6 PM, Sun. 10 AM–6 PM. With Just Us! locally roasted Fair Trade coffee, and tea and other beverages, as well as bagels, panini, soups, and salads.
Wolfville Café (902-542-7731; justuscoffee.com/wolfvillecafe.aspx), 450 Main St., Wolfville. Open Mon.–Fri. 7 AM–11 PM, Sat. 8 AM–11 PM, Sun. 9 AM–10:30 PM. Featuring Just Us! Coffee, premium Fair Trade coffee that is roasted in the same town, this café was started in a partnership with the Acadian Cinema Co-op, turning the movie theater in Wolfville into a center of the area's social life. Panini and breakfast sandwiches. Open mic night every Tuesday from 8 to 11 PM.

Cheese
Foxhill Cheese (902-542-3599; foxhillcheesehouse.com), 1660 Lower Church St., Port Williams. Open year-round, and daily Apr.–Dec., 10 AM–5 PM, Sun. 1–5 PM. The creamy yogurt is a perfect children's treat, or quick lunch, and the cheeses can be sampled for

free from the wide range of this artisan cheese dairy. Herbed Gouda, Havarti, cheddar, Quark (a mild, spreadable fresh cheese), feta, and more are wonderful snacks and souvenirs. Jeanita and Richard Rand were the first to start cheesemaking on a commercial scale in Nova Scotia.

Ran-Cher Acres (902-847-3895; rancheracres.com, Aylesford. Randy and Cheryl Hiltz milk 60 Saanen dairy goats on this farm, using the milk to make yogurt and artisan cheeses—something they have been working at for more than 20 years. Feta, ricotta, cheese curds, fresh chèvre, Quark and Gouda are a few from their list. Randy Hiltz is now making raw milk feta, Gouda, and cheddar, with its more nuanced, livelier flavor. You can buy these cheeses at the farm or at many Nova Scotia stores, and you might find them on the menu at Tempest (above), Jane's On The Common in Halifax, and many other places.

Taproot Farms greens at Noggins Corner Farm Market, Wolfville

Gourmet and Deli Markets

Noggins Corner Farm Market (902-542-5515; nogginsfarm.ca), 10009 Hwy. 1, Greenwich. Noggins Corner Farm near Wolfville sells Taproot Farms greens (part of the excellent salad at Tempest) and other high-quality produce.

The Tangled Garden (902-542-9811; tangledgarden.ns.ca), Grand Pré. Open Apr.–Dec. This business makes fine herb jellies, like basil wine jelly or orange thyme or ginger lime thyme; vinegars like fennel bay vinegar; jams like strawberry lavender and rhubarb angelica conserve; mustards; and liqueurs like dazzling damson plum with a touch of basil. Owners Beverly McClare, a sculptor of natural materials, and George Walford, a painter, also display their artwork in the gallery.

Tempest To Go (902-542-0588, 866-542-0588; tempest.ca), 117 Front St., Wolfville. Enter on Central Ave. Open Mid-May–Oct., daily 11 AM–6 PM. Quality groceries and take-out from a fabulous fine-dining restaurant.

Pubs

The King's Arms Pub (902-678-0066; kingsarmspub.ca), 390 Main St., Kentville. The King's Arms is described by pub aficionado, Bob Connor, author of *Sociable*, *The Elbow Bender's Guide to Maritime Pubs*, as "in many ways simply an expression of the personalities and interests of the two original owners." Two British doctors with a passion for soccer and an appreciation for good beer, they created a handsome place to enjoy a pint and a meal, either by the mahogany bar or outside on the terrace. Look also for a "properly drawn pint of Guinness."

Paddy's Pub (902-678-3199; paddyspub.ca), 42 Aberdeen St., Kentville; also (902-542-
0059), 460 Main St., Wolfville. Open daily at 11 AM in both locations. A brewpub since
1995, both of Paddy's brew pubs are the source of Acadian Cream Ale and Raven Ale,
overseen by head brewer Wayne Shankel. Live entertainment, and pub food from mussels to burgers.

Union Street Café and the Wick Pub (902-538-7787; unionstreetcafé.ca), 183
Commercial St., Berwick Open daily at 11 AM. Saturday brunch and "Around the World"
pizza—two for one on Wednesday, in 2008—are more reasons to arrive here, but the
music performed might be even more persuasive. The Friday-night Kitchen Party presents many well-known Maritime musicians, and more music is performed on some
Saturday nights. The café serves house-made dishes based on local produce and ingredients, and the pub hosts a free mussel bar on Fridays.

Wineries

Blomidon Estate Winery (902-582-7565, 877-582-7565; blomidonwine.com), 10318
Hwy. 221, Canning, NS B0P 1H0. This small winery makes an Estate L'Acadie Blanc that
has picked up silver medals at All Canadian Wine Championships in the past.
Complimentary tastings, and tours by appointment.

Domaine de Grand Pré (902-542-1753; grandprewines.com), 11611 Hwy. 1, Grand Pré,
NS B0P 1M0. Open May–Oct. for tastings, and tours for $6, including a wine-tasting, at
11 AM, 3 PM, and 5 PM. The tastings of L'Acadie Blanc, made with a Nova Scotia grape, and
Maréchal Foch as well as many other Grand Pré wines, are offered for a small fee, vary-
ing with the choice of wines sampled. Five dollars covers the basics. The tour goes
through the vineyards and introduces visitors to wine grapes unique to Nova Scotia.

Gaspereau Vineyards (902-542-1455; gaspereauwine.com), 2239 White Rock Rd.,
Wolfville, NS B4P 2R1. Wine tours mid-May–mid-Oct., daily at 12 noon, 2 PM, and 4 PM;
winery is open shorter hours Apr.–Dec. Gina Haverstock is the winemaker at up-and-
coming Gaspereau Vineyards, a quick drive from the village of Wolfville. Thirty-five
acres of vineyards began to be planted in 1996 on a slope beside the winery, which
makes delicious wines like Seyval Blanc, a slightly fruity white perfect with summer
meals; Riesling; ice wine; and Lucie Kuhlmann, a dry red.

CULTURE

Galleries

ROSS CREEK CENTER FOR THE ARTS
902-582-3842
artscentre.ca
555 Ross Creek Rd., P.O. Box 190, Canning, NS B0J 1H0
Open: Hours vary
Admission: Free

An artists' colony that works with aboriginal communities, offering programs for adults
and for children, Ross Creek holds exhibitions of artists' work through the year; it's also
the base camp for a theater group, see below.

Historic Buildings and Sites

GRAND PRÉ NATIONAL HISTORIC SITE

902-542-3631, 866-542-3631
pc.gc.ca/lhn-nhs/ns/grandpre/
P.O. Box 150, Grand Pré, NS B0P 1M0
Open: Mid-May–mid-Oct., daily 9 AM–6 PM; grounds always open
Admission: Adult $7.80, senior 65 and older $6.55, children 6–16 $3.90

In front of Memorial Church at Grand Pré Memorial Park stands the well-known statue of Evangeline, the symbol of the deportation of the Acadian people. Her story, recounted in the poem of her name written by Henry Wadsworth Longfellow, has introduced people to her history—and the story of the deportation ordered by the British—for more than a hundred years. The statue was placed here in 1920, when the land was owned by the Canadian Railroad company. A year later the Société Mutuelle de l'Assomption built the church with money raised from scattered Acadians throughout North America. Canada bought the park in 1957, and it was designated a National Historic Site in 1961. In this region French people, the Acadians, came to live between 1682 until they were forcibly exiled by the British government from 1755 to 1762. Exhibits about the history of the Acadians are shown at the Visitor Reception and Interpretation Centre, and a movie about the history is shown in the theater.

Museums

CHARLES MACDONALD CONCRETE HOUSE MUSEUM

902-678-3177
concretehouse.ca
19 Saxon St., Centreville, NS B0P 1J0
Open: late June–late Aug., daily 10 AM–6 PM
Admission: Free

The museum has a gallery of the paintings of Charles Macdonald, but the whole building is his creation, from the concrete animals in the garden to the newel post inside. Another gallery exhibits contemporary artwork by others, and an antique show is held every September.

JAMES HOUSE MUSEUM

902-665-4530
town.bridgtown.ns.ca
12 Queen St., P.O. Box 645, Bridgetown, NS B0S 1C0
Open: End of May–Aug., Mon.–Fri. 10 AM–4 PM
Admission: Free, donations accepted

Inside this 1835 house is the Memorial Military Museum, with artifacts of World War I and II on loan from the Royal Canadian Legion, Branch 33. Changing exhibits show the history of Bridgetown and the surrounding areas.

RANDALL HOUSE MUSEUM

902-542-9775
wolfvillehs.ednet.ns.ca
259 Main St., Wolfville, NS B4P 1C6
Open: Mid-June–mid-Sept., Mon.–Sat. 10 AM–5 PM, Sun. 1:30–5 PM
Admission: Adults $2, children 12 and under free

Glass, china, paintings, and a collection of Victorian greeting cards are on exhibit inside Randall House, a 1800 farmhouse owned by the Randall family for three generations. A garden of Nova Scotia plants, a library and local history research office on second floor, and more are cared for by the Wolfville Historical Society. In 2008 an afternoon tea was served from 3 to 5 PM Friday afternoon from mid-July to mid-September, with tea in china cups, fresh-baked tea biscuits, clotted cream, and local jams ($5); they are planned for 2009.

Music

THE ST. MARY'S CONCERT SERIES

berwickanglicanchurch.com/stmarysindex.htp
St. Mary's Anglican Church, Auburn, NS B0P 1A0
Open: Through the summer
Admission: Varies

The Venite Exultemus concerts offer classical and choral music, and The Joyful Noise concerts bring an "eclectic mix" of music to the church sanctuary every summer.

Theater

CENTRESTAGE THEATRE

902-672-3502, Reservations 902-678-8040
centrestagetheatre.ca
61 River St., P.O. Box 742, Kentville, NS B4N 3X9
Open: Check production schedule
Admission: Adults $10, students and seniors $9, children $5

With a season of eight productions every year, including musicals, children's shows, and classics, CentreStage Theatre is a community resource. Acting workshops, summer children's programs, dinner theater, and concerts are also on the schedule. This is a community theater run entirely by volunteers, vibrant and lively since 1984.

TWO PLANKS AND A PASSION THEATRE COMPANY

Ross Creek Center for the Arts
902-582-3842
artscentre.ca
555 Ross Creek Rd., P.O. Box 190, Canning, NS B09 1H0
Open: Check site or call for performance schedule
Admission: Varies

Productions of *Our Town* and *Jerome: The Historical Spectacle* were part of the 2008 season. Theatre Off The Grid, a group of summer-theater productions, takes place in some spot of the more than 250 acres at Ross Creek. With puppets, huge props, stilts, and more, drama unrolls as it might have done thousands of years ago—an eagle flying overhead during a performance of the *Odyssey*, played the role of Zeus. No technology is involved.

Seasonal Events

April
Annapolis Valley Music Festival (avmf.ca/), Wolfville. Pianists, bands, and other musicians compete for awards during this two-week festival held in a variety of venues.

July
Mud Flat Days (902-542-7000, 877-999-7117; downtownwolfville.com), Wolfville. History, music, skateboarding and other sports events, and more.

RECREATION

Beaches
Horton Bluffs, between Avonport and Hantsport. Follow the Avonport road on the backway to Hantsport, and take the turn located near where the railroad tracks cross the road. Look for fossils on Blue Beach, where you may stumble across finds similar to those at the UNESCO site in Joggins. A small fossil museum is another find ("Museums," above). On a New Year's Day one local resident saw guys ice-climbing down the cliffs. The book called *The Last Billion Years*, about the Maritimes, mentions Blue Beach. Campsites.

Camping
The Look-Off Family Camping Park (902-582-3022, lookoffcamping.com), Rte. 358, Canning. With a café and ice cream, a guest room, and campsites, this camping park has the advantage of a great location. There's even in-room massage in the one guest room ($110–$120). Camp cabins are furnished, but require you to bring your own bedding ($60).

Golf
Eagle Crest Golf Course, Centreville. Eighteen-hole golf course built on land that was previously owned by Nova Scotia Lieutenant Governor Clarence Gosse.

Hiking
Cape Split (novatrails.com/annapvalley/trails/capesplit/), Scot's Bay, is a 1.75-hour hike over fairly level terrain to the end of a point. According to Nova Trails, the inland trail is easier, about 16 kilometers or 10 miles round-trip, requiring at least five hours to hike out and back. But for those that do, the reward will be magnificent scenery that will take in the full expanse of the low tides of the Bay of Fundy; the hikes should be timed to coincide, allowing a visitor to hear the roaring sound of the water over the seafloor rocks and caves.

Parks

Blomidon Provincial Park (902-582-7319; novascotiaparks.ca), on Cape Split. Picnicking and hiking are fantastic on top of the 600-foot cliffs overlooking Minas Basin. Trails total 13.4 kilometers or 8.5 miles, interconnecting different points overlooking the ocean to the inland spruce forest, with Look Off Trail affording one of the best views of the mudflats and eroding sandstone of the cliffs. Migrating hawks, owls, and other birds pass over nearby North Mountain, and others feed on the exposed ocean floor, enjoying the clams and slipper limpets.

Waterfront Park, Wolfville With a gazebo and a plaque to help explain the waterfront, this is a sweet. small place to take in on a walk in Wolfville; but at low tide, when the mud just in front of you is heaped and carved in lovely patterns, the mosquitoes are on a rampage.

Rock Hunting

Goldmines Rock Shop (902-538-9759; goldmines.ca), 2718 McNally Rd., Woodlawn. Eight miles northwest of Berwick. Custom tours offered by Tom Metcalf seek out fine minerals and engage in gold-panning, in places he knows well. Metcalf introduces his clients to the geology of the region and explains why you are able to pick up specimens of amethyst, agate, and zeolites, in some locations, during the mineral-collecting tour.

Rob's Rock Shop (902-678-3194; robsrockshop.com), 677 West Main St., Kentville. Owner Robert Baird hosts a Web site that offers a lot of information on areas where you can hunt for semiprecious stones. Baird started serious rock-hounding in 1985. He sells only Nova Scotian material; he makes jewelry with gold and silver that shows off local stones like silica, quartz, amethyst, citrine, rose quartz, smoky quartz, and a green crystal—something the books don't recognize as made in nature. Agates and jaspers formed in this area are unique, with 11 major eruptions and 30 minor ones, he said. Black opals and fire opals are also found here—at least by Baird.

SHOPPING

Bookstores

Blue Griffin Books (902-363-2665; bluegriffinbooks.com), 30 Commerical St., Middleton. The stock here holds almost every genre and category, from mysteries to cooking, children's books to Canadiana.

Books Galore (902-679-9816), Coldbrook Centre, Coldbrook. Steve Franey sells a massive selection of used books, with well-organized used mass-market paperbacks that customers are grateful for, and hardcover nonfiction. "No doubt it's the largest one in the valley," said Franey, who opened in 1991.

Marchandise (902-542-4419), 11491 Hwy. 1, P.O. Box 51, Grand Pré. A good collection of Acadian and Nova Scotian books adds to the selection of travel, gardening, and general interest books and postcards sold here.

The Odd Book (902-542-9491), 112 Front St., Unit 118, Wolfville. An intellectual bent focuses this collection of exemplary used books, with foreign-language sections (mostly French), theology, sociology, and more. In the large fiction section, you'll likely find the volume of Alice Munro that you've been missing—or pick up a new one, to realize all over again what a genius this Canadian writer is.

Clothing

deWeever's Wovens (902-847-9270; deweeverswovens.com), 3486 Hwy. 1, Aylesford. Hilda deWeever is well known for her special weaving techniques, and her deep-hued cardigans and coats are investments that will make winter almost something to look forward to. She has been weaving since 1979.

Galleries

Harvest Gallery (902-542-7093; harvest gallery.ca), 462 Main St., Wolfville. Open year-round. Art, crafts, jewelry, sculpture, and more are on display here, created by area artists.

Gifts

Blomidon Inn (800-565-2291; blomidon.ns.ca), 195 Main St., Wolfville. This shop sells Canadian crafts, kitchen items, gardening accessories, hats, and more.

Jewelry and Stone Samples

Fancy Jewellers (902-245-2431; scalloppearl.ca), 57 Water St., Digby, and at (902-532-5185), 318 S. George St., Annapolis Royal. The source for "scallop pearls" set in gold and available only here.

Goldmines Rock Shop (902-538-9759; goldmines.ca), 2718 McNally Rd., Woodlawn. Eight miles northwest of Berwick. Limited jewelry, but more rock samples, among 500 specimens both from Nova Scotia and away, are available here. By appointment or by chance.

Rob's Rock Shop (902-678-3194; robsrockshop.com), 677 West Main St., Kentville. Local quartz, jasper, and more. See the longer description under "Rock Hunting," above.

Yarn

Gaspereau Valley Fibres (902-542-2656; gaspereauvalleyfibres.ca), 830 Gaspereau River Rd., Wolfville. With registered Cotswold sheep in the field nearby, this shop sells Canadian, local, and organic yarns and fiber, along with spinning and weaving equipment.

Painting St. James United Church, in Great Village

Truro and the Upper End of the Bay of Fundy

Mudflats and Fossils

The Glooscap Interpretive Centre in Truro is devoted to Mi'kmaq culture, offering workshops and demonstrations of quill embroidery, drumming, and dancing. The Glooscap Trail in this area follows the eastern shoreline of the Bay of Fundy around Minas Bay, where carved rocks tower overhead at low tide, carved around their base into the "flowerpots" they resemble.

Nova Scotia's largest provincial park is in Cape Chignecto, where a 30-mile hiking trail curves around the Bay of Fundy above its cliffs. The tidal bore, a 2-foot wave that glides up the rivers inland, is surfed and rafted on Shubenecadie River and other rivers in this area.

Lodging

Windsor

CLOCKMAKER'S INN
Sarah and Sean Arthur and Debbie and
Rick Dunham, innkeepers
902-792-2573, 866-778-3600
theclockmakersinn.com
1399 King St., Windsor, NS B0N 2T0
Price: $75 to $175
Credit cards: Yes
Handicapped Access: None
Special Features: Wi-Fi, afternoon tea

All the up-to-date amenities are thoughtfully included in the rooms at Clockmaker's Inn, from DVDs to coffee makers to a microwave and fridge in the suites. The honeymoon suite features a king-size sleigh bed, a large airjet tub, and an electric fireplace. The walk-in two-person shower and two sinks will make the beginning of anything rosy. Parquet risers on the stairs and a stained-glass window show the lavish use of fine decoration in this 1894 Victorian inn. A full breakfast is included, with a menu offering six items, eggs Benedict, pancakes, french toast, and omelets. The inn is named after *The Clockmaker*, a book by local well-loved author Chandler Haliburton.

THE FIDDLEHEAD B&B
Don and Betty Sheehan, innkeepers
902-798-2659
bbcanada.com/5660.html
307 King St., P.O. Box 3087, Windsor, NS
B0N 2T0

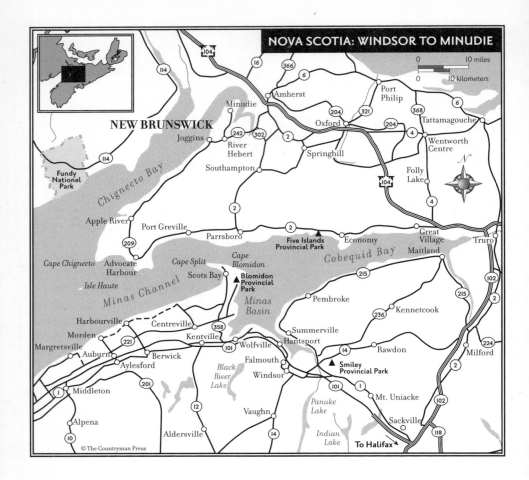

Price: $95 to $110
Credit cards: No
Handicapped Access: None
Special Features: Plug-in for broadband
Internet access

Blueberry pancakes, Scottie's Nest Eggs
(egg cooked in a cup-shaped slice of ham),
or a vegetarian breakfast are served in the
morning at the Fiddlehead, where two
rooms come with private baths. An
inground pool is available to the guests. The
downstairs room with a sitting room and a
television is like a little apartment.

THE WOODSHIRE INN

Marilyn MacKay, Scott Geddes, and Mike
McCabe, innkeepers
902-472-3300
thewoodshire.com
494 King St., P.O. Box 2318, Windsor, NS
B0N 2T0
Price: $89 to $140
Credit cards: Yes
Handicapped Access: None
Special Features: Wi-Fi

Handcrafted cedar bedsteads with canopies
and feather duvets make the bedrooms of

this inn unique, as do the glass and tile bathrooms. The inn's building has a long history: It was once known as the Paulin Residence, when it was the home of a local bank president and his wealthy family. Later, as the Sherwood Inn, it had a reputation for fine hospitality from the 1950s to the mid-1970s. A tiled double entrance, framed by leaded glass windows, and a marble fireplace in the dining room of the restaurant Cocoa Pesto are more details of the past, set inside this modernized interior. Two rooms were available in 2008; another seven additional rooms, with modern décor, should be available in 2009.

TRURO

BAKER'S CHEST BED & BREAKFAST

Maarten and Nelly Schuurmans, innkeepers
902-893-4824
bakerschest.ca
53 Farnham Rd., Truro, NS B2N 2X6
Price: $95 to $120
Credit cards: Yes
Handicapped Access: None
Special Features: Wi-Fi, AC

Located just outside of Truro, the Baker's Chest works well for people who want to explore the Bay of Fundy. The Estey Room, looking out on the garden, has a king-size sleigh bed and a soaker tub in its private bath. The smaller Thomas Room is set under skylights in the eaves, with a queen-size bed in an attractive slat, dark-wood bedstead. The owners from Holland speak Dutch, German, and French. The full breakfast might include a Dutch paperkoek, a breakfast cake that's spicy with ginger and lemon zest. Maarten will not give out the recipe—he says people will have to come here and try it.

BELGRAVIA BED & BREAKFAST

Anne McDonah, innkeeper
902-893-7100, 866-877-9900
belgravia.ca
5 Broad St., Truro, NS B2N 3G1
Price: $100 to $110
Credit cards: Yes
Handicapped Access: None
Special Features: Plug-in Internet access or Wi-Fi

Cheerful colors and wallpaper brighten the rooms at Belgravia. The room called Minuet uses pink and white to advantage, setting off the mahogany double bed and rocking chairs. In the middle of the upstairs hall, where the three rooms available here are located, is a couch, bookcase, and a guest computer for checking in with the Internet and your e-mail. Serenade has a pretty antique dresser and mirror and flowered and striped wallpaper. Breakfast might be eggs Florentine, with tomato and spinach, along with fresh fruit, muffins, yogurt, juice, and more.

PARRSBORO

GILLESPIE HOUSE INN

Lori Lynch and David Beattie, innkeepers
902-254-3196, 877-901-3196
gillespiehouseinn.com
358 Main St., Parrsboro, NS B0M 1S0
Open: May–Oct.; off-season by reservation
Price: $119
Credit cards: Yes
Handicapped Access: Yes
Special Features: Wi-Fi

With a large garden and shady maple trees, the grounds of this fine 1890 inn are as much a place to relax as are the handsomely decorated rooms. The Whitehall Room, with its hickory sleigh bed and handicapped-accessible bathroom, is on the ground floor. The seven bedrooms all have a private bath, and five fireplaces and a library are other keys to a delightful stay. Fresh fruit, yogurt, freshly baked muffins, and whole-grain breads are on the menu for breakfast, along with blue-berry pancakes with local maple syrup, cinnamon French toast, or scrambled eggs with fresh herbs from the garden. Two resident dogs.

MAPLE INN

Ulrike Rockenbauer and Johannes Hiesberger, innkeepers
877-627-5346
mapleinn.ca
2358 Western Ave., Parrsboro, NS B0M 1S0
Price: $90 to $175
Credit cards: Yes
Handicapped Access: None
Special Features: Wi-Fi

This Italianate house built in 1893 holds eight accommodations for travelers. The Empire Suite has an ocean view, a living room with Viennese antiques—older than the house, brought by the owners, who are from Vienna—and an air-jet tub. The Delivery Room—part of the house was a hospital for more than 30 years, and half of Parrsboro was born inside the house between 1943 and 1978—has a queen-size bed, along with an original bassinet that was here in the earlier days, with a little blue cross for a baby boy. Breakfast offers a choice of eggs or French toast or pancakes with blueberries in season, or a fruit bowl with yogurt.

AMHERST

THE REGENT BED & BREAKFAST

Jim and Gwen Kerr, innkeepers
902-667-7676, 866-661-2861
theregent.ca
175 East Victoria St., Amherst, NS B4H 1Y6
Price: $105 to $160
Credit cards: Yes
Handicapped Access: None
Special Features: Wall-plug Ethernet

Hardwood floors, antique or reproduction furniture, a comfortable bed—these are a

few of the basics covered at The Regent. One extra touch is the pair of reading lights above the beds, allowing you to enjoy the novel or history you have brought with you without disturbing your partner. The Chandler room is warmed by its deep-red walls and deep-red velvet curtains, a warmth that the thick light duvet will make even more delicious. An Aboriginal art collection decorates the house, and breakfast, served on fine china, might include buttermilk pancakes that you can be sure will have local maple syrup to go along with them.

RESTAURANTS

WINDSOR

COCOA PESTO

902-472-3300
thewoodshire.com
494 King St., P.O. Box 2318, Windsor
Open: Lunch Mon.–Fri. 11:30 AM–2 PM;
dinner daily 5–9 PM; brunch Sat.–Sun.
11:30 AM–2 PM
Price: $17 to $29
Credit cards: Yes
Cuisine: International
Serving: L, D, Brunch
Handicap Access: Yes
Special Features: Mon. night all-you-can-eat ribs

Barbequed ribs are a specialty, always accompanied by hand-cut fries and employing a dry rub or the restaurant's signature sauce to enhance the tender meat. The sauce has a tomato base, with cayenne and a touch of vinegar—and that was all co-owner Marilyn MacKay would share about her secret recipe. An applewood smoker makes the southern-style smoked ribs particularly good. Nova Scotia's best seafood is represented: Digby scallops served with garlic and lemon butter, or haddock with cherry tomatoes and scallions. A lamb shank and pork schnitzel are additional meat entrées. Vegetarians might find a dish of roasted red peppers and grilled portobellos with cheddar, white beans with roasted garlic and caramelized onions and sweet potato fries with curry mayonnaise, which sounds like a feast.

TRURO

THE JOHN STANFIELD INN

902-895-1505, 800-561-7666
johnstanfieldinn.com
437 Prince St., Truro
Open: Daily 5–9 PM
Price: $21 to $36
Credit cards: Yes
Cuisine: Modern fine dining, with Maritime seafood
Serving: D
Handicap Access: Limited

A Caesar salad might come with a parmesan "cracker" and duck bacon, and the pile of arugula might be topped with goat cheese. There's seafood chowder standing at the ready as a classic, and New York striploin with celery root puree and Stilton or Nova Scotia rack of lamb. Annapolis Valley pork with mustard cream might be served with an apple and barley risotto and sage pork cracklings. The menu changes weekly and features fresh, local food; in the summer you might find Millbrook arctic char. In 2008, Shaun Goswell was the chef and Steven Donnelly the executive chef at this ambitious dining room.

✪ MURPHY'S FISH AND CHIPS

902-895-1275
murphysfishandchips.com
88 Esplanade St., Truro
Open: Mon.–Thurs. 11 AM–7 PM, Fri.–Sat. 11 AM–8 PM, Sun. 12–7 PM
Price: $6.35 to $19.29
Credit cards: Yes
Cuisine: Maritime seafood and burgers

Serving: L, D
Handicap Access: Yes

Gerard's secret batter coats the deep-fried scallops, Digby clams, and fish at this seafood resource. Poached haddock is thoughtfully provided for anyone wanting something else, as is roast turkey, grilled liver and onions, and a large hamburger served with whipped potatoes or fries, a vegetable, and coleslaw. Fried onions are extra. "Everything we do we try to do locally," said Dave Anderson, a co-owner with his brother, Gerard, who said everything is made fresh. The recipes are original, the kind of oil used is a secret, and the fish providers are secret too. The oil is cleaned every day and frequently changed; each kind of seafood is cooked in its own deep fryer. "We've never followed anyone's lead." If you have had a better piece of fried fish in your life, Anderson said, he will give you your deep-fried fish for free. Coconut cream and butterscotch pies are made here every day.

PARRSBORO

BARE BONES CAFÉ AND BISTRO

902-254-2270
151 Main St., Parrsboro
Open: May–Oct. 1, Tues.–Wed. 10:30 AM–7:30 PM, Thurs.–Sun. 10:30 AM–9 PM.
Price: Dinner entrées $15 to $32
Credit cards: Yes
Cuisine: Modern French with Maritime seafood
Serving: L, D
Handicap Access: No
Special Features: Outdoor patio

Lunches feature hickory-smoked corn chowder. A lightly curried chicken and apple salad sandwich is on ciabatta and excellent chili. Pasta dishes are available at lunch and dinner, for example a vegetable pasta with zucchini, onions, peppers, cherry tomatoes, spinach in garlic cream sauce. Chicken, tuna, and certified Angus beef from Alberta are central to the dinner menu. Striploin with smashed new potatoes and peppercorn brandy demiglace is also available. Glenn Wheaton learned cooking at Nova Scotia Community College and cooked at The Five Fisherman and The Halliburton House Inn, both in Halifax.

BOUILLABAISSE CAFÉ & BAKERY
902-254-3371
121 Main St., Parrsboro
Open: May–Oct., daily 11 AM–8 PM
Price: $10 to $25
Credit cards: Yes
Cuisine: French, with an emphasis on seafood
Serving: L, D
Handicap Access: Yes

Patti Rithamel, co-owner, said everything here is made fresh daily, and that includes desserts like blueberry pie, rhubarb pie, lemon meringue, as well as breads and rolls. A soup might be Italian Wedding Soup with little meat balls—a favorite—or turkey vegetable, both accompanied by white or whole-wheat bread or rolls. The bouilla-baisse is made from the café's own recipe, with fish, clams, lobster, crab, sometime haddock, and more. Sandwiches are made with the fresh bread—the fabulous meatloaf sandwich might be even better than the lobster club. Seafood fettuccine and the three-mushroom fettuccine are both made with cream.

HARBOR VIEW RESTAURANT
902-254-3507
145 Pier Rd., Parrsboro
Open: Mid-Apr.–mid-Oct., daily 6:30 AM–9 PM, till 10 PM on weekends
Price: $4 to $20
Credit Cards: Yes
Cuisine: Fried seafood and burgers
Serving: L, D
Handicap Access: Yes

Clams, fresh lobster, scallops, and flounder are all local. The gulf shrimp, the one seafood not local, is grilled with garlic butter. Scallops can be pan fried or deep fried, and the same applies to the haddock or flounder. Grilled chicken Caesar salad, roast beef, and turkey are options for people tired or averse to seafood. Nothing is made from a mix, said Judy Wheaton, who has been here since 2002. A covered deck with a view of Minas Basin and the beach spread out before you allows a customer to watch the tide come and go every day.

NEAR AMHERST

MARSHLANDS INN
506-536-0170
marshlands.nb.
55 Bridge St., Sackville, New Brunswick
E4L 3N8
Open: Daily, breakfast 7–9:30 AM, lunch 11:30 AM–2 PM, dinner 5:30–8:30 PM
Price: $18.50 to $24
Credit cards: Yes
Cuisine: Fine Maritime dining
Serving: B, L, D
Handicap Access: Limited, ramps available to enter front door
Special Features: Antiques-filled inn with elegant parlors and rooms

In this beautifully restored old inn on the route to Nova Scotia, dinner is taken seriously. Scallops with Pernod is one French classic that is right at home with Maritime shellfish. Lobster, scallops, and shrimp folded up in a crêpe makes good sense too. Pork tenderloin is served with shrimp and cashews, and the steak comes with a classic mushroom peppercorn sauce. Crêpes are on the lunch menu, along with a chicken Caesar salad or smoked salmon on a bagel with cream cheese. You could start a dinner with a cocktail on the veranda.

Food Purveyors

Bakeries
Bouillabaisse Café & Bakery (902-254-3371), 121 Main St., Parrsboro. Open May–Oct., daily 9 AM–7 PM. Pies, breads, and specialty desserts—a chocolate peanut butter ball is one of them. Marshmallow squares, date squares, classic doughnuts from scratch.

Cafés and Cheeses
That Dutchman's Farm (902-647-2751; thatdutchmansfarm.com), 112 Brown Rd., Upper Economy. Open daily Father's Day–Labour Day. Maja and Willem van den Hoek produce Farmstead Gouda. The excellent Dragon's Breath Blue is a favorite on good restaurant menus throughout Nova Scotia. The farm can have it shipped to the friend you know will appreciate such a pleasure. This farm is a destination also for its walking trails and water gardens. Before a stroll, you can order one of the two sandwiches, Broodje Kaas, a Dutch roll with cheese, or Broodje Ham, a Dutch roll with ham, in the café, or try the appel tart.

Gourmet and Deli Markets
Masstown Market (902-662-2816; www.masstownmarket.com), 10622 Hwy. 2, Masstown, near Truro at Exit 12 from the Trans Canada Highway. Open daily 9 AM–9 PM. Baked goods, fruits, and vegetables at this thriving business that started as a farm store. You will also find chowders, soups, cheeses, and 48 flavors of Scotsburn ice cream, made at a local dairy, plus other goodies, like pecan pie. There's also a restaurant on the premises.

Honey
Sweetness and Light Honey Shop (902-261-2212), 9686 Hwy. 215, South Maitland Honey, chocolates, candles, and quilt work.

Microbreweries and Pubs
Duncan's Pub (902-660-3111; duncanspub.ca), 49 Victoria St., Amherst. Open daily from 11 AM. The local seafood is a focus of the menu, including a seafood casserole and fish and chips. Drunken haddock is baked with white wine, and the scallop dinner can be seared or pan fried. Pub burgers, a lobster roll served with fries, and a veggie wrap are also on the menu. Keith's IPA, Guinness, and single-malt whiskeys are a few things to drink.

The Spitfire Arms Alehouse (902-792-1460; spitfirearms.com), 29 Water St. (Exit 6 off Hwy. 101), Windsor. Open daily from 11 AM. Owner Troy R. Kirkby plans to open more traditional alehouses, displaying architectural memorabilia, military history, and motorcycles. In 2008 his one pub, The Spitfire Arms, focused on World War II fighter planes, like the Supermarine Spitfire. There's also an unrestored 1956 Francis-Barnett Cruiser 68. The pub serves smoked salmon, beer-batter onion rings, seafood chowder, and big salads. McAuslan Apricot Wheat Ale on draft is from Montreal, and so is St. Ambroise Oatmeal Stout, two among many high-quality Canadian and imported beers.

Tearoom

Baker's Chest Tearoom (902-893-4824; bakerschest.ca), 53 Farnham Rd., Truro. Attached to a bed & breakfast (described in the Lodging section, above), The Bakers Chest Tearoom serves lunch and teas between 11 AM and 3 PM. Owner Maarten Schuurmans is the son of a Dutch baker and makes the pastries and bread with the help of his wife, Nelly Schuurmans.

Wineries

Sainte-Famille Wines (902-800-565-0993; st-famille.com), RR #2, Falmouth. Open Mon.–Sat. 9 AM–5 PM, Sun. 12–5 PM; Jan.–end of Mar., closed Sun. Seyval Blanc, Acadie Blanc, Riesling, Siegfried, Michurinetz, Baco Noir, and Maréchal Foch are some of the grapes grown here, on 30 acres of vineyards. No fee for tastings, and all 17 of the wines can be tasted, unless they are sold out. Tours are given at 10 AM and 2 PM, May to October. A maple wine and an apple wine are newer choices.

CULTURE

Heritage Center

GLOOSCAP HERITAGE CENTRE
902-843-3496
glooscapheritagecentre.com
65 Treaty Trail, Truro Power Centre, Millbrook, NS B6L 1W3
Exit 13A off the Trans Canada Hwy. (Hwy. 102)
Open: Mid-May–mid-Oct., Mon.–Fri. 8:30 AM–7:30 PM, Sat.–Sun. 10 AM–6 PM; mid-Oct.–mid-May, Mon.–Fri. 8:30 AM–4:30 PM
Admission: Adults $6, seniors 65 and older $5, children 6–17 $3.50

Created by a lightening bolt that struck sand, the original man in the Mi'kmaq tradition is named Glooscap, and he possessed enormous powers. With his teaching, the Mi'kmaq nation became intimates of their environment, feasting for generations off the bounty of sea and land, living a traditional life in harmony with the seasons, and producing the graceful porcupine quillwork, weaving, and other artifacts like what the center has on exhibit. With European settlement, Mi'kmaq people found ways to work together with the newcomers, using their beads to make work to sell, and offering them insight into how to live in the woods and find the animals they needed. The Visitor's Information Centre, in this building, is a resource for travelers in the area.

Historic Buildings and Sites

ELIZABETH BISHOP MEMORIAL PLAQUE
Great Village, NS
Open: Always
Admission: Free

The American poet Elizabeth Bishop (1911–79) spent several years growing up in Nova Scotia after her father died and her mother was institutionalized with mental illness. She

The Elizabeth Bishop memorial in Great Village provides a summer refuge.

was brought up by her grandparents in Great Village, where she lived close to the woods and encountered creatures who would appear in her work in later years. A pergola-like structure beside the river in the center of Great Village holds several panels that describe her years here, when she lived in a house just a few doors down the street. One holds the text of her poem, "The Moose," set in Great Village. The installation, adjacent to Wilson's Service Station, is the result of a collaboration between the Great Village Historical Society and the Elizabeth Bishop Society of Nova Scotia, based in Halifax.

THE BLOCKHOUSE AT FORT EDWARD NATIONAL HISTORICAL SITE
902-532-2321, in July and Aug. 902-798-4706
pc.gc.ca
Fort Edward St., Windsor
Open: Guide service July–Aug., grounds open year-round
Admission: Free

Canada's oldest standing military structure, this blockhouse was built in 1750 by Major Charles Lawrence. British soldiers manned it to protect the road from Halifax to Annapolis Royal, only leaving in 1820. But aside from fending off external enemies, the British used this site in 1755 to organize the deportation of 1,200 Acadians from Pisiquid—and those they couldn't force to leave were sometimes jailed here in subsequent years.

FORT BEAUSÉJOUR–FORT CUMBERLAND
506-364-5080
bc.gc.ca
111 Fort Beauséjour Rd., Aulac, New Brunswick E4L 2W5

Open: June–mid-Oct., daily 9 AM–5 PM
Admission: Adults $3.90, seniors 65 and older $3.40, children 6–16 $1.90

The Visitors' Centre holds exhibits and artifacts about the military history of the area. Between 1751 and 1783 the area was passed back and forth between France and Britain, and this site, on the trail that Mi'kmaq had been following for centuries, was part of an important trade route. The fort was built in 1751 to watch over French interests, but after France lost its control, it was used to manage the deportation of the Acadians. As Fort Cumberland it was attacked by native tribes and Americans in the beginning of the American Revolution, but the assault failed.

Interpretive Centers

AGE OF SAIL CENTRE
902-348-2030
ageofsailmuseum.ca
8334 Hwy. 209, P.O. Box 14, Port Greville, NS B0M 1S0
Open: July–Aug., daily 10–AM–6 PM; June and Sept.–Oct., Thurs.–Mon. 10 AM–6 PM
Admission: Adults $3, seniors and students $2, under 6 free

Located at the site of former shipyards, the Age of Sail Centre looks out on Greville River, a tidal river that you can watch rise and fall from the Port Hole Café & Gift Shop. The center holds an amazing collection of hand-crafted wooden boat models as well as many word-working tools used to make ships, including the largest collection of hand planes in Canada. Pictures, paintings, photographs of sailing ships, and panels that explain the different kind of ships built here, as well the kind of wood they were made of, make these displays fascinating. Port Brazil Lighthouse is on the property, as is a blacksmith shop and a band saw from an old sawmill.

FUNDY TIDAL INTERPRETIVE CENTRE
902-261-2298
southmaitlandns.com
9865 Hwy. 236, South Maitland, NS B0N 2H0
Open: May–Oct., daily by mid-summer
Admission: Adults $2.50 or $7.50 for a family

This center is located at the end of a former rail line of the Dominion Atlantic Railway, with a great look-off spot to watch the tide come in. The tidal bore during the inrushing tide is a favorite spectacle, and staff can tell you when it occurs. The Web site also offers a tide schedule. Panels in the building describe the tide, the area, and its history.

JOGGINS FOSSIL CLIFFS & INTERPRETIVE CENTER
902-251-2727, 888-932-9766
jogginsfossilcliffs.net
100 Main St., Joggins, NS B0L 1A0
Open: Mid-May–mid-Nov., daily 9:30 AM–5:50 AM; off-season by appointment only
Admission: Adults $8, students and seniors $6, children under 5 free

Named a UNESCO World Heritage Site in the summer of 2008, the Joggins Fossil Cliffs hold a vast treasure of fossils from the world that existed 300 million years ago, during the Coal Age. The United Nations Educational, Scientific, and Culture Organization examined the site extensively before deciding to add it to the list that includes the Grand Canyon and the Galapagos Islands. A 13,000-square-foot Joggins Fossil Centre, built on the site of an old coal mine, brings the fossils up close without a trek on the beach, but both methods of exploration are educational. Reptile skeletons found by 19th-century geologists here are the oldest ever found in the world. Guided tours are offered for a fee, and there's a gift shop, café, an outdoor maze, and more. The rising and falling tides continue the erosion of the cliffs, constantly exposing new fossils that visitors discover every day. Once a year or so, a rare one is discovered.

Museums

FUNDY GEOLOGICAL MUSEUM

902-254-3814, 866-856-3466
museum.gov.ns.ca/fgm/
162 Two Islands Rd., P.O. Box 640, Parrsboro, NS B0M 1S0
Open: Mid-May–Oct., daily 9:30 AM–5:30 PM; late Mar.–mid-May, Mon.–Sat. 8:30 AM to 4:30 PM
Admission: Adults $6.25, seniors 65 and older $5, children 12 and under must be accompanied by an adult; family rates $9

Dinosaur skeletons, 200 million years old, and an array of gems draw visitors to this museum in Parrsboro. The remains of several Prosauropods have been found here, and specimens are under glass. Exhuming the fossilized bones from sandstone is a long, painstaking process described in detail on the museum's Web site: ethanol is used to soften the stone and expose the bones of a Prosauropod. Curatorial field trips are offered during the summer on Fridays and Saturdays; start at the museum, or on the beach where the tour begins, and walk three to six hours, learning about the region's geology and the history of human habitation too. Anyone who sees bones, teeth, or tracks on Parrsboro shore is asked to call the museum; it is illegal to remove fossils, which are protected in Nova Scotia under the Special Places Protection Act.

HALIBURTON HOUSE MUSEUM

902-798-2915
museum.gov.ns.ca/hh/index.htm
414 Clifton Ave. Windsor, NS B0N 2T0
Open: June–mid-Oct., Mon.–Sat. 9:30 AM–5:30 PM, Sun. 1–5:30 PM.
Admission: Adults $3.25, seniors 65 and older and children 6–17 $2.25

The former home of Judge Chandler Haliburton, who wrote Sam Slick stories—humorous tales featuring a fast talker who said, "Facts are stranger than fiction"—includes a collection of clocks, including a clockwork spit in the open fireplace. Children can play games, and walking trails on the property can take you to the next museum on your trip, Shand House Museum. Parents eager to leave the present day behind, with its GameBoys and DVDs, can arrive on the day scheduled for Play in the Past, which features painting, kite-making, nature walks, and more.

LAWRENCE HOUSE MUSEUM

902-261-2628
museum.gov.ns.ca/lh/index.htm
8660 Hwy. 215, RR #1, Maitland, NS B0N 1T0
Open: June–mid-Oct. Mon.–Sat. 9:30 AM–5:30 PM, Sun. 1–5:30 PM
Admission: Adults $3.25, children 6–17 and seniors 65 and older $2.25

Starting with his wits and 30 pounds sterling in the 1850s, William D. Lawrence created a shipbuilding business that made him wealthy and led to the construction of the largest sailing ship built in Canada, named after him, which was launched in 1874. Handsome furniture and international pieces brought back on his ships show off the heights he achieved. Day camps and a garden party are held every year.

SHAND HOUSE MUSEUM

902-798-5619
museum.gov.ns.ca/sh/
389 Avon St., P.O. Box 2683, Windsor, NS B0N2T0
Open: June–mid-Oct., Mon.–Sat. 9:30 AM–5:30 PM, Sun. 1–5:30 PM
Admission: Adults $3.25, children 7–17 and seniors 65 and older $2.25

Built in 1890–91, this late-Victorian mansion was stuffed with then-contemporary luxuries, like electric lights. Original furnishings and children's things, like a trophy for a three-wheeled bicycle race, are on display. Summer teas are held frequently, and local girls take advantage of some formal-dress events by dressing up in pretty Victorian dresses—at which, the Web site explains, "English accents are optional."

OTTAWA HOUSE BY THE SEA MUSEUM

902-254-2376
ottawahouse.org/pages
1155 Whitehall Rd., Parrsboro. NS B0M 1S0
Open: Late May–late-Sept., daily 10 AM–6 PM
Admission: Adults $2, children under 12 free

Luncheons and teas are often on the calendar, but a general tour is always on offer in this gracious house overlooking the sea. In mid-July on Sunday, there is a strawberry tea; Lady Tupper Tea is the mid-August Wednesday. Sunday afternoon at 2, the Sunday series presents entertainment or a tea.

The main building of this house may have been built in the 1770s and might have been one of two hotels in the town. Later in its storied existence it was a summer home, belonging first to Cumberland Railway general manager R. G. Leckie, and then his successor, general manager J. R. Cowans—who in 1910 supposedly required an entire railroad train to move in, with horses, servants, family, and supplies. Before it was a museum, it was an inn.

SPRINGHILL MINERS' MUSEUM

902-597-3449
145 Black River Rd., P.O. Box 1000, Amherst, NS B0M 1X0
Open: June–Sept., daily 9 AM–5 PM
Admission: Adults $5.25, seniors and children 7–18 $4.50, children 3 to 6 years old $3

A helmeted tour guide who knows all about the mining, years ago, will take you 300 feet down inside the mine for about twenty minutes. He or she will tell you the story of the subterranean fire that burned in 1916, and will also describe other disasters—in 1956, when 39 men were killed, and in 1958, when 75 men died during an earthquake that pancaked one area of the mine. Nine days later, survivors who had endured the darkness inside small openings walked out into daylight. The museum gives a lump of coal away to everyone who asks for one.

Theater

MERMAID THEATRE OF NOVA SCOTIA
902-798-5841
mermaidtheatre.ns.ca
132 Gerrish St., P.O. Box 2697, Windsor, NS B0N 2T0
Open: Schedule varies
Admission: Prices vary

A theater for children that tours North America and the world, the Mermaid Theatre also performs in Windsor, usually either before going on tour or just when returning. The events are posted on the Web site under the tab at the left labeled "Mermaid Imperial Performing Arts Centre."

SHIP'S COMPANY THEATRE
902-254-3000
shipscompany.com
18 Lower Main St., P.O. Box 275, Parrsboro, NS B0M 1S0
Open: July–Sept.
Admission: Adults $26, youth 6 to 17 and seniors 60 and older $23, except previews $10 and Sun. nights $17 for everyone.

This company began performing on a ship called the *M. V. Kipawo*, which has now been set above the tideline, so that it forms part of the theater lobby. Big productions, shorter-run shows, and concerts are held here, as are children's shows and programs, like a drama camp run every summer. The 2009 season will be the 25th-anniversary year, with a full schedule to celebrate.

TANTRAMAR THEATRE
902-667-7002
tantramartheatre.ca/
98 Victoria St. East, Amherst, NS B4H 1X6
Open: Year-round
Admission: Tickets $12

Presenting live theater, dinner theater, and children's programs, Tantramar Theatre has a season that goes year-round. Christmas dinner theater catered by Patterson's Family Restaurant, Sackville, New Brunswick, presents a different production every year. Brown bag theater offers an hour-long play that can be enjoyed over lunch.

Seasonal Events

August
Nova Scotia's Gem and Mineral Show, Lion's Recreation Center, Western Ave., Parrsboro. Workshops, demonstrations, exhibits, and fossils, minerals, jewelry, and more for sale.

October
Launch Day, Maitland. A commemoration in late October honoring the 1874 launching of the *William D. Lawrence*, a 2,459-ton sailing ship that was the largest built in Canada up to that time. Enjoy a parade, a launching of a model of the ship, and skits.

Pumpkin Regatta (worldsbiggestpumpkins.com), Windsor. Paddlers negotiate the river in hollowed-out giant pumpkins.

RECREATION

Golf
Amherst Golf and Country Club (902-667-8730; amherstgolfclub.ca), John Black Rd., Amherst. Eighteen holes in a pastoral setting.

Avon Valley Golf & Country Club (902-798-2673; avonvalleygolf.com), Falmouth. An 18-hole course with small greens covers a hilly landscape. Canteen and bar, equipment rentals, pro shop.

Brookfield Golf Club (902-673-3352; nsga.ns.ca/brookfield/bf.htm), RR #2, Brookfield. An open, flat course with the challenge of a winding brook. Snack bar and rentals available.

Mountain Golf Club (902-893-2841; mountaingolf.ca), 1195 Pictou Rd., Truro. With views of the area, café, and pro shop.

Truro Golf Club (902-893-2508; trurogolfclub.com), 86 Golf St., Truro. An 18-hole course designed by Stanley Thompson and hosting tournaments for many years. Restaurant and pro shop.

Hiking
Kenomee Hiking Trails, 35 miles east of Parrsboro, off River Phillip Rd., Economy. There is a network of trails with wilderness campsites. One hour to Economy Falls, and 18 kilometers or 12 miles for the Kenomee Canyon Trail. Also nearby on the Economy River is the **Thomas Cove** trail, with views of the coast.

Partridge Island Trail, 3 kilometers or 2 miles from Parrsboro, is a short trail that brings a hiker to the other side of Partridge Island, looking across to Cape Blomidon.

Ward's Falls Hiking Trail. Eight kilometers or 5.6 miles west of Parrsboro, this 3-kilometer or 2-mile trail leads to Ward's Falls.

Horseback Riding
Boulderwood Stables (902-791-1215, 866-499-9138; boulderwood.com), 7321 Hwy. 1, Ardoise. Trail riding, and lessons, as well as a swimming pool and hot tub, tennis court, and play area.

Kayaking

NovaShores Adventures (902-392-2761, 866-638-4118; novashores.com), P.O. Box 111, 20 School Lane, Advocate Harbour. Tours of the Bay of Fundy near Cape Chignecto take a visitor up close to the eroded sandstone cliffs of this region. The strong tides of the bay make a tour guide a good idea for novices.

Parks

Burncoat Head Park (902-369-2669; nslps.com), Noel. With a replica lighthouse constructed after local urging and fund-raising, on 3 acres set above Cobequid Bay, this day-use park with walking trails is free to the public. The lighthouse holds panels about the bay and its tides.

Cape Chignecto Provincial Park (902-392-2085; capechignecto.net), 1108 West Advocate Rd. (Rte. 209), Advocate Harbour (45 kilometers or 28 miles west of Parrsboro). The dramatic landscape and sea cliffs are the phenomenal pleasures of a visit here, which all visitors begin with a registration at Red Rocks Visitor Centre in West Advocate. The 185-meter or 600-foot cliffs are especially dramatic at low tide, along the 29 kilometers or 18 miles of coastline contained in this park. Wilderness camping, with no drive-up sites, and hiking trails inland and along the cliffs. Most of the trails here are rated difficult. A day-use park in Eatonville Harbour (via West Apple River Road) was officially opened in 2008, with trails accessible for the physically challenged and young children not up to a long hike. Two trails go to distinctive features, one called the Three Sisters (three "sea stacks" cut from stone by the water), and the second Squally Point, a terrace raised up over the sea that was once a beach—underneath the enormous weight of a glacier.

Five Islands Provincial Park (902-254-2980; novascotiaparks.ca/parks/fiveislands.asp), 618 Bentley Rd., Lower Five Islands (25 kilometers or 15 miles east of Parrsboro). Open mid-June—early Sept. With 90-meter or 300-foot-high cliffs along the sea, this park has many vantage points from which to contemplate the acres of mudflats at low tide. According to Mi'kmaq legend, Glooscap, the original man, threw five rocks at a beaver that was angering him—and created these five islands. Campground, unsupervised beach, playground, and washrooms.

Shubenacadie Provincial Wildlife Park (902-758-2040; wildlifepark.gov.ns.ca), off Rte. 2 (Exit 11 off Rte.102), Shubenacadie. With 33 species of mammals and 65 kinds of birds, this wildlife park has 2 kilometers or 1.3 miles of paths for visitors to stroll, and many panels to read. Western Canadian cougars, the little swift fox, lynx, a pine marten, and other creatures bring the woods of the region alive. A playground, picnic area, and washrooms are available.

Skiing

Ski Martock (902-798-9501; martock.com), 370 Ski Martock Rd., Windsor, NS B0N 2T0. A place to ski and snowboard with seven trails and a quad, two T-bars, and one rope tow. Usually open in mid-December to end of March.

White Water Rafting

Shubenacadie River Adventure Tours (902-261-2222; 888-878-8687; shubie.com), 10061 Hwy. 215, South Maitland. Riding the Bay of Fundy tides is exciting—and can be drenching. Bring dry clothes and a towel. Offered daily June to September, this 3.5-hour tour stops at a midpoint lodge for a break and refreshments, a swim in a pool, or horseshoes. A barbeque meal is part of the tour, with hamburgers and hot dogs. A chance to mud slide is another once-in-a-lifetime opportunity—the Bay of Fundy leaving behind four inches of soft, warm mud.

Shubenacadie River Runners (800-856-5061; tidalborerafting.com), 8681 Hwy. 215, Maitland. A steak barbecue is part of the trip, which starts at the mouth of the river and lasts a full or half day. Rain gear and rubber boats are provided during trips operated between May and September. Depending on the height of the tide, you will encounter a big tidal bore—the surge where the incoming tide meets the still outgoing water—or a small one. Rapids form on the top of the sand bars as the water floods over them, and they're fun to traverse; the operators of this tour promise that even a fall from the boat won't injure a passenger, since there are no rocks to hit.

SHOPPING

Antiques
Great Village Antiques (902-668-2149; greatvillageantiques.ca), 8728 Hwy. 2, Great Village. A wide-ranging collection of furniture, glassware, and collectibles.

Bookstores
Amy's Used Books (902-667-7927), 51 South Albion St., Amherst. A huge selection, without much organization— but patience may be rewarded.

The Book Nook (902-893-7766), 8 Dominion St., Truro. Maritime books and local authors in addition to general stock from all categories.

Clothing and Accessories
Turbine (902-798-3966; turbine.ca), 1901 Hwy. 1, Falmouth. A high-fashion store and café, selling coats, clothing, handbags, knitware, and accessories. Owner and designer Lisa Drader-Murphy makes custom clothing with vintage fabrics and designs equestrian garments as well. Organic-when-available meals and fine coffees and teas served.

Great Village Antiques

Rocks and Minerals

The Parrsboro Rock & Mineral Shop & Museum (902-254-2981; 3.ns.sympatico.ca/
eldon.george/), 349 Whitehall Rd., Parrsboro. Open for more than half a century, this
shop is run by fossil collector Eldon George, and it shows off some of his best finds.
The smallest dinosaur footprint was one of them, a half-inch print from a Coelophysis
he found in 1984. See zeolites, stillbites, chalcedony, amethyst, and other fine crystals
that were encountered on nearby beaches. Fern fossils, more dinosaur prints, and
trilobite fossils are in the museum.

Tysons' Fine Minerals (902-728-8364; tysons-minerals.com), Parrsboro. Open mid-
May–mid-Oct., Thurs.–Mon. 10 AM–5 PM; Tues.–Wed. and off-season by chance.
Focussed on mineral specimens, many from Canada. Jewelry with natural stone beads
is made here. Pieces sometimes include wood, pearls, and some gemstones.

Montrealers waiting for the PEI ferry in Caribou, Nova Scotia

PICTOU AND NEW GLASGOW

The Northumberland Shore

Set on the Sunrise Trail, these towns hug Northumberland Strait where the warm waters flow that make Prince Edward Island across the way and this coast of Nova Scotia such a friendly spot for swimming. The beaches here have the warmest water found in the province. Lorneville lies near the western border of Nova Scotia and New Brunswick; from that town 280 miles of red sand beaches unfurl to the east.

Pictou welcomed its first Scottish immigrants in 1773; their boat, the *Hector*, has been re-created and lies at anchor along the waterfront. During the summer months, costumed guides on the Pictou Quay will show you how to do the carpentry of the 1800s, or deal with life on board a small ship.

The Caribou-Woods Island Ferry to Prince Edward Island leaves from north of Pictou, making the area a regular destination for visitors passing through. It's great to know about New Glasgow's pub, The Dock, for a meal on the way back home.

Scottish heritage is the theme of the Highland Games in Antigonish every summer, but for much of July and August theater-lovers are also flocking there for the shows presented every night, on multiple stages.

LODGING

LORNEVILLE

THE STUART HOUSE BED AND BREAKFAST

Shelly and Brian Tanner, innkeepers
902-661-0750
stuarthousebedandbreakfast.com
5472 Rte. 366, Lorneville, NS B4H 3X9
Open: May–Oct.
Price: $80
Credit cards: Cash or travelers checks only
Handicapped Access: None
Special Features: Wi-Fi

The raspberry bushes next to the vegetable garden will be fruiting in August, a fine time to visit and take advantage of raspberry muffins at breakfast at the Stuart House. Four generations of the same family have lived here; the house was transformed into a B&B in 1991. An antique dresser and headboard in the Princess Patricia Room has also been in this family for four generations. Three rooms have private baths, and all have quilts made by Shelly Tanner, her mother, and her grandmother. The old section of the house was built by Tanner's great grandfather; today it's two houses built together.

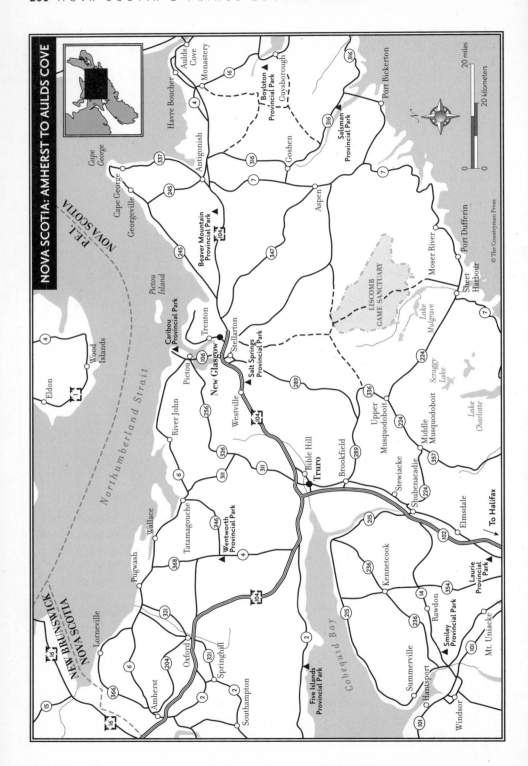

NOVA SCOTIA: AMHERST TO AULDS COVE

The Stuart House Bed and Breakfast

WALLACE

FOX HARB'R GOLF & COUNTRY CLUB

902-257-1801, 866-257-1801
foxharbr.com
1337 Fox Harbour Rd., Wallace, NS B0K 1Y0
Price: $300 to $400
Credit cards: Yes
Handicapped Access: Yes
Special Features: Wi-Fi, fine dining

A "semi-private" resort, Fox Harb'r provides six suites in each of the 12 guesthouses, outfitted with top-of-the-line beds, linens, towels, and bathrobes. The heated granite floor in the bathroom is par for this upscale course, as is the wet bar, mini-fridge, and private balcony. The larger suites have propane fireplaces and three rooms. A wellness center holds a small pool, mineral pool, and hot tub. Tennis, basketball, croquet, mountain biking, kayaking, beach volleyball, snow-shoeing, and cross-country skiing are activities that can be arranged in season. This resort is owned by the former owner of the Tim Horton's chain.

TATAMAGOUCHE

GREEN DRAGON FARM

Stephan and Gerlinde Hederich, innkeepers
902-657-0081
greendragon@ns.sympatico.ca
3082 Balmoral Rd., Tatamagouche, NS B0K 1V0
Price: $75
Credit cards: Cash or checks only
Handicapped Access: None
Special Features: An organic farm

Natural materials were used in the 2004 renovation of this farm, for tourists with chemical sensitivities. The host can give a tour of the farm and introduce the llamas and the fallow deer, chickens, goats, as well as serve an organic breakfast with eggs, jams, sausage, pancakes. "The only thing I buy is the coffee and butter," said Gerlinde Hederich. She makes feta, cream cheese, and Gouda, which are also part of breakfast. A couple of times people stayed on as volunteers and weren't charged for their room. The one room available for rent shares a bathroom.

TRAIN STATION INN

James and Shelley LeFresne, innkeepers
902-657-3222, 888-724-5233
trainstation.ca
21 Station Rd., Tatamagouche, NS B0K 1V0
Price: $100 to $170
Credit cards: Yes
Handicapped Access: None
Special Features: Wi-Fi

Stay in one of seven cabooses, turned into cushy nests with fireplaces, TVs, and private baths by the adventurous entrepreneurs at Train Station Inn. Some of the accommodations have a kitchenette or two bedrooms, several are paneled with pine and include a gas fireplace. But anyone not quite ready to be railroaded can stay in the Station itself, in the Belyea, a Victorian-style room with a four-poster double bed, or perhaps Penny, with its antique furnishings. A railway museum in the former waiting rooms, a café, and a gift shop are also located in the first floor of this building. Restoration of the train car Alexandra for a cocktail lounge may be done in 2009.

PICTOU

CUSTOMS HOUSE INN

David and Douglas DesBarres, innkeepers
902-485-4546
customshouseinn.ca
38 Depot St., P.O. Box 1542, Pictou, NS B0K 1H0
Price: $109 to $129
Credit cards: Yes
Handicapped Access: Yes
Special Features: Wi-Fi, AC

The 1870 brick and sandstone building was gutted and renovated in 1997; the result is eight rooms with private baths, some with a kitchenette, and two that are handicapped accessible. The high ceilings, original doors and molding, hardwood floors, and non-working marble fireplaces are features from the past. A large continental breakfast with cereal, fresh fruit, homemade bread for toast, and tea or coffee is included.

EVENING SAIL BED & BREAKFAST

Gail and Michelle LeBlanc, innkeepers
902-485-5069, 866-214-2669
eveningsail.ca
279 Denoon St., P.O. Box 209, Pictou, NS B0K 1H0
Price: $79 to $129
Credit cards: Yes
Handicapped Access: None, but one ground-floor room
Special Features: Wi-Fi

The bright, pretty colors of the rooms of this inn are inspired. For example, green walls and green and rose quilts make Driftwood, with its shady deck and fireplace, as luminous as a seashell. Blue and white Jacob's Dory, set under the eaves, has its own sunny deck, a gas fireplace, a couch and two upholstered wingback chairs, and a table with painted wooden chairs in multiple shades of pastel in a little kitchen. "The most important things at a B&B are the bed and the breakfast," said Michelle LeBlanc, who has invested in high-quality beds and memory-foam top pads. Breakfast might be a casserole with a potato crust made of cheese, mushrooms, peppers, and ham.

WILLOW HOUSE

Debbie and Jamie MacLean, innkeeper
902-485-5740, 800-459-4133
willowhouseinn.com

11 Willow St., P.O. Box 1900, Pictou, NS
BoK 1Ho
Price: $80 to $120
Credit cards: Yes
Handicapped Access: None
Special Features: Wi-Fi

Rooms at the Willow House are furnished
with antique, dark-wood furniture, and
some beds are draped with white translu-
cent curtains. The two-bedroom suites on
the third floor are set below the eaves.
Located on the second floor are four guest
rooms, all with private baths and sitting
areas. In three of the rooms you can find
three upholstered love seats. The large
house was built in 1840 by barrister and
Pictou mayor David Matheson. Debbie
MacLean makes a breakfast something
fresh baked like jam-filled buns, and a hot
dish like peach-stuffed french toast, or a
croissant stuffed with scrambled eggs,
always served with fresh fruit.

ANTIGONISH

ANTIGONISH EVERGREEN INN
Bill and Lynne Vasil
92-863-0830, 888-821-5566
antigonishevergreeninn.com
295 Hawthorne St., Antigonish, NS B2G
1B9
Price: $100
Credit cards: Yes
Handicapped Access: Yes
Special Features: Wi-Fi, AC

The eight units cared for meticulously by
Bill and Lynne Vasil were brought back
from disrepair and neglect in the winter
and spring of 2008. Now they all shine with
handsome wood flooring, new paint, and
pretty furniture. Each one has a big picture
window looking past well-kept buildings to
a stretch of farmland—and likely as not
you'll get to taste something grown nearby
if you head out for dinner. Big, clean bathrooms, with full baths and tiled floors, are

in each room, and some of the units have
a full kitchenette to keep guests self-
sufficient. You'll receive a free copy of the
Chronicle Herald; from June through
September a cup of very good coffee, fruit,
cereal, toast and yogurt are set out from
8 to 9 or 9:30 AM.

ANTIGONISH VICTORIAN INN
902-863-1103, 800-706-5558
antigonishvictorianinn.com
149 Main St., Antigonish, NS B2G 2B6
Price: $110 to $170
Credit cards: Yes
Handicapped Access: None
Special Features: Wi-Fi

Oak paneling and flooring greet you as you
enter this historic property built in 1904 by
Duncan Kirk. He owned hardware and
department stores in Antigonish and Nova
Scotia, and with his earnings he set out to
build this house with its corner turret and
elaborate trim. In 1943 the building was
sold and transformed into a hospital; later,
until 1997, it was a bishop's residence
owned by the Catholic Church. Five acres of
gardens border the East River and the fields
that are home to the town's famous
Highland Games. Twelve rooms are furnished in a variety of styles, and three have
wood-burning fireplaces. On the third
floor the bathrooms are across a hall.

RESTAURANTS

PUGWASH

SANDPIPER RESTAURANT
902-243-2859
Rte. 6, Pugwash
Open: Apr.–Oct., daily 11 AM–8 PM, off-
season till 7 PM
Price: $9 to $20
Credit cards: Yes
Cuisine: Seafood and Maritime standards

Serving: L, D
Handicap Access: Yes

Deep-fried clams, from Five Islands, are one specialty of the Sandpiper Restaurant. Lobsters come boiled or deluxe, served on toast with a cheddar cheese sauce. The Sandpiper Special is a grilled lobster and cheddar-cheese sandwich. Roast turkey and roast beef dinners are available every night. Pies might be apple, blueberry, lemon, or coconut cream. Another dessert sometimes served is blueberry Boston cream cake, a cake with a cream filling and stewed blueberries on top.

WALLACE

JUBILEE COTTAGE INN
902-257-2432
jubileecottage.ca
13769 Hwy. 6, Wallace
Open: Tues.–Sun. at 5 PM, reservation only
Price: $38 for four-course menu
Credit cards: Yes
Cuisine: Changing themes
Serving: D
Handicap Access: No
Special Features: BYOB, bring your own wine or beer

Fire of the Caribbean night is on Thursday, International Fusion on Sunday, and so it goes for every night of the week this dining room is open. "Because I've lived in different countries I couldn't decide on one, so I've got them all," said chef and co-owner, Carol Dee. Chimoola shrimp, pan-seared maple trout with apple-turnip compote, honey orange and lime salmon, pan-seared Digby scallops, grilled vegetables, and the signature dessert, tiramisù, with whipped marscapone cheese and Kahlua, are a few items from past menus. Dee, who is from Trinidad, met her husband in Toronto. Then she and he went to Australia for 26 years before moving to Nova Scotia.

TATAMAGOUCHE

SUNRISE MERCANTILE GOURMET FOODS AND CAFÉ
902-657-1094
sunmerc.com
1631 Rte. 6, Tatamagouche
Open: June–Labour Day, Mon.–Sat. 8 AM–8 PM, Sun. 1–8 PM; Nov.–Apr., till 6 PM, but call to confirm
Price: $5 to $15
Credit cards: Yes
Cuisine: Maritime with Asian influences
Serving: B, L, D
Handicap Access: Yes, but a gravel parking lot can be a challenge
Special Features: Shop with specialty foods

Crab cakes, salmon and shrimp pâté, and a sunrise salad made with farmers'-market greens and edible flowers are some of the inspired ways to begin a meal at this café. So are Thai ginger eggrolls. Wraps and deli sandwiches are substantial meals, and a lobster salad in a whole-wheat tortilla is a great take on a lobster roll. Kicking Horse Coffee, chai, and blueberry juice are also served, and the cakes and pastries look irresistible.

EARLTOWN

✪ SUGAR MOON FARM
902-657-3348, 866-816-2753
sugarmoon.ca
Alex MacDonald Rd., Earltown
Open: July–Aug., daily 9 AM–5 PM; weekends year-round
Price: $11
Credit cards: Yes
Cuisine: Pancakes, omelets, and sandwiches
Serving: B, L
Handicap Access: Yes
Special Features: Maple syrup demonstrations

This farm is the site of a sugaring operation that employs a wood-fired evaporator and uses wood harvested with the help of draft horses. Pancakes made with Red Fife flour, buttermilk, and eggs are ready for the maple syrup you will have learned about, or not, when you visit. Frittatas, a breakfast sandwich, and fresh-fruit parfait were added to the menu of classic breakfast dishes in 2008. But you can always count on pancakes with local sausages, maple baked beans, and seasonal fruit topping, served all day. Hikes through the sugarbush are part of the visit. Maple cocktails provide a pleasant way to transition to lunch; try the Irish Maple Syrup, just Irish whiskey and maple syrup on ice. A store sells pancake mix made with Red Fife Flour, syrups, and more.

PICTOU

MURPHY'S FISH AND CHIPS

902-485-2009
91 Water St., Pictou
Open: Mon.–Thurs. 11 AM–7 PM, Fri.–Sat. 11 AM–8 PM, Sun. 12–7 PM
Price: $6.35 to $19.29
Credit cards: Yes
Cuisine: Maritime seafood and burgers
Serving: L, D
Handicap Access: Yes

A branch of the exceptional seafood restaurant in Truro, this Murphy's Fish and Chips follows the same excellent practices, with the same menu. Gerard Anderson's secret batter coats the deep-fried scallops, Digby clams, and fish, all cooked fresh and to order. Poached haddock is thoughtfully provided for anyone who prefers not to eat deep-fried food, and you can also dine on roast turkey, grilled liver and onions, or a large hamburger served with whipped potatoes or fries, a vegetable, and coleslaw, "fried onions extra." Natalie Anderson, sister of the Anderson brother owners, runs the Pictou location. Customers can enjoy their meals on a big deck within full view of the water, at this location next to the DeCoste Center.

PICTOU LODGE

902-485-4322
pictoulodge.com
172 Lodge Rd., Braeshore
Open: Mid-May–mid-Oct., breakfast 7–11 AM, Sunday 7–10; lunch 12–2 PM (June–Oct.) except Sun.; dinner (reservations required) 5:30–9 PM (mid-May–Oct.);Sun. brunch (mid-June–mid-Oct., reservations required) 11 AM–2 PM, live music
Price: $20 to $30
Credit cards: Yes
Cuisine: Continental and Maritime
Serving: B, L, D
Handicap Access: Yes
Special Features: A screened, outdoor terrace for dining in good weather

A curiosity about haggis would serve you well on a visit to this dining room, where "haggis, tatties, and neeps" are served with Balvanie whiskey sauce. But a fine reputation for good meals at Pictou Lodge works for everything else too. A lobster Napoleon sandwiches lobster in chive and brandy cream with layers of puff pastry. For a main course there's maple-planked salmon, roasted on a cedar board and basted with maple syrup and butter, then served with maple mustard sauce. Pictou Lodge's kitchen decided that scallops can share the good fortune of its pairing with bacon, wrapping halibut in bacon and serving it with a tart apple sauce and balsamic reduction. For a vegetarian, the coulibiac made with layers of tofu, peppers, onions, glass noodles, and puff pastry sounds like a winner. Tuesday night Prime Jazz, from mid-June to mid-October, features prime rib on the menu and local jazz musicians.

NEW GLASGOW

BISTRO ON BACK STREET

902-752-4988
thebistronewglasgow.com
216 Archimedes St., New Glasgow

Open: Tues.–Sat. from 5 PM
Price: $14 to $29
Credit cards: Yes
Cuisine: Italian and Asian
Serving: D
Handicap Access: No

Chef/owner Robert Vinton and partner Heather Poulin opened this bistro in 2002 for the previous owners, and they took it over themselves in 2006. Vinton trained in French cooking and worked in Italian and French restaurants in Calgary and Toronto plus; he's Asian-Scottish and grew up eating Asian food. He's developed his own good recipes for Asian classic cuisine; the trick with dumplings, he says, is to boil them first and pan-fry them. His pork dumplings are made with Sicilian sausage and scallion and served with a three-pepper salsa. From another tradition—one he may have started—the seared scallops come with Frangelico cream, peaches, and toasted hazelnuts. Dinner could be pork tenderloin wrapped with Serrano ham, or curried haddock, or Thai noodles with steak, shrimp, mushrooms, and snow peas.

HEBEL'S RESTAURANT

902-695-5955
hebelsrestaurant.ca
71 Stellarton Rd., New Glasgow
Open: Tues.–Sat. from 5 PM
Price: $19 to $32
Credit cards: Yes
Cuisine: Continental
Serving: D
Handicap Access: Yes

Peter Hebel is the chef at Hebel's, which he opened in 2006. He arrived in Nova Scotia from Germany after a career in European, Caribbean, South Pacific, and Maritime kitchens. His menu might start with fried calamari with a garlic and yogurt dip, or a seafood strudel. For the main course, grilled swordfish and mango papaya salsa with sweet potato fries is his twist on fish and chips. His chicken cordon bleu is stuffed with ham and Swiss. Apple fritters with vanilla ice cream, or a wine-poached pear with chocolate sauce, are desserts.

ANTIGONISH

DRAGONFLY CAFÉ

902-863-2574
dragonflycafe.ca
Lower South River, Antigonish
Open: Mon.–Fri. 6 AM–6 PM, Sat. 7 AM–6 PM, Sun. 7AM–3 PM
Credit cards: Yes
Cuisine: Bistro standards
Serving: B, L
Handicap Access: No

Suzanne Benoit's cafe makes fresh soup every day. The house salad dressing might be vinaigrette with some strawberries in it that she picked up at the Saturday farmers' market. She buys as much local produce as possible, looking for things to inspire her lunch specials, like chanterelle mushrooms for a pasta dish. The fresh flowers on the table might come from the market too. Benoit studied pastry arts and culinary arts at Nova Scotia Community College's Akerly campus, and she praises her staff of about 18 for their excellent skills, from the chefs to the servers. Some of them assist at the local weddings and business lunches that she caters too.

GABRIEAU'S BISTRO

902-863-1925
gabrieaus.com
350 Main St., Antigonish
Open: Mon.–Fri. 11 AM–9 PM, Sat. 4–9 PM, closed Sun.
Price: $17 to $30
Credit cards: Yes
Cuisine: French and Italian, with Asian influences
Serving: L, D
Handicap Access: Yes
Special Features: Sidewalk tables

When we visited, black tablecloths and red napkins added sophistication to the interior of Gabrieau's—even as the pale green light reflected from a tractor-trailer load of hay flashed through the windows. The Domaine de Grand Pré Léon Millot is a simple, smooth red wine, nicely cutting the cream of the appetizer, mussels with tarragon and white wine, so delectable I ate every last one. The seafood vindaloo held a half tail of lobster, scallops, gulf shrimp, salmon, haddock, and swordfish, in a spicy sauce with green and red peppers and celery. Ripe strawberries with whipped cream on puff pastry made a wonderful end, the puff pastry sugared and crisp and the cream definitely real. I would be eager to try anything else on the menu here, from the beef and shrimp stir-fry to a pairing of grilled lamb and braised lamb with wild-mushroom risotto. Owned by chef Mark Gabrieau and his wife Karen, Gabrieau's opened in 1999.

FOOD PURVEYORS

Cafés and Coffee Shops
Dine and Dash (902-695-3300), Main St., Trenton. Open daily, weekdays 11AM–8 PM, weekends 8 AM to 8 PM. Fish cakes are a specialty, along with good chowder, and corned beef and cabbage on Thursdays. Milk shakes are the old-fashioned kind. For dessert there's chocolate cake with boiled frosting and pies like apple, strawberry rhubarb, and many more.

Gram's Place (902-752-1002), 225 Foord St., Stellarton. Open Mon.–Sat. Homemade bread is used in the excellent sandwiches. This expanding café and bakery is well known for fresh rolls and homemade soups like tomato cheddar soup, made every day. There are sandwiches like roast beef, chicken salad, tuna, egg, and turkey. Scotch cookies, squares, and cherry cheesecake are some of the desserts.

Sunrise Mercantile Gourmet Foods and Café (902-657-1094; sunmerc.com), 1631 Rte. 6, Tatamagouche. Coffee, tea, spices, jams, dessert sauces, snacks, housewares and much more. A café inside the shop allows some taste tests.

Candy
The Appleton Chocolates Company (902-548-2323; appletonchocoaltes.ca), 567 Lake Rd., Wentworth (Rte. 4 to Wentworth from Exit 11 off the Trans Canada Highway if traveling north from Truro, or Exit 7 if south from Amherst). The fine chocolates you can find here are made with Callebaut chocolate from Belgium and Cacao Berry chocolate from France. The Wild Blueberry and Rum chocolate combines historic ingredients to make a mouthful of information anyone can learn from. Centers of candied wild blueberries are made with maple fondant.

Wild Blueberry and Maple Center (902-447-2908; town.oxford.ns.ca/visit/wbmc.htm), 105 Lower Main St., Oxford. Open May–Oct. daily 10 AM–6 PM. Exhibits reveal the ways wild blueberries are harvested, and a case with bees demonstrates their important work of pollination. Maple syrup exhibits show how trees are tapped and how the watery sap is turned into liquid gold. A self-serve corner allows a sampling of the flavors of both local pleasures, and the shop is stocked with plenty you can buy for a wonderful souvenir.

Meats

Roseland Farm Bavarian Meat Shop (902-657-0374; roselanefarm.com), Denmark , south of the coast and between Tatamagouche and River John. Open Apr.–Oct., Fri.–Sat. 9 AM–6 PM. Manfred and Doris Bauer, came here from Unterschüpf, Germany, in 1998; a year later they opened the meat shop, with 70 kinds of meat and sausages made with locally raised pork. Gelbwurst with herbs, Lyoner, Jagdwurst, smoked German salami, or Cabanossi, are some names from the long list of products.

Microbreweries and Pubs

The Dock (902-752-0884), 130 George St., New Glasgow. Open Mon.–Sat., weekdays from 11:30 AM, Sat. from 12 noon. The Dock is inside a restored sandstone heritage house built in the mid-1800s. Shelley Lockehart is the chef who returned home from Montreal; she cooks the fresh seafood that arrives three times a week. The owner, Carmel Margeson, bakes fresh soda bread daily. Margeson, who is from Cork, said that going into a pub was second nature to her; when she moved to New Glasgow, it seemed like a woman on her own would feel uncomfortable doing that here. But now children and women will feel right at home. "We're slowly changing people's idea about a public house in New Glasgow," she said. Her wonderful group of regulars, she said, includes Canadian tourists who make sure to return to The Dock on trips to Nova Scotia. Corned beef and cabbage and Irish stew are specials more likely to be offered in the winter.

Seafood Take-out

Boyd's Seafood Galley (902-863-0279), Cribben's Point Wharf, Antigonish. Fried seafood and more. A long menu, and indoor seating, makes this a good place for dinner on a cold night.

Fish 'N' Ships (902-870-5207), Ballantynes Cove Wharf, Rte. 337, Ballantynes Cove Open July–Oct., daily 12 noon–8 PM. This take-out spot has good fish and chips, fried scallops, and seafood chowder. It's set on an exceptionally lovely wharf, with tables and chairs next to it for sitting and enjoying your meal. Also serving hamburgers, ice cream, and milk shakes. The cove is 1.2 miles southwest of Cape George Lighthouse, off Rte. 337 and heading to Antigonish.

Tearoom

Mrs. MacGregor's Tea Room and Restaurant (902-382-1878; mrsmacgregors.com), 59 Water St., Pictou. Open daily 11 AM–3 PM, Thurs.–Sat. also open 5–8 PM. Teas with shortbread, cheesecake, and butterscotch pie, or lunch and suppers of Scots Meat Pie or pan-seared haddock. The sticky toffee pudding is one more reason to make this a destination.

Wineries

Jöst Vineyards (800-565-4567; jostwine.com), 48 Vintage Ln. (between Malagash Mines and Malagash Centre), Malagash, NS B0K 1E0. Open mid-June–mid-Sept., daily 9 AM–6 PM; May–Dec. 23 daily 9 AM–5 PM, Dec. 24.–Apr. Mon.–Sat. 9 AM–5 PM. Complimentary wine tastings and tours mid-June to mid-September at noon and 3 PM. Forty-five acres of grapes are under constant care, pruned, tied, suckered, weeded, trimmed, and harvested, year-round. Jöst Vineyards contracts with growers to care for another 130 acres of vineyards, using those harvests to make its good wine. Both at Jöst and at its contracted fields, grapes that excel in this area are cultivated, including Maréchal Foch, L'Acadie, Luci Kuhlmass, Mischurnitz, Maréchal Joffre, Severnyi, Seyval Blanc, Canadice, Baco Noir, Léon Millot, and several more. Some imported grapes are also used, for instance Cabernet Sauvignon in a Cab and Maréchal Foch blend. The 2005 Léon Millot was a double gold winner at the 2007 All-Canadian Wine Championships.

CULTURE

Historic Buildings and Sites

HECTOR HERITAGE QUAY
902-485-4371, 877-574-2868
townofpictou.com/the_experience.html
33 Calladh Ave., Pictou, NS B0K 1H0
Open: Mid-May–mid-Oct. daily
Admission: Adults $7, seniors and students $5, children 6–12 $2

The centerpiece of this historic site is the replica of the *Hector*, the rotting ship—without the rot—that brought the first 189 Scots into New Scotland, the English translation of the Latin name, Nova Scotia, on September 15, 1773. Smallpox had killed some of the children, and storms had blown them off course, but the arrival of this ship heralded the beginning of an influx of Scots that turned the entire region into a reproduction of their native land. Scottish settlers here and on Cape Breton continue to honor their heritage with the language of the Celts, Gaelic, and the tartans, bagpipes, games, and other traditions.

The reproduction of the *Hector* was built by volunteers and local craftsmen, some descendents of those first 189. "New Scotland Days," celebrated from mid-July to September 15, brings costumed interpreters on board. In the shipyard, workers keep a fire burning at the blacksmith's shop, and hammer chisels in the carpenter's shop. The studio of artist David MacIntosh is open to visitors; his paintings chronicle the building of the modern *Hector*.

Lighthouses

CAPE GEORGE LIGHTHOUSE
parl.ns.ca/lighthouse
Lighthouse Rd. (off Rte. 337), Cape George Point
Open: May–Nov.
Admission: Free

The 1908 structure, rebuilt in 1968, is a white octagonal tower with a red lantern. Views of Cape Breton and Prince Edward Island can be enjoyed from this spot overlooking St. George's Bay, and interpretative panels tell the history of the lighthouses built here. Trails.

Museums

CREAMERY SQUARE MUSEUM AND ARCHIVES
902-657-3500
creamerysquare.ca
257 Main St., Tatamagouche, NS B0K 1V0
Open: July–Aug. daily; call for off-season hours
Admission: To be set with opening of the new building

Displays of the Anna Swan Museum, the Brule Fossils, Creamery Museum, Sunrise Trail Museum, and North Shore Archives are all inside the newly renovated buildings, including the Creamery, where a million pounds of butter once were churned. Anna Swan, the Tallest Woman in The World at 7 feet, 5.5 inches, who toured with P. T. Barnum's museum, supposedly weighed 19 pounds when she was born in 1846, near Tatamagouche. A door from her house in Seville, Ohio, is on display: it's 8 feet, 6 inches tall.

The Brule Fossils—and the re-creation of a 290-million-year-old forest, with models of animals whose tracks were discovered on the beach within 7 kilometers or 5 miles of the museum—are part of the new exhibits. Boiler Bob is a resident ghost who will appear and tell tales about the creamery.

MALAGASH AREA HERITAGE MUSEUM
902-257-2407
1926 North Shore Rd., Malagash, NS B0K 1E0
Open: Mid-June–mid-Sept., Tues.–Sat. 10 AM–5 PM, Sun. 12–5 PM
Admission: Adults $2, seniors $1.50, and students $1

The museum depicts the history of the first rock-salt mine in Canada. From 1918 until 1959, salt was mined from 300 meters or 1,200 feet below the surface. Rock salt is as hard as cement; it was formed in a large seam. Several tons of this material were hauled out each day by an underground railway. Sample chunks are available for visitors to take away, but they are from a salt mine in Pugwash.

NORTHUMBERLAND FISHERIES MUSEUM
902-485-4972
northumberlandfisheriesmuseum.com
71 Front St., Pictou, NS B0K 1H0
Open: July–Aug., daily 10 AM–5 PM; June and Sept. opens later
Admission: Adults $5, students and seniors 65 and older $3

With exhibits about the fishing industry, the museum operates out of a former Canadian Railway Station. Within the next two years, it will move to a new waterfront building. A replica of a fisherman's bunkhouse, a 28-foot open-top fishing boat called the *Silver Bullet*, and a live-lobster tank with blue and green and other unusual lobsters are all on display. The **Lighthouse Exhibit**, at 7 Caladh Ave., on the waterfront, has a 6-foot map with lighthouses flashing at their spots along the coast. It's inside a full-size replica lighthouse, still a work in progress, and it's open 12–7 PM daily in summer, with free admission and a gift shop.

NOVA SCOTIA MUSEUM OF INDUSTRY
902-755-5425
museum.gov.ns.ca/moi/
147 North Foord St., Stellarton, NS B0K 1S0
Open: June–Oct. 15, Mon.–Tues. and Thurs.–Sat. 9 AM–to 5 PM, Wed. 9 AM–8 PM, Sun.
12–5 PM; Oct. 16–May, Tues. and Thurs.–Sat. 9:30 AM–5 PM, Wed. 9:30 AM–8 PM (and free
after 5), Sun. 1–5 PM, closed Mon.
Admission: Adults $7.50, seniors 65 and older $4.50, children 6–17 $3.25

The largest of the 27 museums in the Nova Scotia museum group, Nova Scotia Museum of
Industry lets visitors get to work with rug-hooking, quilting, and at an assembly-line
challenge. Kids like to pump water into the waterpower exhibit—if you pump enough,
the grindstones will turn or the carding machine will get underway. The Samson Steam
Locomotive on display was built in 1838; large pulleys nearby demonstrate the steam power
in a machine shop. Pressed glass made in Pictou County in the late 1800s was fired with
coal.

SUTHERLAND STEAM MILL AND BALMORAL GRIST MILL
Sutherland: 902-657-3365
steammill.museum.gov.ns.ca
3169 Rte. 326, Denmark, NS
Mail: RR #5, Tatamagouche, NS B0V 1K0
Open: June–mid-Oct. Mon.–Sat. 9:30 AM to 5:30 PM, Sun. 1–5:30 PM
Admission: Adults $3.25, children 6–17 and seniors 65 and older $2.25
Balmoral: 902-657-3016
gristmill.museum.gov.ns.ca
660 Matheson Brook Rd., Balmoral Mills, NS
Open: June–mid-Oct., Mon.–Sat. 9:30 AM–5:30 PM, Sun. 1–5:30 PM
Admission: Adults $3.25, children 6–17 and seniors 65 and older $2.25

These two mill museums, both part of the Nova Scotia Museum Group, are located within
10 kilometers or 6.2 miles of each other. Sutherland Steam Mill used a steam boiler for its
power source, making shingles, boards, trim, sleds, and carriages. Balmoral Grist Mill
once took advantage of the water power in Matheson's Brook to grind wheat, oats, and
buckwheat, and it still does just that for museum visitors, when it's in good working order.
Oat flour, wheat flour, and buckwheat flour are for sale in the store. The Christine
MacDonald Trail, 1 kilometer or .62 mile long, is next to the mill.

Music

SUMMER MUSICAL SHOWCASE
902-485-6057
Visitor's Marina Stage, Waterfront, Pictou, NS
Open: July–Aug., Sun.–Mon. at 6 PM
Admission: Free

Outdoor concerts are held in the summer.

SUMMER SOUNDS OF NOVA SCOTIA

902-485-8848, 800-353-5338
decostecentre.ca
deCoste Centre, 85 Water St., P.O. Box 39, Pictou, NS B0K 1H0
Open: July–Aug., Tues.–Thurs. at 8 PM
Admission: Adults $16, students, $8

Ceilidhs (Gaelic for kitchen party), with fiddlers, bagpipes, dancers, and other traditional Maritimes musicians and singers, are held on some Tuesdays, Wednesdays, and Thursdays of July and August—check the schedule or call for performances.

Theater

FESTIVAL ANTIGONISH SUMMER THEATRE

902-867-3333, 800-563-7529
festivalantigonish.com
Bauer Theatre, St. Francis Xavier University, P.O. Box 5000, Antigonish, NS B2G 2W5
Open: Through the summer
Admission: Seats range from $28 to $5, depending on stage and time

More than 100 performances of 12 shows are scheduled for the two months of the summer season. Theatergoers under 30 years old can get $10 tickets, less than half price and a wonderful way to start enjoying live drama. Passes are also available with four show tickets you can use however you wish, for substantial savings.

Seasonal Events

July

Antigonish Highland Games (antigonsihhighlandgames.com), Antigonish. Musicians, dancers, and athletes arrive here every July to compete, just as they have done since 1863.

Gathering of the Clans (pugwashvillage.com), Pugwash. Bagpipes, drums, dancing, and fireworks.

New Scotland Days (902-485-6057; townofpictou.com/special_events.html), Hector Heritage Quay, Pictou. Celebrated from mid-July to September 15 and honoring the arrival of the *Hector* with the first Scots to land in what would become their new land.

Pictou Lobster Carnival (pictoulobstercarnival.com), Pictou. Chicken barbeque and lobster supper is held in the town center.

August

Festival of the Tartans (festivalofthetartans.ca), New Glasgow. Four days celebrating Scottish culture, with pipe and drum competitions, highland dancing, ceilidhs, a tea, and more.

Hector Festival (902-485-8848, 800-353-5338; Decostecentre.ca), DeCoste Centre, 85 Water St., P.O. Box 39, Pictou, NS B0K 1H0. This five-day festival re-enacts the arrival of the *Hector* in 1773, with entertainment, displays, and demonstrations.

Pictou North Colchester Bluegrass Festival (902-382-2166), Exhibition Grounds, Pictou. Three days of bluegrass music.

Riverfront Music Jubilee (jubilee.ns.ca), New Glasgow. A four-day music event held in the outdoor amphitheater on the New Glasgow riverfront.

Wild Blueberry Harvest Festival (wildblueberryfest.com), Central Nova Scotia.

RECREATION

Amusement Parks

Magic Valley Family Fun Park (902-396-4467; magicvalley.ca), 4488 Hwy. 4, Greenhill (9.5 kilometers or 6 miles west of New Glasgow). Open early July–Labour Day daily. Riders on the long and high waterslide must be 36 inches tall or more. There's a swimming pool, railroad train, pedal boats, and bumper boats. The paradrop was out of commission in 2008. The miniscrambler and bunny hop are for small children only. Story Book Village is a walk through a wood full of familiar fairy tales, like the old woman who lived in a shoe, and you can also visit Old MacDonald's Farm petting zoo.

Beaches

Blue Sea Beach Provincial Park, Malagash. A mile-long beach suitable for children and for swimming. Picnic tables, sandbars, a salt marsh, and changing rooms.

Cape John Fisherman's Beach Park, Cape John Rd., River John. A commercial fishing wharf is alongside at this beach, reached by a steel stair. Flat rock makes up the ground under the water, but the beach is sandy. Views of Amet Island and Brule Shore are beautiful, and the beach itself is private and quiet.

Fox Harbour Provincial Beach Park, Fox Harbour. Red-sand beach with changing rooms and toilets.

Gulf Shore Provincial Park Beach, Pugwash. Warm water and a sandy beach with picnic tables, changing rooms, and toilets.

Heather Beach Provincial Park, Port Howe. This beach can get crowded; the water is supervised in midsummer. Changing rooms and toilets.

Melmerby Beach, east of New Glasgow, and 16 kilometers or 10 miles north of Hwy. 104, Exit 25. The favorite beach of many in the area, Melmerby Beach has 2 kilometers or 1.25 miles of supervised reddish sand beach and boardwalks. There are changing rooms and salt-rinse showers. Stop at Harbor Beach Market before you arrive for good pizza or a picnic lunch.

Rushtons Beach Provincial Park, east of Tatamagouche. This sandy beach features warm ocean water and picnic tables, sandbars, and a salt marsh that birds love. A bird observation deck overlooks the marshland. Changing rooms, toilets, boardwalks, and views of Amet Island and Cape John cliffs.

Skinner's Cove Beach, Skinner's Cove East Rd., Melville. Views of red cliffs and Prince Edward Island. This beach has no facilities, but it's quiet and secluded.

Golf

Abercrombie Golf & Country Club (902-752-6249, 888-758-6350; abercrombie golf.com), Abercrombie Rd., New Glasgow. A host to provincial and national tournaments, Abercrombie Golf Course is undergoing renovations to six of its 18 holes, improving the looks and structures of the course.

Fox Harb'r Golf & Country Club (902-257-1801, 866-257-1801; foxharbr.com), 1337 Fox Harbour Rd., Wallace. An 18-hole course on Wallace Bay, available to members and guests of the resort only. The course is also considered the most expensive in the Maritime Provinces.

Northumberland Links (902-243-2808; northumberlandlinks.com), 1776 Gulf Shore Rd., Pugwash. Blustery conditions can add a challenge to this handsome course overlooking the ocean. At the fourth hole, some balls have been known to slide into the sea.

Hiking

Antigonish Landing Trail, Antigonish. A 4-kilometer or 2.5-mile hike on an estuary holds two observation platforms where hikers can watch for osprey, eagles, and ducks.

Cape George Trail (sunrisetrail.ca/places/Cape-George-Trail.htm), Cape George. A 33-kilometer or 22-mile network of trails brings hikers out to the sea and inland up and down the hills, with benches on the trails. Three kilometers or 2 miles of trail is on the ocean. Trail heads are located at Cape George Heritage School, Ballantyne's Cove Wharf, and Cape George Day Park.

Tidnish Dock Provincial Park (902-424-4321), Rte. 366 at Tidnish Cross Roads. The marine railway was once located here, a failed project that was intended to transport ships by rail to the Bay of Fundy. But now the **Henry Ketchum Trail and Cable Bridge** is completely successful—at getting folks out walking and enjoying the scenery. The 4-kilometer or 2.6-mile trail runs between Tidnish Dock Provincial Park and the Tidnish Bridge Vistor's Centre, on the old route of the Chignecto Ship Railway, across an old bridge and over the Tidnish River on a modern cable suspension bridge.

Trans Canada Trail (902-425-5450, ext. 325; trailtc.ns.ca), located in Tatamagouche behind the Train Station Inn, this trail takes a walker across French River from Nelson Memorial Park Campground.

Wallace Bay Nature Wildlife Trail, Old Bidou Rd., Wallace. A 582-hectare or 1450-acre wildlife area with trails running through marsh, woods, and fields.

Parks

Amherst Shore Provincial Park (902-661-6002; parks.gov.ns.ca), Rte. 366, between Lorneville and Northport, west of Puwash. A 2.5-kilometer or 1.5-mile trail runs beside Annabelles Brook to the beach. Sandpipers, blue herons, osprey, and ducks like to visit, and triploid blue-spotted salamanders are found only in this area. Tidal flats heated by the sun bring up the temperature of the already mild ocean water here. Forty-two sites at the campground.

Arisaig Provincial Park (902-863-4513; novascotiaparks.gov.ns.ca), Rte. 245, Arisaig. The rocks are the stars at this coastal park. Eroded by the sea, the Silurian rocks of this area include dark and light lava and pyroclastic flows, and embedded in them are fossils of creatures that lived 400 million and more years ago. A 1.6-kilometer or 1-mile trail has a viewing platform at the beach and places where you can walk down to the rocks and maybe find a fossil.

Caribou-Munroes Island Provincial Park (902-485-6134; parks.gov.ns.ca), off Rte. 6, Caribou. Located close to the Caribou-Woods Island Ferry to Prince Edward Island,

Caribou-Munroes Island Park has camping, group camping sites, unsupervised swimming, showers, and washrooms. A 2-kilometer or 1.2-mile trail follows the sandspit out to Munroes Island and at the end gives a hiker a great view of the arriving and departing ferry. A stand of beech on the island is unique among the softwoods that dominate. A search of the tidal pools will likely turn up hermit crabs, jellyfish, and shellfish that Great Blue Herons visit the park to dine on.

Nelson Park (902-657-2730), Tatamagouche. Campgrounds, beach, and a canteen on 47 acres of land alongside the ocean. A pool, children's play area, and more.

Shopping

Bookstores

Bookends (902-863-6922), 342 Main St., Antigonish. More than 30,000 books range from fiction to nonfiction, children's books, and rarities.

Downtown Exchange (902-752-1216), 168 Provost, New Glasgow. New and used books, CDs, and movies. Local authors and books about Atlantic Canada are a specialty.

Galleries

Alice Reed Studio Gallery (902-386-2501), Pomquet, RR #7 Antigonish. Watercolor paintings that are vividly detailed take nature and animals as their subjects. Call ahead to view original work, reproductions, and cards.

Knives

Grohmann Knives (902-485-4224; grohmannknives.com), Factory Outlet Store, 116 Water St., Pictou. Open Mon.–Sat. 9 AM–5 PM, Sun. in summer. Beautifully crafted hunting knives, an extensive range of chef's knives, and some outdoor clothing. Fifteen- to 30-minute tours of the factory are offered Monday through Friday 9 AM– 3 PM, but call to confirm. The business began here with the creation of the D. H. Russell Belt Knife #1, for hunters.

Lavender

Beach Lane Lavender Farm (902-351-2601, 800-294-9530; anitacarlson.com), 147 Carlson Lane, River John. Open Mon.–Sat. 10 AM–4 PM. Visit the certified organic farm to walk in the lavender fields, and later stop by the shop to consider the bath and body care products, aromatherapy pillows, and lavender jelly made with roses, red currants, and raspberry. You can also purchase lavender plants. The farm hosts a Lavender Festival every summer.

Pottery

Sara Bonnyman Pottery (902-657-3215; sarabonnymanpottery.com), 326 Maple Ave., Tatamagouche. Open July–Sept., Mon.–Sat. 10 AM–4 PM, off-season by chance or appointment. Functional pottery with earth tones and graceful organic shapes. A "moss scuttle" has proved to be a popular new piece—it's used for wet shaving and has a handle and lip for lathering a shaving brush.

Woodworking

Peter and David MacLean (902-863-2922, or 902-863-2739; macleanbroswoodwork
  ing.com), 225 Old Beaver Rd., James River, Antigonish. Call ahead of a visit. Kitchen-
  ware and gifts made out of silky, polished bird's-eye maple; also custom furniture and
  cabinetry.

Wool

Lismore Sheep Farm (902-351-2889; lismoresheepfarmwoolshop.com), River John, just
  off Rte. 6. A sheep farm with 300 sheep, mostly Dorset/Finn sheep with soft fleece. The
  farm uses the fleece to make blankets, sweaters, hats, wool mattress pads, and more.
  During the summer you can visit the barn.

8

CAPE BRETON ISLAND

Fiddlers Serenade the Mountains and the Sea

This chapter is divided into regions to help a reader make sense of Cape Breton Island—while it's possible to travel around the Cabot Trail in a day, it's far more fun to stay in each area and explore.

First from the western end of the Canso Causeway, which divides the island from the mainland, to the top of the western coast of the island in Pleasant Bay, you encounter Scots and Acadians, entering the southwestern corner of the Cape Breton Highlands National Park at about midpoint. The Ceilidh Trail threads through the Scots settlements of the turn of the 19th century, in a region famous for its love of traditional music and the source of the "Cape Breton Sound."

The beginning of the Cabot Trail moves through the Margaree River valley, where you can fish for wild salmon. Where the trail touches down on the western coast, and before it climbs the steep coastal mountains, you will find Acadian towns like Chéticamp, with artisans' shops and informal restaurants serving Acadian specialties.

The next section of this chapter describes the northern tip of Cape Breton Island, where a drive beyond the Cabot Trail rewards the curious with magnificent views in Meat Cove, delicious fresh oysters at Hideway Campground, and the southern town of Baddeck.

Finally, in the third section of this chapter, the Bras d'Or Lakes, Louisbourg, and Isle Madame again mix up the French and the Scots, who live peacefully these days, working together to promote this pretty area that is a delight to explore.

The Fortress of Louisbourg National Historic Site was another outpost of

The indigenous pitcher plants of the bog are on display along the Bog Walk in Cape Breton Highlands National Park.

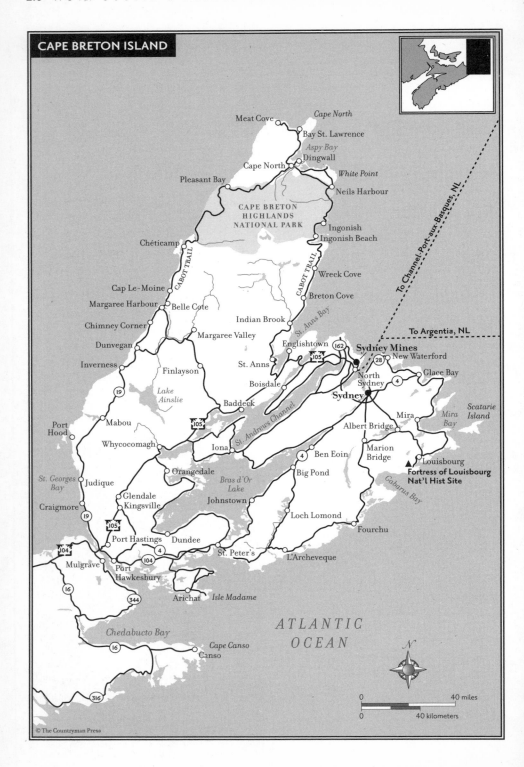

CAPE BRETON ISLAND

Meat Cove
Cape North
Bay St. Lawrence
Aspy Bay
Cape North
Dingwall
White Point
Pleasant Bay
Neils Harbour

CAPE BRETON HIGHLANDS NATIONAL PARK

Chéticamp
Ingonish
Ingonish Beach

CABOT TRAIL

Cap Le-Moine
Wreck Cove

Margaree Harbour
Breton Cove
Belle Cote

CABOT TRAIL

Chimney Corner
Indian Brook
Margaree Valley

Dunvegan
St. Anns Bay
Englishtown
162
Sydney Mines
New Waterford
105
28

Inverness
Finlayson
St. Anns
North Sydney
Glace Bay

19
Lake Ainslie
Boisdale
Sydney
4

Mabou
Baddeck
Mira
Scatarie Island

Port Hood
105
Albert Bridge
Mira Bay

Whycocomagh
Iona
St. Andrews Channel
Marion Bridge

Ben Eoin
Louisbourg
Orangedale
▲ **Fortress of Louisbourg Nat'l Hist Site**

St. Georges Bay
Judique
Bras d'Or Lake
Big Pond

Craigmore
Glendale
Johnstown
Cabarus Bay

Kingsville
Loch Lomond

19
105
Port Hastings
Dundee
Fourchu

104
St. Peter's
L'Archeveque

Mulgrave
Port Hawkesbury
104

16
344
Arichat
Isle Madame

Chedabucto Bay
Cape Canso
Canso

ATLANTIC OCEAN

16
316

To Channel Port-aux-Basques, NL

To Argentia, NL

N

0 — 40 miles
0 — 40 kilometers

© The Countryman Press

Acadia—and lost its battle to stay that way in the mid-1700s. Although destroyed, its stone shipped off to construct buildings elsewhere, it was rebuilt in the 1960s. Today Fortress Louisbourg is a flourishing cultural destination from May to October.

Western Cape Breton Island to Pleasant Bay

Lodging

Port Hood

HAUS TREUBURG COUNTRY INN
Georg and Elvi Kargoll, innkeepers
902-787-2116
haustreuburg.com
175 Main St., P.O. Box 92, Port Hood, NS
B0E 2W0
Price: $95 to $135
Credit cards: Yes
Handicapped Access: Yes, one cottage
Special Features: Wi-Fi

The Berlin Room has a fully paneled bathroom, and paneling forms the headboards of its two double beds with down duvets. Paneled ceilings are another feature, notably in the Munich Room, with its queen-size beds and down duvet. A suite has a room for relaxing as well as a paneled bedroom and private bathroom. The house holds a well-thought-of restaurant and serves a German breakfast to its guests ($11.50 in 2008), with homemade bread, sourdough rye or white, plus tea, bacon, cheese, tomatoes, cereal, homemade yogurt, fresh fruit, and perhaps a zucchini omelet or pancakes.

Glenville

GLENORA INN & DISTILLERY RESORT
800-839-0491
glenoradistillery.com
Rte. 19 (Ceilidh Trail), Glenville, Cape

Sometimes you can see whales just by pulling off the Cabot Trail near Pleasant Bay and scanning the ocean below.

Breton, NS BoE 1X0
Open: May–mid-Oct.
Price: $120 to $295
Credit cards: Yes
Handicapped Access: Yes
Special Features: Wi-Fi, distillery

The inn has nine rooms built beside a flowering courtyard. Elsewhere, on the hillside, are six pine-paneled chalets with front decks and two-person airjet tubs. Guests are given a discounted rate for the tour that takes you through the distillery—$5 instead of $7. The inn rooms are not as attractive as the rooms in the chalet. Ask about room rate specials.

MARGAREE VALLEY

THE NORMAWAY INN
David MacDonald, innkeeper
902-248-2987, 800-565-9463
normaway.com
691 Egypt Rd., P.O. Box 121, Margaree Valley, NS BoE 2C0
Price: $100 to $270, MAP rates available
Credit cards: Yes
Handicapped Access: Yes
Special Features: Wi-Fi, bicycles, half-mile paved private airstrip a short hike away

Ten rooms in the inn, all with private bath, some under the eaves and some with a single pull-out sofa, are the least expensive accommodations. The White Cabins, built in 1945 and updated, are furnished with painted wood furniture and tartan curtains. The pine-paneled Green Cabins, 6 one-bedroom and five larger versions, all have a woodstove or fireplace, screened or glassed-in porch, and a porch swing. Top of the line are the MacPherson House suites with either one or two bedrooms and decorated with original art. Trails for hikes, a lawn for croquet, and a horseshoe pit take care of any moments left over after fly fishing on the Margaree River for some of North America's only thriving wild Atlantic salmon.

BELLE CÔTE

ISLAND SUNSET RESORT AND SPA
866-515-2900
islandsunset.com
19 Beach Cove Ln., Belle Côte
Mail: P.O. Box 27, Margaree Harbor, NS BoE 2B0
Price: $145 to $205
Credit cards: Yes
Handicapped Access: Yes, one
Special Features: Fireplaces, Wi-Fi

Set beside the ocean, five buildings with suites in each total 18 exceptional accommodations; each has a fireplace, an outfitted kitchen, a whirlpool tub, hardwood floors, a front deck with wooden lawn chairs, and high-quality furnishings. They are all basically the same inside; the Sunset Royal Suite has a view of the ocean from many of its windows. A sandy beach can accommodate swimming. A stay of seven consecutive nights or more will bring a 5-percent discount. Spa treatments run the gamut from lash tinting to massage.

CHÉTICAMP

ALBERT'S MOTEL
Tom Delosa, innkeeper
902-224-2077, 877-220-2077
15086 Cabot Trail, P.O. Box 68, Chéticamp, NS BoE 1H0
Price: $55 to $85
Credit cards: Yes
Handicapped Access: None
Special Features: Wi-Fi

Tom Delosa has completely updated his simple motel in the middle of Chéticamp, across the street from the Acadian Restaurant. Three of the rooms have two double beds and one has a double and a queen; all of them hold new furniture, a fridge, and a microwave. You can sit on the deck and look out across the street to the water; in the early part of the day the white sheets will be on the clothesline, drying in the sun.

Albert's Motel in Chéticamp is small and immaculate.

L'AUBERGE DOUCET

Ronnie Doucet, owner, Lida Babineau, manager
902-224-3438, 800-646-8668
aubergedoucetinn.com
14758 Cabot Trail, P.O. Box 776, Chéticamp, NS B0E 1H0
Open: May–mid-Nov.
Price: $60 to $150
Credit cards: Yes
Handicapped Access: Yes, one
Special Features: Wi-Fi in dining room after breakfast, and in some of the rooms

Seven plain and clean rooms with two double beds, others with one queen or double, and two housekeeping suites make up the accommodations here. Number 14, the suite, and Rooms 1, 3, 5, and 7 are all on the water side with a good view. A full breakfast, served from 7:30 to 10 AM, can be enjoyed in the restaurant and might include eggs any style with a choice of ham, bacon, or sausage, plus toast; or pancakes or french toast, or oatmeal; and coffee or tea and juice. The bilingual owners can find a route for your adventures the next day, or help with recommendations, at this inn just outside of Chéticamp

OCEAN VIEW MOTEL AND CHALETS

Guillaume and Paulette LeBlanc, hosts
902-224-2313, 877-743-4404
oceanviewchalets.com
15569 Cabot Trail, P.O. Box 419, Chéticamp, NS B0E 1H0
Price: $100 to $220
Credit cards: Yes
Handicapped Access: Yes, one with lower counter, barrier-free shower
Special Features: Wi-Fi

Comfortable, clean, nicely furnished, and well maintained, the accommodations at Ocean View are the priciest in this little town, but considering the spectacular location, they're hard to criticize. Duplex units in six buildings and a motel are located just north of the village of Chéticamp, two chalets with fireplaces and whirlpool tubs, motel units with sitting areas, and all with mini-kitchens. Ocean View is also right across the street from Le Portage Golf Club, one of Cape Breton's four best, and offers a special for golfers. Free laundry facilities and a nightly campfire. The motel owners offer discounts for whale watching. Visit Hometown Kitchen next door, for breakfast at 7 AM, and then walk down the seaside boardwalk to the village.

RESTAURANTS

PORT HOOD

HAUS TREUBURG COUNTRY INN
Georg and Elvi Kargoll, innkeepers
902-787-2116
haustreuburg.com
175 Main St., Port Hood
Open: May–Aug., daily at 6 PM, or earlier if preferred
Price: $39 for a four-course meal
Credit cards: Yes
Cuisine: German
Serving: L, D
Handicap Access: No

Featured on *The Great Canadian Food Show* in 2000, Haus Treuberg Inn makes a wonderful German-style dinner and is a resource for any traveler planning to be in this area. A first course might be salmon smoked at the inn or flammkuchen, an Alsatian specialty that resembles pizza, with cream, onion, and sautéed mushrooms. Next comes a salad with greens from a local farmer.

Lobster (with a higher price), beef Stroganoff with homemade Champagne spaetzle, poached salmon with spinach and either wild rice or a potato pancake called krusti are some of the main courses served here. Dessert is apple strudel. German wines served here come from a small winery in Germany, Weingut Mussler, whose wines you cannot find or buy in North America.

GLENVILLE

GLENORA INN & DISTILLERY RESORT
800-839-0491
glenoradistillery.com
Rte. 19 (Ceilidh Trail), Glenville, Cape Breton
Open: May–mid-Oct., breakfast 7–9 AM, lunch 11 AM–3 PM, dinner 5–9 PM
Price: $20 to $24
Credit cards: Yes
Cuisine: Nova Scotia and North American
Serving: L, D
Handicap Access: Yes
Special Features: Outdoor terrace, whiskey distillery

With both a restaurant and a pub for visitors touring the distillery and guests in the inn and chalets, Glenora Inn upholds the Celtic tradition of hospitality, though the bar may close early. A menu from a culinary weekend special started with a salad with goat cheese, pear, and figs soaked in Glen Breton whiskey, and then went on to whiskey-cured salmon. Musical entertainment daily in season.

INVERNESS

TOMMY CAT BISTRO
902-258-2833
15693 Hwy. 19, Inverness
Open: June–Oct., daily 11 AM–10 PM, Nov.–May, Thurs.–Sun.
Price: $8 to $20
Credit cards: Yes
Cuisine: Italian and seafood
Serving: L, D
Handicap Access: Dining room accessible, but no accessible washroom
Special Features: Outdoor patio

Frankie MacKinnon, who took over the bistro in 2008, is serving fish and chips, pizza, pasta, steak, and lobster for lunch and dinner. Crab cakes, fish cakes and subs, sandwiches, soups, and chowder are from the lunch menu—both the lunch and dinner menus are served all day long. The bread is freshly baked, and desserts include coconut cream pie and cheesecake. Mac-Kinnon had been the chef for the previous eight years before he made the former owner an offer to buy the business.

MARGAREE VALLEY

THE NORMAWAY INN
902-248-2987, 800-565-9463
normaway.com
691 Egypt Rd., Margaree Valley
Open: Mid-June–third week of Oct., break-fast 7:30–10 AM, dinner 6–9 PM
Price: $34.50 for a three-course dinner, entrées $16 to $30
Credit cards: Yes
Cuisine: Country gourmet and seafood
Serving: B, D
Handicap Access: No accessible washrooms in dining room

Porridge bread is a specialty, encountered at breakfast. Atlantic-farmed salmon is on the menu, unless you've tagged your own wild salmon after catching it yourself in the Margaree River and cleaned it first.

Haddock and meatloaf made with beef from the inn's own Highland cattle are usually on the menu. Lamb chops might be seasoned with garlic and Dijon mustard and grilled; but the menu changes every day. Seafood coquille served here held scallops, shrimp, lobster, and halibut in white-wine cream sauce, topped with cheese and broiled. Your dessert might be an ice-cream pie with chocolate sauce, or blueberry cream cheese crisp with ice cream. Wine and cocktails are served.

BELLE CÔTE

ISLAND SUNSET RESORT AND SPA
866-515-2900
islandsunset.com
19 Beach Cove Lane, Belle Côte, Margaree Harbor

Open: June–Sept., dinner daily at 4 PM; Oct., weekends only
Price: $10.50 to $29.50
Credit cards: Yes
Cuisine: Maritime
Serving: D
Handicap Access: Yes
Special Features: Tues.-night ceilidh, outdoor deck overlooking ocean

Haddock served à la grenobloise, or in the style of Grenoble, with a sauce of brown butter, capers, parsley, lemon juice, and little croutons, is the favorite main course of one local. The dining room prepares pasta, perhaps with spinach and wild mushrooms and basil pesto, or with shrimps and scallops in cognac lobster sauce. You can count on an upscale lobster dinner with a beurre blanc to dip the tender lobster meat in; or try the rack of lamb instead. Bourbon pecan pie with toasted pecan and bourbon caramel sauce beckons on the dessert menu—consider a long walk adequate penance, and order it.

CHÉTICAMP

RESTAURANT ACADIEN
902-224-3207
co-opartisanale.com
15067 Main St., Chéticamp
Open: Mid-May–mid-Oct., 7 AM–9 PM
Price: $10 to $14
Credit cards: Yes
Cuisine: Acadian
Serving: B, L, D
Handicap Access: Yes
Special Features: Costumed Acadian servers, craft shop

Blond-wood chairs and tables and pale blue walls are in keeping with the sun streaming in and the white caps and long white aprons of the servers. Looking for a taste of the local cuisine, I ordered the sauce de boudin, blood pudding, "un recette bien de chez nous," and enjoyed a plate of dark,

The women who serve tables at Restaurant Acadien

smooth spiced meat. Flavorful, savory, and touched with a spice like clove, it was like the same thing I had enjoyed at a restaurant in Paris a year earlier. Big, white fresh rolls come with every meal, which could also be stewed chicken, fish chowder, or meat pie. Lobster salad plate is something on the menu for us tourists.

PLEASANT BAY

RUSTY ANCHOR
902-224-1313
23197 Cabot Trail Rd., Pleasant Bay
Open: End of May–Oct., daily 10:30 AM till end of dinner
Price: $6 to $24
Credit cards: Yes
Cuisine: Seafood, burgers, and more
Serving: L, D
Handicap Access: Yes
Special Features: Outside deck with a sea view—sometimes of whales

Lobster and crab duo—with five crab legs—is usually on the menu at night. Snow crabs with ten legs are caught right off the coast. Pasta dishes and vegetarian dishes, like a wrap with mixed greens, strawberries, and poppy seed dressing, offer more variety. Cape Breton fish and chips come with grilled haddock, without the batter coating, and Jöst wines are served. Fruit pie with strawberries, blackberries, raspberries, apples, and rhubarb is made here; it can come with ice cream and is a wonderful way to end a meal.

Food Purveyors

Bakeries
Aucoin's Bakery (902-224-3220), Chéticamp (2 kilometers or 1.3 miles from Cape Breton Highlands National Park). Acadian meat pies, pastries, and bread.
Shining Waters Bakery (902-945-2728), 11497 Main St., Mabou. Also an eatery favored by locals, where you can pick up fresh-baked cinnamon rolls, muffins, squares, cookies, and scones. Breakfast is served; sandwiches, salads, and soup are for lunch, and all of it can be enjoyed at the picnic tables outside.

Candy and Jam
Galloping Cow, 59 Justin Rd., Port Hood (Halfway between Mabou and Port Hood just off Rte. 19). Ron and Joanne Schmidt make jam and fruit preserves.

Cafés and Coffee Shops
The Dancing Goat Café and Bakery (902-248-2308), 6335 Cabot Trail, Northeast Margaree. The best coffee on Cape Breton Island? Well anyway, it's right up there with

the best, so the Dancing Goat is an essential stop for some of us when we are traveling. Fresh-baked bread, sandwiches, pies, and more.

Distilleries

Glenora Inn & Distillery Resort (800-839-0491; glenoradistillery.com), Rte. 19 (Ceilidh Trail), Glenville, Cape Breton, NS B0E 1X0. Open May–mid-Oct. Tours ($7 in 2008) instruct visitors in the art of whiskey-making and include a taste of the Glen Breton made here.

Pubs

✪ **The Red Shoe Pub** (902-945-2996; redshoepub.com), 11533 Rte. 19, Mabou, Inverness County. Open June–mid-Oct., from 11:30 AM, Sun. from 12 noon. Music, music, and more music in the nighttime here, every night of the week, with a Friday-night ceilidh, Gaelic for party and likely to mean dance. Fish and chips and poutine, fries with cheese curds and gravy, might be worked off in the course of a long night of dancing. Since you are in The Red Shoe, that will be almost inevitable. The Red Shoe burger is served with roasted onion mayonnaise; the Mabou chowder has sweet corn with its seafood and is served with warm cheddar biscuits.

CULTURE

Galleries

Joe's Scarecrow Village, Cap Le Moine, just south of Chéticamp. As it comes into sight, you might experience a hallucinated moment, as if there were crowds of performers along-side the road. But these politicos are always smiling and waving to passersby, and even the real ones take a break now and then. Stop and say hello.

Museums

LES TROIS PIGNONS: MUSEUM OF THE HOOKED RUG AND HOMELIFE
902-224-2642, 902-224-2612
lestroispignons.com
15584 Main St., (on the Cabot Trail), P.O. 430, Chéticamp, NS B0E 1H0
Open: Mid-May–mid-Oct., daily 9 AM–5 PM; July–Aug. till 7 PM
Admission: Adults $5, seniors 65 and older $4, students $3.50

This building is the visitor's information center for the area, but it would be a shame not to take a tour of the museum and its gallery of hooked rugs by Elizabeth LeFort. Born in 1914, this native got her start selling hooked rugs when a barnyard scene she had made for her sister, with 28 shades of brown, so impressed a shopkeeper that he offered to buy all her work. She set up shop in his store in Margaree Harbour and made hundreds of pieces, some reproducing famous paintings, like Leonardo da Vinci's *Last Supper*. A museum guide will demonstrate rug hooking and help visitors try their hand at it.

Local collector Marguerite Gallant did the work needed to fill the other part of Les Trois Pignons today with furniture, accessories, antique dolls, and kitchen tools from the old ways of life in Chéticamp.

MARGAREE SALMON MUSEUM
902-248-2848
margaree.net/salmonmuseum/
60 East Big Intervale Rd. (off the Cabot Trail), North East Margaree, NS BoE 2Ho
Open: Mid-June—mid-Oct., daily 9 AM—5 PM
Admission: Adults $2, children $ 1

Old fishing poles, records of the biggest salmon caught—it was 52.5 pounds, caught in 1927—and an aquarium of brook trout and smelt are on view at the Margaree Salmon Museum. Anglers caught salmon in 2008 that might have reached 20 pounds. In 2006 someone released one that was reported to be 49 pounds. Salmon that exceed 63 centimeters (24.8 inches) or longer must be released. On the Margaree River in 2008, when you bought a salmon-fishing license, you were allowed four tags for any fish caught from June 1 to October 31. In October, fishing with barbless hooks was allowed. Until 1982, commercial salmon fishing took so many salmon they couldn't return up the rivers to spawn. Catch-and-release fishing started in 1982, and since then the salmon population has grown. Even so, many people don't catch a thing. Fishing in waders is how it's done in this small river.

Music

THE BARN AT THE NORMAWAY INN
902-248-2987, 800-565-9463
normaway.com
691 Egypt Rd., P.O. Box 121, Margaree Valley, NS BoE 2Co

Inside the Barn or by the fire in the inn, weekly ceilidhs or kitchen parties are held at 8 PM on Wednesdays in July and August, and on Fridays in June, September, and October.

Seasonal Events

October
Celtic Colours International Festival (902-562-6700; celtic-colours.com), 850 Grand Lake Rd., Suite 8, Sydney, Cape Breton Island. A nine-day festival with hundreds of musicians performing all over the island. Workshops and concerts, as many as eight in one day, might be held in a local fire station or a reconstructed French chateau. Gaelic singing, Cape Breton fiddling, and bagpiping are certainly performed, and when the concerts are over, the Festival Club at the Gaelic College at St. Anns opens for informal concerts by invited musicians, who play into the morning hours.

RECREATION

Fishing
See **Margaree Salmon Museum** above for details on salmon fishing here.

Golf
Le Portage Club de Golf (902-224-3338; leportagegolfclub.com), 15580 Cabot Trail Rd., Chéticamp. A golf course with an Acadian history, Le Portage is set in woods, fields, and

farmland on Chéticamp's highlands. The 16th hole is called Le Père Fiset after the clergyman who built l'Église St. Pierre in Antigonish.

Horseback Riding

Little Pond Stables (902-224-3858), between Chéticamp and the entrance to Cape Breton Highlands National Park, on the Cabot Trail. Three-hour mountain rides, bilingual guides, and pony rides.

Whale Watching

Captain Mark's Whale and Seal Cruise (902-224-1316, 888-754-5112; whaleandseal-cruise.com), Pleasant Bay. Open June–mid-Oct., from 11:30 AM, Sun. from 12 noon. Captain Mark Timmons guarantees a whale sighting, and why not? His location in Pleasant Bay is near their cruising grounds. With more than 20 years of experience on the sea, Timmons has been taking visitors out to see whales since 1994. A whale researcher from Dalhousie University is the guide on the 1.5 to 2-hour trip, which is likely to pass alongside pilot, minke, finback, and humpback whales. There's an onboard washroom on this 42-foot boat with a spotting tower. A 25 percent discount is given on the 9:30 AM and 5 PM trips by reservation only. A second tour is done in a zodiac-style inflatable boat, and it might include sea cave explorations.

Westley's Whale Watch (866-999-4253; novascotiawhales.com), Pleasant Bay. Open June–mid-Oct., from 11:30 AM, Sun. from 12 noon. This whale-watching company leaves the dock in a two-level passenger boat with padded seats and a protected lower level. Of course, you are guaranteed to see a whale. Pilot whales that travel together in pods of 10 to 15 whales are your best bet. A 25 percent discount on tickets is given to customers with a National Park Pass, or it was in 2008; for others, a 25 percent discount on the 9:30 AM and 5 PM trips is available by reservation only. The little lighthouse on the wharf is the company's ticket booth.

Pleasant Bay Whale Watch companies are lined up at the dock.

SHOPPING

Gift and Specialty Shops

Belle Meade Farm (902-945-2256; bellemeadefarm.ca), 166 Rankinville Rd., Mabou, Cape Breton Island. Open June–mid-Oct. This shop on a dairy and sheep farm sells sheepskins, yarn, blankets, hand-knit hats, mittens, and socks. The wildflower honey comes in jars decorated with tartan.

Hooked Rugs and Acadian Handwork in Chéticamp

Co-op Artisanale (902-224-2170; co-opartisanale.com), 15067 Main St., Chéticamp. Open Mid-May–mid-Oct., 8 AM–8 PM. Hundreds of hooked rug mats range in size from tiny to large, ready to cover a dresser or hang on the wall. Kits to make your own are also for sale.

Flora's (902-224-3139; floras.com), PO. Box 316, Point Cross. Original designs and hand-dyed yarns are used for the hooked rugs of all sizes that are here. A floral coaster set or table runner would be the perfect souvenir from this Acadian part of the Cabot Trail. **Flora's Ice Cream** is conveniently located next to the shop, with chocolate and butterscotch dips, sundaes, toppings, and more.

Jean's Gift Shop (902-224-2758 or 902-224-1223), 10 Old LaPrairie Rd., Cabot Trail, Chéticamp. Hooked rugs of every size, sweaters, quilts, and souvenirs. Traditional patterns of hooked rugs, and also modern and original patterns, with lovely scenes.

Pottery

Cape Breton Clay (902-235-2467; capebretonclay.com), Margaree Valley. The main shop is off the Cabot Trail at the Margaree Valley exit, on East Big Intervale Road. Another shop is on the Ceilidh Trail in Chimney Corner at 2521 Shore Road. Yet one more is in Baddeck, at 503 Chebucto Road #2 (beside the Court House). At any of these spots you will find the elegant work of Bell Fraser, with local icons like lobster artfully integrated into a bowl as a handle, and mussels and crabs encrust the outside of a bowl.

EASTERN CABOT TRAIL FROM NORTH HARBOUR TO BADDECK

LODGING

CAPE NORTH

OAKWOOD MANOR
Hansel and Sharon MacEvoy, innkeepers
902383-2317
capebretonisland.com/oakwood
250 North Side Rd., Box 1, Comp 9, Cape North, NS BoC 1Go
Open: May–Oct.
Price: $65 to $105

Credit cards: Yes
Handicapped Access: None
Special Features: Wi-Fi

This is the longest-running bed and breakfast in Canada—underway since 1973. You can bet the owners know what they are doing. Over the years the accommodations have evolved into self-contained suites and rooms with every amenity—though back in the beginning, Sharon MacEvoy recalls waiting with her young children on the stair for the bathroom to be empty, so she could get them off to school.

Today this charming house holds a suite with a whirlpool tub of its own, a gas fireplace, a private entrance with a gas grill, a large deck, and three rooms.

In the 1940s and 1950s, Hansel MacEvoy's father cut the trees that were made into paneling for the dining room, living room, and entrance hall. The narrow bird's-eye maple and oak boards are perfectly fitted, creating a uniquely beautiful downstairs. Homemade jam arrives with the full breakfast every morning.

TWO TITTLE BED & BREAKFAST

Cyril and Marguerite Dunphy, innkeepers
902-383-2817, 866-231-4078
twotittle.com
2119 White point Village, NS B0C 1G0
Price: $60 to $90
Credit cards: Yes
Handicapped Access: None
Special Features: Wi-Fi

Perhaps the whales will be sounding, outside the breakfast-room window, when you sit down for your bacon and eggs. There are quilt-covered beds in the three rooms and a cottage (no kitchen). Nine kilometers or 6 miles, round-trip, on the White Point Trail begins at the driveway of this B&B, with ocean views all along the way. It's 9.6 kilometers or 6 miles to Neil's Harbor for a good place for dinner (see below).

NEIL'S HARBOUR

SEYMOUR HARBOUR VIEW BED & BREAKFAST

Steve and Roxy Coutts, innkeepers
902-336-2543, cell 902-285-4949
capebretonisland.com/northernhighlands/
seymour/
31 Seymour Ln., Neil's Harbor, NS B0C 1N0
Price: $80
Credit cards: Cash or travelers checks only

Handicapped Access: None
Special Features: Wi-Fi, deck with a great view, washer and dryer (fee)

Room 2, with its queen bed and patio doors that open on an ocean-view deck, and Room 3, with a double and a day bed, both have private baths. The somewhat small rooms are each outfitted with sturdy, new furniture, TVs, DVDs, a small refrigerator, and a closet, and the bathrooms feature sturdy acrylic tub enclosures. But perhaps the best feature here, after Roxy and Steve's friendly, down-to-earth hospitality, is the harbor view. The open second-floor deck holds three little tables and chairs for each room, and it looks over the top of the houses set below on the hill, across the road and straight out to sea. The winter of 2007–08 brought record snow to this region, and the top of windy Pleasant Mountain near Pleasant Bay was a tunnel enclosed by 20-foot snow drifts, according to Roxy Coutts. Let the province worry about the special equipment to get the snow out of the way, and consider a ski trip; the ski hill in Ingonish has found a buyer, and though closed until 2008, it will be open again now.

INGONISH AREA

KELTIC LODGE

902-285-2880, 800-565-0444
kelticlodge.ca
Middle Head Peninsula, Ingonish Beach, NS B0C 1L0
Open: Mid-May–mid-Oct.
Price: $228 to $301
Credit cards: Yes
Handicapped Access: Yes
Special Features: Wi-Fi

One main lodge room I visited had a beige and red coverlet on the bed, and the décor of a good motel, with a tiled bathroom. A huge closet partly made up for the smallish room, located on a long hallway with

The expansive lobby of the Keltic Lodge wears its age well.

flowered wallpaper. A big dining room, called the Purple Thistle Dining Room, with a wide view of the glorious coast, serves breakfast and dinner, and guests can add meals to their room rates. Atlantic Restaurant serves a more casual dinner and sells ice cream for take-out snacks, and the Highland Sitting Room is a lounge with a light menu and nightly entertainment. Outside the main lodge, with its 32 bedrooms, is the Inn at Keltic, with 40 rooms, and two- to four-bedroom cottages, all with a fireplace. There is a swimming pool, tennis courts, a spa, and an 18-hole golf course, which is many folks' reason to arrive.

LANTERN HILL & HOLLOW BEACH-FRONT COTTAGES AND SUITES

Sharon Harrison, innkeeper
902-285-2010, 888-663-0225
lanternhillandhollow.com
36845 Cabot Trail, P.O. Box 235, Ingonish Beach, Cape Breton Highlands, NS B0C 1L0
Open: Late May–late Oct.

Price: $160 to $245
Credit cards: Yes
Handicapped Access: Yes
Special Features: Wi-Fi

Private beachfront and a supervised 3-kilometer or 1.7-mile sandy beach are outside the door, with picnic tables for an alfresco meal and bonfires at night. Three large suites in the guest house share a sitting room and a screened veranda; all rooms have small refrigerators as well as TVs, hardwood floors, and ceiling fans. The biggest has an electric fireplace. Six cottages are well furnished and brand new, with private patios and grills for each one.

INDIAN BROOK

ENGLISH COUNTRY GARDEN BED & BREAKFAST

Penny Steele and Ian Green, innkeepers
866-929-2721
capebretongarden.com

45478 Cabot Trail, Indian Brook, St. Anns
Bay, NS B0C 1H0
Credit cards: Yes
Handicapped Access: Yes, in the cottage
Special Features: Wi-Fi, dinners by
reservation

Penny Steele and Ian Green have done a lot
of traveling, and their familiarity with other
cultures is one source of the charm at their
small B&B. Modest gardens and exteriors
belie the glories that await inside, where
the Russian room, with its elaborate upholstered headboard, gives you the impression
you've fallen into the novel *Dr. Zhivago*. A
two-person tub with airjets and a view of
MacDonald Pond (and an occasional
moose), as well as the TVs with DVD players
in all rooms, binoculars, and more make
this a refuge and a place to recuperate from
the last hike you've attempted in Cape
Breton Highlands National Park.

The Rose Cottage is a rarity in Nova
Scotian B&Bs, handicapped accessible,
which means for anyone with or without a
handicap it is wonderfully spacious.
Breakfast in July might include strawberry
muffins and always includes fruit and a hot
dish; all are served on fine china at private
tables, so guests who like a quiet morning
meal can enjoy one here.

BADDECK AREA

BELLVIEW BED & BREAKFAST
Denise and Bill Mulley, innkeepers
902-295-2334, 877-234-1333
bellview.baddeck.com
713 Bay Rd., Baddeck Bay, NS B0E 1B0
Price: $120 to $149
Credit cards: Yes
Handicapped Access: None
Special Features: Wi-Fi

Double whirlpool tubs are the norm in the
four rooms at Bellview, named for its setting alongside the Bras d'Or Lakes and
overlooking the bay. The rooms are somewhat formal, with four-poster beds, but
comfortable, with chairs to relax in inside
each room and more outside in view of the
water. A full breakfast might include
omelets and French toast with fruit and
yogurt—"The whole nine yards," said owner
Denise Mulley.

CASTLE MOFFETT
Linda Moffat, innkeeper
902-756-9070, 888-756-9070
castlemoffett.com
11980 Hwy. 105, Bucklaw, P.O. Box 678,
Baddeck, NS B0E 1B0
Open: Early May–late Oct.
Price: $250 to $1,000
Credit cards: Yes
Handicapped Access: Huge apartment with
large bathroom, $1,000, only
Special Features: Wi-Fi, spa services, gar-
dens, grand piano in great room

Every one of the nine suites is deluxe at
Castle Moffett, and each one holds separate
baths and showers, canopied or four-poster
queen- or king-size beds, a sitting area
with a fireplace, antiques and original art,
and a view of the Bras d'Or lakes. A breakfast of eggs or waffles or pancakes (not
included in the rates) is served in the dining room. Dinners, served Tuesday through
Sunday, might start with lobster bisque, or
a salad with pear, blue cheese, and toasted
walnuts on greens, and go on to haddock
almondine or maple-glazed salmon. The
Dungeon Lounge and Wine Cellar is the
right spot to brood over the beauties of the
landscape while savoring a single-malt.
Massage, a sauna, and an exercise room are
available in the spa.

LYNWOOD INN
Gerald and Lynn Dunlop, innkeeper
902-295-1995, 877-666-1995
lynwoodinn.com
441 Shore Rd., Baddeck, Cape Breton, NS
B0E 1B0

Price: $100 to $140
Credit cards: Yes
Handicapped Access: Yes, two with large walk-in shower, lower sinks, and more
Special Features: Wi-Fi

Twenty-eight suites each hold two queen-size beds, and each offers a good view of the lakes or gardens. Some have a balcony. The new building that holds these accommodations was built to resemble the inn, with steep gables and red siding. The newer rooms at Lynwood Inn are the most up-to-date accommodations in this area, and both the old and new rooms and the grounds are well maintained and highly recommended. Three suites in the older main house are more distinguished, with antique furniture and more formal details and Victorian décor, and one has a queen sleigh bed. A two-bedroom housekeeping cottage is another option.

TELEGRAPH HOUSE

Shawn Dunlop, innkeeper
902-295-1100, 888-263-9840
baddeck.com/telegraph
479 Chebucto St., Box 8, Baddeck, NS B0E 1B0
Price: $99 to $109
Credit cards: Yes
Handicapped Access: None
Special Features: Live entertainment in dining room every night in July and Aug.

This old inn has maintained its character over the years, with Victorian rooms with flowered wallpaper and antique chairs in the style of a hundred years ago. Alexander Graham Bell stayed here in the late 1880s, when having a private bathroom was extraordinary. Rooms in the motel hold mid-20th-century furnishings and are plain but comfortable, with exposed beam ceilings.

RESTAURANTS

NEIL'S HARBOUR

CHOWDER HOUSE

902-336-2463
Lighthouse Rd., Neil's Harbor
Open: June–Sept., 11 AM–7 PM, sometimes as late as 8
Price: $5 to $16
Credit cards: Yes
Cuisine: Seafood, hamburgers
Serving: L, D
Handicap Access: No
Special Features: Everything is made here, from the chowder to the pies

When I arrived, nets were stretched out to dry on the flowering clover beside the restaurant, benefitting from the strong wind that just might always blow here, at the edge of a bluff on the edge of the sea. The Chowder House in Neil's Harbor is a plain brown building set next to the sea, just past a lighthouse and just around the corner from the little protected harbor where the fishing boats are moored. The four mackerel filets I ate ($7.99) had no doubt been caught by one of the nets outside; their dense meat was flavorful, benefiting from the lemon on the plate. Tender, crisp fresh-cut french fries, and little plastic containers of stewed green tomato and pickled beets completed the simple dinner.

INGONISH AREA

ATLANTIC RESTAURANT AT THE KELTIC LODGE

800-565-0444
kelticlodge.ca/keltic_cuisine.html
Middle Head Peninsula, Ingonish Beach
Open: Mid-May–mid-Oct.
Price: $9 to $26
Credit cards: Yes
Cuisine: Casual Maritime standards
Serving: L, D

Handicap Access: Yes
Special Features: Great views

Chicken and baby back ribs are one of the dishes of the menu. Eight snow crab legs come with melted butter potato salad, coleslaw, and rolls. The nachos appetizer and the Highland Club, made with roasted chicken, bacon, lettuce, Canadian cheddar, fried egg, tomato, and pesto mayo, are mainstays of the lunch. Two outdoor decks both overlook the water. One is close to a playground, where children can escape the meal table.

MAIN STREET RESTAURANT & BAKERY

902-285-2225
37764 Cabot Trail, Ingonish Beach
Open: May–mid-Oct., daily 7 AM–9 PM
Price: $10 to $15
Credit cards: Yes
Cuisine: Seafood and casual standards
Serving: B, L, D
Handicap Access: Yes

The seafood chowder is creamy, lightly thickened, and full of sweet, North Atlantic shrimp, scallops, haddock, and more, with bits of carrot and cubed potato in a fresh and pure-tasting soup. The light, tender tea biscuit alongside is perfect, especially spread with butter. One meal ended with a strawberry rhubarb pie full of big chunks of rhubarb and its bright, tangy taste. With a streetside covered deck, this plain, well-lighted restaurant has a high-ceilinged dining room and metal chairs around its uncovered tables.

BADDECK AREA

BADDECK LOBSTER SUPPERS

902-295-3307
baddeck.com/lobstersuppers/
17 Ross St., Baddeck
Open: June–mid-Oct.
Price: $30

Credit cards: Yes
Cuisine: Seafood
Serving: L, D
Handicap Access: Yes

The best way to enjoy lobster is in a straightforward place like this. Unlimited mussels, chowder, salad, dessert, and beverage are all served alongside the one- to one-and-a-quarter pound lobster for a classic lobster supper. Two other dishes are on the menu: plank-roasted salmon served with all the sides listed above, or for someone who doesn't like seafood, a ham plate for $19. Lunch items include fish chowder, pizza, and hot dogs for the kids, a lobster roll, and an egg-salad platter. It's all served in a plain, casual dining room.

LYNWOOD INN

902-295-1995, 877-666-1995
lynwoodinn.com
441 Shore Rd., Baddeck
Price: $8 to $19
Credit cards: Yes
Cuisine: Maritime classics, a smattering of Italian, and more
Serving: B, L, D
Handicap Access: Yes
Special features: Entertainment, nightly in summer, outside deck

The mussels in this old-fashioned dining room are served with melted garlic butter, and a good follow-up might be the fish cakes and homemade beans. A boneless trout is served with roasted corn salsa, and the lobster platter includes mussels and coleslaw. The great thing about the Lynwood Inn's menu is its range, because no one will have to sacrifice a preference in order to dine here. Lasagna, hot turkey sandwiches, linguine with sautéed shrimp and olives, chicken stir-fry, a burger and a T-bone steak are all here, along with tempting desserts like ice cream pie, bread pudding, and fresh ginger cake.

THE WATER'S EDGE INN, CAFÉ & GALLERY
902-295-3600, 866-439-2528
thewatersedgeinn.com
22 Water St., Baddeck
Open: May–mid-Oct.
Price: $5 to $12.50
Credit cards: Yes
Cuisine: Seafood with Mexican Indian, and vegetarian items
Serving: L, D
Handicap Access: No

MacIver's quesadilla with sautéed peppers, tomatoes, green onions, garlic, cheddar, and mozzarella are grilled in a whole-wheat tortilla and served with salsa and sour cream—or you can add chicken and bacon—for an appetizing meal. The chowder is filled with seafood, combining little clams, salmon, haddock, scallops, shrimp, and lobster. A meal of chicken tikka is made with yellow split peas, garlic, ginger, cardamom, cumin, nutmeg, mace, and turmeric, and can be made without the chicken for a good vegetarian meal. But meat-lovers will be grateful for the Cuban, with pork and ham.

FOOD PURVEYORS

Bakeries and Pizzerias
Celtic Touch (902-383-2014), 570 Dingwall Rd., Dingwall. Open Apr.–Nov., 9 AM–9 PM. Ruby Frazer, owner, serves good pizza and fresh-baked bread at this good spot for a meal. Mussels and chowder are for lunch or dinner, and a full breakfast is served starting at 9 AM.

Coffee Shops and Tearooms
The Celtic Tea Room at St. Ann's Bay United Church (902-929-2999), 46685 Cabot Trail, Indian Brook. The square, chewy, good oatcakes made here and a pot of tea might be all you have a hankering for, but the menu also offers salads, chowder, cakes and pies, and more, serving breakfast, lunch, and tea. Teapots and kettles line a shelf set high on the wall over the entrance to this new room, set at the other end of the building from the sanctuary of the church, always open for visitors to sit in contemplation or prayer, should the spirit move them.

CULTURE

Historic Buildings and Sites

ALEXANDER GRAHAM BELL NATIONAL HISTORIC SITE OF CANADA
902-295-2069
pc.gc.ca/lhn-nhs/ns/grahambell
P.O. Box 159, Baddeck, NS BoE IBo
Open: July–mid-Oct., 8:30 AM–6 PM; June, 9 AM–6 PM; May and second half of Oct., 9 AM–5 PM; off-season by appointment
Admission: Adults $7.80, children 6–16 $3.90, and seniors $6.55

Beinn Bhreagh was Alexander Graham Bell's summer home in Baddeck, on Cape Breton Island; the rest of the year he lived in Washington, D.C. This man, famous for the invention of the telephone (and the simultaneous invention of the telephone by others cannot detract from his accomplishment) is honored here with exhibits about his scientific experiments. When he bought himself this summer home in 1885, the telephone patent had already made him rich. But he restlessly pursued other innovations, including developing a hydrofoil that set a world record in 1919—of 71 miles per hour.

Lucky neighbors found jobs at Beinn Bhreagh, some making cells for enormous kites; a prism-shaped triangular box kite first flew in Baddeck in 1901. Bell's wife Mabel Bell had money of her own, and she spent some of it on her husband's ventures, like the Aerial Experiment Station.

GREAT HALL OF THE CLANS—INTERACTIVE MUSEUM
902-295-3411
gaeliccollege.edu
Gaelic College of Celtic Arts and Crafts, Hwy. 105, St. Anns, NS
Open: June–Sept., call for hours
Admission: Adults $7, children $5.60

The history of the migration of Scots from the highlands of Scotland is told in the exhibits here. The clans' costumes, dress and hunting tartans, and early settlement artifacts bring to life the beginning of Gaelic culture and its establishment in Nova Scotia. The museum holds eight interactive stations based on the culture of the Gaels, describing the language, the oral tradition of storytelling, song, dance, and more. The college was founded in 1938, and its mission is to keep alive the Gaelic language, the culture, music, arts, and traditions of Scottish immigrants.

Music

CELTIC TEA ROOM AT ST. ANN'S BAY UNITED CHURCH
902-929-2999
46685 Cabot Trail, Indian Brook, NS B0C 1H0.

Tuesday and Friday ceilidhs (KAY-lees) or house parties are held here through the summer.

OCTAGON ARTS CENTRE
The Markland Coastal Resort
902-383-2246
marklandresort.com
Cabot Trail at Dingwall, NS B0C 1G0

Fridays evenings at 8, Cape Breton fiddlers and singers perform here throughout the summer. Occasionally, classical musicians and singers perform on Sunday at 4:30 PM, but call first to confirm.

ST. ANDREW'S CELTIC CONCERT SERIES
celtic.concertseries@gmail.com
St. Peter's Parish Hall, 37894 Cabot Trail, Ingonish Beach, NS B0C 1L0

Open: May–Sept., schedule varies
Admission: Tickets $25

In 2008, Lennie Gallant, The Irish Descendents, Bruce Guthro, and The Cobblestones performed at this parish hall, one concert each month of the summer, at 7:30 PM.

Seasonal Events

June
Englishtown Mussel Festival, Englishtown. Near the end of June, musicians play while local volunteers cook and serve huge quantities of mussels and chefs enter a contest for best seafood dish.

August
Festival of Cape Breton Fiddling (capebretonfiddlers.com), Gaelic College of Crafts (902-295-3411; gaeliccollege.edu), Gaelic College of Celtic Arts and Crafts, Hwy. 105, St. Anns, Englishtown.

RECREATION

Camping
Hideaway Campground and Oyster Market (902-383-2116; campingcapebreton.com), 401 Shore Rd., South Harbour. The views from this campground are incredible, and the easy access to bushels of fresh oysters is just the thing for anyone with a taste for them. Forty sites for tents or trailers. Two of the four cabins, at $40 for 2, do not have electricity, but do have extraordinary views. "It's basically going camping, but you leave the tent and air mattress at home," said Susan Dunphy, owner with her husband Alex. He's the one who dives for the Aspy Bay oysters. The Dunphys seed their flats themselves—the tiny sprat "looks like pepper in the collectors," she said.

Meat Cove Camping (902-383-2379), Meat Cove. At the topmost spot on Cape Breton Island, inexpensive campsites, a cabin, and kayaks are for rent. Evening crab boils, showers, and firewood are all available, but the stand-out virtue of this place is the landscape and the wildlife. The MacLellans, who run the campground, can tell you all about the hikes and local history, and they offer whale watching and nature tours too. Humpback whales migrate within view of the campground.

Golf
Bell Bay Golf Club (902-295-1333, 800-565-3077; bellbaygolfclub.com), Baddeck. This course was rated the best new course in Canada in 1998—the view from the 18th tee is fabulous. Thomas McBroom is the course designer, and the Bras d'Or Lakes stretch out in front of almost every hole. Clubhouse, pro shop, and a pretty bird's-eye maple bar.

Highlands Links (902-285-2600, 800-441-1118; highlandslinksgolf.com), Ingonish Beach. A gorgeous "Mountains and Ocean" course designed by Stanley Thompson in 1939 and built inside the Cape Breton Highland National Park. Audubon certified, this course has found a middle way to maintain lush greens and sustain the area wildlife and environment. Golfers who walk will find they have traveled across 11 kilometers or

The view from Hideaway Campground and Oyster Market is one of its best features.

7 miles of hilly, spectacular terrain. The loop-style links course is based on traditional Scottish golf courses, and each hole has a Scottish name. The course is owned by Parks Canada.

Hiking
See "Parks," below

Kayaking
Eagle North (902-383-2552, 888-616-1689; kayakingcapebreton.com), 299 Shore Rd., Dingwall. Guides and equipment provided by this reputable company will take you into sea caves and isolated beaches, or over an oyster bed, or to marshlands that birds love, beside gypsum cliffs—with great horned owls and kingfishers living in the cliffs. Fossils of ancient shells are often found. Hear about the shipwrecks still visible off the beach from Michael Fitzgerald, tour guide and owner. Kayaks and canoes are also rented.

North River Kayak Tours (902-929-2628; northriverkayak.com), RR #4, Baddeck. Angelo Spinazzola, a musician, leads kayak tours on the coast of Cape Breton, from half-day trips to five-day adventures. Secluded beaches, a lighthouse, eagles, and more are featured on these tours, which offer some of the best ways to encounter this region.

Parks
Whycocomagh Provincial Park (902-756-2448; parks.gov.ns.ca), Hwy. 105, Whycocomagh (just east of Whycocomagh village). Three trails take hikers up to the top of Salt Mountain, with its views of the inland sea that is the Bras d'Or Lakes. Trail 3 is the most difficult, with 2 kilometers or 1.2 miles of steep trail that then takes you over boulders and rocks. There are 62 camping sites, and showers and firewood are available. On the lake side of Highway 105 is a day-use park with picnic tables and a beach.

Cape Breton Highlands National Park

(902-224-2306; pc.gc.ca/pn-np/ns/cbreton/index), Ingonish Beach.

One of the most scenic places in the world, Cape Breton Highlands rises out of the sea with steep slopes and impervious rock. Take advantage of every scenic pull-off you come to on the **Cabot Trail** in the park, and with just a few stops you will learn, from the panels at each place, about the geological history of the steep-sided land. Arctic plants, rare anywhere but on the Rocky Mountains and the arctic tundra, live in the woods—evidence that some of these hills stood above the glaciers during the repeated ice ages.

Drivers on the Cabot Trail enter the park either north of Chéticamp or in Ingonish Beach—a third of the trail is in the park.

The bilingual information centers, one in Chéticamp, the other at the Ingonish Beach entrance, are open daily from mid-May to mid-October and can help you decide which trail to tackle or what beach to try as well as sell you park permits.

Twenty-five hiking trails offer everyone something to enjoy—from the boardwalk through the bog between Pleasant Bay and Cap Rouge, which is handicapped accessible, to the 9.2-kilometer or 5.7-mile loop of **Skyline**. The easy **Middle Head Trail**, accessible from the Keltic Lodge, quickly brings a hiker upon the dramatic coastline.

Five beaches in the park include both salt water and fresh, and at Ingonish Beach you can walk from one to the other. Black Brook Beach, north of Ingonish and before Neil's Harbour, has a waterfall and a beach with a lifeguard.

Admission rates for sightseeing on the **Cabot Trail** are adults $7.80, seniors $6.80, and children 6–17 $3.90 (but check the Web site for 2009 fees after April 1). Fees paid at the entry points can also include camping fees, golf fees for **Highlands Links** (see "Golf"), and catch-and-release fishing permits for wild salmon.

SHOPPING

Clothing and Accessories

Sew Inclined (902-929-2050 or 902-929-2259; sewinclined.ca), Wreck Cove in Englishtown. Barbara Longva couldn't believe the customer who mentioned he didn't look good in hats. "Everybody looks good in my hats," she said—and it was true. Among her inventive styles from conservative to Mad Hatter, there are hats with earflaps and hats with flowered fabric, hats for Sherlock Holmes, and hats for a queen. In her own line of clothing, she specializes in re-creations of antique styles, with pretty fabrics sewn up in singlets and drapy, flattering styles. Don't miss her original approach and her fine company while you are driving the east side of the Cabot Trail.

Gift and Specialty Shops

Arts North (902-383-2911, off-season 902-383-2632; arts-north.com), Cabot Trail, 3 kilometers or 2 miles west of Cape North Village. Open June–Nov., 9 AM–6 PM. A fabulous collection of local and Nova Scotian artisans' work from extraordinary quilts, fine pottery, and jewelry, to hand-painted floor cloths and more.

Leather Works (902-929-2414; leather-works.ca), 45808 Cabot Trail, Indian Brook. Open May–Oct., daily 9 AM–5 PM, or by appointment. John C. Roberts is a craftsman who has recreated the leather water buckets used by firemen in the past—after waterproofing the interior of the buckets. Today those exquisite buckets are simply emblems of the skill and beauty in the basic necessities of the past. Simple, finely made wallets, purses, belts, leather aprons, and more.

Outdoor Clothing and Gear

Upper Cove Store (902-285-2077), 36432 Cabot Trail, Ingonish. It's good to know there is a place to replace a lost pair of water shoes or pick up a new thermos. This store stocks camping gear, beachwear, and rainwear.

Pottery

Cape Breton Clay (902-235-2467; capebretonclay.com), 503 Chebucto Rd., #2 (beside the Court House), Margaree Valley. This is a branch of the main shop off the Cabot Trail at the Margaree Valley exit, on East Big Intervale Road. Here, as at the main store and another branch on the Ceildh Trail in Chimney Corner, you will find the elegant work of Bell Fraser, with local icons like lobster artfully integrated into a bowl as a handle, and mussels and crabs encrust the outside of a bowl.

Quilts

Quilts at the Sea Shanty (902-929-2992; capebretoncraft.com), 1517 Hwy. 312, Jersey Cove. Open June–Oct., 9 AM–5 PM. Owner and quilter Marsha Smith makes quilts with traditional patterns, some using motifs from Celtic knots, seabirds, and landscapes. The shop sells other Baddeck Quilt Guild members' work, and some artwork.

SYDNEY, LOUISBOURG, AND SOUTH TO ISLE MADAME

LODGING

SYDNEY MINES

✪ GOWRIE HOUSE COUNTRY INN
Ken Tutty, innkeeper
902-544-1050
gowriehouse.com
840 Shore Rd., Sydney Mines, NS B1V 1A6
Price: $145 to $265
Credit cards: Yes
Handicapped Access: No
Special Features: Excellent dinner (see Restaurants), Wi-Fi, but not in Garden House rooms, AC

Room 9 in the Garden House sits on a second floor overlooking the lawn, and if the garden beds are a little thin early in the summer, the old trees and the sense of peace and tranquility have been rooted here for decades. Flowered wallpaper, chintz curtains with a green trellis pattern, a kitchenette, balcony, and gas fireplace combine to make a luxurious hideaway on the coast of Cape Breton Island. Add to that a dinner in the elegant dining room and more rooms in the main house, as well as a cottage, and you can be sure visitors are happy with their choice.

Breakfast at two common tables might begin with fresh strawberries (in strawberry season); yogurt; light, delicate biscuits (like a scone but made with buttermilk and no eggs); and scrambled, fried, or poached eggs served with eight-grain bread and crisp bacon.

Two front parlors are dressed up with antiques and porcelain collections, with blue and white Wedgwood the most ornate. But the place is not stiff or formal, because these rooms also hold modern art, most of it painted by Nova Scotia artists.

The Gowrie House Inn parlor is exceptionally handsome.

SYDNEY

GEORGE AND COTTAGE BED AND BREAKFAST

Carolyn and Bill Hatcher, innkeepers
902-567-6782
georgeandcottage.ca
808 George St., Sydney, NS B1P 1L6
Price: $100
Credit cards: Yes, or cash
Handicapped Access: None
Special Features: Wi-Fi, cable TV, DVD

Following an extensive renovation, George and Cottage B&B opened in 2005 in a 130-year-old house owned by Carolyn and Bill Hatcher. Three rooms are for rent, including The Wentworth, which has a claw-foot tub, substantial dark-wood furniture, and a little sitting area that looks out on peaceful Mill Creek. Breakfast might be fish cakes and eggs, or fresh muffins, and a spot in the garden might be the right place to decide what to do that day. All the rooms have a queen-size bed and a private bathroom. The house is within walking distance of downtown restaurants and shops.

A PARADISE FOUND BED & BREAKFAST

Rick and Connie Bowers, innkeepers
902-539-9377, 877-539-9377
3.ns.sympatico.ca/paradisefound/
62 Milton St., Sydney, NS B1P 4L8
Price: $95 to $110
Credit cards: Yes
Handicapped Access: None
Special Features: Wi-Fi, discounts for multiple night stays

The rooms of this B&B—the Hydrangea Room, with its king-size bed, TV, and chairs; the small Wedgwood room, with a queen-size bed; and the Rose Rooms with either two twin beds or one king bed—all have ceiling fans, phones, and private bathrooms. Pretty flowered wallpaper and older furniture add to the homey décor. A fireplace in the library makes this an inviting spot, and the shelves are full of things to read. Breakfast—a hot dish, fruit, and all the rest—is served in a pretty dining room with a stained-glass window.

A CHARMING VICTORIAN BED & BREAKFAST

Alex and An Pilon, innkeepers
902-564-0921
annsbb.com
115 George St., Sydney, NS B1P 1H9
Price: $85 to $115
Credit cards: Yes
Handicapped Access: None
Special Features: Wi-Fi, cable TV

Built in 1903, this house opened as a bed and breakfast in 1999. Its three rooms have tiled bathrooms and bright, attractive décor. The Pearl Room's flowered bed cover and valence are cheerful. Two reading lamps over the bed—all the rooms have queen-size beds—in the rooms make them a good place to settle in for a long read. But a comfortable chair in the Lace Room is another potential spot for reading, after tours of local attractions like the Miners' Museum. Also nearby is Sydney's Harbour Boardwalk, the casino, and restaurants.

LOUISBOURG

CRANBERRY COVE INN

David and Germaine LeMoine, innkeepers
800-929-0222
cranberrycoveinn.com
12 Wolfe St., Louisbourg, NS B1C 2J2
Open: May–Oct.
Price: $105 to $160
Credit cards: Yes
Handicapped Access: None
Special Features: Wi-Fi

Swank is the word for the parlor and the room called Cranberry Sweet at Cranberry Cove Inn, which offers both a restaurant and a refuge. Ten minutes from the Louisbourg Fortress, this inn brings the imagination to work in its varied décor, styling each of its seven rooms after a theme that doesn't repeat itself. Cranberry Sweet, with different patterned wallpaper and curtains, is furnished with antiques and fitted out with a whirlpool tub and a fireplace. Field and Stream uses a bent twig headboard and other details to create a rustic atmosphere. Breakfast, included with the rate, might include Highland oat toast beside the buffet of cereal and fresh fruit, and a hot dish.

LOUISBOURG HARBOUR INN BED & BREAKFAST

Parker and Suzanne Bagnell, innkeepers
902-733-3222, 888-888-8466
louisbourgharbourinn.com
9 Lower Warren St., Louisbourg, NS B1C 1G6
Open: June–mid-Oct.
Price: $140 to $180
Credit cards: Yes
Handicapped Access: None
Special Features: Wi-Fi

Eight rooms in this B&B are all outfitted with queen-size beds, high ceilings and wood floors at this sea captain's house. The boyhood home of the owner, Parker Bagnell (his room as a kid was Room 1), was built by a descendent of a British officer who laid siege to this town in 1758. Six of the eight rooms have a harbor view, and the fortress and the harbor are both an easy walk from the front door. The owners also manage a sister inn, below. "The biggest difference between them is that one is yellow and one is green," said Bagnell.

LOUISBOURG HERITAGE HOUSE

902-733-3222, 888-888-8466
louisbourgheritagehouse.com
7544 Main St., Louisbourg, NS B1C 1J4
Open: Late June–mid-Oct.
Price: $120 to $180
Credit cards: Yes

Handicapped Access: None
Special Features: Wi-Fi

Solid four-posters and reproduction dark-wood furniture outfit the attractive rooms at Louisbourg Heritage House. Bedside lamps and upholstered chairs add to the comfort level. Matthews Room is set under the eaves on the whole of the third floor, with a skylight in the roof over the king-size sleigh bed. A balcony comes with each room, and in four a guest will have a view of the harbor. Gabriel Room has original flooring, refinished to a pale honey tone. Fruit popovers, strawberry or peach, might be on the breakfast table, along with the oven-baked crêpes.

St. Peters

BRAS D'OR LAKES INN

902-535-2200
brasdorlakesinn.com
10095 Grenville St., St. Peter's, NS B0E 3B0
Open: May–Oct.
Price: $100 to $135
Credit cards: Yes
Handicap Access: Yes
Special Features: Wi-Fi, hot tub, Ceilidhs every week in dining room, beautiful views of southern end of the Bras d'Or Lakes, CAA/AAA 10 percent discount

The twenty plain bedrooms here, some paneled, are stocked with all the important standards, from private baths to a microwave and small refrigerator. But the really stellar part of this inn is its location, on the edge of the Bras d'Or Lakes. A floating dock adds pleasure to the lake swimming, as does the opportunity to explore the water on kayaks or in canoes.

Isle Madame, Arichat

L'AUBERGE ACADIENNE INN

Pauline Bona, innkeeper
902-226-2200, 877-787-2200
Acadienne.com

2375 High Rd., P.O. Box 59, Arichat, NS
B0E 1A0
Price: $71 to $145
Credit cards: Yes
Handicapped Access: Yes, one room, but
gravel drive
Special Features: Wi-Fi

A nine-unit motel is furnished handsomely
with two double beds, and the inn itself
holds eight large rooms, one of which has its
own large hot tub. Bona's Bar and the inn's
restaurant are attractive places for a night-
cap or a meal (see the review in the
Restaurants section, below). Acadian fish
cakes and eggs and homemade preserves
made with strawberries and rhubarb are
served for breakfast to the guests, for an
additional charge, or try the "bonus breakfast" of fried bologna and eggs—a
Newfoundland tradition.

RESTAURANTS

SYDNEY MINES

✪ GOWRIE HOUSE COUNTRY INN

902-544-1050
gowriehouse.com
840 Shore Rd., Sydney Mines
Open: May–Oct., dinner at 7:30 PM;
Nov.–Dec., dinner at 8:15 PM
Price: $55, with complimentary wine
included for guests of the inn
Credit cards: Yes
Cuisine: classic Canadian
Serving: D
Handicapped Access: Limited
Special Features: Limited choice included
two entrees and two desserts, reservation
required

The tables are set with linen, multiple
pieces of flatware ready for the four-course
meal served in the summer season, and
there are flowers just picked from the garden, like a white iris with a lyrical scent and
lemon yellow day lilies. A complimentary
carafe of French table wine is served to
guests at the inn.

On one visit, dinner started with chilled
strawberry soup, a creamy and mildly sweet
puree enriched by crème fraîche and gar-
nished with a sprig of mint. Served in a
soup-rim bowl in an unusually fine, flowered china that held all four courses of the
meal, this was entirely welcome even if it
isn't something most of us would order off a
menu. We should.

A small salad of tender young spinach
and sliced tomato, roasted tomatoes, and a
creamy pesto vinaigrette followed, balancing the mildly sweet with savory and tart flavors. Crusty bread with a little whole-grain
flour and butter were also on the table.

Our entrées were a choice of roast
salmon or marinated Cape Breton lamb.
The lamb, cooked slightly more than my
preference, was yet utterly tender, full of
flavor after marinating in cumin and other
spices. A rich, tender potato au gratin perfectly flanked the meat, and the rest of the
plate was crowded with colorful vegetables,
julienned carrot, broccoli, cauliflower, and
sugar snap peas, as well as a just-picked (I
saw innkeeper Ken Tutty in the chive patch)
purple chive blossom.

Chocolate truffle tart, a bittersweet stiff
mousse on top of a dense cake, thin and
perfect, placed the ace—since I consider
any kitchen that serves bittersweet chocolate my kind of place. A lemon tart with a
gelled lemon filling sandwiched by
whipped cream, on a tender crust, was
almost equally fine. Then it was time to take
cups of coffee out into the garden.

ST. PETERS

BRAS D'OR LAKES INN

902-535-2200
brasdorlakesinn.com
10095 Grenville St., St. Peter's
Open: May–Oct.

Price: $23 to $35
Credit cards: Yes
Cuisine: French with regional specialties
Serving: B, L, D
Handicap Access: Yes
Special Features: Ceilidhs every week, beautiful view of the southern end of the Bras d'Or Lakes

Lunch is served in the side of the restaurant facing the road, unfortunately, but at dinner the full glory of this inn's location, a view of the lake, is part of its appeal. The log frame of the structure is repeated in the furnishings of the dining room, with small logs for legs and backs on the chairs, and split logs polished for a floor.

The chowder is made with salmon, haddock, shrimp, scallops, and a little lobster; full of good seafood flavor, it is also tuned up with a touch of Pernod and many savory leeks. The light, dill-flecked biscuit on the side was hot, and tender with fresh butter.

Dinners range from Atlantic Salmon Oscar—a salmon fillet topped with lobster, crab and shrimp with Hollandaise sauce ($27)—to grilled striploin, or sirloin strip, served with wild mushrooms and sweet-potato fries. Of course you can also find lobster. Dessert could be Gâteau St. Honoré, one of the chef's specialties.

ARICHAT

L'AUBERGE ACADIENNE INN
902-226-2200, 877-787-2200
acadienne.com
2375 High Rd., Arichat
Open: Year-round dinner nightly, off-season Wed.–Sun. only
Price: $26 for three courses
Credit cards: Yes
Cuisine: Acadian
Serving: D
Handicap Access: Yes
Special Features: Ten to 14 local musicians offer entertainment at a kitchen party on Sat. afternoon once a month—and the place is packed

L'Auberge Acadienne Inn serves its house specialties in the summer, like chicken fricot, or Acadian meat pie, or a seafood dish like scallop and shrimp gratinée. Although you can order à la carte, the restaurant offers a table d'hôte $26 appetizer, main course, dessert, and coffee. Jöst L'Acadie from Nova Scotia is the house white wine. Desserts in summer are all about berries and might be a berry apple blueberry crumble.

FOOD PURVEYORS

Farm Stands
Hank's Farm Stand and Miniature Village (902-674-2646), Kings Grove Rd., Millville. (Take Exit 16 from Rte. 104.) Open May–Oct. Early in the season the fresh produce is sketchy, but count on fresh strawberries and rhubarb, radishes and spinach. The bakery makes tea biscuits, cinnamon rolls, granola macaroons, and oat cakes, as well as pork pies; fresh eggs from the chickens are also for sale. Next to the farm is a miniature village that visitors are welcome to look at, with buildings from the area, including the Lick-A-Chick restaurant, re-created in small scale. There are picnic tables, a play area, and pens with goats, rabbits, geese, and even a miniature donkey—at least it looked like one as it ran by.

A miniature village is part of the attraction at Hank's Farm Stand in Millville.

Pubs

Ziggy's Pub & Grill (902-539-8747), Cape Breton Shopping Plaza, 39 Keltic Dr., Sydney. Fresh-cut French fries are one of the major attractions at this pub with live entertainment.

Tearoom

Rita's Tea Room (902-828-2667; ritamacneil.com), 8077 Rte. 4, Big Pond. Open June–Oct. A one-room schoolhouse makes a good stop while on the road heading to Sydney on Route 4, the scenic route that passes the east side of the Bras d'Or Lakes. Rita MacNeil, an accomplished singer and songwriter, shows off her accomplishments with awards and photographs, and in 2008 she served tea, light lunch, and dinner.

CULTURE

Historic Site

MARCONI NATIONAL HISTORIC SITE OF CANADA

902-295-2069
pc.gc.ca/lhn-nhs/ns/marconi/
Timmerman St., Glace Bay

Mail: P.O. Box 159, Baddeck, NS B0E 1B0
Open: June–mid-Sept., 10 AM–6 PM
Admission: Free

In 1901, when Guglielmo Marconi transmitted a Morse-code signal through the air—from an antenna at this site—he ushered in the era of wireless communication. It had been impossible before his invention to send or receive messages without a telegraph cable, an expensive undertaking when it had to be laid under the Atlantic Ocean. In fact, the telegraph companies were furious that their infrastructure could prove unnecessary, and the Anglo-American Telegraph Company stopped Marconi in the midst of his work in Newfoundland. But Marconi was soon to dine with politicians happy to further his inventions. Table Head on Cape Breton Island appealed to him, and with government backing and the attention of the press he set up his work here, erecting 200-foot towers. Within hours of detecting signals, he received messages from the king of England—the news stories were everywhere, and Marconi's fortunes were made. The Cape Breton Marconi station closed in 1946, a victim of improved technologies. The science is explained in exhibits in the Visitor's Centre, and foundations of the original towers at Table Head station can also be seen.

Lighthouses

LOUISBOURG LIGHTHOUSE
nslps.com
Havenside Rd., Lighthouse Point, Louisbourg, NS

The first lighthouse at this site was built in 1734. Although today the lighthouse here is the third one built on this site (in 1923), it stands at the place of the oldest lighthouse in Canada. That lighthouse watched over both of the sieges of Louisbourg, but it had earned its price by guiding French ships into the harbour before those calamities. Cod liver oil fed its flame, which was visible, via lantern panes, for 18 nautical miles. In 1736 the heat of the oil flames started a fire in the lantern; another was built to replace it. In the 1758 siege it was damaged by cannon fire and lay in ruins until 1842. The lighthouse is sited at the head of an oceanside trail.

Museums

COSSIT HOUSE MUSEUM
902-539-7973
museum.gov.ns.ca/ch
225 George St., Sydney, NS B1P 4P4
Open: June 1–to Oct. 15, Mon.–Sat. 9:30 AM–5:30 PM, Sun. 1–5:30 PM.
Admission: Adult $2, seniors and children 6–17 $1, under 6 free.

Sydney's Reverend Mr. Ranna Cossit lived in this 1787 house, the town's oldest, but not for long. His archbishop moved him back to Yarmouth in 1800. The house has been furnished based on an inventory of the contents made in 1815.

FORTRESS OF LOUISBOURG

902-733-2280

pc.gc.ca/lhn-nhs/ns/louisbourg/

259 Park Service Rd., Louisbourg, NS BIC 2L2

Open: July–Aug., 9 am–5:30 pm; Mid-May–June, 9:30 am to 5 pm; Sept.–mid-Oct., 9:30 am–5 pm. Late May & late Oct., no animators, but some access. Closed Nov.–mid-May

Restaurants and bakery open June–Sept.

Admission: Adults $17.60, seniors $14.95, children $8.80

In 1713, when Isle Royale and Isle Saint-John were in French hands, the cod were so big and plentiful in the nearby waters that French fishermen and shippers could get rich on cargoes of salt cod—worth eight times the value of the fur trade, according to the Web site. Louisbourg, the fortress meant to keep British hands off this last treasure, began to be built in 1719, and rumors of its magnificence were soon to follow. At first the greedy British failed to see that the magnificent battery was best defended only on the waterfront of the fort—and that an attack from the land behind the fort had a chance of succeeding. So it proved in 1745, after war had been declared between France and Britain. New Englanders laid siege—and claimed the fort in 46 days. Even so, three years later the kings traded it back again. In 1758 the British took it again in seven weeks—and tore the place apart, hauling away the stone. It would never recover—at least not until Nova Scotia decided to rebuild one quarter of the fortress, in 1961.

In the height of the season, the streets are now filled with musicians, soldiers, bakers, and fisherman—who tend to interact with performances and talk about their activities. Madame DeGannes may be able to teach you a little about lacemaking. If you arrive in late August prepare to celebrate King Louis IX, who was once patron saint of France. When dining at Hotel de la Maine your dinner utensil is a large spoon, and the knife is shared, just as it might have been for travelers more than 250 years ago.

CAPE BRETON MINERS MUSEUM

902-849-4522

minersmuseum.com

17 Museum St., Quarry Point, Glace Bay, NS B1A 5T8

Open: June–Oct., daily 10 AM–6 PM, Tues. till 7 except in Sept.–Oct.; Nov.–May, Mon.–Fri. 9 AM–4 PM

Admission: Adults $5, children $4; mine tour an additional fee, adults $5, children $4

Your admission fee is more than three times what a miner would have earned on Cape Breton in 1873, at one of the island's eight coal companies. You won't think it was anything but a hard, difficult career after a visit to this museum, and especially after the trip down into the room and pillar mine below the museum, guided by a retired miner. Many people make sure to be in the area on a summer Tuesday, to attend a concert by the Men of the Deeps; check the Web site for the schedule. A miners' village beside the museum shows two time periods, the 1850s and 1900, with furniture and artifacts. The **Miners' Village Restaurant** (open from mid-April to October) is a good place to enjoy the Ocean Deeps Casserole, with seafood under mozzarella, or a platter of deep fried clams or fish and chips.

HIGHLAND VILLAGE MUSEUM/AN CLACHAN GAIDHEALACH

902-725-2275, 866-442-3542
museum.gov.ns.ca/hv/
4119 Hwy. 223, Iona, NS B2C 1A3
Open: June 1–mid-Oct., daily 9:30 AM–5:30 PM; shop at Visitor's Centre same hours
Admission: Adults $9, seniors $7 (CAA/AAA discount with card), children 6–17 $4

On 43 acres with views of Bras d'Or Lakes, staff dressed as early Scottish Gaelic settlers work with the farm animals and tools that those settlers would have had, in buildings like those they built. They speak Scottish Gaelic, a language rooted in Old Gaelic, as is modern Irish. Old Gaelic was spoken by the Goidelic Celts who moved into the region of Scotland called Argyllshire, from Ireland's eastern Ulster shore, in the 5th century A.D.

When Scottish immigrants came to Cape Breton in the 1800s, Gaelic was often their only language, and the districts they favored on the island were those already settled by their neighbors from the old country. Dialects from Barra and North Uist, for instance, are still spoken among their descendents on Cape Breton Island.

This museum intends to honor those traditions, researching the history and sustaining the vitality of the dialects

LENOIR FORGE MUSEUM

902-226-9364
cbmuseums.tripod.com/id38.html
Lower Rd., Rte. 206, P.O. Box 223, Arichat, NS B0E 1A0
Open: June–Sept., daily 10 AM–5 PM
Admission: Free

The Isle Madame Historical Society runs this museum, with a collection of 18th and 19th-century blacksmith tools, including an anvil, forge bellows, chisels, horseshoes, and weighing scales. The building was built with red sandstone from Port Hood and timber for the roof. Thomas LeNoir was the blacksmith here in the late 1700s; he worked for ship-owners who needed repairs and anchored in the deep water of the Arichat harbor. The business survived till 1902. The area of Arichat was settled by Acadians uprooted after the 1758 siege of Louisbourg.

Music

MEN OF THE DEEPS CONCERTS

902-849-4522
minersmuseum.com
Birkley St., Glace Bay, NS B1A 5T8
Open: July–Sept.
Admission: Adults $5, children $4

Held in summer on Tuesday nights at the Miner's Museum (see above). The chorus enters the darkened theater with their miner's helmets lighted—and sweeps the theater and music audience off their feet with their powerful singing.

LOUISBOURG PLAYHOUSE

902-733-2996, 888-733-2787
louisbourgplayhouse.com
11 Aberdeen St., Louisbourg, NS B1C 1A2
Open: June–Oct.
Admission: Varies with performances

A building out of history—out of 16th-century London—this recreation of the 1599 Globe Theatre was put up by Walt Disney Studios to film *Squanto: A Warrior's Tale*. Then it was donated to Louisbourg and moved to its present spot, opening in 1994 with music, theater, and more.

Englishtown Ferry

The Englishtown Ferry takes cars across a short stretch of water between Englishtown and a causeway jutting out from Jersey Cove. On the day I took it the new, larger ferry, *Torquil MacLean*, had just begun operating, able to take on two more cars than before with more space for passengers to get out of their cars. It costs $5 to cross in six minutes, and you skip 15 kilometers more driving, if you are heading north on the Cabot Trail.

The pastoral landscape near the Englishtown Ferry dock

Seasonal Events

April
Cape Breton International Drum Festival (capebretoninternationaldrumfest.ca),
  Glace Bay.

July
Bartown Festival, Sydney. Regattas, parades, and activities for children.
Coal Dust Days, New Waterford.

August
Fête de Saint Louis (902-563-4636), Louisbourg. Late August.
The Johnny Miles Festival (johnnymilesfestival.ca), Sydney.
Louisbourg Crab Fest (louisbourgcrabfest.ca), Louisbourg. Fresh mussels and crab din-
  ners served on the first Saturday of August.
Sydney Action Week (www.actionweek) Nine-day festival, with music, parades, children's
  activities, sports tournaments.

RECREATION

Boat Tours
Bird Island Boat Tours (800-661-6680), 1672 Old Rte. 5, Big Bras d'Or, Cape Breton.
  Operating from mid-May to mid-September. Puffin and eagle tours are the focus in the
  early summer. The business is operated by the Van Schaicks, a family that has been
  running tour boats here since 1972. They once took the Princess of Japan out for a tour—
  and anyone who can buy a ticket can see the nesting grounds of Atlantic puffins (the
  world's cutest bird), black-legged kittiwakes, black guillemots, and more.

Golf
Dundee Golf Club (902-345-0420, 800-565-5660; dundeegolfclub.com), Dundee Resort
  & Golf Club, RR #2, West Bay. Designed by Robert Moote and set on the side of a mountain, every moment on this course offers up sweeping views of the Bras d'Or Lakes. A
  new clubhouse is good for a meal whether you play golf or not.

Hiking
Cap Auguet Eco-Trail, Rte. 206, Isle Madame. Beginning at the Boudreauville trailhead is
  a 9-kilometer or 6-mile hike with the ocean to one side and marshland to the other.

SHOPPING

Bookstores
Reynolds Book Store (902-564-2665), 446 Charlotte St., Sydney. New books by local
  authors and a large selection of all categories of new and used books, with some rare
  and first editions.

Gift and Specialty Shops

The Artisan's Market (902-625-0207), 606 Reeves St., Port Hawkesbury. Owned by Nicole Fawcett, a Cape Breton native who paints miniatures, The Artisan's Market sells quilts, pottery, sweaters, and more, all made by local artists and craftsmen.

Cape Breton Centre for Crafts and Design (902-539-7491; capebretoncraft.com), 322 Charlotte St. Sydney. An exhibit of some of the craftwork done on Cape Breton Island is just the beginning: this center is also the source for the Cape Breton Artisan Trail Map that tourists in love with handwork will want to consult every mile of their journey on the island. Jitka Zgola makes functional pottery, which serves to make the moments of the day aesthetic delights. Arlene Christmas, also known as Dozay, paints phantasmagorical images.

La Picasse Boutique (902-226-0149; lapicasse.ca), 3435 Rte. 206, C.P. 70, Petit-de-grat, Isle Madame, Nouvelle Écosse, B0E 2L0. Located at this Acadian center is a boutique of local arts and crafts. Acadian souvenirs like earrings, hats, plates, and more. You might want a little Acadian flag, the French tricolour with a yellow star, that tradition says may represent the Virgin Mary.

9

EASTERN AND CENTRAL PRINCE EDWARD ISLAND

Charlotteville and Kings and Queens Counties

With a population of 35,000 Charlottetown is a modest-sized city; but as host to most of PEI's 1.2 million tourists every year it has developed every kind of entertainment from musical theater and a jazz and blues festival to deep-sea fishing and world-class golf. Ceilidhs are held all over the island throughout the year.

Big bluefin tuna is caught off North Lake. The Confederation Trail, a defunct rail route, takes hiking or biking visitors in three directions. And wherever you go on the island, you will be passing sweeping fields that grow Prince Edward Island's famous crops, from the potatoes of tradition to modern additions that added up to $380 millions worth of agricultural products in 2007.

The year 2008 was the 100th anniversary of the publication of the island's most famous book, *Anne of Green Gables*. Also the subject of long-running musicals, this book draws visitors to the author's home and to a village called Avonlea that copies the story line right down to Anne's red braids. Both are in Cavendish on Prince Edward Island's north shore, along with the fabulous 24-mile-long sandy Cavendish Beach, just a tiny bit of PEI's 1,100 miles of coastline.

EASTERN SHORE AREA

LODGING

MURRAY RIVER

DEEP WATER INN
Gerald and Iris Soloman, innkeepers
902-962-2243, 888-778-9990
deepwaterinn.com
10582 Shore Rd., RR #4 Murray River, PEI
C0A 1W0
Price: $75 to $100

Credit cards: Yes
Handicapped Access: Yes
Special Features: Wi-Fi

This recently built house, designed as an inn, opened for business in 2006. Three big rooms all have large bathrooms, and the first-floor room is built exactly to code for handicapped access, allowing someone with a wheelchair to maneuver easily, and anyone else to feel like a king. An upstairs

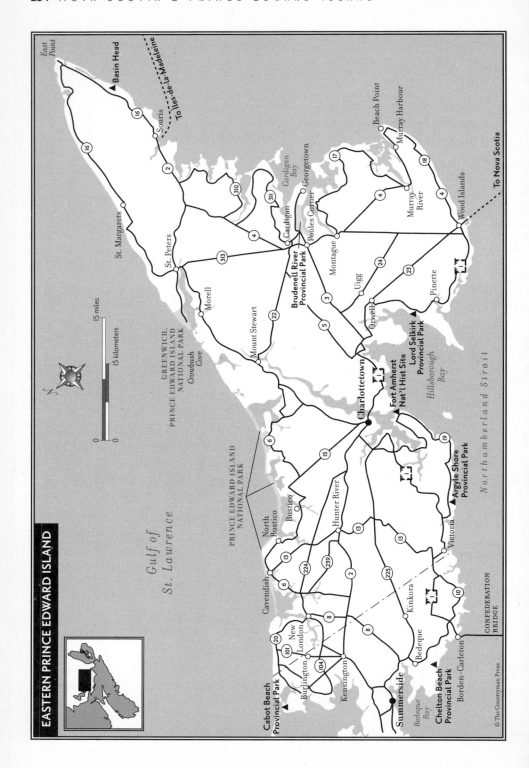

EASTERN PRINCE EDWARD ISLAND

© The Countryman Press

library and computer for guests augments the building's Wi-Fi, and satellite TV makes every room an entertainment center. The Arctic Room is lilac and holds a large bath; the Pacific is large too and has a tub with air jets. Both rooms on the second floor are in the front of the house and look across the narrow road to the sea.

Georgetown

GEORGETOWN INN

Joel Short and Dawn Sadowey, innkeepers
902-652-2511, 877-641-2414
georgetownhistoricinn.com
62 Richmond St., Georgetown, PEI CoA 1Lo
Price: $99 to $149
Credit cards: Yes
Handicapped Access: None
Special Features: Wi-Fi, fine-dining restaurant, breakfast included with room

Eight large rooms include two of the most expansive in the provinces—the Ivy Room and the Forget Me Not Room, with separate bathtubs and showers in their large bathrooms—create a sense of tranquility just by looking inside them. New owners Joel Short and Dawn Sadowey have plans to update the paint in the inn rooms, so these two may evolve from their floral charm, but they can't lose that luxurious quality of space. All eight rooms have access to the second- and third-floor decks and a late-night cup of tea or early coffee.

In the dining room, Joel Short, who earned a culinary degree at Northern Alberta Institute of Technology, has created a menu worth tasting. Your first clue to reserve for dinner might be the chocolate pecan waffles served for breakfast.

Bay Fortune and Spry Point

✪ INN AT BAY FORTUNE

902-687-3745, 888-687-3745
innatbayfortune.com
Bay Fortune, PEI CoA 2Bo

Open: Late May–mid-Oct.
Price: $135 to $335
Credit cards: Yes
Handicapped Access: Yes, Unit 7 and possibly two others
Special Features: Wi-Fi, close to Back Beach and Front Beach, magnificent dinners in the restaurant

The 18 suites and two standard guest rooms have the burnished quality of a well-loved home, and some of that has to do with the old furniture, some with the local crafts. They are mostly different, with a balcony, or a fireplace, and tiled bathrooms with whirlpool tubs. North Tower Suite 3 has a view of the water from a balcony, a king-size bed, propane fireplace, and cathedral ceiling. I stayed in the smallest room available, Room 135 in the South Tower's second floor, but even though my bed filled most of the space, the bathroom was good looking and the windows across from each other let in a sweet breeze over the lichen-covered roof shingles. Breakfast was terrific—buttery scrambled eggs, whole-grain toast, house preserves, and lots of fresh fruit set out on a buffet with other things to supplement the main dish.

INN AT SPRY POINT

902-583-2400, 888-687-3745
innatsprypoint.com
RR #4, Souris, PEI CoA 2Bo
Off Rte. 310, on Spry Point Rd.
Open: mid-June–late Sept.
Price: $185 to $335
Credit cards: Yes
Handicapped Access: Yes
Special Features: Wi-Fi, breakfast and lunch served in the dining room

The location of this wonderful inn on a glamorous 110-acre peninsula sets it in the midst of water—the Northumberland Strait, and Batten Bay. Eleven of the 15 rooms at the Inn at Spry Point have king-size beds, and four have European split-king beds that can be configured as two singles or a king bed. Some of the rooms look out at the garden and others contemplate the sea. Pastel walls, dark-wood four-poster beds, some contemporary, wingback chairs in spacious rooms with high ceilings make these accommodations stand out. Enjoy a breakfast made with fresh organic ingredients.

HERMANVILLE

JOHNSON SHORE INN

Arla Johnson and Julie Shore, innkeepers
902-687-1340, 877-510-9669
johnsonshoreinn.com
9984 Rte. 16, Hermanville, PEI
Mail: RR #3, Rte. 16, Souris, PE CoA 2Bo
Open: May–Jan.
Price: $175 to $350
Credit cards: Yes
Handicapped Access: Yes, one
Special Features: Wi-Fi

Built in 1999, this inn is placed almost as far out to sea as a ship, and the eye lingers on the red cliffs and blue water visible from every room. Colorful Adirondack chairs offer even closer perspectives on the sea, painted red at sunset. Fifty acres of wind-swept grass spread out from the 12 guest rooms, requiring immediate exploration. The white rooms all hold a queen-size bed covered with a quilt (four have an additional twin-size bed), wingback chairs, and private baths, with antiques, art, and a fire in the living room in cold weather. Breakfast, included in the rates, is served from 8 to 10 AM in the ocean-view dining room, perhaps with a smoked salmon frittata or blueberry pecan pancakes. Dinner is served in the dining room, by reservation only.

ST. PETERS

BAYSIDE COUNTRY INN AND COTTAGE

902-961-2954, 866-961-2954
baysidecountryinn.com
P.O. Box 93, St. Peters, PEI CoA 2Ao
Open: May–mid-Nov.
Price: $90 to $175
Credit Cards: Yes
Handicapped Access: None

Simple, clean accommodations offer a next-door restaurant and a great location for getting on the Confederation Trail. The

The Inn at St. Peters is set along the bay with paths through the gardens.

large units are on two floors. The bedroom on the upper floor has a private deck with a view of the bay. Some units have two bedrooms, and all of them have a kitchen and dining area. The two-bedroom condos are just right for a couple traveling together.

THE INN AT ST. PETERS

Karen Davey, innkeeper
902-961-2135, 800-818-0925
innatstpeters.com
Greenwich Rd., RR #1. St. Peters Bay, PEI CoA 2A0
Open: May—beginning of Oct.
Price: $315 to $390, includes breakfast and three-course dinner for two
Credit cards: Yes
Handicapped Access: Yes
Special Features: Wi-Fi, AC

The accommodations at this inn are top of the line—and each one has its own deck and waterview. Eight of the units face the waterfront directly, and the other eight view the water at an angle, with an immaculate, constantly replanted garden stretching out between the main building and the rooms on part of the property's 13 acres. Out in the bay are some of the rafts used for rope-grown mussels, a huge business on Prince Edward Island and a clue that they will be perfectly fresh and good when you try them in the dining room here (see the Restaurants section below). Waterfront Room 9 holds an elaborately carved four-poster bed, a couch, and a rocking chair in front of the fireplace.

DALVAY

DALVAY BY-THE-SEA HERITAGE INN

David Reymond and Michelle Thompson, innkeepers
902-672-2048, 888-366-2955
dalvaybythesea.com
16 Cottage Crescent, P.O. Box 8, Dalvay, PEI CoA 1P0
Off Hwy. 6 at the Dalvay gate to Prince

Edward Island National Park
Open: Mid-June—mid-Sept.
Price: $280 to $390 includes breakfast and three-course dinner for two
Credit cards: Yes
Handicapped Access: Yes, two cottages
Special Features: Tennis courts, kayaks, bikes for rent, croquet, two-hole golf practice range

Some of the rooms at this old inn are paneled from head to foot, and so are some of their private bathrooms. None of the rooms have television, radio, or a phone—a problem 10 years ago, and now a selling point. "It's quiet here at night," said Brandon Rose, night manager. Every room is different in this 1895 "cottage." The queen-bed suite on the corner of this rounded building holds views of water and the front lawn, a plush four-poster, couch, and two wingback chairs, and a claw-foot tub in its bathroom. Most of the cottages, with three bedrooms and paneled rooms, overlook the lake.

RESTAURANTS

MURRAY HARBOUR

BREHAUT'S RESTAURANT

902-962-3141
Murray Harbour
Open: Mon.–Sat. 8 AM–9 PM, Sun. 11 AM–9 PM
Price: $5 to $16
Credit cards: Yes
Cuisine: Seafood and casual classics
Serving: B, L, D
Handicap Access: No
Special Features: Ice-cream cones sold in the front

With upholstered booths downstairs, and more tables up, Brehaut's is built to take care of its visitors. The menu is too, with a mix and match section that lets you devise exactly what and how much of it you would like to eat. A little meal of one piece of fried fish and a small serving of coleslaw barely broke $8 and exactly matched my appetite—more places should follow suit. This style of hospitality shows itself in the friendly service and in the reputation of this restaurant—making it the one restaurant innkeepers and locals recommend to visitors.

Georgetown

CLAM DIGGERS BEACH HOUSE & RESTAURANT
902-652-2466
clamdiggers.ca
7 West St., Georgetown
Open: Year-round, daily 11:30 AM–8:30 PM
Price: In the Beach House, $9 to $20, in the restaurant, $21 to $49
Credit cards: Yes
Cuisine: Seafood and meat with eclectic flair
Serving: L, D
Handicap Access: Yes
Special Features: Three areas offer the choice of casual or white tablecloth dining

The building in which Clam Diggers is located is a replica of a train station, but make no mistake, this is a vital, hard-working town still making its living from the sea at a tug-boat construction company and a seafood plant.

Inside the building are two dining rooms. The Beach House, with multi-colored umbrellas decorating the tall ceiling, offers casual meals like fish and chips ($11, with a homemade remoulade if you'd like), fried scallops ($18), or fried clams ($13).

In the other dining room, the restaurant proper, honey-glazed halibut comes with basil cream, and center-cut pork chops are matched with peach chutney. Chicken, a rib eye, lobster, and salmon are all made special with clever touches.

If you want to eat outside on the deck, you can participate in the cooking of dinner—with a hibachi.

Bay Fortune

✪ INN AT BAY FORTUNE
902-687-3745, 888-687-3745
innatbayfortune.com
Bay Fortune, PEI C0A 2B0
Open: Late May–mid-Oct.
Price: $26 to $38
Credit cards: Yes
Cuisine: Seasonal, inspired, and locally sourced
Serving: D
Handicap Access: No
Special Features: Tasting menu available for $70

Clam Diggers Restaurant has a formal dining room and an informal café on the other side.

A plate of oysters with Champagne vinaigrette beckoned, but so did the tasting menu. I decided to let the chef, Warren Barr, take care of my evening—except for my wish that there be no mackerel and that I finish with strawberries.

The amuse-bouche of lobster salad with a little tomato confit, one purple viola and one branching frond of dill, began the evening with the fresh taste of lightly cooked lobster and more intense tomato. A fish cake, fat and crunchy on the outside, was topped with tomato jam and three crossed young sorrel leaves. The sweetened tomato condiment and the lemony sorrel went well with the creamy fish cake. Next, a small piece of halibut cooked to tender perfection sat in a pool of corn chowder with a touch of bacon—thin, crunchy pieces of potato contrasted with the tender little cubes in the soup.

Maréchal Foch red from Rossignol Estate Vineyard (see below), a Prince Edward Island winery, is curiously smooth and mild, while also scented with mushrooms.

A roast pork tenderloin set on a smear of pureed sweet potato, with crunchy disks of corn bread covered with melted Gouda from The Cheese Lady (see below in the Charlottetown section), with a split spring carrot in a little demiglace, created a winning meal—unlike everything else, this one I could not resist eating every bit of.

The strawberries I'd requested were set on a thin slice of shortbread, with pastry cream, and accompanied by a wafer-thin poppyseed rectangular cookie and a scoop of strawberry sorbet.

St. Peters

THE INN AT ST. PETERS

Karen Davey, innkeeper
902-961-2135, 800-818-0925
innatstpeters.com
Greenwich Rd., RR #1. St. Peters Bay, PEI
C0A 2A0

Open: May–beginning of Oct., daily for dinner; Sun. brunch
Price: $27 to $38
Credit cards: Yes
Cuisine: Upscale seafood and meat
Serving: D, Sun. brunch
Handicap Access: Yes
Special Features: Verandah overlooking the bay and the sunset

The mussels with smoked tomato butter are a standard treat in this dining room, where they come with toasted corn bread as an appetizer. Colville Bay oysters are also on that list, in three preparations: raw, Rockefeller, and fried. For the main course the difficult choice lies among island lobster, pan-roasted salmon, poached beef tenderloin with pommes Anna, or pineapple glazed halibut. Save room for a cheese plate or the trio of house ice creams, or even, ambitiously, the white-chocolate baked Alaska with caramelized banana.

RICK'S FISH 'N CHIPS

902-961-3438
Rte. 2, St. Peters Bay, PEI
Open: July–Aug., daily 11 AM–10 PM; June, daily 11 AM–9 PM; mid- to end of May and Sept., 11 AM to 7 PM except Fri.–Sat. till 9 PM
Price: $6 to $12
Credit cards: Yes
Cuisine: Fried seafood, burgers, and pizza
Serving: L, D
Handicap Access: No

Where are the best French fries on Prince Edward Island? According to many people, the fresh-cut fries at Rick's are the best, along with the island's best fried haddock and best fried clams. It's important to know where to go when the yen for fried seafood takes hold, since it's such a waste to indulge in stuff that doesn't taste great. Count on Rick's kitchen to serve high-quality fried haddock, sole, clam strips or whole clams, scallops and shrimp. Poutine is on the menu for French Canadians and their converts who adore the fries with cheese and gravy specialty, and seafood chowder and marinated mussels are extras to make the meal a feast.

DALVAY

DALVAY BY-THE-SEA HERITAGE INN
David Reymond and Michelle Thompson, innkeepers
902-672-2048, 888-366-2955
dalvaybythesea.com
16 Cottage Crescent, P.O. Box 8, Dalvay, PEI CoA 1Po
Open: Mid-June–mid-Sept.
Price: $25 to $40
Credit cards: Yes
Cuisine: Up-to-date and inventive
Serving: L, D
Handicap Access: Yes
Special Features: A beautiful view

The dining room with its paneled ceiling and windows arching over a water view is a recent addition, built to resemble the rest of the inn with its charming interiors and pretty details. Guests at the inn pay rates that include dinner, and the three-course fine dining offered every night is from the same menu for everyone. The lucky guests receive menus with no prices listed, and they can have lobster every night if they want. No doubt many of them do.

Guests who arrive with a wide experience of the world's restaurants applaud the meals, though generous proportions risk a weight gain. Malpeque oysters, Blue Point mussels, beef, mushrooms, and greens are all from local suppliers. The wild venison short loin with bacon and barley risotto is perfect on a chilly night, and the grilled filet mignon with an onion, mushroom, and blue cheese ragout sounds good anytime. The island's biggest wine list, with 12 wines sold by the glass, spans the globe. Dalvay's sticky date pudding is a date cake served warm with toffee sauce and vanilla ice cream—and according to many it's the best thing in the world.

FOOD PURVEYORS

Bakeries and Cafes
Sheltered Harbour Café (902-687-1997), 2065 Rte. 2, Souris. Open in summer, Mon.–Sat. 7 AM–9 PM, Sun. 8 AM–9 PM. Locals swear by this café tucked into a gas station. "Honey-stung fried chicken" might be why, or the fried fish, clams, scallops, or potato and herb-crusted haddock. Burgers and a roast turkey dinner, Thai spring rolls and pierogies, onion rings and deep fried veggies, chowders, salads, and milk shakes are all served. Owners Ed and Mary Steele take their menu all over the world.
Trailside Café (902-676-3130, 888-704-6595; trailside.ca), 109 North Main St., Mount Stewart. Open Thurs.–Sun. mid-June–mid-Oct., daily; mid-Oct.–mid-June, Fri.–Sun. 4 PM–10 PM. The house seafood chowder is made with salmon, haddock, lobster, and clams. Spanikopita, Digby scallops, and Atlantic salmon are possibilities for a dinner, and an ice-cream crêpe topped with chocolate, raspberry, strawberry, or blueberry sauce is waiting for you for dessert. Thursday to Sunday musical performances through the summer, all inside an old coop that had been a general store but had fallen into disrepair before it was renovated in 1996.

Distillery

The Myriad View Distillery (902-687-1281; straitshine.com), 1336 Rte. 2, Rollo Bay, PEI
C02 2P0. Free tastings and a free tour daily May–Oct.; off-season call in advance. A
German, hand-crafted copper still is the tool that transforms each batch of ingredients
into Strait Shine, Strait Vodka, Strait Lighting, and Strait Gin. Organic coriander, orris
root, angelica root, lemon peel, and anise, steeped in the triple-distilled gin, make its
flavor smooth and bright. The Strait Shine is made by fermenting cane sugar and
molasses—legal moonshine that John Law will leave alone. Moonshine was PEI's traditional drink, according to owner Ken Mill. Prohibition was in effect longer here, from
1901 to 1948, so everyone made shine, and it's still served at local weddings. Pieces of
illegal stills are here on display—donated by locals who say they no longer need to use
them, now that they can buy their moonshine here. Seven milliliters or a little more
than a teaspoon is the maximum amount of tasting, and the spirits are tasted neat.

Winery

Rossignol Estate Winery (902-962-4193; rossignolwinery.com), 11147 Shore Rd., Little
Sands, RR #4, Murray River, PEI C0A 1W0. Open June–Sept., or call ahead off-season.
Located just a few minutes east of the Caribou/Woods Island ferry from Nova Scotia,
this is a delightful way to begin a visit to PEI. Owner John Rossignol is expanding his
vineyards and cultivating another 10 acres in 2009 and 2010 if all goes as planned. His
gold medals for the best dessert wine in Canada—won for three years at the All-
Canadian Wine Championships for his blackberry mead—have been a boost. The Saint
Jean White is a friendly wine with a summer picnic and seafood, and the Isle Saint Jean
Red is a good blend of Maréchal Foch, Baco Noir, and blueberry. But try them for your-
self—the tastings are free—and admire the labels made with prints of Rossignol's wife
Nancy Perkins's paintings.

The vineyard and building at Rossignol Winery in Little Sands

CULTURE

Lighthouses

EAST POINT LIGHTHOUSE

902-357-2106
eastpointlighthouse.com
East Point, PEI
Open: Daily tours given mid-June–Labour Day; call for off-season hours

WOOD ISLANDS LIGHTHOUSE

902-962-3110
woodislandslighthouse.com
173 Lighthouse Rd., Woods Island, PEI CoA 1Bo (next to the ferry terminal)
Open: Early June–early Sept., 9:30 AM to 6 PM
Admission: Adults $5.25, children 6–13 $2.50, seniors $4

The climb to the top of the 18.5-meter- or 54-foot-tall tower will reward you with an instant understanding of the lay of the land. The lighthouse keeper's quarters, including an old bedroom, will acquaint you with the lonely life of the last keeper—and the rumrunning room suggests some of the dangers and excitement on the coast. Another hint is the reported sightings of the phantom burning schooner offshore. Complimentary food is served from the kitchen.

Museums

ELMIRA RAILWAY MUSEUM

902-357-7234
peimuseum.com
Rte. 16A, Elmira, PEI CoK 1Ao
Open: June–Sept.
Admission: Adults $4, students $3

At the easternmost point of the Confederation Trail, the wonderful hiking and biking trail that stretches across the island, the Elmira Railway Museum holds a large model-train collection and tells the history of the railroad.

LOG CABIN MUSEUM

902-962-2201
Rte. 18A, Murray Harbor
Mail: Gen. Deliv., Murray Harbour, PEI CoA 1Vo
Open: July–Labour Day, daily
Admission: Adults $2.50, children 6–12 $.50

This collection is a labor of love, the love of Prince Edward Island and its history in Preston Robertson, who built the building after cutting down the trees he needed to make it. "Two neighbors helped me," Robertson said. Born in 1917, he was 90 years old when I met him in 2008, and he showed me some of the highlights of his collection, like an old comic book that described the life of John F. Kennedy from birth to assassination. "People sold it to me for a quarter because they could come back and see it," he said. Additions to the original building house old horse carriages, like one built in Charlottetown in 1880. A 1930s washing machine works just fine, as does a 1905 Edison Phonograph, with a cylinder recording of "When You and I Were Young, Maggie." Antique jewelry, needlepoint, handkerchiefs ("kept from wear because they were too good to use"), and kitchen tools and stoves are also here.

Theater

KING'S PLAYHOUSE
902-652-2824
kingsplayhouse.com
65 Grafton St., Georgetown, PEI CoA 1Lo
Open: June–Aug. season, 7:30 PM shows
Admission: Varies according to performance

Musical performances, theatrical premiers, and history—like the train that crashed into the original building two years after it was built in 1897. That building went up in smoke in a storm on March 3, 1983. Today's building is also a community center with annual Remembrance Day services and many other events.

Preston Robertson playing "When You and I Were Young," on a 1905 Edison Phonograph, at the Log Cabin Museum

Seasonal Events

August
Wild Blueberry Festival & Homecoming (stpetersblueberryfestival.ca), St. Peters Bay. Teen dance, parade, and pancake brunch.

RECREATION

Bicycling
Kingfisher Outdoors (902-961-2080), Morell. Open July–mid-Sept. This outfit rents bicycles, canoes, and kayaks at both the Park and the Tourism Centre. Morell River is a bird-watching destination, and the Confederation Trail is here too; bike east along St. Peters Bay for a pretty waterside ride.

Plover Bike Rental (902-367-7900; stpetersbay.com/rentals/), St. Peters Bay. Open daily mid-June–mid-Sept.; weekdays May–mid-June and mid-Sept.–Oct. Bike rentals for full-day or half-day include helmet, trail map, water, and a discount in the St. Peter's Bay Craft and Giftware store next door. The Confederation Trail, the former railroad route that runs from tip to tip of the island, is next door, smooth and easy "sailing."

"We have the nicest part of the trail on Prince Edward Island," said owner Ed McKenna—it runs for 11 kilometer or 8 miles right along the water and over a few bridges, away from the highway.

Boating

Cruise Manada Seal Cruises (902-838-3444, 800-986-3444; cruisemanada.com), Montague Marina, Montague. Operating mid-May–Sept. Tours in a covered boat with washrooms cruise up to seal and sea bird habitats and mussel farms, and offer an entertaining narration of the history of the island and the lives of its sea creatures. Another option is the ceilidhs on the water on Friday nights, with musician and singer Gordon Belsher—besides his music, there will be mussels with garlic butter as part of the trip and beer and wine for sale.

Marine Adventure Seal Watching (902-962-2494; sealwatching.com), Murray River. Run daily June–Sept., at 10 AM, 1 PM, and 3:30 PM. A two-hour tour of the Murray River, this narrated trip takes visitors alongside the island's biggest seal colony, and it shows off PEI's enormous mussel farming industry too.

Camping

Campbell's Cove Campground (902-357-2233, off-season 902-687-3246; campbellscove campground.com), Campbell's Cove. A magnificent location at the top of a low cliff and a wide beach, this campground has 52 sites, two cabins, a playground, laundry and kitchen facility, and more.

Farming

Springwater Farm (902-583-2340; springwaterfarm.ca), 697 Rte. 4, Albion Cross (Mail: RR #2, Saint Peters Bay, PE C0A 2A0). George and Melaney Matheson run this busy sheep farm, but if you call in advance you can arrange a hayride and a tour of the farm. The Shepherd's Nook is a store with sheepskins, wool blankets, and more. The farm also offers a farm vacation—for $49 a day you can live on the farm, enjoy breakfast with the family, and do as much or as little as you like, although a hosted farm day will be another $20.

Fishing

MacNeil's Deep Sea Fishing (902-357-2858, 902-357-2454), North Lake Harbour (Mail: Red Point, Souris, PEI C0A 2B0. Operating end of July to end of September. The whales, seals, birds, and coastline are bonuses of an eight-hour trip to catch tuna on *Wendy R5*, a fiberglass fishing boat equipped with a washroom, with Captain Jeff MacNeil in charge.

Golf

In 2007, 361,000 rounds of golf were played on PEI's golf courses. In the 2008–2009 edition of *Best Places to Play*, published by *Golf Digest*, Dundarave and Crow Bush both received a rating of 4.5 out of 5 stars, according to a news release from Prince Edward Island Information Service.

Getting the hay in at Springwater Farm in Albion Cross, where tourists can join in

The Callaway Golf Divine 9 at the Rodd Brudenell River Resort, Roseneath (800-235-8909; golflinkspei.com) With a nine-hole par 30 course, the Calloway Golf Divine Nine is one of PEI's top destination golf courses. It was designed by Dr. Michale Hurdzan and Dana Fry, and it's just a short walk from both the Rodd Brudenell Resort and the Brudenell River Provincial Park. A pro shop, the Callaway Golf Performance Centre, offers custom-fit golf clubs and a range of other golf equipment and apparel.

Dundarave at the Rodd Brudenell River Resort, Roseneath (800-235-8909; golflinkspei.com) is another part of that resort's 45-hole golf landscape. Opened in 1999, this 18-hole course is set on red sandstone alongside the Brudenell River, with greens bordered by pines.

The Links at Crowbush Cove, Rodd Crowbush Golf & Beach Resort, Rte. 350 (800-235-8909; golflinkspei.com). Rated as one of the top two best-value golf courses in Canada, The Links is set in PEI's north shore dunes and offers a skyline of blue water.

Hiking

Confederation Trail (902-368-5540; princeedwardisland.com). The Prince Edward Island Trans Canada Railroad route has been transformed into a hiking and biking trail, and thus transformed into one of the island's most popular resources since it opened in 2000. See above under "Bicycling" for two places to start a bike trip down the trail. But taking it in on foot might be even better, especially on the stretch that borders St. Peters Bay. The trail is flat and covered with crushed gravel. It has its own little bridges; plum-colored gates signal an entry point. Download a copy of the PEI Confederation Trail Cycling Guide or order one by mail from Tourism PEI, P.O. Box 940, Charlottetown, PEI C1A 7M5.

The stable at Brudenell Trail Rides, in Brudenell Provincial Park

Horseback Riding

Brudenell Riding Stables (902-652-2396 in-season, 902-583-2757 off-season). Set inside the Brudenell Provincial Park, this riding stable offers visitors a chance to ride a horse on Brudenell River Beach. A 4.5-kilometer or 2.8-mile ride, lasting an hour, is $45. Five dollar pony rides are also on the list of possibilities, and reservations are recommended.

Parks and Beaches

Greenwich Peninsula, part of Prince Edward Island National Park (902-672-6350; pc.gc.ca), Dalvay. Open year-round. Admission: Adults $7.80, seniors $6.80, children 6–16 $3.90, but check in April for changes. Three hikes in this section of the national park take you through the dunes. The park staff has found 150 unauthorized paths through the dunes; they ask visitors to stick to the marked trails so that the marram grass can regrow and hold the fragile dunes together. The cute red foxes that live in the dunes will be grateful.

SHOPPING

Gift and Specialty Shops

Old General Store (902-962-2459), 9387 Main St., Murray River. Island jams, CDs of island musicians' music, and handcrafted quilts, jewelry, pottery, hooked rugs, and more.

St. Peters Bay Craft and Giftware (902-367-7900; stpetersbay.com/rentals/), St. Peters Bay. Open mid-June–mid-Sept., daily; May–mid-June and mid-Sept.–Oct., weekdays only. Tour the pewter workshop for free, and consider a purchase of pewter jewelry or a personalized golf marker afterward. Island fruit preserves, fruit juices, maple syrup, and free samples.

Charlottetown

Charlottetown and the immediate surrounding region has so many conveniences and attractions within easy reach of one another that it seems best to give them their own section.

Lodging

Charlottetown

CHARLOTTE'S ROSE INN
Maureen and John Crofts, innkeepers
902-892-3699, 888-237-3699
charlottesrose.ca
11 Grafton St., Charlottetown, PEI C1A 1K3
Open: Mid-May–Oct.
Price: $100 to $205
Credit cards: Yes
Handicapped Access: None
Special Features: Wi-Fi

The Confederation bedroom with its high canopy queen-size bed and blue print wallpaper carries the air of the beginning of Canada in 1867, though an Edwardian dresser would have been made after the turn of the century. Five well-equipped rooms, all with private baths, will make a guest comfortable for a night, and the exceptional breakfast will be a welcome event in the morning. A loft suite on the third floor has a walk-out deck on the roof. Fruit at breakfast might be blueberry and peach parfait, or melon cocktail with a vinaigrette. Next a quiche Lorraine or baked peach French toast, and lemon bread, might be on the menu.

CHARLOTTETOWN BACKPACKERS INN
Levi Urman, innkeeper
902-367-5749

charlottetownbackpackers.com
60 Hillsborough St., Charlottetown, PEI C1A 4W1
Open: Apr.–mid-Nov.
Price: $30 for dorm, $70 loft private room
Credit cards: Yes
Handicapped Access: None
Special Features: Wi-Fi, large collection of vintage vinyl records, pool table

This inexpensive option opened in 2007 with four dorm rooms. Two of the rooms hold four beds, one holds five, and one holds six. Two private rooms are great for a family. The Loft private room has a fireplace, air-conditioning (also in the loft dorm room) and a double-size premium mattress. No room has its own private bathroom. Fresh fruit, fresh baked goods like banana bread, jams, toast, honey, and coffee are served every day from 8 to 10 AM. Two common rooms are another resource, one with an LCD for movie watching. Most of the customers are under 30, and many are cyclists. Make a reservation to be sure of a bed.

ELMWOOD HERITAGE INN
Carol and Jay MacDonald, innkeepers
902-368-3310, 877-933-3310
elmwoodinn.pe.ca
121 North River Rd., Charlottetown, PEI C1A 3K7
Price: $110 to $259
Credit cards: Yes

Handicapped Access: None
Special Features: Wi-Fi, complimentary drinks, TVs and video or DVD player

Up under the eaves, the two ends of Rosa's Room have the feeling of a cocoon. The angled ceiling draped with curtains encloses the queen-size bed underneath like a canopy. At the other end, a large air-jet tub has its own large niche, and in between is the electric fireplace and a Victorian rocker and sofa. But back on the first floor, The Library, with a black marble fireplace, wingback chairs and a large ottoman, and a bathroom with both a tub and a separate shower, makes spaciousness seem both commodious and utterly comfortable. The inn is hidden at the end of an elm-lined driveway—there are still 30 tall elms, planted in 1889, shadowing the grounds with their high crowns of leaves.

THE GREAT GEORGE
902-892-0606, 800-361-1118
thegreatgeorge.com
58 Great George St., Charlottetown, PEI

C1A 4K3
Price: $155 to $399
Credit cards: Yes
Handicapped Access: Yes, one
Special Features: Wi-Fi, AC

A boutique hotel set in twelve different buildings, The Great George has 54 different rooms. Modern and traditional décors vary according to the space you choose, with the five Hideaway Suites being the most luxurious, one with black leather furniture and white walls, a fireplace and large tub. The Perkins Suite is set on two levels with an outside balcony, living room, dining room and kitchen, walk-in double shower, two-person airjet tub, and steam room. A complimentary continental breakfast is served in the lobby, with muffins and cinnamon rolls, a hot mini-quiche, fresh fruit, cereal, toast, and more.

HILLHURST INN
Scott Stewart, innkeeper
902-894-8004, 877-994-8004
hillhurst.com

The dining room at Hillhurst Inn, Charlottetown

181 Fitzroy St., Charlottetown, PEI C1A 1S3
Price: $100 to $235
Credit cards: Yes
Handicapped Access: None
Special Features: Dataports, AC

Nine different rooms are available in this 1897 Georgian Revival house with oak and beech paneling and woodwork in the entrance hall. The spacious Fitzroy Room holds a canopy bed and formal upholstered chairs and a sofa, with plenty of room left to move around—perhaps to do the yoga your body is requesting after a long drive. The house was owned by the University of Prince Edward Island between 1970 and 1995, when the university president lived here.

FAIRHOLM NATIONAL HISTORIC INN
Terry O'Malley, innkeeper
902-892-5022, 888-573-5022
fairholm.pe.ca
230 Prince St., Charlottetown, PEI
Price: $129 to $289
Credit cards: Yes
Handicapped Access: None
Special Features: Wi-Fi, AC, fireplaces in every room

The Benjamin Rogers Suite in this 1838 mansion is on the main level and has its own entrance, but the massive dark-wood Victorian bed will endow a night's sleep with a certain magnificence. The Florence Babe Rogers Suite has a soaking tub and separate shower in a wainscoted bathroom. The king-size bed and fireplace share the room with wingback chairs and a settee. Fruit and yogurt start breakfast, and then a hot course is served, like pancakes or eggs Benedict.

BONSHAW

BONSHAW BREEZES
Sharon and Dave Moore, innkeepers
902-675-3479, 877-677-3479

bonshawbreezes.com
293 Green Rd., Bonshaw, PEI C0A 1C0
Price: $125 to $175
Credit cards: Yes
Handicapped Access: None
Special Features: Wi-Fi

The Morning Glory Suite at Bonshaw Breezes, with its own entrance and a high cut-out ceiling, has a living area where you can settle down at the end of a day at the beach for a glass of wine and a moment's relaxation before dinner. The outdoor hot tub is another resource at the end of the day. The Mayflower Suite is an efficiency cottage with two beds—one of them a pull-out bed—and a kitchen—but you still have a breakfast included in the rate, so you don't have to worry about making that meal.

RUSTICO

BARACHOIS INN
Judy and Gary MacDonald, innkeepers
902-963-2129, 800-963-2194
barachoisinn.com
2193 Church Rd., Rte. 243, Rustico
Mail: Hunter River R.R. #3, PEI C0A 1N0
Price: $185 to $275
Credit cards: Yes
Handicapped Access: Yes, one
Special Features: Wi-Fi, spa services

Two houses, one historic and one built recently in a traditional style, hold eight rooms for rent. The older Gallant House rooms are decorated in the Victorian style, with a brass bed and ornate wooden beds, and a soaking tub. In Room 1, the hand-carved walnut bed from the 1840s is massive and gorgeous. The Queen Suite 7 in the MacDonald House, on the second floor, has a view of Rustico Bay and a large, open room with a sitting area, fireplace, wingback chair with ottoman, and a kitchenette. Breakfast is served in the elegant formal dining room, with bacon and eggs or French toast or omelets and more.

RESTAURANTS

CHARLOTTETOWN

CLADDAGH OYSTER HOUSE & OLDE DUBLIN PUB
902-892-9661
claddaghoysterhouse.com
131 Sydney St., Charlottetown
Open: June–Sept., daily 11 AM–11 PM; off-season closed Sun.
Price: $10 to $13
Credit cards: Yes
Cuisine: Seafood and Maritime
Serving: L, D
Handicap Access: No

It's good to know there's a spot that puts together that classic, oysters Rockefeller, with great skill, but first and foremost is the list of the raw version. Malpeques, Colville Bay, Sarah' Shore, Raspberry Point, and Pickle Point oysters are all from PEI, and Beausoliels are brought over the water from New Brunswick. A 25-oyster taster ($45) sounds like the right move. Maybe twice? But island beef tenderloin and fried oysters, or pan-seared scallops, or rack of lamb are other possibilities. Upstairs is the Olde Dublin Pub, with a pub-food menu that lists fish and chips, deep-fried scallops, broiled salmon, and sandwiches and burgers. Live entertainment.

LUCY MAUD DINING ROOM
Culinary Institute of Canada
902-894-6868
dineaid.com/lucymaud/
4 Sydney St., Charlottetown
Open: Tues.–Sat. 11 AM–1:30 PM and 6–9:30 PM
Price: $18 to $24
Credit cards: Yes
Cuisine: Continental
Serving: L, D
Handicap Access: Yes

The students and staff of the Culinary Institute of Canada and Holland College are in charge of this restaurant. The dining room has a view of the harbor, but it's the culinary education that is really enriching this town, with more and more capable chefs, servers, and restaurateurs. The menu is straightforward, with all of the usual favorites. Visit and decide whether the students in the kitchen have figured out the challenge of a good Caesar, or steamed mussels with curried cream. Pancetta-wrapped Cornish game hen with fig sauce, or a bouillabaisse with PEI seafood, get high marks from the locals.

FLEX MUSSELS
902-569-0200
flexmussels.com
2 Lower Water St., Charlottetown
Open: End of May–mid-Oct., daily 11 AM–midnight
Price: $12 to $29
Credit cards: Yes
Cuisine: Seafood and more
Serving: L, D
Handicap Access: Yes
Special Features: Outdoor seating with a view of the harbor and marina

Mussels with lemongrass, mussels with black beans, mussels with chorizo? The 22 versions challenge anyone's decision-making faculties. This spot is making the claim for the best island fries, with its "French method" of twice frying the cut PEI Russet Burbank potatoes. Owned by Robert Shapiro, who also owns Dayboat at Oyster Bed Bridge (below), Flex Mussels does everything that can be done with the island's biggest natural product, grown on ropes in bays around the shore. But a customer isn't limited to mussels every which way—you can also order an oyster po' boy, fried oysters with remoulade on a bun, or a lobster sushi roll, or popcorn clams with jalapeño aioli. Steak, chicken, and BBQ ribs too.

THE MAPLE GRILLE

902-892-4411
themaplegrille.com
67 University Ave., Charlottetown
Open: Mon.–Thurs. 11 AM–9 PM, Fri.–Sat.
11 AM–10 PM
Price: $18 to $26
Credit Cards: Yes
Cuisine: Seafood and steak
Serving: L, D
Handicap Access: No

Steamed clams and seafood chowder are made "à la minute" and are not sitting at the back of the stove all day long. Greek salad and house salads can turn into a meal with chicken or shrimp. Three appetizing steak selections are all certified AAA prime beef and include 10-ounce rib eye and a 6-ounce New Yorker, served with a maple butter glaze. The chorizo pizza looks almost as good. Salmon filet, crab-crusted haddock, rack of lamb, and seared duck are on the dinner menu. Quiet, eight booths on one side, with soft music playing, this is within walking distance of everything.

SIRENELLA RISTORANTE

902-628-2271
sirenella.ca
83 Water St., Charlottetown
Open: Lunch Mon.–Fri. 11:30 AM–2 PM, dinner Mon.–Sat. 5–10 PM; closed Jan.
Price: $13 for pasta dishes to $27
Credit cards: Yes
Cuisine: Italian
Serving: L, D
Handicap Access: No
Special Features: Outdoor patio, house-made fresh pasta

A Northern Italian restaurant, Sirenella offers its own take on gnocchi—made here with PEI potatoes, of course—and other classics. One local innkeeper extols the "Mussels in Love" in Pernod cream sauce with tomato, onion, and garlic. Linguine Scoglio is made with scallops, shrimp, mussels, and hot peppers, putting together a sweet and spicy marinara. Milk-fed veal with capers, white wine, garlic, oregano, fresh mozzarella, and tomato sauce make up the Vitello Pizzaiola. Risotto di Mare, a classic, is a risotto made with saffron, squid, scallops, salmon, shrimp, mussels, clams, and green vegetables.

Owner and chef Italo Marzari immigrated to Canada from Italy in 1967, worked as a busboy in Toronto, and eventually became maître d' at Royal York in the same city. Later, after running a Halifax restaurant and opening his own in New Brunswick, he took a job as a professor at the Culinary Institute in Charlottetown—and then opened Sirenella in 1992. "Slowly, slowly I've been able to get people to understand my special cuisine," he said. With no prosciutto, bocconcini, or fresh mozzarella available at first, he relied on a friend for supplies from Toronto. Now gnocchi, polenta, and carpaccio are enthusiastically enjoyed, as are Limoncello, Campari, and grappa. But rabbit is still a bit of a hard sell.

WATER PRINCE CORNER SHOP AND LOBSTER POUND

902-368-3212
waterprincelobster.ca
141 Water St., Charlottetown
Open: May–mid-Oct., daily 11 AM–10 PM; closes at 8 PM after Labour Day
Price: $7 to $30
Credit cards: Yes
Cuisine: Seafood and a burger
Serving: L, D
Handicap Access: No
Special Features: Ship live lobsters from here

Amid the pictures of visitors and old license plates on the wall, settle in at a table and anticipate the freshest dish of blue mussels around and the meatiest Malpeque oysters on the half shell.

Lobster and mussels, always fresh and always freshly cooked, are the specialty at Water Prince Corner Shop, a small and personal kind of eatery run by Shane Campbell and his family. Campbell knows exactly who can supply him with the freshest seafood. Besides the good lobster dinner with potato salad and mussels, you can dine on fish and chips made with either haddock or halibut, pan-fried sole, a scallop dinner, or a burger.

NORTH RUSTICO TO BRACKLEY BEACH

BLUE MUSSEL CAFE
902-963-2152
bluemusselcafe.com
312 Harbourview Dr., North Rustico Harbour
Mail: 1394 Kingston Rd., Cornwall RR #3, PE PoE 1H0
Open: Mid-June–mid-Sept., 11:30 AM–ca. 8 PM
Price: $19 to $20, lobster $26
Credit cards: Yes
Cuisine: Fresh seafood and steak
Serving: L, D
Handicap Access: No

Blue picnic tables enjoy the shade of a covered deck and protection from the wind, while more tables just below are ready for delightful weather. Inside tables are ready for the really bad days. All have a clear view of the water at this spot, near where the Raspberry Point oysters and the mussels served here came from. Nothing is deep fried. The Rustico Beach is spread out in front of the restaurant, and folks put on their clothes for a lunch or meal. No reservations.

✪ DAYBOAT RESTAURANT
902-963-3833
dayboat.ca
5033 Rustico Rd., Rte. 6, Oyster Bed Bridge
Mail: 5033 Rustico Rd., RR #3, PE C0A 1N0
Open: Late May–mid-Oct., dinner 5–9 pm; July–late Aug., also serves lunch
Price: $24 to $32
Credit cards: Yes
Cuisine: Inventive, creative, and locally sourced
Serving: L, D
Handicap Access: Yes
Special Features: Extensive wine list

Sashimi of dayboat scallops is the ultimate test—the creamy clean taste of the just-harvested raw scallops tells the truth, even drizzled with Japanese lemonade fruit, ginger, pistachio oil, and calendula petals, as they are here. Tempura zucchini blossoms stuffed with Provençal vegetables and goat cheese is yet more proof—there is a genius in this kitchen.

Prosciutto-wrapped halibut with chanterelle polenta and grilled mackerel with chanterelle and lobster butter were two of the main meals. Roasted duck breast with a bacon and potato cake and black currants with honey and pepper sauce was another. Dessert is another trial of temptations—like the crunchy caramel, peanuts, chocolate mousse, and corn cake.

Chef Francois de Mélogue, here in 2008, had most recently been executive chef at Pili Pili in Chicago, ranked as one of the top ten restaurants in the world by *Food and Wine* Magazine, and he is certain to be here in 2009.

✪ THE DUNES CAFÉ AND STUDIO GALLERY
902-672-1883
dunesgallery.com
Rte. 15, RR #9, Brackley Beach
Open: Café June–Sept., 11:30 AM–10 PM
Price: $22 to $32
Credit cards: Yes
Cuisine: Inventive and modern international
Serving: L, D
Handicap Access: No
Special Features: Gardens

Driftwood seats at Dunes Café and Studio Gallery stand in the garden.

The iced coffee is dessert, as I discovered when the goblet of creamy, sweet, chocolate-tinged cold coffee arrived with a cap of whipped cream. It wasn't what I'd expected, but it was irresistible. The grazer's plate minus the cured and roasted PEI pork loin and plus the vegetarian version's red lentil hummus had a grainy, appealing chicken liver pâté and fresh greens, artichoke hearts and slices of the Cheese Lady's best Gouda. After a stroll in the elaborate gardens, packed with sculpture and intriguing plant specimens, a meal in the café is delightful. Dinners could be seafood cioppino with basil pesto or rib eye with porcini and field mushroom sauce and crème fraîche.

FISHERMAN'S WHARF LOBSTER SUPPERS

902-963-2669
fishermanswharf.ca
Fisherman's Wharf, North Rustico

Open: July–mid-Oct., daily noon–9 PM; mid-May–June, 4–9 PM only
Price: $31 with 1-pound lobsters
Credit cards: Yes
Cuisine: Seafood, steak, and chicken
Serving: B, L, D
Handicap Access: Yes

The 400 seats are ready for the crowds who hunger for lobster. Unlimited blue mussels, seafood chowder, rolls and biscuits, salads from the huge salad bar, fresh fruit, soft ice cream, and lemon meringue and coconut cream pies. The lobster may be the most popular entrée, but customers can also order steak, scallops, shrimp, lobster and steak both, snow crab, haddock, and half a chicken. Next to the Lobster Supper is a restaurant for à la carte meals—where it's a little more tranquil. More variety in the seafood, wine and beer, and breakfast and lunch are also available there.

Food Purveyors

Cafés and Coffee Shops

Beanz Espresso Bar (902-892-8797), 38 University Ave., Charlottetown. Good coffee. Good chicken salads, sandwiches, and other salads too.

Cora Breakfast and Lunch (902-569-5681; chezcora.com), 123 Queen St., Charlottetown Open Mon.–Sat. 6 AM–3 PM, Sun. 7 AM–3 PM. A popular place for the best meal of the day—breakfast. Waffles, eggs, French toast, omelets, and crêpes. A strawberry and cream cheese panino is a seasonal treat. A big serving of fresh fruit is part of every plate. This is a franchised business with branches in Ontario and Quebec.

PEI Preserve Company (800-565-5267; peipreservecompany.com), 2841 New Glasgow Rd., P.O. Box 5501, Hunter River. Open late May–mid-Oct.; call for hours. Reservations in the café, 902-964-4301. Fish cakes, vegetarian pasta made with PEI produce, lobster quiche, or a chicken and broccoli crêpe are possibilities for lunch. Cocktails, wine, and beer are served. The desserts are a specialty, like raspberry cream cheese pie, "The World's Tastiest Brownie," and the chocolate potato cake, frosted with ganache. Fruit preserves, marmalades, and wine jelly are some of the products that brought company success.

Urban Eatery (902-566-4848; urbaneatery.ca), The Shops of Confederation Court Mall, downtown Charlottetown. Different stations, each with its own good food, make this unusual place to eat perfect for independent thinkers. Barbecue and rotisserie meats are one possibility; pizza, soup, coffee are three more.

Cheese

The Cheese Lady (902-368-1506), 1423 Rte. 223, RR #9 Stn. Main, Winsloe North, Charlottetown. Open Mon.–Sat. 9 AM–6 PM. The center of the PEI cheese world is this sweet little shop, beside the windmill—decorative only—in the yard. Dozens of kinds of Gouda are for sale, and cheese-making is visible, when it is under way, through the inside windows. Try the fresh yogurt.

Produce at the Best of PEI Market in outer Charlottetown

Gourmet and Deli Markets

Best of PEI Market (902-370-3703; best ofpei.com), 618 University Ave., Charlottetown. This is the second location of Best of PEI (the original is devoted to crafts and is located at Victoria Row, 156 Richmond St.; see under "Gifts and Accessories" in the Shopping section below). This store opened in the spring of 2008 and carries only island-produced and island-made products. Pork, beef, chicken, shellfish, and other seafood are all guaranteed local stuff. The jams, jellies, and spices and herbs make exceptional souvenirs, and cheeses would too if you didn't have too far to go to get home. The store has a deck set in greenery, where customers can taste Prince Edward Island beers. The ice-cream bar, art gallery, and coffee shop are added diversions during a visit.

Ice Cream

Cows (902-892-6969; www.cows.ca), 150 Queen St., Charlottetown. Branches of Cows Ice Cream are all over the island, and they're a welcome sight anytime you encounter them. Also at Peakes Wharf in Charlottetown (902-566-4886), in the PEI Factory Shops in Charlottetown (902-628-3614), and on the Cavendish

Formosa Tea Room in Charlottetown

Boardwalk in Cavendish (902-963-2692). All operate from May to October.

Microbreweries and Pubs

Gahan House Pub Brewery (902-626-2337; gahan.ca), 126 Sydney St., Charlottetown. Open year-round; in summer 11 AM–11 PM for food, weekends till midnight, open Sun. at noon; October–May, 11 AM–10 PM, till 11 PM weekends, open Sun. at noon. Prince Edward Island's only brewery makes seven brews, and 1772 India Pale Ale and Sydney Street Stout are two of them. Perhaps Sir John A's honey wheat ale would be a fine drink on a summer day with the dry ribs roasted with salt and pepper, or the brown bag fish and chips. The steak and cheese wrap might also catch your eye. A costumed guide conducts tours ($8) during July and August, Monday through Saturday at 5 PM and 7 PM.

Tearoom

Formosa Tea House (902-566-4991), 186 Prince St., Charlottetown. Open Mon.–Sat. 11:30 AM–3 PM and 5–8 PM. This Chinese-style tea house with booths and dark wood serves a wide variety of teas including Puerh, Oolong, T Quien-Ying, and more. Cold green tea and taro milk tea are specialties in hot weather. Meals of dumplings, noodles, and stuffed buns are served.

Thai and Taiwanese

Interlude Café (902-367-3055), 88 Kent St., Charlottetown. Taiwanese dishes.

Thai Food, Kent St., Charlottetown. A refreshing change from deep-fried seafood, count on this little place to serve a brilliantly seasoned curry or stir-fry.

CULTURE

Galleries

CONFEDERATION CENTRE ART GALLERY

902-628-6142

confederationcentre.com

145 Richmond St., Charlottetown, PEI C1A 1J1

Open: Mid-June–Sept., daily 9 AM–5 PM; Oct.–mid-June, Wed.–Sat. 11 AM–5 PM, Sun. 1–5 PM

Admission: Free

The art gallery at the Confederation Centre owns 15,000 pieces of art. With six exhibition spaces, it holds special events, public lectures, and art openings for new shows year-round. The collection is a mixture of historic and contemporary art, and exhibitions present them both. In the summer of 2009, *Others Worlds* will offer a variety of exhibitions. Seth, a graphic novelist, will be the subject of one exhibit.

Historic Buildings and Sites

PROVINCE HOUSE NATIONAL HISTORIC SITE

902-566-7626

pc.gc.ca

165 Richmond St., Charlottetown

Mail: 2 Palmer's Ln., Charlottetown, PE C1A 5V6

Open: June–Oct., daily 8:30 AM–5 PM; Nov.–May, Mon.–Fri. 8:30 AM–5 PM

Admission: Free

The birthplace of the Confederation on July 1, 1867, and the second-oldest provincial legislature in Canada, the Province House graces the center of Charlottetown with its beautiful structure. Isaac Smith built the three-story building, with a central portico and massive columns in the Greek style popular in the 1840s. An introductory video and guides on site answer questions, and tours with more information are given to groups if booked in advance. You can observe the provincial legislature when it's in session, in late October for four weeks and again sometime in April or May for six weeks.

FORT AMHERST NATIONAL HISTORIC SITE

902-566-7626

pc.gc.ca

191 Haché Gallant Dr., Rocky Point, PEI

Mail: 2 Palmer's Lane, Charlottetown, PE C1A 5V6

Open: Staffed with tours in summer, grounds open year-round
Admission: Free

Port-la-Joye is another name for this site, where the first Europeans settled on the island around 1720. Aside from an excellent view of Charlottetown harbor, you can see the ruins of the British fort, and interpretive panels detail the history. Staffed daily mid-June to August, tours (adults $3.80) are given, walking the site for about a half hour with a chronicle of the events that took place here. The site's Visitor's Centre reopened in 2008 and hosted The Acadian Celebration, which may become a yearly festival, in August; aboriginal events like a Pow Wow and arts and crafts are held on Labour Day weekend.

Province House in Charlottetown

Museums

BEACONSFIELD HISTORIC HOUSE

902-368-6603
peimuseum.com
2 Kent St., Charlottetown, PEI C1A 1M6
Open: July–Aug., daily 10 AM–4:45 PM; call for off-season hours
Admission: Adults $4.25, student $3.25

Some of the 25 rooms of this 1877 mansion, built by a shipbuilder, are furnished as they would have been in its heyday. Only five years after it was built, James Peake Jr. lost his fortune and his house. His successor lived there for more than 30 years, leaving it in his will as "a refuge and temporary home for friendless young women." Students and young women working in the town lived there till the 1930s, when it became a dorm for student nurses. The province took it over in 1973, and it is now the headquarters of the PEI Museum.

FARMERS' BANK OF RUSTICO AND DOUCET HOUSE MUSEUMS

902-963-3168, off-season 902-963-2304
farmersbank.ca
Church Rd., Rte. 243 North, Rustico
Mail: Friends of the Farmers' Bank, RR #3, Hunter River PE C01 1N0
Open: June–Sept., Mon.–Sat. 9:30 AM–5:30 PM, Sun. 1–5:30 PM
Admission: Adults $4, seniors $3, students and children 13 and older $2

The Farmers' Bank, operating from 1864 to 1894, was the first people's bank. It holds exhibits about natural history, an early library, panels about fishing and the Acadians. The 1772 Doucet House shows visitors early baking in an outside oven, the bare kitchen, and the farmland surrounding the restored log house. A rope-bed stands in the bedroom, and wool carding and spinning might be under way in the hands of women dressed like the Acadians of the early 1800s.

RUSTICO HARBOUR FISHERY MUSEUM

902-963-3799
318 Harbourview Dr., North Rustico, PEI C0A 1X0
Open: Mid-June–Sept.
Admission: Free

At one end of the boardwalk is this small museum devoted to fishing. The *Silver Wave* is ready to be boarded, and lobstering is explained by a video.

Music

BRACKLEY BEACH CEILIDH WITH CYNTHIA MACLEOD & FRIENDS

Brackley Beach Community Center, Brackley Beach, PEI
Open: Late June–mid-Sept., Mon. and Wed. at 7:30 PM
Admission: Adults $8, children 12 and younger $4

An energetic schedule has Cynthia MacLeod performing from Manitoba to Pennsylvania, but her beloved home in Prince Edward Island, where she has been awarded more than a dozen music awards, is the site of regular concerts through the summer. MacLeod's vibrant musical skill endows her fiddle with a voice you will greet like a long lost friend.

CONFEDERATION CENTRE OF THE ARTS
902-628-1864, 800-565-0278
confederationcentre.com
145 Richmond St., Charlottetown, PEI C1A 1J1
Open: Year-round
Admission: Varies according to the performance

The Summer Concert Series is performed on Sundays, once each in June, July, and August. Late night at the Mack, with the Charlottetown Festival cast singing music, is a cabaret with drinks and snacks available. Other musical performances are presented here throughout the year.

Theater

CONFEDERATION CENTRE OF THE ARTS
902-628-1864, 800-565-0278
confederationcentre.com
145 Richmond St., Charlottetown, PEI C1A 1J1
Open: Year-round
Admission: Varies according to the performance

Confederation Centre of Arts has three different physical theaters. From mid-June through September the show *Anne of Green Gables—The Musical* is performed in the Mainstage Theatre, and 2009 will be its 45th season. *The Ballad of Stompin' Tom*, about PEI story-teller and singer Tom Connors, was presented in the MacKenzie Theatre in 2008. Other musicals and concerts are performed here every year as part of the **Charlottetown Festival**, a summer theater tradition. *PEI Presents* is the off-season offering, with local theater and Canadian and international singers and dance companies.

THE GUILD
902-368-4413
theguildpei.com
111 Queen St., Charlottetown, PEI
Mail: 115 Richmond St., Charlottetown, PE C1A 1H7
Open: Year-round
Admission: Varies with performances

Local music, theater, film screenings, dance, and art exhibits are all part of The Guild. In 2008, PEI's top group Celtic Ladies performed on the Guild Main Stage, in the 150-seat theater (wheelchair accessible), every Tuesday in July, August, and September, using the fiddle, singing, and step dance to charm their audiences.

Dinner Theater

FEAST DINNER THEATRE
902-629-2321
feastdinnertheatres.ca
The Rodd Charlottetown, corner of Kent and Pownal Sts., Charlottetown
Mail: P.O. Box 1418, Summerside, PE C1N 4K2

Lucy Maud Montgomery

The hero of Prince Edward Island is an author of a book about a girl. *Anne of Green Gables* was published more than 100 years ago, and its characters—and its author—are the subject of reveries, romances, and amusement parks. The author's family's house is gone, but the Site of Lucy Maud Montgomery's Cavendish home (902-963-2231; peisland.com/lmm), a national historic site open mid-May to mid-October, retains its character—its quiet. That quiet is good thing for a writer, who needs to concentrate and beware of distraction.

Green Gables Heritage Place (902-963-7874; pc.gc.ca), 2 Palmer's Ln., off Route 6 in Cavendish, is another Historic Site, the home of relatives of Montgomery (her grandfather's cousins) that inspired her most famous story. It's open year-round, and in summer daily 9 AM–6 PM and till 8 PM on Tuesday and Thursday. The surrounding area is the landscape of her most famous book. The island was the place her imagination thrived in, as 19 of her 20 novels were placed here. Montgomery was buried in the Cavendish cemetery when she died in 1942.

The Lucy Maud Montgomery Birthplace (902-886-2099), New London, holds exhibits with a replica of the author's wedding dress and some of her writing notebooks. The Anne of Green Gables Museum at Silver Bush (902-886-2884, 800-665-2663; annesociety.org/anne), on Route 20 in Park Corner, offers a horse-drawn carriage ride just like the one Matthew gave. The Campbells, descendents of the author's aunt and uncle, live here, as their family has for 230 years. They display furniture, a patchwork quilt, and photographs hand-colored and developed by Montgomery. Open July and August 9 AM–5 PM, shorter hours May, September, and October.

Anne of Green Gables Chocolates are sold in Cavendish, Borden-Carleton and Charlottetown, and made and sold in Avonlea. An Anne of Green Gables Store is also located in both Avonlea and Charlottetown.

Avonlea (902-963-3050; avonlea.ca) is a theme park open June to September, on Route 6 in Cavendish. Along with costumed people straight out of Montgomery's novel, Lady Baker's Tea Trolley serves traditional teas in the summer Monday to Thursday 2–4 PM.

The yearly production of *Anne of Green Gables The Musical* keeps ticket sales brisk at the Confederation Centre of the Arts (800-565-0278; confederationcentre.com), 145 Richmond St., Charlottetown. King's Playhouse (902-652-2824; kingsplayhouse.com), 65 Grafton St., Georgetown, produced its own dramatization of Montgomery in 2008, *The Nine Lives of L. M. Montgomery*, and may produce it again in 2009. Abegweit Sightseeing Tours (902-894-9966), 157 Nassau St., Charlottetown, offers a North Shore Tour that covers 100 miles and leaves daily at 10:30 AM for a full day at North Rustico and Anne of Green Gables sites.

The fictional character's spirit and adventures are so vibrant that they still fill this area with life—and commercial possibilities. After all, a well-told story can work miracles.

Open: June–Aug., Tues.–Sun. nights

Admission: Adults $35, student and seniors 60 and older $32, children 12 and younger $25

Good light entertainment is on offer at Feast Dinner Theatre, with one show at the Rodd Charlottetown—*The Nearlyweds* played in 2008—and another, *Victoria's Secret*, at the Brothers Two Restaurant in Summerside. The four-course meal starts with salad, and steamed mussels. Choose chicken cordon blue or poached salmon next; both come with mashed potatoes and vegetables. Dessert is cheesecake.

Seasonal Events

February
The Jack Frost Children's Winterfest, Charlottetown. Snow and ice demonstrations, slides, a snow-sculpting contest, outdoor skating rink, carnival rides inside Charlottetown Civic Centre, and much more.

July
PEI Jazz and Blues Festival (902-569-8692; jazzandblues.ca), at three locations in downtown Charlottetown.

September
International Shellfish Festival (peishellfish.com/sf/) shellfish dishes abound at Charlottetown restaurants in late September, and chefs from all over the world compete.

October
Fall Flavours (800-955-1864; fallflavours.ca) Television chef Michael Smith, host of Food Network's show, *Chef Abroad*, is the instigator of this relatively new festival, which offers tours of organic gardens and chef competitions islandwide. Make cheese, press cider, learn to shuck oysters, and eat great island food.

RECREATION

Bicycling
Gowheelin' (902-566-5259; gowheelinpei.com), 6 Prince St., Charlottetown, at the Visitor's Centre. Open May–Oct. Bicycle rentals, delivery service.
McQueen's Island Tours Bicycling Specialists (902-368-2453; macqueens.com), 460 Queen St., Charlottetown. Operating year-round. Guided tours and bicycle rentals.

Boating
Bearded Skipper's Deep-Sea Fishing (902-963-2334), North Rustico Wharf. Operating July–Aug., with trips at 8 AM, 1:15 PM, and 6 PM. Norman Peters, the best-known captain of the PEI fishing boats, offers a three-hour trip with all gear supplied. Mackerel and cod are caught four or five miles offshore; Norman Peters and Doug Ferguson, his one-man crew, clean the fish, and the customers take them home to eat.

Golf

Fox Meadow (902-569-4653, 877-569-8337; foxmeadow.pe.ca), 167 Kinlock Rd.,
Stratford. This new 18-hole course very close to Charlottetown is affordable. Dining
room and ninth-hole canteen, Fox Den Lounge, pro shop, shoulder-season rates, nine-
hole rates, and twilight rates.

Hiking

Confederation Trail (902-368-5540; princeedwardisland.com). The Prince Edward
Island Trans Canada Railroad route has been transformed into a hiking and biking trail,
one of the island's most popular resources since it opened in 2000. The trail is flat and
covered with crushed gravel. It passes through towns and over its own little bridges:
plum-colored gates signal an entry point. Download a copy of the PEI Confederation
Trail Cycling Guide or order one by mail from Tourism PEI, P.O. Box 940, Charlottetown, PEI C1A 7M5.

Parks and Swimming

Prince Edward Island National Park (902-672-6350; pc.gc.ca), Dalvay. Open late June,
11 AM–6 PM; July–Aug., 10 AM–7 PM. Admission: Adults $7.80, seniors $6.80, children
6–16 $3.90, but check in April for changes. Within this park are Green Gables (see the
sidebar above about Lucy Maud Montgomery) and Dalvay by-the-Sea (see the listings
above in the Lodging and Restaurants sections), and more importantly, sand dunes,
barrier island, beaches, sandstone cliffs, and wetlands. Thirteen trails lie inside this
park, and almost all are rated easy. Hike through reeds, across farmlands, into the
woods, or along the beach; stick to the marked trails.

Tours

Abegweit Sightseeing Tours (902-894-9966; www.peisland.com/abegweit/), 157 Nassau
St., Charlottetown. Adults $10, children $2. A double-decker bus takes you on an hour-
long tour of Charlottetown, while a guide narrates the historical details. The North
Shore Tour covers 100 miles and leaves daily at 10:30 AM for a full day at North Rustico
and Anne of Green Gables sites.

SHOPPING

Antiques

The Weathervane (902-621-0070; theweathervaneantiques.ca), 836 Crooked Creek Rd.,
Wheatley River. Open May–Oct., Mon.–Fri. 9 AM–7 PM, Sat.–Sun. 12–7 PM. Island pine
and Canadiana furniture, hooked mats, folk art, and fine art are some of the categories
of items sold.

Bookstores

The Book Emporium (902-628-2001), 169 Queen St., Charlottetown. A large selection of
well-organized books with a friendly and helpful staff.

Gallery 18 (902-886-3201; gallery18.com), 10686 Rte. 6, New London. Antique maps and
prints, collectible books and small antiques. Work by island artist Robert Harris and

Charles and Eileen Bentley, and first-edition novels by Graham Greene. Original prints from 19th-century illustrated newspapers.

J.E.M. Books (902-963-3802), 6922 Rustico Rd., Rte. 6, Rusticoville. Open mid-May–mid-Oct., daily; off-season Sat. only. A pink house with a half-price fiction section, island books, and books for the beach.

Gift and Specialty Shops

The Best of PEI (902-368-8835; www.bestofpei.com), Victoria Row, 156 Richmond St., Charlottetown. Open 9 AM–9 PM except Jan.–Mar., 9 AM–5:30 PM. If you can't make it to every craftsperson's own studio, this store offers many island artisans' crafts, from hooked rugs and quilts to a hand-carved wooden pig and seaweed soap. Honey, wine, and other easy-to-eat items are also sold.

The Dunes Café and Studio Gallery (902-672-1883; dunesgallery.com), Rte. 15, Brackley Beach. Open May–Oct., daily 10 AM–6 PM, and summer evenings. A huge collection of fine crafts by Canadian artisans, from jewelry to glass to ceramics, and sculpture, clothing, and more imported from Thailand and Bali. Peter Jansons, the owner, began with just a studio, but his workplace has grown to an 18,000-square-foot store, two-level café, and studio.

Soap

The Great Canadian Soap Company (902-672-2242, 800-793-1644; greatcanadian soap.com), 4224 Portage Rd., on Rte. 6, Brackley Beach. Open mid-May–Oct., 9 AM–6 PM, except July–Aug. till 9 PM. First of all, you can offer the expressive goats (but what exactly do those wise faces mean to communicate?) a handful of feed from the bucket hanging on the barn wall. They expect you to, when you get out of the car, and they are waiting. Inside the soap store and factory, daily demonstrations of soapmaking take you through every step of the process, and you can get a free sample. The goat's milk soap made with olive oil is moisturizing and wonderful; a bar lasts months when it is allowed to dry between uses.

The goats at The Great Canadian Soap Company can be fed for free.

Moonsnail Soapworks (888-771-7627; moonsnailsoapworks.com), 85 Water St., Charlottetown. Natural ingredients and essential oils go into this company's 25,000 hand-cut bars of soap each year. A start at the farmers' market in 1995 led to this success and to today's shop and factory, where all the products are now made. Watch them stir the liquid soap as it thickens and then cut the cooled bars into just the right size with guitar-string cutters.

10

WESTERN PRINCE EDWARD ISLAND

Summerside, Victoria-by-the-Sea, and Prince County

Loyalists who left the newly United States of America after its revolution moved into Summerside, a 19th-century mercantile town. Its older buildings stand ready for walking tours, in between meals of lobster and PEI's famous mussels. Silver-fox ranching brought another short spell of energy here, after shipbuilding died out, but tourism and farming are today's mainstays. The local College of Piping offers frequent summer stepdance and bagpipe concerts and, of course, ceilidhs, or house parties.

The Confederation Trail is perfect for off-road hiking, and rental shops offer visitors a chance to bike.

The Acadian Museum in Miscouche brings to life the French culture still vibrant on the island. Seaweed pie, made with Irish moss and gathered along shore, can be sampled in Miminegash. Lennox Island's cultural museum displays local Mi'kmaq artifacts and crafts.

LODGING

VICTORIA-BY-THE-SEA

ORIENT HOTEL BED & BREAKFAST
Bob and Bonnie Brammer, innkeepers
902-658-2503, 800-565-6743
theorienthotel.com
34 Main St.,Victoria-by-the-Sea, PEI C0A 2G0
Price: $80 to $150
Credit cards: Yes
Handicapped Access: None to rooms, but tearoom is accessible
Special Features: Mrs. Proffit's Tea Room (see "Food Purveyors, under "Tearoom")

The Flamingo Room, one of the seven rooms for rent, each with private bath, would satisfy any flamingo-lovers reading this book, with its pink, flamingo cut-out headboard on the queen bed. But for the rest of us, the cool blues and pastels in the sweet bedrooms would make for a more tranquil night. The living room makes a fine place to relax, with its deep red walls and white upholstered chairs. Rooms are on the second and third floor of this historic hotel, now run as a bed and breakfast; your breakfast is included in the rates for the rooms.

After lobster season is over in summer, the lobster traps are stored on the wharf.

VICTORIA VILLAGE INN

Stephen Hunter, innkeeper
902-658-2484, 866-658-2483
victoriavillageinn.com
22 Howard St., Victoria-by-the-Sea, PEI
CoA 2Go
Open: Year-round
Price: $75 to $145
Credit cards: Yes
Handicapped Access: None

Four rooms simply and comfortably decorated fill the upper floors of this charming
inn, and the prospect of a good meal is
another attraction. Room 3 is a suite with
two bedrooms, one with a queen-size bed
and the other with two twins. The claw-foot
tub in the bathroom is large—just right
after a day of cycling on the Blue Heron
Coastal Drive. Room 1 has its own entrance
and private deck. Breakfast is made up of

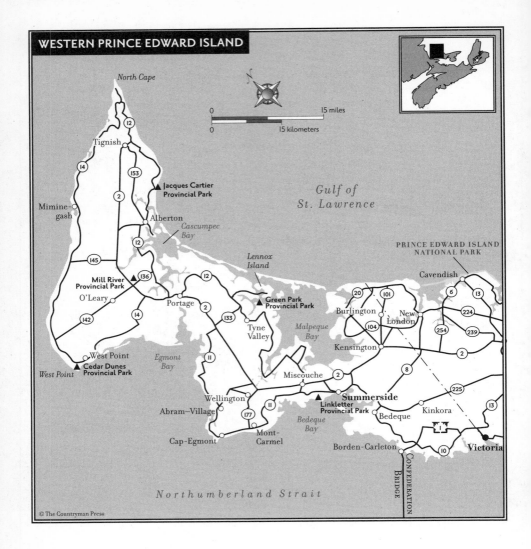

WESTERN PRINCE EDWARD ISLAND

0   15 miles
0   15 kilometers

North Cape

Tignish

Jacques Cartier
Provincial Park

Gulf of
St. Lawrence

Mimine-
gash

Alberton

Cascumpec
Bay

Lennox
Island

PRINCE EDWARD ISLAND
NATIONAL PARK

Cavendish

Mill River
Provincial Park

O'Leary

Portage

Green Park
Provincial Park

Burlington

New
London

Cedar Dunes
Provincial Park

West Point

West Point

Egmont
Bay

Tyne
Valley

Malpeque
Bay

Kensington

Wellington

Abram–Village

Miscouche

Summerside
Linkletter
Provincial Park

Bedeque

Kinkora

Cap-Egmont

Mont-
Carmel

Bedeque
Bay

Borden-Carleton

Victoria

CONFEDERATION BRIDGE

Northumberland Strait

© The Countryman Press

high-quality egg dishes, baked muffins, fruit, and much more.

CAPE TRAVERSE

BLUE HERON RETREAT

Jane and Phil MacKay, innkeeper
902-439-9899
apeiblueheronretreat.com
168 Wharf Rd., Cape Traverse, PEI C0B 1X0
Open: Mid-May to Oct.
Price: $145 to $195
Credit cards: Yes

Handicapped Access: No
Special features: Free mussels on your arrival night

The whole-wheat honey waffles that are part of breakfast seem almost unique on B&B menus—and these waffles are made with local, organic eggs. Breakfast might also be the house gravlox—cured salmon—served on a bagel with cream cheese, capers, and shallots. The Ocean View room with its air-jet tub and view of the Confederation Bridge sounds perfectly acceptable, but the Master Room, with its air-jet tub for two and wide showerhead over a marble bench for two, adding up to what the innkeepers call a water-therapy room, sounds like heaven.

BEDEQUE

BRIARCLIFFE INN

Mary and Bill Kendrick, innkeepers
902-887-2333, 866-887-3238
briarcliffeinn.com
274 Salutation Cove Rd., RR #1, Bedeque, PEI C0B 1C0
Located near the Confederation Bridge
Price: $100 to $150
Credit cards: Yes
Handicapped Access: None
Special Features: Wi-Fi, healing labyrinth

In the Leard Room, a floral print on the duvet and the Roman shades give a summery feeling, but the cooler temperature will only make the warmth from the duvet and the comforter more delicious. Five rooms are for rent, all with private baths and those soft duvets. Mary and Bill Kendrick have a knack for making a visit special—they offer PEI Experiences (see below) and have run some spiritual retreats. Some pigs are running free in the forest area, inside an electric fence, keeping the undergrowth down. After a lobster dinner at the inn, guests like to throw the pigs the shells, which they devour. Later in the year the pigs will become the bacon served at breakfast.

SERENDIPITY BED & BREAKFAST

Dolores Poles and Ross Greig, innkeepers
902-887-3540, 866-887-3540
serendipitypei.com
77 Linkletter Ave., P.O. Box 3956, Central Bedeque, PEI C0B 1G0
Price: $90 to $130
Credit cards: Yes
Handicapped Access: None

The Victorian Suite is the largest accommodation at Serendipity, with two bedrooms and a private balcony with a fine view of the Prince Edward Island's countryside. Light blue and yellow quilts and an antique dresser and chairs add to the comfort of the rooms. The Garden View room is decidedly cozy, with a small bathroom with shower only. Dolores Poles is a restaurant chef, and she prepares pancakes and much more for a full breakfast with fresh fruit. Three cottages are also for rent.

SUMMERSIDE

CAIRNS MOTEL SUMMERSIDE

Aaron and Kendra Wedge, owners
902-436-5841, 877-224-7676
cairnsmotel.net
721 Water St. East, PEI C1N 4J2
Open: May–Oct.
Price: $59 to $69
Credit cards: Yes
Handicapped Access: Limited
Special Features: Wi-Fi, phones with free local calls, AC or cross-ventilation

Inexpensive, simple, and clean, this is the spot to be when what you need is a good sleep. Good-quality mattresses and disciplined management that keeps the flower beds immaculate and the rooms spotless give more proof of the motel's value. A trail takes you to the Confederation Trail, so this

Cairns Motel in Summerside

The Silver Fox Inn in Summerside

is also a good spot for bicyclists and hikers. Continental breakfast in May and in October.

SILVER FOX INN

902-436-1664
silverfoxinn.net
61 Granville St. Summerside, PEI C1N 2ZE
Price: $105 to $140
Credit cards: Yes
Handicapped Access: None
Special Features: Wi-Fi, hot-water bottles

Situated on a leafy street in the midst of older, large houses, The Silver Fox Inn has its own special dignity. The 1890 Queen Anne Revival architecture gives it high-ceilinged rooms and a living room made warm by its walnut woodwork and its large fireplace. Its own tearoom is open from noon to 4 PM, ready to serve you a light meal or tea and a snack. The Black Fox Room, with its deep-hued wallpaper and Victorian love seat, has a king-size bed and a carved desk, the perfect spot to get the last draft of your novel into better shape.

TYNE VALLEY

THE DOCTOR'S INN BED & BREAKFAST AND ORGANIC MARKET GARDEN

Jean and Paul Offer, innkeepers
902-831-3057
peisland.com/doctorsinn
Rte. 167, P.O. Box 92, Tyne Valley, PE C0B 2C0
Price: $45 to $60
Credit cards: Yes
Handicapped Access: None
Special Features: Workshops about gardens, composting, and herbs

An organic market garden spreads across 2 acres, and chickens and geese make another part of the picture, at The Doctor's Inn. The more than 50 kinds of vegetables and fruits, flowers, and herbs grown here are sold at Charlottetown's farmers' market, a must-see event every Saturday morning. Old-fashioned and comfortable, with spindle chars and wood floors, the rooms are both inexpensive and attractive.

RESTAURANTS

VICTORIA-BY-THE-SEA

LANDMARK CAFÉ

902-658-2286, off-season 902-626-3459
victoriabythesea.ca/landmark.html
Victoria-by-the-Sea
Open: May–Oct., daily from 11:30 AM
Price: $14 to $30
Credit cards: Yes
Cuisine: Continental with Maritime
favorites
Serving: L, D
Handicap Access: No

Eugene Sauvé owns this highly thought of
café in charming Victoria-by-the-Sea,
serving meat pie, quiche, seafood, lasagna,
and tempting desserts. He began business
in 1989 and has turned his spot into a destination for a day trip. Organic ingredients
play a large role in the soups and entrées.
Reservations recommended.

VICTORIA VILLAGE INN

Chef/owner Stephen Hunter
902-658-2484, 866-658-2483
victoriavillageinn.com
22 Howard St., Victoria-by-the-Sea
Open: Early June–Sept., daily 5–10 PM; off-
season by reservation
Price: $20 to $28
Credit cards: Yes
Cuisine: Modern continental
Serving: L, D
Handicap Access: No

Dinner and theater packages are one draw,
with the Victoria Playhouse a few steps
away. Local produce and island lamb are
another. Bar clam and sea scallop chowder
comes with a smoked salmon crouton, and
the smoked salmon tartar, another appetizer, is complemented by red onion jam. A
main course might be pan-roasted halibut
with herb and lemon butter, or roasted
pork tenderloin with smoked Gouda and

seasonal vegetables. The beef tenderloin
might come with Béarnaise sauce.

KENSINGTON

HOME PLACE INN & RESTAURANT

902-836-5686
thehomeplace.ca
21 Victoria St. East, Kensington
Open: May–Labour Day, daily 11:30 AM–
9 PM (dinner menu at 4 PM); off-season
Thurs.–Sat., ask about hours
Price: $13 to $23
Credit cards: Yes
Cuisine: Maritime
Serving: L, D
Handicap Access: No

Pan-fried Malpeque oysters are a mainstay
of the menu at this favorite local eatery, and
oysters also come on the half shell with
lemon, simple and perfect. Steamed mussels are made with cream, wine, and garlic.
The thoughtful provision of "light entrées"—
fish cakes with green tomato chow, for
example—makes it easier to indulge in
dessert. Atlantic salmon or beef tenderloin
are larger dinners. Coconut cream pie, an
island favorite, and crêpes are for dessert.

SUMMERSIDE

LOBSTER HOUSE RESTAURANT AND OYSTER BAR

902-436-8439
lobsterhouserestaurant.ca
Shipyard Market Building, 370 Water St.
West, Summerside
Open: Dinner daily 4–9 PM, Sun. brunch
11 AM–2 PM
Price: $17 to $19, more for lobster
Credit cards:
Cuisine: Classic seafood and meat with
inventive touches
Serving: Brunch, D
Handicap Access: Yes

An enclosed deck on the water, just inside
the waterfront walking trail, lets you savor

the lobster you ordered with your eyes resting on a distant blue horizon.

Consider the plate of raw oyster on the half shell, a must on this island with its many good oyster beds just offshore. The chowder is a smooth and rich appetizer, or make a light meal of it with the chewy grilled flatbread that comes with smoked salmon, cream cheese, capers, and red onion. The PEI pork tenderloin with blue cheese and bacon vies with the seared halibut with black olive tapenade. Of course, the lobster suppers are ready for anyone, traditional, baked, or served with pasta.

TYNE VALLEY

THE DOCTOR'S INN
902-831-3057
peisland.com/doctorsinn
Rte. 167, P.O. Box 92, Tyne Valley

Open: Year-round; closed Fri. (to prepare for farmers' market)
Price: $50 for guests, $60 for outside reservations, wine included
Credit cards:
Cuisine: Continental
Serving: D
Handicap Access: No
Special Features: Reservation only, for inn guests or others

Dinners for a maximum of six are served by reservation only—and the inn takes only one reservation each night. Paul and Jean Offer work together in the garden and the kitchen making salads from their favorite varieties of lettuce. They might serve cocquilles St. Jacques provençal, tournedos Rossini, or Cornish game hen for dinner. You can make sure that your meal is exactly to your liking, because the menu is decided in advance, when the reservation is made.

FOOD PURVEYORS

Cafés

❂ **Seaweed Pie Café** (902-882-4313), 11318 North Cape Coastal Dr. (Rte. 14), Miminegash, C0B 1S0. The dessert to try is the high, creamy seaweed pie, with a choice of raspberry, strawberry, or blueberry sauce. The base of the pie is a layer of sponge cake, and the center is made with Irish moss gel and whipped cream. The chef, Nick Doucette, boils Irish moss, a frilly white seaweed, with water and strains it, to make liquid gel. It has no calories at all and vitamins like A, B1, B2, and minerals. The thickener in Irish moss is called carrageenan, used in ice cream, beer, toothpaste, and many other products, and harvested on the beaches of Prince Edward Island. Lou Anne Gallant runs this business for Women in Support of Fishing, a group she is a member of, as are her chef and a server at the café. The group started up in 1982 when the prices for Irish moss fell, as a way to help support themselves. An Irish moss interpretive center, a gift shop, and a full menu are all here. You can dine on seafood chowder, mussels, fisherman's lunch with fish cakes, beans, buttermilk biscuits; or try lobster quiche, salmon pie, or Myrtle's Acadian meat pie (made by a relative of Gallant). Beer and wine available.

Candy

Island Chocolates Company (902-658-2320), Main St.,Victoria, PEI C0A 2G0. Open June—Sept. Handmade Belgian chocolate is for sale, and workshops are on offer. Coffee, hot chocolate, cold tea.

Fruit Farms

Cackleberry Farms (902-854-3306; cackleberryfarms.com), RR #1, Richmond. The fruit that grows on this farm's 130 acres is wonderfully fresh and scrumptious in jams—the Cackleberry Preserves made with cherries and brandy store up a PEI summer day, and they make a mouth-watering souvenir. Strawberry rhubarb, raspberry rhubarb, and rhubarb with ginger are other fine fruit spreads. U-pick strawberries in late June and July, raspberries in late July and August, and apples in late September to October. On October Sundays from 1 to 4 PM, kids are entertained with pony rides, face painting, apple bobbing, and more.

Ice Cream

Cows (902-888-4441), 23 Water St., Summerside. This branch of Cows Ice Cream is open May–Oct. Another with the same schedule is at Gateway Village, Borden-Carleton (902-437-6883).

Tearoom

Mrs. Proffit's Tea Room (902-658-2503; theorienthotel.com), inside The Orient Hotel Bed & Breakfast, 34 Main St., Victoria-by-the-Sea. Open Wed.–Mon. 11:30 AM–4 PM; closed Tues. This traditional English tea room serves afternoon high teas and its own blend of loose leaf tea—which you can also buy it to take home.

CULTURE

Historic Buildings and Sites

THE BOTTLE HOUSES/MAISON DE BOUTEILLES

902-854-2987, off-season 902-854-2254
bottlehouses.com
6891 Rte. 11 (North Cape Coastal Dr.), Cap-Egmont
Open: Mid-May–mid-Oct., daily 10 AM–4 PM; July–Aug., till 6 PM
Admission: Adults $5, students and seniors $4, children 6–16 $2

Édouard Arsenault had a vision—of light and color created by glass. In 1980 he began to live his dream, constructing a six-gabled house with 12,000 bottles. In 1982 he built

---

EXPERIENCE PEI
866-887-3238
experiencepei.ca
275 Salutation Cove Rd., RR #1, Bedeque, PEI C0B IC0
Open: Year-round
Admission: $35 to $120, depending on the experience and number of participants

From a morning spent making moonshine—at a perfectly legal distillery, of course—to a day with the Gillis family collecting Irish moss with special rakes, participants have the chance to really get their imaginations to work in another world—the world of Prince Edward Island. Marine botanist Dr. Irene Novaczek describes how to identify seaweeds and which are edible or medicinal powerhouses. Lunch is vegetable sea-plant soup and dulse biscuits.

Another day might be spent harvesting oysters from a dory by tonging. Or join the Piping Plover patrol, helping to protect this little bird from the predators and humans likely to disturb its nests. Make paper, candles, or cheese, or learn how to tie a fly. Twenty-four experiences, lasting 2.5 to 3 hours, are waiting.

the second structure, a hexagonal tavern—where souvenirs were sold. Nowadays it houses the bottle collection of this bottle collector, who kept the best out of the walls. The chapel went up in 1983; Arsenault died just before completing its steeples and front pew. Renovations in the early 1990s saved the structures from crumbling, and they attract people ready to marvel. Arsenault's daughter is in charge of the gardens, which spread around the structures and are maintained with the help of her sister and a gardener.

LENNOX ISLAND ABORIGINAL ECOTOURISM
866-831-2702
lennoxisland.com
P.O. Box 134, Lennox Island, PEI C0B 1P0
Open: May–Oct.
Admission: Varies according to the program

Four hundred members of the Mi'kmaq nation live on Lennox Island. This organization started up in 1999, to take advantage of the tourist industry and introduce its own approach, sensitive to both all the residents of the island, human and otherwise. Visitors can learn about the Mi'kmaq culture and history at the Lennox Island Mi'kmaq Cultural Centre. The Path of Our Forefathers is a walk of either 3 or 10 kilometers (2 or 6 miles) with interpretive panels about local and Mi'Kmaq history.

Museums

THE ACADIAN MUSEUM
902-432-2880
peimuseum.com
Rte. 2, Miscouche
Mail: 2 Kent St., Charlottetown, PE C1Z 1M6
Open: Year-round
Admission: Adults $4.50, students $3.50

The Acadians called Prince Edward Island Île-du-Prince-Édouard, but they first called it Île Saint-Jean, and they arrived here in 1720. Acadians also arrived in flight from the British expulsion of Acadians from Nouvelle Écosse, across the Northumberland Strait. Some traveled the world before finding a permanent home here on PEI. But as Catholics, they were not allowed to vote in the early 1800s. At this museum, a video presents that long history and the story of the culture, and artifacts show visitors the tools and world of the Acadian past.

EPTEK ART & CULTURE CENTRE
902-888-8373
peimuseum.com
Waterfront Mall, Harbour Dr., Summerside, PEI
Open: July–Aug., Mon.–Sat. 9 AM–5 PM, Sun. 12–4 PM; call for off-season hours
Admission: Adults $4, students $3

Exhibits presented at this center can be about art and history. Island artist Dr. Georgie Read Barton's work is on permanent display. She painted "the inspiring beauty and magnificence" she found every six months when she returned to Prince Edward Island to paint and teach until her death in 1994.

PRINCE EDWARD ISLAND POTATO MUSEUM

902-859-2039
peipotatomuseum.com
1 Dewar Ln., O'Leary, PEI C0B 1V0
Open: Mid-May–mid-Oct., Mon.–Sat. 9 AM–5 PM, Sun. 1–5 PM
Admission: Per person $6

The largest exhibit of potato artifacts in the world, according to the Web site, is inside this museum, and no doubt the best known is the giant potato at the entrance. The wild food of South America has evolved through many harvests over centuries to become the favorite crop of PEI, and the history of this food is a history of the world, all explained in the Amazing Potato Exhibit.

VICTORIA SEAPORT MUSEUM

victoriabythesea.ca
Open: Daily in summer
Admission: Free

This operating lighthouse is the second-oldest on island. An exhibit inside tells the story of Victoria-by-the-Sea.

Music

THE COLLEGE OF PIPING AND CELTIC PERFORMING ARTS OF CANADA

902-436-5377, 877-224-7473
collegeofpiping.com
619 Water St. East, Summerside, PEI C1N 4H8
Open: July–Aug.
Admission: Highland Storm performances adults $24, seniors $20, children 16 and younger $15, mini-concerts $5, children 6 and under free

The Highland Storm is the famous part of the summerlong Celtic Festival, presenting performances of singing and dancing, bagpipe playing, and more at the Mary Ellen Burns Amphitheatre in The College of Piping. Concerts are on Tuesday, Wednesday and Thursday at 7:30 PM during July and August. Mini-concerts are performed Monday to Friday, three times daily: 11:30 AM, 1:30 PM, and 3:30 PM.

MACKINNON FAMILY SCOTTISH CONCERT SERIES

902-854-2245
31228 Rte. 2, Richmond, PEI C0B 1Y0
Open: Mid-May–mid-Oct.
Admission: Adults $10, seniors $9, youth $7, children $4

Two or three members of the MacKinnon Family perform in a small building down a narrow track off the main highway—park on the grass outside and come in. The sister and brother I listened to could play and sing both traditional Scottish tunes and original music, like "The Frost Has All Gone Away," a paean to spring. Fiddle-playing, piano, guitar, a jig or two, and some anecdotes, including one about a cow that swallowed an important item once when one young MacKinnon was loading his truck with manure.

The MacKinnon Family Scottish Concert is held frequently in summer, in Richmond.

SPINNAKERS LANDING
902-888-8364, off-season 902-436-6692
spinnakerslanding.com
150 Harbour Dr., Summerside
Mail: 24 Spring St., Summerside, PE C1N 3C8
Open: Visitor's Information Centre
July–Labour Day, daily 9 AM–9 PM; June and Sept., 9 AM–5:30 PM

Free concerts with folk, rock, country, and other kinds of music are held at this outdoor site on Friday, Saturday, and Sunday in the summer.

Theater

VICTORIA PLAYHOUSE
902-658-2025, 800-925-2025
victoriaplayhouse.com
P.O. Box 83, Victoria-by-the-Sea, PEI C0A 2G0
Open: July–Sept. performances nightly, off-season concerts and amateur plays
Admission: Adults, $24, students $18, seniors $22

The Victoria Community Hall in Victoria-By-The-Sea is also Victoria Playhouse.

Comedies were the four shows performed in the summer of 2008, in this historic hall that has rung with laughter and applause for almost 100 years. Contemporary Canadian drama and music are presented from July to September. Off-season plays are performed by the Victoria Playhouse Drama Club, an amateur group.

Dinner Theater

FEAST DINNER THEATRE
902-888-2200
feastdinnertheatres.ca
Brothers Two Restaurant, 615 Water St. East, Summerside
Mail: P.O. Box 1418, Summerside, PE C1N 4K2
Open: June–Aug., Tues.–Sun. nights
Admission: Adults $35, children 12 and younger $25, student and seniors 60 and older $32

Good, light entertainment is on offer at Feast Dinner Theatre, with one show at the Rodd Charlottetown—*The Nearlyweds* played in 2008—and another, *Victoria's Secret*, at the Brothers Two Restaurant in Summerside. The four-course meal starts with salad and steamed mussels. Choose chicken cordon bleu or poached salmon next; both come with mashed potatoes and vegetables, or lobster. Dessert may be layered chocolate mousse cake, strawberry cake, or lemon layer cake.

Seasonal Events

All Summer
Indian River Festival (indianriverfestival.com), St. Mary's Church, Indian River. Chamber music, jazz, Celtic music, and choral concerts held in July and August.
Highland Storm, part of the summerlong Celtic Festival, presents singing and dancing and bagpipe music at the Mary Ellen Burns Amphitheatre, The College of Piping, during July and August.

June
Tignish Irish Moss Festival, Tignish.

July
Lobster Carnival Week, Summerside. Lobster suppers, parade, spelling bee and cardboard boat races.
Potato Blossom Festival (peipotatomuseum.com), O'Leary.

August
L'Exposition agricole et le Festival acadien de la région Évangéline (902-854-3300; exhibitions-festivalspeiae.com/evangelinefestival.html), Abram-Village.

The rows of potatoes in this field in North Tyron curve like the hill they're on.

RECREATION

Golf

Andersons Creek Golf Club (902-886-2222, 866-886-4422; andersonscreek.com), Hunter River. Prince Edward Island's newest course, designed by Graham Cooke, is located near Cavendish. The course crosses its namesake creek four times and has water hazards on nine of its holes. Mussels are complimentary, and bagpipers are on staff to enliven your game.

Mill River Golf Course at the Rodd Mill River Resort, Mill River (800-235-8909; golflinkspei.com). Lakes and streams punctuate this wooded 18-hole course, located beside the Mill River Provincial Park.

Hiking

Black Marsh Nature Trail, North Cape. A 2.7-kilometer or 1.7-mile trail takes you through a blustery landscape of marshland, likely to be populated by birds and with fascinating plants, to the edge of Northumberland Strait, where a long rock reef that sticks out into the water has caused many shipwrecks. The huge windmills of the future are already in place here at the Atlantic Wind Test Site and Wind Farm. The Interpretive Center (902-882-2230) shows how electricity is generated by the revolutions of the wind mills.

Confederation Trail The Prince Edward Island Trans Canada Trail has been transformed into a hiking and biking trail, and it has been one of the island's most popular resources since it opened in 2000. The trail is flat and covered with crushed gravel. It passes through towns and over its own little bridges: plum-colored gates signal entry points. Snowmobilers use it in the winter. The 125-kilometer or 77-mile section from Tignish to Kensington goes through Acadian country, farmland, and woods.

Parks and Beaches

Cabot Beach Provincial Park (902-836-8945), Rte. 20, 16 kilometers or 11 miles north of Kensington. Open June–late Sept. The largest park on Prince Edward Island, Cabot Beach is set on Malpeque Bay. A staff naturalist offers guided nature walks, and an activity center has children's programs.

Cedar Dunes Provincial Park (902-859-8785), Rte. 14, 24 kilometers or 18 miles south of O'Leary. Open mid-June–early Sept. Long, long beaches and supervised swimming with nature walks and a staff naturalist who gives guided walks. West Point Lighthouse, also an inn, is located here, and camping sites are available.

Green Park Provincial Park (902-831-7912), Rte. 12, 6 kilometers or 4 miles west of Tyne Valley. Open mid-June–early Sept. Once a shipyard, Green Park is now a place to relax, with a playground, riverside camping sites, and a river beach.

Jacques Cartier Provincial Park (902-853-8632), 5 kilometers or 3.5 miles east of Alberton. Open June–Sept. Supervised ocean beach on the Gulf of St. Lawrence; campers store and campground.

Skiing

Brookvale Ski Park (902-658-7866), Brookvale, PEI (Mail: P.O. Box 4000, STN Central, Charlottetown, PE C1A BV7). Ten alpine ski trails and three lifts, as well as 24.5 kilometers or 15 miles of groomed cross-country ski trail, tubing runs, a snowshoe trail, and a hill for sledding are all at this pretty, small winter park. A rental shop and canteen are in the upper level of the main lodge, and the ski school is below.

SHOPPING

Bookstores
Abegweit Books (902-836-4334), 6 Commercial St., Kensington. Used hardcovers and paperbacks, CDs, DVDs, and some new board games.

Galleries
Studio Gallery (902-658-2733; studiogallery.ca), 2 Howard St., Victoria-by-the-Sea. The studio of Doreen Foster features her watercolors and work by other local artists and crafts people.

Gift and Specialty Shops
La Coopérative d'Artisanat, Handcraft Co-op (902-854-2096), 2181 Canontown Rd., Abram-Village. Open June–Sept., Mon.–Sat. 9:30 AM–5:30 PM. A quilting room and quilters who make the stock together are on hand to help. Also weaving, hooked rugs, Acadian cotton shirts, and embroidery.

Island Traditions Store (902-854-3063; islandtraditionsstore.com), Rte. 2 (at junction with Rte. 131), west of Summerside and south of Richmond. Baskets, woodworking, woolen socks, and pottery. Demonstrations and a museum offer a lover of basketry a fine way to spend the afternoon.

MacAuslands Woolen Mills (902-859-3005; macauslandswoollenmills.com), Bloomfield (just west of O'Leary). Open year-round, weekdays 8 AM–5 PM except Fri. closes at 4 PM. An islander I spoke to recalled saving up all her used wool clothes, too worn to wear, and bringing them here to be transformed into a new blanket. That thrifty practice is no longer possible, but the blankets made here are thick and long-lasting—queen-size blankets range in price from $81 to $85.

Quilts
The Quilt Gallery (902-859-1888, 800-889-2606; quiltgallerypei.com), O'Leary Guardian Drug, Main St., O'Leary. Open May–mid-Oct., Mon.–Fri. 9 AM–9 PM, Sat. 9 AM–5 PM, Sun. 1–4 PM. A huge selection of fabrics and supplies for quilt-making. Also, hooked rugs and quilt gallery.

INFORMATION

Nuts and Bolts

What follows is a brief compendium of generally useful information that is not provided elsewhere in this book

Ambulance, Fire, Police
The emergency 911 system is in effect throughout Nova Scotia and Prince Edward Island.

Area codes
902 is the area code for both Nova Scotia and Prince Edward Island.

Climate and Weather Reports
Contact 902-426-9090, or go to ns.ec.gc.ca for current forecasts.

Handicapped Services
The Nova Scotia League for Equal Opportunities (902-455-6942; novascotialeo.org) can locate inns and restaurants with accessible accommodations.

Hospitals
Hospital locations are marked on highways and roads in Nova Scotia with a symbol of a bold, blocky **H.** You can also ask for help from the local operator by dialing 0.

Magazines
Provincial Tourism departments publish their own directories of accommodations and attractions, updated annually. *Doers and Dreamers* comes from Nova Scotia Tourism (800-565-0000, novascotia.com); *Your Island Guide, Prince Edward Island, The Gentle Island* comes from PEI (902-368-4801, gentleisland.com). *Coastal Discovery*, with articles about Maine and Maritime Canada, is published by Saltscapes Publishing Limited in Dartmouth, Nova Scotia.

Money
All dollar amounts are given in Canadian dollars, and that dollar varies daily in value compared to the dollar. After years of being valued much less, in the summer of 2008 the Canadian dollar equaled the American dollar. Check the exchange rate whenever you are thinking of a trip in the future, as its value changes daily.

The classic narrow gable is a charming detail on southern Nova Scotia houses.

One central experience of travelers will inevitably be the (unpopular) **TAXES**. What is called the GST, the Canadian goods and services tax, is charged in combination with a provincial sales tax. In Nova Scotia this tax is now known as the HST, the "harmonized sales tax," and totals 13 percent.

Look for rates that say "no tax" in this book and anywhere you seek information about places to stay in Canada. Otherwise, expect to pay the HST.

In Prince Edward Island in 2008, the provincial sales tax (including GST) totaled 10.5 percent. Some items for sale, notably clothing and shoes and groceries, are exempt from the provincial sales tax, or PST.

Cobbler potatoes for sale on the honor system on PEI

Newspapers

The Chronicle Herald (902-426-3031; thechronicleherald.ca), the daily newspaper published in Halifax, NS.

The Guardian (902-629-6000; theguardian.pe.ca), the daily newspaper published in Charlottetown, PEI.

Passports

Although American citizens had been allowed to travel by sea to Canada without a passport through 2008, a change in federal law in the summer of 2009 will mean that all Americans traveling to Canada will need to have a passport to return to the United States.

Tourist Information

With provincial tourism Web sites and phone numbers, you can book a room, or order a copy of the government-sponsored guides to all kinds of travel and opportunities in the province.

For **Nova Scotia Tourism,** go to novascotia.com or call 800-565-0000.

For **Prince Edward Island Tourism,** go to gov.pe.ca/visitorsguide, or call 902-368-4801.

General Index

Lodging by Price

Inexpensive: Up to $110
Moderate: $190 to $130
Expensive: $120 to $200
Very Expensive: $149 and up

Nova Scotia

Inexpensive

Inexpensive–Moderate

Inexpensive–Expensive

Moderate

Moderate–Expensive

Moderate–Very Expensive

Expensive

Expensive–Very Expensive

Very Expensive

Cape Breton Island

Inexpensive

Inexpensive–Moderate

Inexpensive–Expensive

Moderate

Dining by Price

Inexpensive: Up to $16
Moderate: $12 to $24
Expensive: $21 to $38
Very Expensive: $60 or more

Nova Scotia

Inexpensive

Inexpensive–Moderate

Inexpensive–Expensive

Moderate

Moderate–Expensive

Expensive

Very Expensive

Cape Breton Island

Inexpensive
Chowder House, 232
Main Street Restaurant & Bakery, 233
Water's Edge Inn, Café & Gallery, 234

Inexpensive–Moderate
Lynwood Inn, 233
Restaurant Acadien, 223–24
Rusty Anchor, 224
Tommy Cat Bistro, 222–23

Inexpensive–Expensive
Atlantic Restaurant at the Keltic Lodge, 232–33
Island Sunset Resort and Spa, 223

Moderate
Glenora Inn & Distillery Resort, 222

Expensive
Baddeck Lobster Suppers, 233
Bras d'Or Lakes Inn, 243–44
L'Auberge Acadienne Inn, 244
Normaway Inn, 223

Very Expensive
Gowrie House Country Inn, 243
Haus Treuburg Country Inn, 222
Normaway Inn, 223

Prince Edward Island

Inexpensive
Brehaut's Restaurant, 257–58
Claddagh Oyster House, 270
Olde Dublin Pub, 270
Rick's Fish'N Chips & Seafood House, 259–60

Inexpensive–Expensive
Clam Diggers Beach House & Restaurant, 258
Water Prince Corner Shop and Lobster Pound, 271–72

Moderate
Home Place Inn & Restaurant, 289
Lobster House Restaurant and Oyster Bar, 289–90
Lucy Maud Dining Room, 270

Moderate–Expensive
Blue Mussel Cafe, 272
Flex Mussels, 270
Landmark Café, 289
Maple Grille, 271
Sirenella Ristorante, 271
Victoria Village Inn, 289

Expensive
Dayboat Restaurant, 272
Dunes Café and Studio Gallery, 272–73
Fisherman's Wharf Lobster Suppers, 273
Inn at Bay Fortune, 258–59
Inn at St. Peters, 259

Very Expensive
Dalvay By-The-Sea Heritage Inn, 260
Doctor's Inn, 290

Dining by Cuisine